D0550759

Learning and Development

THIRD EDITION

Rosemary Harrison is chief examiner, learning and development, the Chartered Institute of Personnel and Development (CIPD), a Fellow of the CIPD, and a leading academic and writer in the field. After graduating from King's College London with an honours history degree, she worked for some years as a training officer in the National Health Service before joining the (then) Newcastle Polytechnic to lecture in personnel management and organisational behaviour and act as course leader of the Institute of Personnel Management's professional qualification programme. In 1989 she joined the University of Durham Business School as Lecturer in Human Resource Management, and subsequently became director of the Human Resource Development Research Centre at the university. She is an experienced consultant and speaker at conferences and universities in the UK and abroad.

• Other titles in the series

The Chartered Institute of Personnel and Development is the leading publisher of books and reports for personnel and training professionals, students, and all those concerned with the effective management and development of people at work.
For details of all our titles, please contact the Publishing Department:
tel 020 8263 3387
fax 020 8263 3850
e-mail publish@cipd.co.uk
The catalogue of all CIPD titles can be viewed on the CIPD website:
www.cipd.co.uk/bookstore

Learning
and
Development

THIRD EDITION

Rosemary Harrison

Chartered Institute of Personnel and Development

This book is for my father
John Park
Born 30 December 1907
Died 11 April 1995

©Rosemary Harrison 1997, 2000, 2002

First edition published 1997
Reprinted 1998, 1999
Second edition published 2000
Reprinted 2000
This edition published 2002
Reprinted 2002

Design by Curve

Typeset by Fakenham Photosetting Ltd, Fakenham, Norfolk

Printed in Great Britain by
The Cromwell Press, Trowbridge, Wiltshire

British Library Cataloguing in Publication Data
A catalogue record of this book is available from
the British Library

ISBN 0 85292 927 7

The views expressed in this book are the author's own and may not
necessarily reflect those of the CIPD.

CIPD Enterprises Ltd has made every effort to trace and acknowledge
copyright holders. If any source has been overlooked, CIPD Enterprises
would be pleased to redress this for future versions.

Chartered Institute of Personnel and Development, CIPD House,
Camp Road, London SW19 4UX
Tel: 020 8971 9000   Fax: 020 8263 3333
E-mail: cipd@cipd.co.uk Website: www.cipd.co.uk
Incorporated by Royal Charter. Registered Charity No. 1079797.

• Contents

• Editor's foreword

HRM is now more important than ever. Organisations increasingly compete with each other on the basis of effective people management and
development by tapping into the ideas of workers and organising their
work in more efficient ways. Much of this relies on line managers in their
day-to-day interactions with the people who work for them. However, line
managers are busy individuals who need the support of HR specialists –
internal or external to the organisation – to help them make sense of
what is happening in the field. Contemporary initiatives in learning and
development, recruitment and selection, employee relations, reward
management, appraisal and performance review need to be interpreted
for different organisational contexts. HR specialists not only need to dis-
play a sound understanding of the main HR issues, but also show awareness of business issues and have an acute sensitivity to how change can
be managed effectively. In addition, HR specialists need to demonstrate
a commitment to professional and ethical standards, and be able to provide sound advice based on an extensive knowledge of high-quality
research and contemporary organisational practice.

With this in mind, the CIPD is publishing a series of books designed to
address key issues in people management and development. This book
is one of the series focusing on the CIPD Standards in People
Management and Development, Learning and Development, Employee
Relations, People Resourcing, and Employee Reward. The series provides essential guidance and points of reference for all those interested
in learning more about the management of people in organisations. It
covers the main sets of CIPD Standards in a systematic and comprehensive manner, and as such is essential reading for all those preparing
for CIPD examinations. In addition, however, the books are also excellent
core texts for those studying for courses in human resource management at postgraduate and advanced undergraduate levels. Moreover,
practitioners should also find the books invaluable for information and
reference to sources of specialist advice. Underpinning the series is the
CIPD notion of 'the thinking performer' that is central to the
Professional Development Scheme.

People Management and Development: HRM at Work, written by Mick
Marchington and Adrian Wilkinson, analyses the essential knowledge
and understanding required of all personnel and development professionals. The book comprises a number of sections, commencing with
an examination of the factors shaping HRM at work – including the legal
and institutional forces as well as the changing nature of work and
employment. A recurring theme throughout the book is the integration
of HRM with business objectives and the degree to which it is able
to add value. Later chapters in the book consider each of the main

components of HRM at work, seeking to show how these interrelate with each other in a wide range of differing organisational contexts. The authors are both well-known researchers and professors of HRM at two of the UK's premier management schools – UMIST and the University of Loughborough. Professor Marchington is also Chief Moderator, Standards for the CIPD.

Learning and Development is written by the CIPD's Chief Examiner for the subject, Rosemary Harrison. Building on her extremely popular previous book on training and development, this also provides an extended analysis of learning and development that is based on the CIPD Standards. The book focuses on the main areas of the field – national policy frameworks, professional and ethical considerations, the delivery of learning and development, and career and management development. Given the comprehensive treatment of learning and development in this book, it is also eminently suitable for students on all courses – including CIPD – as well as for practitioners.

Employee Reward has also been fully revised and restructured to address the CIPD Professional Development Scheme Standards in the area. The author, Michael Armstrong, is a well-known and experienced writer and consultant in employee reward, and he was one of the CIPD's chief examiners until 2001. The book is divided into nine sections, each of which analyses a key component of reward management. This includes chapters on reward processes, job evaluation and competency frameworks, pay structures and systems, performance management and employee benefits. The book provides a highly practical and systematic coverage of employee reward that is likely to offer students an invaluable resource as well as give practitioners vital sources of information and ideas.

Employee Relations, like all the other books in the series, has been thoroughly updated in order to cover the CIPD Standards in the subject. The authors, John Gennard and Graham Judge, have an immense amount of academic and practical experience in employee relations, and they have combined forces again to offer students on CIPD courses an unparalleled text. The book deals systematically with all of the key components of employee relations. It provides an overview of the economic, corporate and legal environment and it focuses on the increasing influence of the European Union on employee relations. Subsequent parts of the book examine the processes and policies used by organisations, and the practice and skills required of HR professionals. John Gennard is Professor of HRM at the University of Strathclyde and Graham Judge is an independent consultant.

People Resourcing is written by Stephen Taylor, who is a senior lecturer at Manchester Metropolitan University, one of the CIPD's centres of excellence. This is an updated version of his earlier book on employee resourcing, and it provides a highly practical and accessible text for students taking CIPD examinations. All the main elements of people resourcing are examined in detail in the book. There is a particular focus on human resource planning, recruitment and selection, performance management, dismissal and redundancy. A wide range of examples drawn from different sectors and occupational groups illustrates the core concepts. The author is one of the CIPD's national examiners for Core Management and has a wide range of experience marking scripts in the people management and development area.

Essentials of Employment Law, now in its seventh edition, is firmly established as the most authoritative textbook on employment law for all students of human resource management. The authors are both from Middlesex University – David Lewis is professor of employment law and Malcolm Sargeant is reader in employment law. The text covers the CIPD employment law specialist elective and is an invaluable source of reference to students studying any area of HRM. It covers the key areas of employment law from the formation of contracts of employment to human rights and discrimination issues.

In drawing upon a team of such distinguished and experienced writers, this series provides a range of up-to-date, practical and research-led texts essential for those studying for the CIPD qualifications. Each of the books provides a systematic and comprehensive analysis of their subject area and as such can be used as core texts for all students on post-graduate and advanced undergraduate courses.

Mick Marchington
CIPD Chief Moderator, Standards

• Preface to the Third Edition

The aims of the third edition

One of the aims of producing a third edition of my 1997 Core Text was to provide theoretical and practical guidelines for the CIPD's new Learning and Development Standards (CIPD, 2001). However, the book is also intended to reach a wider student and practitioner market, as Figure 1 shows (opposite). So although it maintains a consistent focus on the CIPD Standards, it is never dominated by them. I write – as I have always done – as an independent author. To question, reflect and evaluate are vital tasks for anyone who wishes to become professional (in the widest sense) in their work, and it is my essential task to promote those qualities without attempting to subordinate them to any particular set of concepts or norms. I stress throughout the book that all customary ways of thinking and doing must be regularly challenged if equity is to be achieved and progress to be made.

Such challenge is vital in the field of learning and development (L&D), since it is constantly under fire and is also both complex and dynamic. The criticisms regularly levelled against practitioners may sometimes be unfair. That, however, is to miss the point. They are publicised, and they gain a wide hearing. The professional response should not be defensiveness but a determination to gather the facts, assess them objectively, and take action accordingly.

However, although I identify and analyse poor L&D practice and its contributory factors in this book, I also draw attention to practice that is good and innovatory, and to the L&D field's powerful theoretical base. I therefore hope that whoever reads this book – students, practitioners, academics – will find much in it to engage their interest, and to stimulate both reflection and action.

The structure of the book

Part 1 frames the rest of the book with an overview of the L&D process, an outline of national vocational education and training policy and its implementation, and a generalised strategic framework for L&D in organisations. It also introduces the CIPD's new Learning and Development Professional Standards (examined in more detail in Part 2, Chapter 8).

Part 2 focuses on the business partnerships that L&D practitioners need to forge if they are to be effective in their work. It explores issues of L&D strategies to add value, of ethics and professionalism, and of the

Figure 1 Route maps for readers

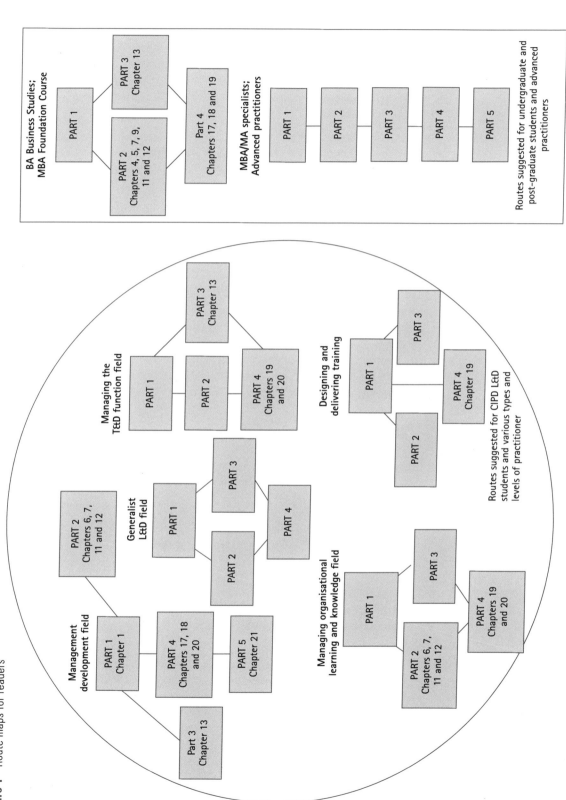

functional management of L&D. It discusses the leadership, standards and organisation of those who have responsibility for L&D activity, assesses ways of integrating new technology into the L&D process, and closes with an exploration of L&D in small to medium-sized organisations in which approximately 90 per cent of the UK's employed labour force is to be found.

Part 3 deals with ways in which L&D practitioners can tackle their vital role of helping to build and sustain human competence and organisational capacity through a developmental performance management process and skilful facilitation of learning processes and initiatives.

Part 4 centres on the role of the L&D process in preparing the organisation for the future. It looks at how careers and managers can be developed in order to optimise the contribution that valued employees can make to organisational progress. It explores the role of L&D practitioners as change agents, and it opens up the complex field of workplace learning and knowledge development.

Part 5 is primarily intended for advanced practitioners and students. It returns to Part 1 of the book, first by expanding the external policy framework to incorporate international dimensions, and then by offering a conceptual framework linking learning and knowledge processes to the strategic direction and progress of the organisation – a theme that completes the circle of discussion that commenced in Chapter 1.

Learning materials

This third edition incorporates many learning aids, intended particularly to help those coming new to the field. These include:

- *chapter objectives* at the start of each chapter, reviewed at its end – these provide each chapter's focal points

- *checkpoints* to review readers' understanding

- *tasks* to place learning in a real-life context and provide the opportunity to apply theory to practice

- *case studies*, real-life and fictional, to illustrate and challenge key issues covered in the text

- *review questions* at the end of each chapter. Their aim is to test readers' achievement of chapter learning objectives. They are in the style of questions set in Section B of the CIPD's PDS generalist examination, but they are relevant for all readers, representing the type of on-the-spot queries that L&D practitioners constantly have to face in real life.

- *useful reference sources* at the end of each chapter. These suggest reading and web-based material to expand on the material covered in the chapter.

Tutors using the book for their study programmes can also access a Tutors' Manual on the CIPD's website (www.cipd.co.uk). This contains many additional learning aids, together with a specific guide for CIPD tutors on how to relate the book's contents to the CIPD's new Learning and Development Generalist Standard (Appendix 1) and to its associated revised specialist standards.

Keeping up to date

In such a dynamic field it is essential to keep abreast with change. This third edition has been effectively re-written for two reasons: to ensure coverage of content relevant to the CIPD's new L&D Generalist Standard, and to incorporate developments in the field since the second edition was produced.

Although each chapter contains reference sources, readers should regard these only as starting-points. Academic journals identify and explain new theories and challenges to the old. Professional journals and reports evaluate current policy and practice (and with the needs of CIPD students particularly in mind I refer regularly to the CIPD's journal, *People Management*, and to its research projects and other publications). The Web is a crucial information source. Here, the Institute's On-line Training Digest is a particularly useful facility and the Department for Education and Skills website provides essential updating on national policy developments. (The Department for Education and Employment was reorganised in June 2001 – see Chapter 2. Although at the time of writing, January 2002, the title is still used on parts of the official website, the appropriate reference now is www.dfes.gov.uk.)

Starting out

Throughout the third edition there is a consistent emphasis on the need for L&D operations to achieve strategic focus and impact. That is appropriate because the L&D process has so much strategic potential (as the CIPD Professional Standards and the National Occupational Standards produced in 2001 underline). Yet to those starting out on a career in people management and development, such discussion may seem of only theoretical interest. Few will have any influence on strategic players in the organisation or on 'strategy' in its more obvious guises.

To think in this way is to miss a vital point – that for those new to the field what is important is not to take strategic action but to think strategically. This is why the CIPD in its 2001 Standards stresses the need for people and development (P&D) professionals to be 'thinking performers', reflecting on what is going on around them, looking outwards to identify and anticipate threats, challenges and opportunities, and promoting ways in which P&D processes and initiatives can help to move the organisation forward.

A growing understanding of 'what is going on here' will equip L&D students and practitioners increasingly well to show how the L&D process at their organisational level can provide added value. Strategy is about looking to the future and building towards what must be achieved. Even newcomers to the L&D field can achieve a good deal by helping to introduce and embed initiatives to improve performance against those targets.

By making a mark in modest ways and providing added value for the business and for individuals in whatever activity they organise, even the most inexperienced practitioners with L&D responsibilities will gain respect. Their influence will grow as people learn to trust their judgement and their professionalism. By working in partnership with stakeholders, benchmarking appropriate activities and processes, and demonstrating a real understanding of the organisation and its business environment, they will build up their credibility. When the opportune moment comes, they will be well equipped to become strategic players.

Rosemary Harrison
Chief examiner, Learning and Development
January 2002

• Acknowledgements

All real-life material reported in the book relates only to situations current at the time. Unless otherwise indicated, comments on such material are my own, and do not represent any official views within or by the organisations concerned. I acknowledge with thanks the organisations that have allowed me to publish accounts of their business and human resource policies and practice – in particular, Cummins Engine Co. Ltd, Darlington, Egg plc and Harris Associates, Birmingham, and Hydro Polymers, Newton Aycliffe – and the permission granted by Cambridge Strategy Publications to reproduce at various points in the book material from *The Training and Development Audit* (R. Harrison, 1999).

I am grateful to the Foundation for Corporate Education in the Netherlands and the University of Durham's HRD Research Centre for funding that enabled me to undertake much of the research into HRD and strategic capability that underpins this book. I also owe thanks to Dave Bevan at Harris Associates for his help with the Egg plc case study in Chapter 6, to Sheila Grimes at the Employment National Training Organisation for advice on National Standards in Chapter 8, to Alan Rutter for originally providing financial insights that I have continued to apply in Chapter 10, to Jim Walker for some stimulating general perspectives, to the anonymous reviewers of my first draft for most helpful comments, and to my CIPD editors, Anne Cordwent and Robert Foss, for their invaluable support throughout this project.

Above all, I am indebted to my husband for his patient and good-humoured encouragement.

• Glossary of terms

adding value To add value, the L&D process must achieve outcomes that significantly increase the organisation's capability to differentiate itself from other, similar organisations, and thereby enhance its progress. It must also achieve those outcomes in ways that ensure, through time, that their value will more than offset the costs that they have incurred.

assessment centre 'A systematic approach to identifying precisely what is required for success in a particular job and then labelling these requirements in terms of a short-list of tightly defined criteria' (Stevens, 1985). Data collected in this way is used primarily to feed into decisions about promotion or some other form of employee redeployment.

business partners When applied to HR practitioners, the term is a way of emphasising that in all their activities they must add value for the business, and cannot do this on their own. They must collaborate with others in the business – especially managers – in working for outcomes that will benefit that business.

competencies The set of character features, knowledge and skills, attitudes, motives and traits that comprise the profile of a job-holder and enable him or her to perform effectively in his or her role.

competency framework A construct of core competencies that provides a template against which teams as well as individuals can be developed.

computer-based training A term that covers both e-based learning (see below) and such computerised learning tools as CD-ROMs.

develop To unfold more fully, bring out all that is contained (Onions, 1973). To make or become bigger or fuller or more elaborate or systematic advancement (Pearsall and Trumble, 1996).

development centre A methodology by which participants take part in a variety of job simulations, tests and exercises in front of observers who assess their performance against a number of predetermined job-related dimensions. Data thus generated is used to diagnose individual training needs, facilitate self-development or provide part of an organisational development audit (Rodger and Mabey, 1987).

dialogic learning A style of learning that involves interacting with others in ways which produce a growing understanding of the culture of the organisation, and of how that organisation typically achieves its goals (Mezirow, 1985).

double-loop learning A concept to describe the style of learning that involves questioning why certain problems occur in the first place and identifying and tackling root causes instead of only surface symptoms (Argyris, 1977). Contrast with *single-loop learning* (qv).

educate To bring up from childhood so as to form habits, manners, mental and physical aptitudes (Onions, 1973). To give intellectual, moral and social instruction to, especially as a formal and prolonged process (Pearsall and Trumble, 1996).

e-learning Learning via electronically based technology. 'E-learning is emerging as the term referring to ... training or learning delivered or received mainly through the Internet, intranets, extranets or the Web. [Thus] for example, the use of CD-ROMs should not properly be described as "e-learning"', (CIPD, 2001a).

evaluation of learning A process to identify the total value of a learning event or process, thereby putting the event or process into its organisational context and aiding future planning.

explicit knowledge Knowledge that has been articulated and codified.

external consistency Applied to L&D activity, a term that refers to the commitment, shared purpose and perceptions of stakeholders that can be achieved through actively involving them in the planning, design, delivery and evaluation of learning events and processes (Kessels, 1996).

implementation The process by which strategy and plans are put into action in the workplace.

instrumental learning Learning how to do the job better once the basic standard of performance has been attained. It is helped particularly by learning on the job (Mezirow, 1985).

internal consistency Applied to L&D activity, a term that refers to the outcome achieved by the effective application of a systematic approach to planning, design, delivery and evaluation tasks (Kessels, 1996).

job training analysis A process of identifying the purpose of a job and its component parts, and specifying what must be learned in order for there to be effective work performance.

job training specification A key outcome of job training analysis. It describes in overall terms the job for which training is to be given, or the key problem areas in a job which training will enable learners to tackle. It then specifies the kinds and levels of knowledge, skill and, where relevant, attitudes ('the KSA components') needed for effective performance, together with the performance standards for the job and the criteria for measuring achievement of the standards.

knowledge Knowledge can be viewed as a type of commodity – something 'out there' that can be searched out and acquired, assessed, codified and distributed across the organisation. In this sense, it is an intangible asset that can have unique competitive value for an organisation. Yet knowledge can also be viewed as a process, emerging from within the individual but intimately shaped by relations with others. In this sense knowledge is dynamic, changing as the individual's understanding and interpretation of the world around him or her changes.

knowledge economy A way of describing a world in which 'knowledge' has become the key to wealth. In this world, the application of knowledge adds more value than the traditional factors of capital, raw materials and labour, and the 'knowledge worker' has unique status.

knowledge productivity A term that refers to an organisation's ability to generate, disseminate and apply knowledge to products, processes and services. Knowledge productivity should therefore enable an organisation to continuously adapt and improve and to regularly innovate.

knowledge workers Those who apply knowledge to the improvement of operating procedures, products, services and processes, and who use knowledge to innovate.

KSA components *see* **job training specification**

L&D *see* **learning and development**

learning A qualitative change in a person's way of seeing, experiencing, understanding and conceptualising something in the real world (Marton and Ramsden, 1988). Also a process whereby such change occurs.

learning and development (L&D) An organisational process to aid the development of knowledge and the achievement of organisational and individual goals. It involves the collaborative stimulation and facilitation of learning and developmental processes, initiatives and relationships in ways that respect and build on human diversity in the workplace.

learning and development function The way in which the whole body of L&D activity is structured in an organisation.

learning technology A term that refers to the way in which learning media and methods are incorporated into the design and delivery of a learning event and interact with those participating in the event.

media of learning The routes, or channels, through which learning is transmitted to the learner.

methods of learning The ways in which learning is transmitted.

mission The detailed (and usually written) articulation of *vision* (qv), which acts as an inspiration and a guide for action.

monitoring of learning 'Taking the temperature' of a learning event or process from time to time, picking up any problems or emerging needs.

organisational context The internal and external organisational circumstances that directly influence, help to explain, or have any other clear bearing on, the organisational situation being examined. Often, organisational context is summarised by reference to culture and structure, but they are themselves outcomes of something more fundamental – the interplay of at least three primary factors. Those factors are: top management's vision and values, management's style and actions at different organisational levels, and HRM policy and practice and the employment system of the organisation.

paradigm shift A complete and permanent change in the established pattern of thinking by organisational members about their work organisation. A shift in the way they understand their world.

pluralist system A term that refers to the concept of an organisation as a system in which there are many and often conflicting interests, and therefore in which conflict itself is a natural occurrence. Contrast with *unitary system* (qv).

self-reflective learning The kind of learning that leads individuals to redefine their current perspective in order to develop new patterns of understanding, thinking and behaving. It requires unlearning as well as new learning (Mezirow, 1985). See also *double-loop learning* (qv).

single-loop learning A concept to describe the style of learning involved in taking a problem at its face value and therefore tackling its surface symptoms but not its root causes (Argyris, 1977). Contrast with *double-loop learning* (qv).

strategic capability 'Strategic capability provides the vision, the rich and sustained learning and knowledge development, the integrity of purpose and the continuous direction and scope to the activities of the firm that are needed to secure long-term survival. It is based on a profound understanding of the competitive environment, of the resource-base, capacity and potential of the organisation, of the strategy process, and of the values that engender commitment from stakeholders to corporate goals' (Harrison, 2002).

strategy A route that has been chosen for a period of time and from a range of options in order to achieve organisational and business goals. It is also a dynamic process by which that chosen route is frequently changed, sometimes abandoned, as changes occur in the organisation's external and internal environment.

tacit knowledge Knowledge that is embedded deep in the individual or the collective subconscious, expressing itself in habitual or intuitive ways of doing things that are exercised without conscious thought or effort (Nonaka, 1991).

technology The particular way in which, in a workplace, technical systems, machinery and processes are designed to interact with human skill and knowledge in order to convert inputs into outputs.

theories Constructs that are the products of reflections on, testing of, and generalisations from, experience. Theories help to aid initial understanding, to give structure to ideas, to suggest explanations of actions and events, and to improve skill in problem-solving and practice in the 'real world'.

thinking performers Practitioners who are knowledgeable and competent in their various fields, and able to move beyond compliance to provide a critique of organisational policies and procedures, and to advise on how organisations should develop in the future (CIPD, 2001).

train To instruct and discipline in or for some particular art, profession, occupation or practice; to exercise, practise, drill (Onions, 1973). To teach a specified skill especially by practice (Pearsall and Trumble, 1996).

unitary system A term that refers to the concept of an organisation as a system in which there is one overriding goal or set of interests, and in which consensus, not conflict, is the expected norm. Contrast with *pluralist system* (qv).

validation of learning An assessment of the extent to which learning objectives have been achieved.

vision The picture that people hold in their minds about what kind of organisation theirs should be.

• List of Figures

• List of tables

LEARNING AND DEVELOPMENT IN CONTEXT

• Introducing Learning and Development

CHAPTER OBJECTIVES

After reading this chapter you should:

- have an overview of 'learning and development' (L&D) as an organisational process
- know something about the historical background of L&D
- be aware of some of the current trends and challenges in the L&D field
- appreciate the more important issues that relate to its practice.

Introduction

In *Barnaby Rudge*, Charles Dickens wrote:

> *Chroniclers are privileged to enter where they list, to come and go through keyholes, to ride upon the wind, to overcome, in their soarings up and down, all obstacles of distance, time and place.*

What he didn't add is that some chroniclers find it hard to decide on exactly 'where they list' as they start their chronicle. 'Begin at the beginning,' Alice in Wonderland would have said. But where *is* the beginning of learning and development?

Task 1

Before going further, what is *your* starting-point? What do you understand the L&D process in an organisation to be? Try to produce your own initial definition, no matter how little you may feel you know at this stage about L&D. Then keep it by you to compare it with those we will be looking at as we move through the chapter.

This chapter starts by opening four different gateways into the L&D field. It then explores some of its past and present territory in order to perceive the challenges faced by its practitioners.

Gateways into the learning and development field

Terminology

The first gateway into the L&D field is terminology. A quick explanation is required as to the use of the term 'learning and development' (L&D) as the title for this book and as a generic term for all L&D processes and activity in an organisation. L&D is a significant change in terminology from the more traditional terms 'human resource development' (HRD) and 'employee development' (ED). It has been chosen as this book's title and as the title of a set of new professional standards produced by the Chartered Institute of Personnel and Development (C1PD) in 2001 because it more powerfully conveys the importance of learning in an organisation. It better emphasises that those who work in and for organisations should be regarded as learners rather than as 'human resources'. Other points explaining its choice are that:

- like HRD, it conveys the scope of activity that can extend beyond those who work in the organisation to those who, although not legally its 'employees', nonetheless make an essential contribution to its success – for example, voluntary and contracted-out workers and suppliers. Responding to the learning needs of these stakeholders is an important way of acknowledging mutuality of endeavour and of interest. Such learning networks also help to stimulate new ways of thinking that can be essential to an organisation's future progress.

- it creates a positive impression of the organisation as a context within which all forms of learning are approached on a partnership basis. Use of the term 'employees' is being replaced in many organisations now by such terms as 'associates' and 'colleagues'.

Fundamental terms to do with the learning process include:

learning: a qualitative change in a person's way of seeing, experiencing, understanding and conceptualising something in the real world (Marton and Ramsden, 1988)

develop: to unfold more fully, bring out all that is contained in (Onions, 1973)

educate: to bring up from childhood, so as to form habits, manners and mental and physical aptitudes (Onions, 1973)

train: to instruct and discipline in or for some particular art, profession, occupation or practice; to exercise, practise, drill (Onions, 1973).

What do these terms suggest? Two things in particular:

- that education and training are major routes to learning and development. Education is the longer-term process that is to do with the rounded formation of the whole individual. Training is the shorter-term activity that helps an individual acquire competence in a specific task, process or role.

- that learning is not context-free. It takes place in a 'real world' and is grounded in ongoing experience. In an organisation, that world is the workplace. If the learning process is to be effective, it must take full account of the aids and barriers to learning that the workplace context presents.

By using the gateway of terminology, we are already beginning to form a view of the L&D process. But a word of warning – definitions are not neutral. They come from, and are used by, individuals who have their own values and viewpoints. For example, I have selected definitions that match some of my own perceptions of the L&D process – but I could have chosen others which might well have suggested something rather different.

Let us look at another set of terms, and see where they lead us:

Task 2

learning: knowledge acquired by study

develop: make or become bigger or fuller or more elaborate; systematically advance

educate: give intellectual, moral and social instruction to, especially as a formal and prolonged process

train: teach a specified skill, especially by practice

These definitions come from the *Oxford English Reference Dictionary* (OERD: Pearsall and Trumble, 1996).

What are the most significant ways in which these definitions differ from the definitions we looked at previously – and from your own initial definition?

Which definition/s contribute/s most to your understanding of the L&D process – and why?

You may have noticed that the OERD definition of learning links it to 'knowledge'. It is a definition that is narrow, since it refers only to knowledge gained through study. But knowledge gained through no matter what kind of learning is precisely what the learning process should produce. If the L&D process is to offer full benefit to the organisation as well as to individuals, then it should be a source of potentially valuable knowledge for that organisation. For this to happen, learning should be pursued not as an end in itself but as a process that can expand or regenerate the organisation's stock of knowledge – its 'knowledge base'. One commentator (Coulson-Thomas, 2001), with this in mind, has claimed that:

For many years before its break-up, Rover had championed learning at all levels in the organisation. But what was learned did little to enhance the company's competitiveness, as events subsequently proved.

This is an overly simplistic explanation of Rover's eventual break-up by BMW, but the fundamental point is valid. Learning will not add value for the organisation unless it yields knowledge that enhances the organisation's capability to operate effectively in its environment.

No added value for the organisation can emerge, either, from situations where learners are not motivated or able to learn, or where the workplace throws up barriers to the sharing of new knowledge, or where the culture is such that existing knowledge cannot be challenged.

To summarise: our exploration of L&D terminology thus far has suggested that:

- learning is a process that enables the development of the organisation and of individuals within it

- learning should produce and expand knowledge that is valuable for the organisation as well as for the individual

- although formal education and training are important vehicles for learning, so too is everyday experience in the workplace

- the workplace environment therefore has a direct influence on learning, and on the development and use of knowledge. (This is a topic we will come back to.)

Terminology has been a useful starting-point for this chapter, but we have seen that it is not a neutral one. Depending on the terms chosen, our notions of the L&D process will vary. Yet there is nothing neutral in that process either. It is all to do with human beings, and so it is never entirely predictable in its outcomes.

Statements of purpose

Terminology cannot take us much further. What we need now is a framework – a statement that can pull our ideas together by clarifying the purpose and potential benefits of L&D as an organisational process. The CIPD's statement of that purpose is shown in Appendix 1 (at the end of the book). Like many such statements, it emphasises the significance of L&D as a critical business process, whether in for-profit or in not-for-profit organisations. It also recognises the need to obtain the active commitment of the learners. You cannot force people to learn, but you can work with them in ways that encourage and help them to do so.

I define L&D's purpose as:

*The primary purpose of learning and development as an organ-
isational process is to aid the development of knowledge and the
achievement of organisational and individual goals. This involves
the collaborative stimulation and facilitation of learning and
developmental processes, initiatives and relationships in ways
that respect and build on human diversity in the workplace.*

This statement of purpose emphasises the importance of the L&D
process as a contributor to individual and societal well-being as well as
to organisational success. A difficult balancing act is involved here, the
importance of which is often overlooked. In using learning to meet
organisational ends we are intervening in a human process that goes to
the heart of an individual's identity. It is vital that personnel and development practitioners understand their responsibility in the matter. It
goes beyond their organisation, being shaped by the ethics and standards of their professional body and by the contribution they must make
to society at large as well as to the organisation that employs them at
the particular point in time.

Checkpoint

● Briefly define *four* key terms that relate to learning and development.

● Outline the purpose of L&D as an organisational process.

● Why does that purpose involve a 'balancing act'?

Theories

A third gateway into the field of L&D is provided by theoretical frameworks – 'constructs' as they are sometimes called. L&D constructs
abound but, like terminology, they emerge from particular viewpoints
and sets of values. We will shortly look at a construct about learning.
First, however, four points:

● Theories are the products of a) reflections on experience, b) the
testing of experience, and c) generalisations from experience.

● Theories help to aid initial understanding, to give structure to
ideas, to suggest explanations of actions and events, and to
improve skill in problem-solving and practice in the 'real
world'.

● Theories about L&D are not rules, and should not be treated as
such. There are no rules of human behaviour, no theories that
explain beyond dispute how people think, learn and acquire knowledge. There are no black-and-white L&D prescriptions to be
applied, because there are no certainties about whether, or how,
people will learn and develop in different contexts.

Figure 2 The experiential cycle of learning (based on Kolb, Rubin and McIntyre, 1974)

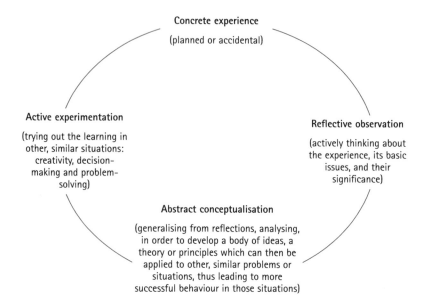

Concrete experience

(planned or accidental)

Active experimentation

(trying out the learning in
other, similar situations:
creativity, decision-
making and problem-
solving)

Reflective observation

(actively thinking about
the experience, its basic
issues, and their
significance)

Abstract conceptualisation

(generalising from reflections, analysing,
in order to develop a body of ideas, a
theory or principles which can then be
applied to other, similar problems or
situations, thus leading to more
successful behaviour in those situations)

- Theories about L&D have a valuable function in helping people to interpret events and situations, and to respond to them in a considered way.

As newcomers to the L&D field test out L&D theories in an increasing range of organisational situations, they should become more confident in applying their own reasoning, common sense and lessons of past experience to new challenges. In such ways all of us through time can become more skilled in assessing where theory works, where it does not, and how best to tailor it to the particular situation.

Figure 2 outlines a well-known theory about learning. It reappears in Chapter 13. Here, its presence is by way of introduction. Of course the diagram is simplistic. The learning process is more complex than this, and does not in reality move through four neatly separated and sequential stages. The circular shape is just a way of emphasising the dynamic nature of learning, and the importance of experience, reflection, analysis and action in the overall learning process.

Stories

We have now opened three gateways into the field of L&D: terminology, statements of purpose, and theories. Yet something is still missing. It is to do with the *feel* of L&D – the lived experience of learning and of developing. This is the relevance of our fourth gateway: that of stories.

Stories, or 'narratives' as they are usually called in the literature, bring alive the relationship between theory and practice. Without them, we may study theory yet be unable to relate it to the real world. Even for the most experienced practitioner, narratives of situations and contexts that they have not yet encountered can give an invaluable extra dimension. Through them we can gain an emotional understanding of the L&D process.

To illustrate this, here is a narrative that made an important contribution to theories about workplace learning. It contains a compelling example itself of the power of storytelling.

CASE STUDY: The photocopier technicians

A group of photocopier technicians had to repair machines in customers' locations. They had been given detailed instructional manuals and training to enable them to perform their tasks. However, it soon became clear to them that this formal knowledge was not enough. The people who had designed the machines had not understood the different social settings in which the machines would have to be used. They had therefore ignored many of the uniquely human foibles that could cause machines to break down.

The technicians quickly realised this and got together to work out for themselves how best to solve the wide range of repair problems that they met in various photocopier locations.

To do this, they made use of what has been called 'tacit' knowledge – that which all of us have, and which is embedded deep in our subconscious. It expresses itself in habitual or instinctive ways of doing things that we seem to exercise without conscious effort (Nonaka, 1991). The technicians shared their tacit knowledge particularly by exchanging stories of similar problems they had encountered in the past, and narrating how they had resolved them. By comparing their tacit knowledge born of intuition, habit and past experience with their formal knowledge gained through training and repair manuals, they began to develop unique insights into different kinds of repair problem. Uncertainty, the need to know, the excitement of discovery, ultimately produced in the group a detailed understanding of the machines. This understanding had been helped as much by the social relationships that existed within the group as by its technical know-how.

Researchers Brown and Duguid, analysing this study in 1991, described the learning that had gone on in the group of photocopier technicians as being 'situated' in a 'community of practice'. Other academics took the research further, and today the body of theory about learning situated within communities of practice in the workplace has a powerful influence on L&D thinking and practice (Vygotsky, 1978; Lave and Wenger, 1991; Sternberg, 1994; Matthews and Candy, 1999).

Source: Orr, 1990

Checkpoint

- An experienced part-time student in her first few weeks on a human resource management course says to the lecturer, 'You academics are always drowning us in theories – but in real life we have to get on and *do* things!'

  You want to convince her of the practical value of theories. So what do you say to her?

- What type of learning did the stories that the technicians told each other in Orr's photocopier study provide that they could not gain from their training or manuals?

Some commonly asked questions about L&D

Having opened four different gateways into L&D's territory, we now need to ask questions that will deepen our understanding. Each of the following six questions relates to an area of enquiry that is examined more fully in subsequent chapters.

What does the L&D role involve?

L&D practitioners may be human resource (HR) generalists combining L&D work with other responsibilities. They may be specialists or external consultants. They may be line managers or team leaders. There is no single role that those with L&D responsibilities are likely to perform – but as a generalisation we can say that:

- in a small or medium-sized organisation, one person may have to plan and organise the developmental process right across the business, with no specialist support to help or manage him or her in the work

- in larger organisations, inexperienced L&D practitioners often work alongside unit managers, while reporting to a senior HR professional or line manager. Like line managers with developmental responsibilities, they may have to plan and organise the provision of L&D in the workplace.

- those with more L&D experience may have to advise on, organise and evaluate unit-wide or corporate L&D strategies and plans, employ and oversee training providers, and run – or help to run – an efficient and 'value-adding' L&D function.

A detailed examination of roles and standards for those with L&D responsibilities is contained in Chapter 8.

Table 1 Building learning and development into the business

Strategic level	L&D's strategic focus is on:	L&D must:	Crucial processes for L&D:	L&D specialist/manager needs to:
1 Corporate	• formulating L&D mission, goals and strategy to achieve corporate goals • influencing and developing strategic thinking and planning	• 'fit' with wider HR strategy • be aligned with corporate strategy • help to secure appropriate balance between corporate goals for survival and for advancement • produce L&D strategy that is capable of implementation at Level 2	• collaboratively developing mission and goals for L&D • strategic planning and thinking • influencing key stakeholders • adding value through L&D activity	• have board-level position/access and skills • be pro-active as well as reactive • have deep knowledge of competitive environment • fully understand the value chain and strategic assets of the business • speak the language and logic of the business • work in business partnerships
2 Business unit/managerial	• developing L&D policies and systems in line with strategic needs of the business unit • ensuring achievement of business targets • influencing and developing strategic thinking, organisational capacity and human capability	• 'fit' with wider HR policies and systems • be aligned with business unit policy • have a clear plan within the overall business plan, with agreed evaluation measures • ensure feedback on policies to Level 1	• working with HR and business unit managers to produce policies and plans for acquisition, retention, growth/redeployment of workforce • developing key performance indicators • strategic thinking and business planning • adding value through L&D activity	• work in business partnership with managers and others • have collaborative relationships with other HR specialists • have deep knowledge of competitive environment of company and of business units • fully understand how strategic assets can be developed • speak the language and logic of the business units
3 Operational	• ensuring individual and team performance targets are met • improving acquisition, quality and motivation of people for the business.	• adapt to needs of the business and needs and aspirations of people • ensure L&D activity is expertly carried out and appropriately evaluated • ensure feedback of outcomes to Level 2.	• working with teams and individuals to implement business plans for L&D • appraisal, personal development planning to achieve targets and improve core competencies and capabilities.	• working in partnership with internal and external stakeholders • have effective and efficient systems and procedures • have deep knowledge of culture of the workforce • be expert and continuously self-developing.

What are the core responsibilities of L&D practitioners?

L&D responsibilities vary with the given role and with organisational context. As a starting-point, we can note the claim made by the CIPD in its 2001 Professional Standards that all personnel and development practitioners must be 'thinking performers'. That is to say (CIPD, 2001: 4–8), their central task is to:

> *be knowledgeable and competent in their various fields, and be able to move beyond compliance to provide a critique of organisational policies and procedures, and to advise on how organisations should develop in the future.*

In its L&D Standard the CIPD has identified 10 main areas of L&D responsibility. These are shown in Appendix 1. They are underpinned by a theme that recurs regularly in this book – the importance of achieving a truly strategic thrust for L&D in the organisation by integrating L&D practice vertically with organisational goals and horizontally with other HR processes in the organisation. The Standard emphasises the collaborative processes by which to achieve this strategic and functional integration.

Table 1 provides not a starting- but a finishing-point here. It illustrates how L&D can be both business-led and strategically integrated. At this point, much of the content of this table may be unfamiliar to you, and much of its meaning will therefore be unclear. By the end of the book, however, you should have acquired the language and the knowledge to make full sense of it, and to be able to relate its content to your own organisation or to any with which you have to deal. We return from time to time to this table, since it offers us a basic 'map' with which to chart L&D territory.

Other important statements of L&D responsibilities – each underpinned by a particular view of the L&D process and its purpose – are examined in Chapter 8.

Task 3

Take any organisation with which you are familiar, and obtain information that enables you to answer convincingly the following questions:

What kind of L&D roles can you identify in the organisation, and who holds them – personnel and development generalists, L&D specialists, line managers, or others?

How many of the CIPD's core L&D responsibilities do they appear to involve?

What is the national context for L&D?

National vocational education and training (NVET) policy and its international context are examined in detail in Chapters 2 and 21. Two introductory points may, however, be made here:

- In the UK at government level there is an increasing recognition of the fundamental role that planned learning at individual, organisational and national levels must play if sustained economic growth and societal well-being are to be achieved. Against a changed economic backcloth and the increasing globalisation of businesses, most of the national training policies, initiatives and institutions established in the late 1980s have now been scrapped. The government is emphasising the need for everyone to have access throughout life to opportunities for learning that will benefit themselves and the economy, and is giving special support to workplace learning initiatives (see Chapter 2).

- NVET policy in the UK is struggling to come to grips with the human implications of the developing knowledge economy – that is to say, an economy in which the application of knowledge adds more value to the business than the application of traditional factors of capital, raw materials and labour. (This concept is explored further in Chapter 11.) By 2010, it is likely that around 30 per cent of job growth will be in knowledge-based jobs. However, many companies in Britain are still producing low-specification products that need only low-level skills. In such companies, skills training may be the only investment made to develop people. If British-based organisations are to compete successfully, that kind of investment will not be enough. In a knowledge economy, the capacity to develop and apply new knowledge rests equally with everyone. That means there must be a sustained drive for the long-term education, training and development of the nation's current and potential workforce.

What is the organisational context for L&D?

We look at the meaning of the term 'organisational context' in Chapter 6. Here, we can note that the organisational framework, or 'context', for the L&D process is provided primarily by:

- top management's vision and values, goals and leadership

- management style and actions that shape people's activity and interactions across the organisation

- the organisation's human resource (HR) policy and practice, and its employment system.

For many commentators – and certainly for the CIPD in its Professional Standards – there are two major implications here for the L&D process:

- It must 'fit' by adapting effectively to the needs and demands that organisational context and environment generate.

- It must be 'integrated' by ensuring that its goals and operations are in line with business and HR goals.

Such adaptation can be difficult – sometimes pretty well impossible – to achieve. We return to the issues involved here in Part 2 of the book.

What is the HR policy context for L&D?

It would seem to be entirely logical to treat L&D as one of a family of HR processes, each of which – under the umbrella of the organisation's HR policy – directly affects people's motivation, performance and expectations in the workplace. As we shall see in Chapter 4, not all HR practitioners share this view. In particular, there is a body of trainers that, failing to understand the true meaning of 'family of processes' here, appears at times to be calling for a separation rather than the integration of 'training' and 'personnel'. In contrast, I argue throughout this

Figure 3   The wheel of HRM and the business

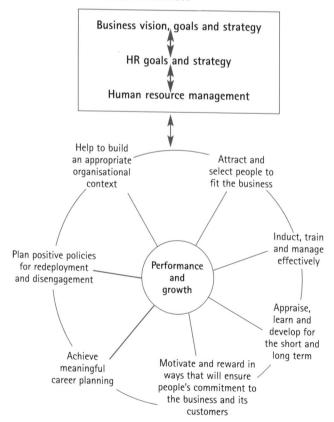

Based on Harrison, 1993a: 40

book that there is a necessary interdependency between HR processes even though, as in many families, relationship problems can occur. In the case of the L&D process, this interdependency is illustrated by the fact that every aspect of HR policy may have outcomes that either facilitate or undermine people's learning and development in the workplace.

Figure 3 introduces the family of HR processes in the form of a wheel. The notion is expanded in Chapter 3.

Why should L&D practitioners be 'business partners'?

The term 'business partners' applied to L&D practitioners is a way of emphasising that in all their activities they must contribute added value to the business, and that they cannot do this on their own. They need to collaborate with others in the business – especially managers – in working for outcomes that will benefit that business. There is more about 'adding value' towards the end of this chapter, and Chapters 4 to 6 deal with the practical tasks involved in these interrelated themes of adding value and of forming and maintaining business partnerships.

Checkpoint

- Identify and outline your responses to *one* of the listed questions commonly asked about the L&D process.

- What is meant by the statement that the L&D process must achieve good 'fit'?

In this section, six commonly asked questions about the L&D process have been identified. In order to more fully understand that process, we should now look at its history and its present position. That is the aim of the following section.

The L&D process: an historical overview

Human resource development and the L&D process

'L&D' is a relatively new term, used to indicate a field that is more generally known in the academic literature as human resource development (HRD). For that reason the term HRD is used throughout most of this section.

A sense of history is vital in seeking to understand the human condition. An historical perspective is a path to wisdom. Taken here, it can help us to appreciate the forces that have made the L&D process what it is, and to argue convincingly about the kind of contribution it can make to society, to organisations, and to individuals.

The study and practice of L&D will always be challenging. Its history, meaning and organisational role are complex. The needs it serves are often contradictory and their boundaries are disputed. The demands made on the process on the one hand by 'the business' and on the other hand by 'the individual' cannot always be reconciled. For such reasons many students find L&D a frustrating subject, and many practitioners struggle for success in the field. Yet it is its challenges that make L&D one of the most exciting and rewarding of the HR processes. I hope that some of its excitement comes through in this book, no matter how many of its readers may be new to its territory.

Meanings

In the USA, the term 'HRD' first came into common use in the 1970s, but its focus then was somewhat generalised. It was defined by one of its most famous commentators (Nadler, 1970: 3) as:

> *a series of organized activities conducted within a specified time and designed to produce behavioural change.*

By the 1980s, some writers were taking a longer-term view of HRD. They saw it as essential to an organisation's strategic progress, and emphasised this strategic element as core to its meaning. Hall (1984: 159) had this to say:

> *Strategic human resource development is the identification of needed skills and active management of learning for the long-range future in relation to explicit corporate and business strategies.*

By the early 1990s, the HRD field had in the USA developed into a recognisable profession, and many (including Burack, 1991: 88) were focusing not only on its strategic orientation but on HRD as change agent:

> *HRD people have been charged to blueprint and lead the way to organization and individual renewal.*

In the UK the picture was less clear-cut. A survey commissioned in 1998 by the (then) Institute of Personnel and Development (Darling, Darling and Elliott, 1999: *xii*) found that training and development practitioners were:

> *affected by the confusion of meanings and boundaries between such terms as human resource management, human resource development, training, learning and development.*

There are so many meanings attached to the developmental process that it is in a sense arbitrary to select any one definition of HRD. Nadler (1992) pronounced that 'there is still no universally accepted definition', and the same remains true today. Some feel that the root cause of this is HRD's interdisciplinary nature. For others – including myself – that is simplistic. Many factors are at work here, as the next section reveals.

Checkpoint

At the start of this chapter, I suggested that you produce your own definition of L&D. In the light of the various definitions of HRD that we have just noted, would you now make any changes to your definition? Briefly explain your answer.

Foundation years

During the last century, there were three distinct strands to HRD's early development.

World War II: the growth of industrial training
For those who see the HRD process as being essentially about 'training', HRD's historical starting-point is clear. During World War II, training as a work-field developed a business profile in both the USA and the UK. In the UK, training officers came into being as a distinct category of staff, and the influential personnel writer G. R. Moxon (1943) linked education with training to form one of the 'six categories' of personnel management work. By 1996 the professional field in the UK had officially broadened to incorporate HRD at levels 4 and 5 of the new National Occupational Standards in training and development.

The post-war years: organisational psychology and systems theory
For those who believe that the development of people who work in and for an organisation encompasses far more than merely 'training', the true historical starting-point of HRD is more likely to be a little later.

During the 1950s and 1960s in the USA, organisational psychologists like Argyris (1957), McGregor (1960), Likert (1961) and Hertzberg (1966) were popularising the developmental process. In the UK, researchers at the Tavistock Institute of Human Relations were exploring organisations as systems, the interaction of whose human and technical elements determined the overall capability of an organisation to adapt to its environment (Trist and Bamforth, 1951). This organic view drew attention to the importance of organisational learning as an adaptive process, thereby adding a major perspective to HRD.

Organisational psychology and systems theory had a powerful impact on the subsequent development of 'learning organisations' theory (Senge, 1990; Nonaka, 1991). So was the mid-twentieth century HRD's starting-point? There are those (including myself) who would not agree that it was. They would place it much earlier – in fact, at the turn of that century.

Early twentieth century: scientific management
The work of the mid-century American organisational psychologists was essentially the continuation of pioneering work on industrial management carried out notably by the American engineer F. W. Taylor

(1856–1915), and expanded in later years by colleagues who contributed to what came to be known as Scientific Management. Taylor believed that the application of rational, fair and systematic forms of management and organisation would lead to mutuality of interest and effort between management and worker, thereby leading to improved efficiency and productivity for the business. If we locate the true origins of organisational HRD here, we can more easily understand those tensions in purpose and values that still bedevil the L&D process in many organisations today. They arise from trying to combine a business imperative with a genuine concern for the well-being and development of the individual.

The growth of the business imperative

As the HRD field developed, the business imperative grew steadily stronger, particularly in the USA. Human capital theory was by then widely known, largely due to the writings of the economist G. Becker (1975). This theory presented people as organisational assets whose economic value derived from their skills, competence, knowledge and experience. Becker argued that investment in training and education led to increased productivity, and thence to increased wages and business earnings. This made HRD a value-adding process. Becker also believed that education was a powerful means of creating a more numerate, literate and informed society. Through its transformational power, HRD could therefore add value to society, as well as to the organisation and the individual.

The business imperative expressed itself most obviously in a drive for performance improvement, and this drive has continued to dominate HRD practice in the USA. In the UK, HRD's early development was more fragmented, but here too a performance-driven approach began to gain ground during the 1980s, notably in larger and multi-divisional organisations. A sustained period of recession had been accompanied by a collapse in manufacturing and by a rapid decline in the country's skill base as apprenticeship numbers were slashed. The outcomes of these crises highlighted the need for performance improvement and skills development. At the same time, much publicity was being given to training strategies being practised in competitor countries where HRD was treated as a vital business process.

For some, the growing emphasis on HRD as a business-driven process aroused concern. In the USA in the early 1990s a group of HRD academics and practitioners established the Academy of Human Resource Development. It was not a physical institution but a body of people committed to the research and practice of HRD. They were disturbed at what they perceived to be the narrowness of focus, the commercial thrust and the restricted research-base of the influential American Society of Training and Development – itself a body distinct from the US Association of Human Resource Managers.

The Academy's membership rapidly expanded. It now has strong partnership ties with the more recently established University Forum for HRD in the UK, whose network of over 20 universities conducts research and provides postgraduate master's-level HRD programmes. Both Academy and Forum collaborate with EURESFORM, a European network of research, education and training institutions and individuals engaged in training HRD managers and professionals. The aim of this partnership is to improve research and practice in HRD in order to achieve a better and more durable balance of benefit for society, organisations and individuals. There is a particular concern that HRD activity should focus on life-long learning and on the development of knowledge that will expand the capabilities and creativity of individuals as well as of the business and the economy.

Checkpoint

- Where do you think HRD's historical origins lie – and why have you come to that view?

- What is meant by the term 'business imperative' applied to HRD?

Finding a strategic role

By the late 1980s, many business strategy academics were researching and writing on the unique internal capabilities of an organisation as sources of competitive advantage. This was accompanied by a concern to improve the contribution of HR processes to the business. HRD figured large here, as Noel, James and Dennehy (1991: 19) observed:

> HRD professionals must work with top management, focusing on the organisation's strategic initiatives and seeking ways to leverage the development of employees to achieve these objectives, in creative and impactful approaches.

In the USA and the UK in the last two decades of the twentieth century, consultants and academics called frequently for practitioners to align HRD more closely with business strategy. Disappointingly, researchers continued to find little evidence for such an alignment in most UK-based organisations (Keep and Mayhew, 1994; Skinner and Mabey, 1995). However, at national level the government was making progress as it attempted to break the old pattern of a 'stop-go' approach to vocational education and training (VET) and achieve a more coherent, strategic approach. Long-term VET objectives were established, driven by a clear purpose. Reforms in the vocational qualifications system were set in train, and an implementation framework was produced at national, sectoral and local levels (see Chapter 2). The business-focused Investors in People Standard was introduced. It became one of the few national training initiatives to gain significant support in the field.

In the UK, by the closing years of the century HRD may not have become a strategic function in many organisations, but it had a more business-focused identity as HR and training issues moved towards centre stage in organisations' search for competitive edge (Darling *et al*, 1999).

L&D: current trends and challenges

It is impossible in a brief section to identify all the important trends and challenges that currently face the L&D process. Here I have chosen some that, taken together, do two things: they help to explain why the L&D territory can be treacherous to traverse; and they demonstrate, too, why success in that journey brings vital benefits for the organisation, for the individual, and for society at large.

Practice in the field

At organisational level, there are disturbingly regular criticisms of L&D practice. Most are about a perceived lack of business relevance and value, and poor planning, design and delivery of training initiatives. More worrying (because so often the underlying cause of these problems) are the attitudes towards training and development that continue to prevail in many organisations and even within the HR profession.

Seventeen years ago, a damning report on training in the UK was published. I mentioned this report – *Challenge to Complacency* (Coopers & Lybrand, 1985) – at the start of my first book on training and development, to draw attention to the dangers inherent in 'a combination of complacent, ill-informed and sceptical attitudes to training at all organisational levels, including that of personnel practitioners themselves' (Harrison, 1988: 2). In 2001, the accusation of complacency returned to haunt us, as the following case study shows.

CASE STUDY: The Paddington rail crash

On 5 October 1999, in the morning rush-hour, a Thames train went through a red signal and collided with an oncoming express near the Ladbroke Grove junction; 31 people died, and 500 were injured.

In June 2001, following a public enquiry, the Cullen Report on the Paddington rail disaster was published. The *Daily Telegraph* published an article (Marston, 2001) identifying the Report as:

> an alarming portrait of a rail industry riddled from top to bottom with complacency, inertia and indifference to safety improvements.

The article described how, amongst staff in the three companies concerned (Railtrack, Thames Trains and the Rail Inspectorate), the Report had found widespread 'incompetent management and inadequate procedures' and a 'lamentable' failure to act on the recommendations of inquiries into two previous incidents in the area. A 'deep-seated *laissez-faire* culture' had prevailed across the system.

This culture was particularly evident in relation to driver training. According to the Report (Marston, 2001), Thames Trains, despite having being involved in more cases of drivers going through red signals than any other company, had a safety culture related to driver training that was 'slack and less than adequate'. The Report's indictments were devastating. Training programmes were unsystematic. Instructors essentially did what 'each of them thought best'. The crash driver had not been adequately instructed in the various signalling layouts and their risks, and:

> His assessments had not covered route knowledge in the Paddington area, despite the fact this was the major terminus for Thames services.

The Report stated that the driver's main instructor had not considered route learning 'to be part of his job'. Training managers involved had communicated poorly with one another. No outside body had validated the content of the training material.

Source: Marston, 2001

In October 2001 Railtrack was placed in administration by the government. By then, much more had emerged about the sorry state of the UK's privatised rail system, and about government policies that must also take a share of the blame for tragedies like Paddington (for by then there had already been one further incident involving fatalities – the Hatfield crash). In that month, the Crown Prosecution Service announced that there was insufficient evidence to bring prosecutions, despite 'a history of corporate failings'. It found no link between inadequate training and the driver going through the critical Signal 109 at danger (McIlroy, 2001).

Nevertheless, the account of complacency at all levels horrifies. But this, you may say, is an exceptional case. Unfortunately, the Cullen Report made it clear that, basically, it was not an exceptional case. Complacency, coupled with hopelessly confused organisational structures, conflicts of interests and lack of adequate co-ordination and co-operation at every level, from government downwards, had all combined to produce a situation in which a crash was waiting to happen. Despite two previous critical incidents, no adequate lessons had been learned.

In such a context, perhaps the organisational disarray surrounding the training function can partly explain its grave deficiencies. But only partly – and in any event this is no isolated example of bad practice. In recent years signals of alarm about the state of training have been raised in many other contexts, including the police force, local authorities, the prison service, and nurse and teacher training. Again, of course, there are factors that can partly excuse the situation:

- The complacency of powerful managers and employers makes it difficult – sometimes impossible – for the concerns of L&D practitioners to be heard or taken seriously.

- Making L&D more business-focused is difficult in those organisations where there is no clear business strategy, or where immediate profits are the only bottom-line that counts with the employer.

- Adding value is likewise problematic where HR practice in the workplace does not support L&D initiatives and processes.

- It can be hard for a L&D function to achieve meaningful organisational outcomes if – as may often be the case – it is a minor and stand-alone function.

- Trends to decentralise, de-layer and downsize sit uneasily with commitments to 'invest in our people' and 'empower the workforce'.

- The downside of the 'flexible firm' – cheap, vulnerable and easily manipulated workers – puts a question mark against the kind of role that L&D is being made to play in many organisations.

Yet when all such factors have been duly considered, they should not be used as a smokescreen. The task of L&D practitioners is not just to execute orders. It is also to ask questions, no matter how awkward for management those questions may be. It is to identify and advise on ways of tackling barriers in the organisation to relevant and necessary training, learning and development. It is to take an ethical approach to the practice of their profession, no matter how difficult that may prove to be.

This is what it means, in real life, to act as 'thinking performers', that core task of personnel and development practitioners referred to on page 12. No matter at what organisational level they are working, those with L&D responsibilities must have an understanding of policy-making and of the kind of strategies that the organisation needs. They must know what it is feasible, as well as relevant, to do in a particular situation. They must be effective business partners. They must consider the needs of their ultimate client, and strive to ensure that those needs are met. They must recall and be unafraid to act on their responsibilities to individuals and to society at large.

This is an awesome agenda, but it is a necessary one. In the 16 years that elapsed between *Challenge to Complacency* and the Paddington rail disaster, too many vital lessons had not been learned across too many organisations. If those who preach the gospel of L&D cannot practise it themselves, then who can – or will? In Chapter 7 we return to such questions, in an examination of professionalism and ethics as they relate to the L&D field.

Task 4

Identify some examples of both good *and* bad practice in L&D in an organisation with which you are familiar. Then obtain information to enable you to identify in those examples the factors that explain the good practice, and the factors that appear to have led to the bad practice.

The control factor

The UK economy has for many years now been relatively low-wage, with a consistently low inflation rate, deregulated labour force and low level of unemployment. At the same time, management's power over employees has been boosted by a relaxation of employment legislation and by an increase in organisational restructuring and in harmonisation of terms, conditions and pay grades.

Such trends can encourage a controlling approach to employees that reduces L&D's scope to its most short-term component – training to remedy immediate skill deficits. As will be explained in Chapter 4, it is difficult, often impossible, to combine such an emphasis with a push to achieve a longer-term, more developmental focus.

Adding value

One of the main challenges for L&D practitioners in today's turbulent and highly competitive business environment is that their operations must add value for the business. To add value in this sense, the L&D process must:

- achieve outcomes that significantly increase the organisation's capability to achieve its goals or even to set new goals that originally would have been unrealistic

- achieve those outcomes in ways that ensure, through time, that their value will more than offset the costs that they have incurred.

UK research has revealed concerns by a number of chief executives that there is 'scattergun' investment in training in their organisations, such training being poorly focused and weakly linked to analysis of skills gaps (Guest and King, 2001). In Chapter 4 the practical ways in which L&D can become a value-adding process are clearly outlined.

Workplace learning

We saw earlier in the case study of the photocopier repair technicians an instance of the rich learning that is latent within communities of practice in the workplace. The importance of workplace learning has now been officially endorsed by the government, which is committed to putting more resources into its expansion and improvement.

As will be made evident in Chapter 20, workplace learning is one of the most powerful sources of organisationally valuable knowledge. One writer (Zuboff, 1998: 395) has claimed that:

> *The [truly successful] organization is a learning institution, and one of its principal purposes is the expansion of knowledge . . . that comes to reside at the core of what it means to be pro-ductive. Learning is the heart of productive activity. To put it simply, learning is the new form of labor.*

Workplace learning, if effectively facilitated and co-ordinated, can also offer many benefits to those who are involved in it day by day. It can become a 'value-adding' process for the individual, whose expertise and potential it can significantly enhance.

For all these reasons, workplace learning has become a crucial area of responsibility for the L&D professional. The tasks involved are challenging and have a clear ethical dimension (as examined in Chapter 7). They become increasingly important as organisations have to operate in a more knowledge-based economy. In Chapter 11 some of the issues such an economy raises for learning in the workplace are explored.

Enhancing employability

There are, then, many ways in which workplace learning can benefit an individual. In a world where few organisations can offer their employees long-term job security, there is a strong business as well as ethical case for providing work environments in which individuals can regularly acquire and practise new skills and knowledge. This is more fully explored in Chapter 20, but for now we can note that:

- employers increasingly need a workforce that can be more pro-ductive, more customer-focused, more adaptable, and more inno-vative

- it is difficult to gain and maintain employee commitment, however, when long-term contracts are not on offer; in that situation, the employer has to forge a new kind of psychological contract with the employee – one focused on mutuality of interest and of benefit

- through enhancing employability, the employer can offer benefit to employees and receive in return benefit for the organisation.

For all governments, it is essential to increase the employability of those in and out of work because of the need to improve a situation in which 'whole segments of the population have been virtually shut out of the job market' (Graham, 1994). The USA has a more dynamic rate of job creation than other Group of Seven leading industrial nations, yet the income gap between the better-trained and educated and the less well-trained had widened dramatically by the mid-1990s (Graham, 1994). It is still the skilled who get the good jobs there, and the unskilled who remain the economy's underclass.

Task 5

In your own organisation, how far – if at all – is 'employability security' offered through L&D initiatives? Produce recommendations for practices that you would like to see introduced there, and provide a convincing business case for them.

Clarifying the boundaries

But where should we draw the boundaries between the organisation and wider society? An increasing number of social issues are becoming the legitimate concern of the L&D function. This is in part for legal reasons. It is also because those issues now so directly affect people's drive and capacity in the workplace.

One such issue relates to stress. Much stress stems from domestic rather than organisational causes, yet its consequences can directly affect employee sickness and turnover rates, morale and productivity. For example, in 1989 Gilley and Eggland observed that as demographic trends result in steadily ageing workforces, HRD initiatives may have to help valued employees to acquire coping skills to adjust to constantly changing home environments (Gilley and Eggland, 1989: 354). Today in the UK, one in eight members of any workforce is a carer, many receiving so little employer support that they give up their jobs completely. By 2010 the situation will be significantly worse, with one fifth of the population likely to be caring for elderly or disabled relatives. This accelerating trend points to the importance of training and other human resource policies that can ease the stress for carers and help to retain their skills for the business (Arksey, 2001).

Other examples of social issues that have implications for the employer include these:

- Many young entrants to employment have low educational standards yet clear potential for the organisation. In response to this problem, some organisations are adding basic skill and literacy training to their traditional range of job-related programmes.

- In a similar way, the development of analytical, problem-solving and team skills are now frequently part of induction and basic skills programmes for new graduates. In the view of their employers, a university education has left many ill-equipped as regards these basic work-related competences.

- Some employers provide free training places for local unemployed people on certain of their skills training courses. The aim is to contribute to an increase in local skills, and – when relevant vacancies occur – to recruit pre-trained personnel who have a particular commitment to the organisation because of the opportunity it has given them for re-employment after periods out of work.

Such examples demonstrate the difficulty of drawing a clear boundary between life at work and life outside it. That presents a fresh challenge to those with L&D responsibilities in an organisation.

Checkpoint

Identify and briefly explain *one* kind of L&D initiative that could tackle high stress levels in a workplace with which you are familiar.

L&D: appearance and reality

Problems of uncertainty

You will notice throughout this book regular statements like 'there is evidence to suggest', 'there are statistics to indicate', 'it is logical to conclude that', or 'it may seem that'. These are all indicators of uncertainty. They suggest an inability to provide a clear answer to the question 'What is really going on here?' They are right to do so. Consider the following:

- British academics Bratton and Gold (1994) claimed that the machine model of organisation still dominates Western industrial society, leaving little place for the consideration of attitudes, feelings and personal development.

- An American writer (Soloman, 1999) has argued that with a diversified workforce, workplace learning can have a 'potentially repressive power' instead of liberating the individual through developing their talents. (We shall be looking at this claim in Chapter 7.)

- Centuries ago, a famous theologian (St Augustine, *Confessions*, Book 3:9) wrote – naturally in a rather different context, but producing insights very relevant to this discussion –

The appearance of what we do is different from the intention with which we do it, and the circumstances at the time may not be clear.

Where, then, does the truth lie? How can we be sure that we know the 'intentions' behind L&D activity, or that we understand the 'circumstances at the time'? Certainly in the HR literature there is often little hard information about actual practices in real contexts. John Storey (1992: 17) told of visits to companies heralded in the literature as having made radical innovations, 'only to discover that the "breakthrough" was viewed as a peripheral trial, was hardly recognizable to the participants on the ground, or had been abandoned altogether'. So the mundane reality in those cases was very different from the expressed intent. In many research studies, too, the methodology underpinning findings is unconvincing, leaving uncertain the answer to the question 'How much of this can we trust?'

Such questions indicate the challenges faced by those researching practice in the field. As we shall see in a review of auditing in Chapter 5, we must give careful thought to how best to capture the intention, the appearance and the reality of the L&D process in the workplace.

CONCLUSION

Having read this chapter, and completed its checkpoints and tasks, you should now:

- have an overview of L&D as an organisational process

- know something about the historical background of L&D

- be aware of some of the current trends and challenges in L&D

- appreciate the more important issues that relate to its practice.

To test yourself against these objectives, what short answers would you give to the following questions?

Review questions

What do you regard as the main purpose of the L&D process in an organisation?

Explain in outline *one* important current trend in the L&D field.

A manager says sceptically, 'All you L&D people do is produce knee-jerk reactions – you don't contribute any added value to the business.' What might you do to avoid this criticism?

Useful reference sources

BOUD D. *and* GARRICK J. (eds) (1999) *Understanding Learning at Work*. London, Routledge.

VROOM V. H. *and* DECI E. L. (eds) (1970) *Management and Motivation: Selected readings*. Harmondsworth, Penguin.

• National Policy and Framework

Introduction

L&D professionals must be able to advise on L&D activity appropriate to their organisations. As part of this responsibility, they must understand NVET policy and the way in which it is implemented nationally and locally. In this chapter the aim is not to present specialist knowledge in the complex and changing NVET field. It is to promote a generalised understanding of that field that will be of help to L&D students and to those with L&D responsibilities in the workplace.

A vision of NVET embedded in lifelong learning was set by the Conservative government in 1991. UNESCO had adopted lifelong learning as its mission in the 1970s, and the European Community espoused it in the early 1990s. Global initiatives followed, including the World Initiative on Lifelong Learning and the European Lifelong Learning Initiative (Homan and Shaw, 2000).

The Labour government that came into power in 1997 announced its commitment to lifelong learning in its 1998 Green Paper *The Learning Age*. There, it defined lifelong learning as the continuous development of the skills, knowledge and understanding that are essential for employability and fulfilment (DfEE, 1998).

Investment in human capital will be the foundation of success in the knowledge-based global economy of the 21st century. That is why the government has put learning at the heart of its ambition.

Another Green Paper in the same year, *Lifelong Learning* (DfEE, 1998a), claimed that nothing could be more important than such learning for the future of the economy, for social cohesion and for the development of individuals' potential.

This vision of learning, whose purpose is both economic and social, is rooted in human capital theory. It is therefore unsurprising that it raises the same question examined in Chapter 1: how, and at what cost, can such duality of purpose be achieved? It is a question that has dogged NVET policy and practice throughout the latter part of the twentieth century and into the twenty-first.

To understand the issues here, we must explore three main themes in this chapter. The first is the problem of skills supply. The second is the ongoing overhaul of the pre-16 UK educational system. The third relates to the 2001 post-16 NVET strategy and framework. In outlining changing government policies, I have had to simplify the scenario by ignoring the many different opposition party policies on NVET. These belong to a different discussion which, although it would be fascinating, I have no space to pursue here.

The problem of skills supply

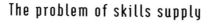

Improving the economy's skill base

In 1991, seven aims were set for post-16 NVET policy, in order to improve the UK's skills base and ensure a fuller contribution to the economy by all individuals. Those aims still guide national policy today. The seven aims of national training policy listed in the White Paper *Education and Training for the 21st Century* (1991) were:

1. to ensure that high-quality further education or training becomes the norm for all 16- and 17-year-olds who can benefit from it

2. to increase the all-round levels of attainment by young people

3. to increase the proportion of young people acquiring higher levels of skill

4. to ensure that people are more committed to develop their own skills throughout working life, and more willing to invest their own time, money and effort in doing so

5. to help the long-term unemployed and those at other kinds of disadvantage to make their full contribution to the economy

6. to ensure that trainers and teachers remain responsive to the needs of individuals and business, working closely with business and widening individual choice

7. to encourage and increase employer commitment to training by having effective enterprise plans that complement work.

Serious skills shortages have been endemic in the UK for many decades. A Trades Union Congress report published in 1999 revealed that the country had more poorly qualified employees and fewer young people in training than most of its European competitors (TUC, 1999). In 2001 Eversheds, the law firm, found in an employment survey of 150 companies that 91 per cent identified skills shortages as a key issue for their businesses (Kemeny, 2001). The methodology used in such surveys often lacks rigour, but the continued existence of a serious skills gap cannot be denied. Determination to close that gap constitutes the central thrust of government policy across the whole NVET area.

Improving the education and training of young people is critical to the success of this policy. By the end of the twentieth century it had become abundantly clear that the education and training system in the UK could not deliver the high-quality foundation learning that young people require for employability and citizenship. In a detailed and damning report produced for the then Institute of Personnel and Development in 1997, Evans, Hodkinson, Keep, Maguire, Raffe, Rainbird, Senker and Unwin called for a new programme of work-based education and training to be put into place as a matter of urgency. What was required was (pvi):

> *a broad-based traineeship of at least two years [to] provide a planned range of work experience, vocational and citizenship education, sectoral and occupationally-relevant training and acquisition of key skills.*

While welcoming the aspirations contained in the White Paper Learning to Compete (DfEE, 1996), the researchers were certain that its goals could not be achieved by market-based policies. Although in subsequent years much has been done to improve the quality and delivery of apprenticeship training and to open up improved work-related training opportunities of other kinds for young people especially, those doubts remain. We return to them at the end of the chapter.

The government sees learning representatives as another key to making its skills strategy work (Rana, 2001). Following the publication of the government's Green Paper *The Learning Age* in 1998 (DfEE 1998), the TUC proposed establishing a network of learning reps to stimulate individuals to learn and to access new skills. By September 2001 the network had grown to 2,000, supported by the government-backed Union Learning Fund.

In its response in March 2001 to the 1999 Moser report (which found that one in five British adults was 'functionally illiterate'), the government emphasised the learning reps' vital role in raising interest in training and development, especially among the lowest-skilled workers. It announced measures to further encourage and strengthen this role, including ensuring that training could lead to formal accreditation. However, the TUC was sceptical about the extent to which reps could make an impact on the national skills gap. Its research in 2000 identified powerful barriers to such an impact in the widespread lack of formal support from employers for the learning rep role.

Incentives for individuals to seek training

There is far less to encourage individuals to invest in training than in many competitor countries, notably Germany, where increases in wages and career prospects are linked to training and qualifications, and where young people are not distracted by high-pay temptations (see Chapter 21). Since the early 1990s some progress has been made by the government to encourage both unemployed and employed individuals to participate in work-related learning. One innovation was the introduction in 1999 of individual learning accounts (ILAs), later open to all. However, in November 2001 the ILA scheme was closed after enquiries into allegations of fraud, and the government announced a period of consultation before the introduction of a new-look ILA. It has yet to come.

A major step in establishing a legal framework of individual rights covering work-related education and training was taken quietly with the passing of the Teaching and Higher Education Act 1998. It established the right of working teenagers between the ages of 16 and 17 who have not attained a certain standard of education and training to paid time off in order to study for specified qualifications. In 1999, the right was incorporated into the Employment Rights Act 1996. Then, in 2000, a substantial financial grant was established for students from the poorest homes, claimable on a weekly basis over two years. The range of allowable courses under the legislation is wide, and includes vocational as well as educational qualifications. The only criterion to satisfy is that they must enhance applicants' employment prospects (Aikin, 1999).

Yet continuing difficulties in the take-up of training opportunities by individuals cannot be resolved by such incentives alone. Older people, the long-term unemployed and ethnic minorities still experience particular difficulties in finding work, whatever their qualifications. Regardless of young people's qualification levels, their unemployment trend rises sharply whenever overall unemployment rises. The wider question therefore remains: how far can any incentives for individuals make a real impact on their motivation to train when qualifications, no matter how relevant, are not rated highly in the job market?

The stance of employers

In the UK, short-termism still dominates the financial base of most organisations and the structure of industry generally, and there is a persistent over-reliance by employers on market forces to provide their skill supply. In October 2001 new research from the British Chamber of Commerce revealed that training investment in the manufacturing sector had fallen to its lowest level, owing partly to the critical slump in manufacturing sales and growth (Taylor, 2001).

Access to training is also unequal. In sectors where low-paid workers form substantial elements of the workforce, training is particularly inadequate despite skills shortages in areas vital to the national economy (Whitehead, 1999). Such trends substantiate the claim that 'managers and professionals or those with a degree [are] up to five times more likely to receive work-based training than people with no qualification and/or in an unskilled job' (Westwood, 2001: 19).

In 1998, Labour introduced the 'welfare-to-work' programme, the New Deal. It was claimed to be the first employment scheme to actively promote equality of opportunity and outcome for people of all ethnic and racial groups (Smith, 1999). That has been disputed, and on a wider front the New Deal has failed to live up to its promise. In 2000 a report by the National Institute of Economic and Social Research, commissioned by the DfEE, showed that only 10 per cent of successful New Deal job placements were due to the programme itself. More damning, of the 191,000 people 'placed' in jobs since the New Deal began, more than 50,000 were back on benefits within three months (Smith, 2000). Meanwhile, the quality of training in the New Deal and the bureaucracy of the system are widely criticised, bringing to mind the concerns of the 1997 IPD report to which reference has already been made.

How can progress be made?

Despite a call in 1999 by the Trades Union Congress report for a legal framework of obligations and of financial incentives for employers to provide training and lifelong learning (Rana, 1999), there seems to be no intention to reintroduce a levy-grant system. The government's philosophy is one of stakeholder partnerships to achieve a learning society by fundamental reform of the pre-16 educational system, and by radical changes to standards and provision of post-16 vocational education and training. These reforms are reviewed in the next section.

Checkpoint

- Over the past decade successive governments have been committed to improving the country's skills base. Explain some of the reasons the problem remains acute.

- Outline *two* of the incentives introduced in recent years to encourage young people to become better trained, and specify whether they are – or should be – used in your organisation.

Reforming the pre-16 education system

The problem of national skills shortages in the UK is rooted in an inefficient, under-achieving, non-vocationally oriented education system.

Despite attempts to improve them, education standards at primary and secondary levels have for half a century been woefully deficient. Until those standards are transformed, they will prevent the success of any attempts to improve the post-16 education system. The government recognises where the fundamental problems lie, and appears to be ready to invest for the long haul. The years ahead represent a route beset with difficulties, but radical changes that have been introduced at the start of the twenty-first century – for most of which the way had been paved by previous Conservative government policies – offer the best hope yet for real progress.

Pre-2001 reforms

Over a decade of the most fundamental overhaul of the state education system since the Butler Education Act 1944 began with the Education Reform Act 1988. Then and thereafter, the Conservative government sought to systematically transform education standards and delivery in the primary and secondary education systems, to reorganise the governance, funding and management of schools – particularly through a dramatic reduction in the powers of local education authorities – and to introduce greater parity of esteem between post-16 vocational and academic pathways.

However, confusion set in from the start. On the one hand, the changes introduced in and after 1988 improved the chances of all children to participate successfully in further or higher education, thereby offering the hope of ultimate substantial improvement in national skills supply. On the other hand, both Conservative and Labour governments introduced more centralisation. In part this was a consequence of nationalising the curriculum and introducing tests to regularly assess pupils across all age ranges. In part it was due to the Labour government's action in 1998 of returning significant power to local education authorities (LEAs). This centralising drive led many to believe that the education system did not and would not permit sufficient educational diversity, choice or quality. As we shall see at the end of the chapter, that fear remains.

Post-2001: 'Raising standards, promoting diversity, achieving results' (Woodward, 2001)

In February 2001 the Education Green Paper *Schools: Building on Success* announced fundamental changes to the entire education system. In an all-embracing policy statement that covered early years and primary schools, the transition to secondary schools and on to higher education or the jobs market, the dominating themes were higher achievement for all, excellence through diversity, and targeted money.

Primary level
Primary schools are Labour's great success story to date. In 1995, more than half of 11-year-olds were behind the expected standard for

their age in English and maths. By early 2001, owing to the success of earlier initiatives (the literacy hour, daily maths lessons and reduced class sizes), Labour was well on course to hit key targets that had been set for 2002. Building on this achievement, the Green Paper announced that these targets were to be increased.

Secondary level

At the heart of the Green Paper lay the determination to achieve greater choice and competition at secondary level (Watson and O'Leary, 2001). To improve the transition between primary and secondary schools, where there is evidence of a real dip in ability, the Green Paper announced measures focused on new targets, catch-up lessons, better teaching, the development of a distinctive ethos in every school, and the delivery of tailored learning to each pupil. The literacy and numeracy strategy that had been so successful in the primary sector was now to be introduced in the secondary sector also.

Another major plank was to extend the successful *Excellence in Cities* programme to one third of secondary schools by September 2001. It provided learning mentors to tackle truancy and the disruptive, and a national academy for talented youth, following a US model, in order to improve provision for gifted children.

Two other planks were intensely controversial – the expansion of specialist schools, and a major increase in the number of faith schools. The proposals (Watson and O'Leary, 2001) in summary were these:

- The number of specialist schools was to be increased to reach a total of half of all secondary schools by 2006, and selection for them was to take place at age 11. Behind this the aim was to increase skills supply in the critical areas of engineering, science, business and enterprise. The fear here is that such schools may result in a two-tier system such that half the secondaries receive a major boost to funds but the other half receive no such benefit. There are also accusations that selection has been reintroduced on a major scale.

- The government was to encourage the immediate establishment of around 100 new faith schools in areas where there was local demand, including for the first time Muslim, Sikh and Greek Orthodox schools. Faith schools have a consistently good record of academic success and of disciplined and motivated pupils. The hope was that their increase would push up standards of achievement, morale and commitment.

Some have welcomed the expansion as a much-needed step to promote tolerance and diversity, and to underpin education with moral values – while also warning against the dangers of perpetuating 'ethnic exclusion or narrow fanaticism' (*Times*, 2001). Others see it to be 'the reverse of what should be happening in a secular multi-cultural society'. They point to the very different treatment of diversity in the USA, where it was 'state schools which helped bind together hyphenated Americans with their different languages, religions and culture' (*Guardian*, 2001).

Amongst the most radical initiatives announced in the Education Green Paper related to the government's hope of changing the law in order to allow private-sector and other external sponsors to take over schools that fail – and even successful schools. We shall look at this issue separately.

The teaching profession

In the Education Green Paper, Labour set out its proposals to recruit and retain entrants to teaching, offering increased financial inducements, on-the-job training in high-cost areas, school placements during university teacher-training courses, and incentives for those with a teaching qualification to return. Overall, the Green Paper promised secondary school heads more freedom to manage their schools, and teachers the prospect of improved working conditions and greatly expanded recruitment. As is made clear at the end of this chapter, these measures have so far proved insufficient to allay teachers' concerns.

Checkpoint

- In the 2001 Education Green Paper Labour pledged to 'empower' individual pupils and schools. Identify *one* key way in which it proposes to do this in the secondary sector, and briefly explain why the success of such measures is vital to government policy to improve the economy's skills base.

- Some of the 2001 Education Green Paper measures have been criticised as divisive. What are your own views on this matter?

Tackling failing schools

Across the whole of the primary and secondary education system, one problem has remained intractable – that of failing schools. There is a significant educational underclass in the UK. National reports have regularly catalogued the widening educational gaps between richer and poorer, and between north and south, as well as deep-rooted gender and ethnic disparities related to educational attainment. Educational league tables have focused further attention on such gaps, which lead ultimately to an underclass in the labour market also.

Most failing schools are located in inner cities, where some of the worst socio-economic conditions in the UK exist. Initiatives like *Educational Action Zones* (25 established in 1998) and the *Fresh Start* programme have had little success. However, the *Excellence in Cities* scheme by which extra money is available to schools in tough city areas has led to markedly improved GCSE pass-rates in those areas.

Under that scheme, a new *City Academies* initiative was announced in 2000 and confirmed in the Education Green Paper of 2001. Hundreds of failing schools may now be taken in their entirety under the control of businesses, churches, voluntary bodies and philanthropists, and out of the control of local education authorities. The new sponsors could employ and determine the pay of teachers, and depart from the national curriculum (Clare, 2000). Modelled on the Conservative government's highly successful 15 City Technology Colleges (CTCs) set up in the 1980s, these academies must, however, admit pupils across the whole ability range and achieve performance targets set by the government. As with the CTCs, the 'sponsors' must also make significant capital investment in the schools, to match or exceed government funding.

City Academies represented a fundamental u-turn in Labour policy. In 1998, the government had brought back grant-maintained schools under the LEA umbrella. Now, the same government was giving City Academies élite status, a high level of autonomy from both LEA and government control (although the academies would remain in the state system), and major injections of government as well as private-sector funding. David Blunkett, Education Minister at the time, made no apology, presenting the u-turn as a 'new approach to diversity' (Blunkett, 2000).

The Academies comprise a brave attempt to tackle inner-city problems. As of October 2001, six projects had been approved, but it will be some time before their likely impact can be assessed. Private-sector involvement is the key ingredient in funding the Academies, expected to cost £10m each. In January 2001, the government was therefore severely embarrassed to be told by the private educational trust that had undertaken to sponsor the Lambeth City Academy project that it could not raise the money required (O'Leary, 2001). However, it is still early days to assess the likely success of the Academies – after all, CTCs took more than 10 years to become firmly established.

Local education authority control
As noted at the end of the chapter, local education authorities (LEAs) remain for many the real barrier to progress in the 'vast majority' of schools (*Daily Telegraph*, 2000), often retaining a large proportion of funding that should be going to schools and disbursing it for other purposes. Their power will be reduced by City Academies and by the expansion of faith schools, but the scope of those is relatively narrow. In much of the overall vision and thrust of education policy, the Conservative and Labour governments since the late 1980s have thought and acted alike. It will be interesting to see how far, in the area where they have so strongly differed – the LEAs' power and control, Labour's policy will be sustained or will change over time.

Task 1

The first City Academy was due to open in September 2001. Using the Web and other information sources, find out what progress the first six projects have made, what performance targets they are aiming to achieve, and the difficulties and successes that they are encountering as they become established.

Reforming the GCSE system

A major plank in Labour's education strategy is the overhaul of the GCSE system that was introduced in 1985 in England, Wales and Northern Ireland. The need is to achieve a more coherent system of vocational study. (The Scottish system under devolution is likely to be significantly different from that in England and Wales, since the Scottish parliament has complete responsibility for devising and implementing education and employment strategies, and for the delivery system.) Despite sporadic attempts since the 1945 Education Act, no government has carried through the concerted reform needed to approach the integrated vocational education and training system in Germany (detailed in Chapter 21).

Progress has been made in improving low educational standards at GCSE. In 2000 the target of 50 per cent of pupils achieving at least five top-grade GCSE passes was missed by only a whisker, two years ahead of the 2002 target date. There continue to be widespread criticisms of 'dumbing down' of GCSE syllabuses and examinations, and concerns at the spread of bad behaviour and regression of pupils in their first year of secondary schooling. However, one other key statistic is promising – the number of those leaving school without any qualifications dropped between 1997 and 2001 from 45,000 to 33,000 (Garner, 2001).

Much more than this, though, is needed. Too many vocationally focused initiatives introduced from the 1980s onwards have failed to achieve their intended impact. The General National Vocational Qualification (GNVQ), introduced in 1993, was the most radical attempt to achieve parity of esteem between the academic and vocational pathways and to end the multiplicity of qualifications. The 1996 Dearing Report into 16- to 19-year-old vocational qualifications dealt a body-blow to its hopes. It found the academic/vocational divide alive and flourishing, 'damaging to the national interest and to the optimal development of the wide range of talents among young people' (Clare, 1996). The national vocational qualification system comes under our microscope on p41.

Vocational A-levels were introduced in the new post-16 curriculum in September 2000, but from the start they were highly controversial, and there is a fear that there will be widespread rejection of AS-levels. In 2001 a far more important change was announced at GCSE level.

Vocational GCSEs had already been targeted for introduction in 2002 to address skills shortages, and these were meant to lead to foundation apprenticeships for 16- to 18-year-olds and on to post-18 modern apprenticeships (Woodward, 2001). In January 2001 a major expansion of the initiative was introduced. State schools were to be able to let their brightest students take GCSEs at 15, so that they could go on to take more A-levels, AS-levels and the new advanced extension awards (Woodward, 2001). From 14, pupils could take a vocational route and ignore some or all traditional subjects, with the exception of English, maths and science.

This move provoked more accusations of a 'two-tier' qualification system, but it represented the most determined attempt so far by Labour to achieve greater parity of esteem between academic and vocational pathways. Yet O'Leary, a respected educational commentator, was pessimistic, alleging (O'Leary, 2001a) that:

- GNVQs have not proved popular with schools or with employers. They have had to be relaunched to encourage a greater take-up, and the more specific workplace courses are in decline. So far, small employers in particular have been reluctant to recognise the intermediate vocational GNVQs, which are still perceived as being less demanding than GCSEs.

- Unless there is 'sustained investment and the close involvement of employers' – rather than leaving the system mainly in the hands of further-education colleges – they will not succeed. The reason for the success of vocational courses in Germany and other European countries is not to do with 'parity of esteem'. It is because they lead to prestigious, well-paid careers. Until that happens in the UK, the vocational route cannot flourish.

Task 2

The introduction of a vocational route at age 14 is vital to Labour's policy to close skills gaps. Carry out some research in your local area to discover how school heads and teachers views this initiative, and the extent to which it is being taken up in their schools.

From the evidence you collect, produce your own conclusions on the likely success of the initiative.

The post-16 education and training system 1990–2000

The Conservative government's intention in the late 1980s and the 1990s was to create a unified framework for the provision of education and training for post-16-year-olds, applying to it the same principles of local autonomy and competition in an open market that underpinned parallel reforms taking place in the primary and secondary education sectors. Throughout this period the providers of post-16 provision – bewildering in their number and complexity – were subjected to rapidly escalating changes resulting from expansion in student numbers, government legislation and official enquiries.

The further- and higher-education system

Under the sweeping changes produced by the Education Reform Act 1988 and the Further and Higher Education Act 1992, all universities, polytechnics and major colleges of higher education came together within a single structure for higher education, with power to award their own degrees. This ended the binary line that had divided universities from other major higher-education bodies for 25 years. Remaining further-education and sixth-form colleges were given independent corporate status, and were to be funded by the government through the Further and Higher Education Funding Councils.

In March 1996 the Dearing Report on post-16 qualifications set out recommendations for a new national framework of qualifications to take the place of the existing jungle of academic, applied and vocational examinations. In response, the government introduced a range of initiatives in 1997 to achieve syllabus change, improve teaching quality, set new performance targets, reduce the number of examination boards and ensure a wider diversity of qualifications. In 1999 a country-wide review of National Occupational Standards and of the NVQ system was launched (see next section).

In 1997 another Dearing Report identified the key role of higher education in enhancing UK competitiveness. The Report was to shape future national educational strategy in fundamental ways, but its most immediate impact on the incoming Labour government's educational policy was to argue convincingly that more money was needed to maintain high-quality higher education. Contrary to Dearing's recommendations, that government decided to waive tuition fees for poorer students while axing maintenance grants in favour of a loan-maintenance package – a highly controversial move that may now be reconsidered (January 2002).

The government also ignored pay structures, and this left critical issues related to staff training, reward and motivation unresolved. Post-16 educationalists at the workface must increasingly manage and work in teams, carry budget responsibilities, generate revenue for their organisations and fight for their position in the marketplace. They must acquire or improve those skills against a backdrop of expanding workloads, a constant squeeze on funding, a fight for educational standards, and salary scales that are a cause of bitter complaint.

The National Vocational Qualification system

The introduction of the NVQ system in 1986 offered Britain for the first time in its history a structure of occupational qualifications comprising agreed national standards of competence across every recognised occupational area [see Appendix 2, p451]. NVQs are intended to be the 'currency of the labour market'. Since performance in the workplace, or activities that realistically simulate it, is integral to the NVQ assessment system, that system relies on a close partnership between colleges, training organisations and/or employers. Yet despite this, many employers see NVQs as irrelevant to their in-house needs.

Take-up has been faster in educational institutions, but many still run traditional and NVQ routes in parallel, and there are problems to do with delivery. The system was meant to ensure progression from education into work and qualifications for those in work. In practice, the settings offered by educational providers are seen by many employers to lack credibility. Furthermore, the cost of providing an NVQ route in a college is so high – in terms of staff training, time and materials – that, as resource constraints and work overload bite harder into the education system, the feasibility of offering that route comes into question for many centres.

In 1996 the Beaumont Report found widespread employer support for the NVQ/SVQ concept but also serious deficiencies to do with a costly and imperfect delivery system, excessive bureaucracy and jargon, inconsistency in funding arrangements, and differences in the interpretation of standards by key parties across the system [Beaumont, 1996: 7]. In 1997, in response to both the Dearing and the Beaumont Reports of the previous year, the Schools Curriculum and Assessment Authority (responsible for GCSEs and A-levels) and the National Council for Vocational Qualifications [see Appendix 2] were merged to form the Qualifications and Curriculum Authority (QCA), with the aim of achieving an administratively more integrated national education and vocational training system. In 1999 a two-year consultative review process was set in motion in England and Wales, in order to produce revised National Occupational Standards and an improved national qualification structure.

A similar process took place in Scotland in 2001, highlighting many assessment problems that were to be reviewed in detail. However, the Scottish system has proceeded more smoothly than that in England and Wales for a variety of reasons, but particularly because 95 per cent of NVQs are awarded by one body, the Scottish Vocational Education Council (SCOTVEC), which also has the accrediting role now held by the QCA in England and Wales. The pattern of the future Scottish NVET system will be determined by the Scottish parliament.

The attractions of NVQs

Whatever the criticisms of the NVQ system, many organisations in the

UK are now making acquisition of NVQs part of the strategic development of their workforces. The Accreditation of Prior Learning process
(APL, see Appendix 2) can be of great benefit to individuals by recognising existing areas and levels of competence that they have achieved in
their jobs, and giving credit in terms of units of a qualification. For a relevant case study demonstrating the value of NVQs, see the Egg plc programme in Chapter 6 (p132).

For organisations like Egg, the attraction of NVQs is that they offer:

- improved profitability and economic performance by raising performance standards and giving employees a better understanding
  of, and ability to do, tasks central to their work in the organisation

- a more adaptable workforce, enabling and encouraging updating
  and modification of skills through the credit accumulation and
  transfer system (CATS)

- increased individual motivation, understanding of competency
  standards and commitment to the organisation

- improved recruitment of competent staff by the organisation using
  the universal standards embedded in NVQs as guidelines for selection

- the opportunity to set clear and consistent goals across an organisation, or units of it, for continued learning and development.
  These goals, when used as part of employee development strategy
  in an organisation, can make a powerful contribution to improving
  business performance

- help to organisations to retain valued employees by building NVQs
  into L&D activity and career-planning systems.

Checkpoint

- As a training manager you want to promote NVQs in your organisation, but you expect to encounter resistance from other managers and their staff. How would you deal with the most typical
  criticisms they are likely to make of NVQs?

- What is 'APL', and what advantages does the process offer for
  individuals?

THE 2001 NVET strategy and framework

A new strategy for NVET

In 1998, two Green Papers heralded a radical change in government
strategy across the whole NVET territory. One was *The Learning Age*
(DfEE, 1998), the other *Lifelong Learning* (DfEE, 1998a). The first

announced the need for new patterns of delivering and achieving learning targets. The second called for a national culture that would stimulate and support lifelong learning and individual initiative in relation to that learning. Both papers had major implications for the further- and higher-education sectors. In July 1999 the DfEE produced its *Learning to Succeed* White Paper to explain how the changes heralded in the two 1998 Green Papers would be implemented (DfEE, 1999).

The new framework was duly put into place in April 2001. Its key features are identified and examined below.

Abolition of the Training and Enterprise Council system

The cornerstone of the national training system between 1989 and 2001 was the Training and Enterprise Council (TEC) system: 82 councils provided the NVET framework at local level in England and Wales – their equivalent in Scotland and Northern Ireland were Local Education Councils (LECs). They were legally autonomous bodies that controlled the public funds allocated to them, could raise private funds and were employer-driven. Their aim was to make national training policy sensitive to local needs and thereby have a real impact on business growth. However, TECs' funding and audit arrangements, their duality of purpose (caught always between the pull of local needs and the tug of national training priorities) and their tangled structural arrangements fatally hampered them in their tasks. In 2001 they were abolished.

The National Learning and Skills Council

In England, the new cornerstone of the NVET framework announced in the White Papers and established in April 2001 is a single, non-departmental public body called the National Learning and Skills Council (NLSC). Its 47 local operating arms are known as Learning and Skills Councils (LSCs).

Goals
The NLSC has four goals:

- to encourage young people to stay on in learning until at least age 19, and to achieve at least a level 2 qualification

- to increase demand for learning by adults

- to maximise the contribution of education and training to economic performance

- to raise standards in teaching and training, supporting the QCA in its efforts to rationalise qualifications.

Responsibilities
In order to achieve these goals, the NLSC has been given responsibility for the funding, planning, quality assurance and delivery of all post-16 education and training up to but not including higher education. Its scope covers:

- further-education colleges and school sixth-forms

- work-based learning for young people (responsibility for work-based learning for unemployed adults has been transferred to the Employment Service, in order to integrate these programmes with the New Deal)

- workforce development – with a special focus on ensuring that the thousands of staff involved in delivering and assessing government-funded learning are competent and appropriately qualified (there is more on this in Chapter 20)

- adult and community learning (working in partnership with local authorities), and information, advice and guidance for adults

- education–business links.

Structure and funding arrangements
A new independent inspectorate covers all work-related learning and training for those over 19, to ensure coherent provision with high standards. A separate inspectorate – the existing Ofsted – covers 16-to-19 provision in addition to its schools' inspection responsibilities. At sectoral level, the 73 state-owned but employer-driven national training organisations (NTOs) were originally key players in the Labour government's reforms of post-16 education and training. However, late in 2001 it was announced that they would be replaced in March 2002 by Sector Skills Councils that would identify skills shortages and deliver action plans.

The NLSC will be accountable for £6 billion of government funds in order to provide education and training for 6 million people. It is intended that this radical restructuring of the national vocational education and training system will achieve much-needed cuts in bureaucracy and delivery costs, and will save at least £50 million.

Crucial to the achievement of the NLSC's goals is effective partnership with employers in order to ensure relevance to local needs. Employers have the single biggest representation on LSC boards at both national and local level, joined by trade unions, government and other voluntary groups (Rana, 1999a). Together, this group constitutes proportionately 40 per cent of representation from 'employment'.

Delivery of training and development
The highest-priority tasks for the NLSC are to build a national database, to identify where specialist training is needed, and to decide where to target funding (Kemeny, 2001). Training and development are delivered or promoted through:

- NVQ frameworks for employees

- Foundation and Advanced Modern Apprenticeships

- support in attaining the Investors in People standard

- support for innovative approaches to workforce development.

Checkpoint

● Outline the goals and scope of the 2001 NVET system and indicate why the reform was needed.

● Why is it so important for LSCs to work collaboratively with employers?

The Investors in People Standard

The IiP Standard was introduced in 1990 to improve the links between training and business goals. Under the TEC system it did not make its intended impact, and it was revamped in 2000 to focus on results rather than inputs and processes. It now has (Rana, 2000):

● more straightforward language

● a focus on results, not processes, by assessors

● 12 instead of 23 performance indicators

● an explicit commitment to equal opportunities

● more flexibility in the way companies and assessors can provide and assess evidence

● more feedback by assessors

● a reduction in paperwork for employers.

IiP-accredited organisations have a choice of a yearly audit or reassessment every three years. The Standard is now delivered through Business Link and Learning and Skills Councils, and a specially tailored version for small firms has also been introduced.

The University for Industry

The University for Industry (UfI, branded *learndirect*) is a key element in the government's new strategy to tackle the acute shortage of basic skills and to achieve innovative and flexible approaches to learning. It was launched on a pilot basis late in 1999, opening 70 development centres prior to its official launch in September 2000.

The UfI is not a university in the conventional sense. It does not offer its own qualifications, and it is not exclusively for industry. It will ultimately operate through a network of 1,000 'learning centres' run by a consortium of bodies – employers, unions, voluntary groups, and so on – in accessible (rather than traditional educational) locations. It aims to cover learning at every level from elementary to postgraduate by linking businesses and individuals to information-technology-based education and training underpinned by a national learning grid. The grid is intended to carry high-quality networked learning and information services to schools, libraries and museums at low cost.

The Ufl thus promises new forms of delivering learning and better advice and information about learning opportunities, especially through its free *learndirect* telephone helpline. The Internet and the Web are its key learning tools, enabling learners to interact, and to have easy access to learning packages best suited to each individual.

Emerging concerns

It is natural that in the early years of any radical reform, many concerns will surface. Among those expressed about the changes introduced by Labour since 1997 are:

Reforms in primary and secondary education

At this point, the future seems to hold promise – although the signs are mixed. The increased tests and the raised education targets for 11- and 14-year-olds that have been introduced in Labour's second term continue to attract much criticism in the teaching profession and elsewhere, yet their rationale is powerful. Labour believes that unless there is a fundamental improvement in knowledge of the basics, discipline, and standards in under-achieving schools, its attempt to create a sea change in standards in secondary schools cannot succeed (Ryan, 2001). It is here that, arguably, progress is more crucial than anywhere else in the education system.

On another, related front, there are worrying signs of disaffection in the teaching profession. In August 2001 a report by Demos, 'a Blairite think-tank' (Clare, 2001), was published by the National Union of Teachers. It concluded that teaching has become an 'unsustainable profession' and will have to change radically if it is to attract a new generation of graduates. The reasons for poor recruitment and retention rates include 'poor pay, low status and falling morale allied to high levels of stress, bureaucracy and pupil misbehaviour'. However, it is the lack of classroom autonomy in a system that is still heavily centralised that explains why '40 per cent of trainee teachers never entered the profession and 50 per cent of those who did left within five years' (Clare, 2001).

The further- and higher-education sectors

In September 2001, universities offered 2,000 places on 40 vocation-oriented courses that aimed to bridge the gap between employment and higher education. Many are worried that education will become increasingly 'dumbed down' in favour of training-led vocational programmes. There is greater worry, however, about how expansion is to be paid for. In 1998 an extra £165 million was provided by the DfEE, but that was to come largely out of anticipated income from student fee contributions introduced in that year. The future scenario is unclear.

For higher education in particular, there has been frustration at the absence of a 'realistic analysis' (Court, 1998) of how to afford the involvement in workplace learning urged on the higher-education system by the Green Paper *The Learning Age*. The omission of the higher-education sector from the NLSC system is puzzling, and the intention to have two separate inspectorates to oversee quality of provision threatens to result in further duplication and bureaucracy. The NLSC is responsible for co-ordination and strategic planning mechanism relating to the FE sector, but many college principals fear more waste and red tape.

Further-education colleges are also concerned about how to cope with the additional numbers of students due to enter the system by 2002, and how to improve their links with employers and individuals. One important issue here is how the *learndirect* helpline will operate. It is there to help people to make the right learning choices, with advice about qualifications to be given in easily understandable form. But will it tend simply to redistribute students, steering many to Ufl centres rather than to traditional further-education institutions (Kingston, 1999)? Will it confuse, rather than clarify, the territory of post-16 education and training?

Serious discontent across the whole education system was indicated by three key resignations during 2000–2001: by Chris Woodhead, HM Chief Inspector for Schools in England, because of his dissatisfaction at the government's failure to take a harder line on poor educational standards in schools; by John Randall, chief executive of the Quality Assurance Agency for Higher Education, because of the government's decision to scrap most of the inspection system established in 1997; and by Nick Tate, chief executive of the Qualifications and Curriculum Authority, who subsequently changed his views on the controversial AS-levels being taken for the first time by 17-year-olds, admitting that he and other government advisers had not thought through available options adequately (Hackett, 2001). Like many others, he believes that there is now excessive testing.

The NLSC system

Before identifying some specific concerns, it is important to note that major doubts remain about the validity of any system relying essentially on the market to provide the stimulus needed to learning and development that will improve national skills gaps. To quote from one discussion paper that asks disturbing questions about NVET policy and its implementation (Keep, 2001: 28): skills and training are together not a 'magic bullet that [can], on its own, transform economic performance or deliver social inclusion':

Skills policies have to come to nest within and support broader policy goals and be promoted and delivered accordingly

Many employers fear that the LSC structure will prove centralised and rigid. Latchford (1999) commented that the NLSC, like the new small business service, is a government agency. It therefore differs significantly from TECs in its constitution and in the way it can operate. It has a duty of local consultation, but such agencies can become 'safe, inflexible rule-followers'. The Confederation of British Industry would have preferred a devolved, employer-driven system with access to local spending power.

Unions welcomed the 1999 White Paper proposal because it included them on the boards of national and local LSCs, whereas they had been excluded from TECs. However, some fear that employer domination of the new system could lead to a short-term and narrowly focused view of skills needs that ignores national priorities (Rana, 1999b).

From another quarter, there is a worry that the transference of training for the unemployed to the Employment Service may divide training provision between that for the employed and that for the unemployed. This would be counterproductive at a time when many are moving repeatedly between spells in and out of work as the employment market experiences rapid and continuous change (Roy Harrison, 1999).

The UfI appeals to many as an innovative concept, but it begs large resource questions. Development centres will be able to realise their potential only when fully operational IT and support systems are established. The UfI has no funding of its own to disburse. It can act solely as a broker, attracting people to learning and pointing them to the most relevant provider. Its funding lies in the NLSC's hands, and it remains to be seen how adequate and well-targeted that funding will prove to be.

Youth training

It is too early to be able to predict the extent to which the measures introduced in 2001 to improve, access to and the quality and delivery of youth training, especially through the apprenticeship system, are likely to work. Much will depend on how far the attempts to reform the education system by opening up a vocational route from 14 years upwards are successful. Employers' commitment must also be obtained, especially by giving them a significant voice in the design and operation of apprenticeship schemes both locally and through participation in sectoral agencies. However, as long as the market-led system of vocational training continues, together with a funding focus on outputs rather than on the quality of learning and training processes, the fears expressed in reports like that of the IPD in 1997 (see p31) must remain.

Adult learning

Despite the government's policy commitment to lifelong learning, the current post-16 education system still lacks the flexibility needed to give adults adequate access to learning throughout their lives rather than just for three years after leaving school. One basic barrier to access is that while those who can study full-time receive direct financial support from the public purse, those who study part-time have to pay their own tuition fees and study costs. There is a parallel need to significantly expand opportunities for part-time study. For single parents, the lack of state support for childcare is another barrier to undertaking training or education that could lead to entry or re-entry into the employment market.

If easy access for adult learners is to become a reality, there must also be better transfer between universities. By 1994, about 85 per cent of UK universities had some system of credit accumulation, or plans to introduce it, but there is still much ground to cover. Other imperatives are regular availability of career breaks, continuous opportunity to follow courses while working, and support to take up learning opportunities for the out-of-work who have carer responsibilities.

Government policy clearly acknowledges that greater adult participation in education is no longer an option but a necessity. That participation must be provided in new, less costly, more accessible ways, and must cover social and intellectual as well as practical skills. Yet the primary thrust of the NLSC is aimed at 16–19-year-olds and those in employment. If adult learning is left mainly to local discretion, this will perpetuate the failure of decades of UK education policy to achieve any powerful focus on an area vitally affecting the country's skills base.

Lifelong learning

Although lifelong learning is the Labour government's central plank of policy, the translation from vision to reality is fraught with difficulty. One of the reasons is to do with continuing barriers to adult learning, as already outlined. Another is the present divide in respect of access to training in the UK (see p33). Yet another is the multiplicity of interested parties involved in lifelong learning planning and provision. These parties include government, organisations, individuals and the education sectors. Each has its unique characteristics, culture and history. Within each there are many stakeholders, all with different ends to serve and contributions to make (Homan and Shaw, 2000). Securing commitment to a shared way forward is a Herculean task.

Attaining the goal of lifelong learning for all is particularly difficult when so many of the social discrepancies that the 1993 Moser Report (NCE, 1993) identified in educational attainment remain. The question Peter Drucker posed in that same year is now more pertinent than ever: in an increasingly knowledge-based society, how can those who are educationally disadvantaged join in fully, not only at work but also as citizens?

One option to improve the social balance might have been to extend the Individual Learning Accounts system to give people the power to spend as they wish instead of continuing to fund educational institutions from the centre. That option is no longer open. The abolition of ILAs (see p32) 'dealt a severe blow to lifelong learning in England and Wales' and may have 'shattered the confidence of both learners and genuine training providers, [threatening] the success of any similar government initiatives in future' (Taylor, 2001). It is in any case far more to the point to look to progress with reforms in the primary and secondary education system. Until more socially disadvantaged individuals have the ability to gain the necessary entry qualifications, the social profile of university and college applicants is unlikely to change. This takes us back to that radical overhaul announced in the Education Green Paper in February 2001. Only if that succeeds can there be any chance of achieving the economic and social aims of NVET policy outlined at the start of this chapter.

Checkpoint

- A colleague who knows little about NVET policy hears you talking about LSCs and comments: 'LSCs – never heard of them. Another layer of government bureaucracy, I suppose, just like the TECs. Or can you convince me to the contrary?' Outline a convincing reply.

- Identify and comment on the implications for NVET policy of some of the pressures now being experienced in higher- and further-education institutions.

Challenges ahead

In the UK, the NVET system has always been flawed by its exposure to political expediency. Educational provision is still beset by disparities between academic and vocational pathways, poor standards, a multiplicity of providers, resource constraints, tensions between forces of centralisation and decentralisation, and intractable 'underclass' problems that are intensified when under-achievers enter the employment market. The advancement of lifelong learning to sustain the economy and innovative capability, and the enhancement of education to ensure society's cultural life and its well-being are not aspirations that sit comfortably together. Strains grow as needs intensify.

To tackle these issues effectively there must be a fundamental shift of resources and priorities. It remains to be seen whether that will be achieved – or, indeed, attempted. Specifically, the government must ensure:

- a powerful integrating vision driving NVET policy overall, which can be realised, resourced and sustained at the practical level

- partnership between education providers who are responsible for opening up a wide variety of routes to lifelong learning

- improved standards across the whole education system, and the significant reduction of the 'underclass' problem.

At this point the portents are confused, and the picture continues to change. In June 2001 the DfEE was rebranded the Department for Education and Skills (DfES) with its responsibilities for employment transferred to the new Department for Work and Pensions. Only six years before, there had been the long-overdue integration of the Department for Education and Science and the Department for Education to form the DfEE. This bringing together of workforce and vocational training and of education, and their merging with employment, had been widely welcomed. Now there is concern at a possible threat to education's relationships with employment and business. The official explanation is that the transfer will enable the government to pursue a more coherent and active approach to getting people back to work (Midgley, 2001). However, there are fears that it will prejudice the relationship between New Deal and other work-based training, and that post-16 policy will now be insufficiently framed within an employment context. The chief executive of the LSC has expressed confidence in the strong links being built up between the LSC and the employment service both locally and nationally . . . but the fears persist.

Doubts about the structure through which NVET is co-ordinated and delivered are symptomatic of a much deeper concern that 'the UK's vocational education and training system remains in crisis' (Westwood, 2001) . Some believe that a radically new vision, policy and system are needed if there is to be any hope of avoiding a repetition of the 'jumble of traditional skills supply initiatives that were still around when the new century dawned' (Keep, 2001: 19).

This chapter has been wide-ranging in scope and is in consequence the longest in the book. I have therefore produced the following task to pull its threads together and also to stimulate a start to the necessary process of regularly updating all NVET material.

Task 3

Use your own local sources of information and those shown at the end of this chapter to discover:

- the national learning targets set for achievement by 2002

- the first annual report to be produced by the NLSC, and the business plan of your local LSC

- the extent and nature of involvement with *learndirect* in your organisation and others known to you

- practical ways in which your local further- and higher-education institutions are opening up adult access to lifelong learning opportunities.

CONCLUSION

Having read this chapter and completed its checkpoints and tasks, you should now:

- understand government vision and policy for national vocational education and training (NVET)

- be able to explain key features of NVET strategy and its implementation framework

- be able to advise on general features of the national vocational qualification system

- be able to advise on NVET initiatives at national and local level that can bring benefits for the organisation and for individual employees.

To test yourself against these objectives, what five-minute answers would you give to the following questions?

Review questions

Outline and justify some arguments to persuade senior managers and human resource professionals in your organisation to form close links with local schools and colleges.

While you are giving a lecture to some HR students on NVET policy, one of them interrupts you to say, 'It's clear that governments are always bringing in new strategies and telling us that they will work, then over-turning them a year or so later. Maybe the truth of the matter is that *nothing* governments plan will work, and that instead of meddling, they should leave L&D to the free market.' How will you reply?

What external sources of information would you use in order to dis-cover national and local education and training initiatives that could bring benefits to your organisation and its employees?

Useful reference sources

The following are recommended for updating information:

- the CIPD's publication *People Management*, which contains reliable, accessible and up-to-date information

- the quality press – and especially the Sunday 'heavies' and *The Financial Times* – for their regular articles and editorials on matters relating to the field of secondary and tertiary

> education, and national training; educational supplements in the quality press should also be consulted regularly
>
> - local libraries, chambers of commerce and Learning and Skills Councils, all of which have valuable up-to-date information; the LSC website is at www.lsc.gov.uk
>
> - *learndirect*'s website at www.ufiltd.co.uk; information about the Ufl can also be obtained through the free helpline 0800 100 900
>
> - the Department for Education and Skills website at www.dfes.gov.uk, a source of comprehensive information about NVET policy and progress in England, with links to websites for Northern Ireland, Scotland and Wales; you can also phone the Employment NTO on 0116 251 7979 or email: info@empnto.co.uk
>
> - the CIPD's website for students and members: www.cipd.co.uk, which has links to its online *Training Digest*.

Endnote: NVET in Scotland, Wales and Northern Ireland

There has not been the scope in this chapter to cover NVET policy and systems in Scotland, Northern Ireland or Wales, but CIPD students in those countries are expected to be familiar with them so that they can relate exam answers on NVET to their own country's system if they wish to do so.

Qualifications approved in Wales, Scotland and Northern Ireland, can with few exceptions, also be offered in England. The Scottish parliament has complete responsibility for devising and implementing education and employment strategies, and for the delivery system. The National Assembly for Wales Training and Education Department is responsible for delivering all publicly funded education, training and skills activities in Wales. In Northern Ireland, the NI Department of Education, the Training and Employment Agency and the Economic Development Network are the relevant bodies. Useful websites include:

- www.scotland.gov.uk. Also www.sqa.org.uk (the Scottish Qualifications Authority website)

- www.wales.gov.uk

- www.ednet-ni.com. The Economic Development Network for NI provides a single reference-point for all business and economic information, including that relating to training. Also www.deni.gov.uk.

3 • The Internal Strategic Framework

CHAPTER OBJECTIVES

After reading this chapter you will:

- have an understanding of major theoretical approaches to strategy, and of their practical implications for the strategy process in organisations

- understand the factors that aid or inhibit human resource management (HRM) in gaining strategic status and credibility

- understand the general principles that aid L&D's strategic orientation in the organisation.

Introduction

Co-operating with stakeholders in producing and implementing L&D strategy is a key process, yet often an unsatisfactory one. Part of the reason for this lies in the ambiguous nature of strategy itself. The word 'strategy' has military origins, and has come to be identified with 'the rational expectations of those wishing to direct and manage an organization' (Whipp, 1999: 13). Strategic management focuses on achieving for the organisation a clear and powerful vision, relatively long-term goals, planning and direction, and well-implemented polices to support that direction. Seen in this way, the management of L&D in an organisation can be likened to a military activity, with a set of goals, an overall strategy for achieving them, and short-term tactics to tackle different contingencies.

Why is it, then, that in reality when we enter the field of strategy we walk on such uncertain ground? Time and again the maps offered to us by academics fail. We cannot find our way forward, and the paths across the strategic territory of human resource (HR) management and development seem especially treacherous. Indeed, three human resource practitioners (Maling, Wright and Hessey, 2000), reflecting on their experience, advise:

 Don't be daunted by the unrealistic ideas of commentators and textbook authors.

And another HR commentator (Baron, 2000: 31) writes:

> *It seems that few now doubt that people management can make a difference. They merely question how the difference can be achieved. It appears that we do not yet know enough about translating strategic intentions into implementation and action, or why a particular course of action might prove successful in one situation but not in another.*

Why, after so many years of painstaking research, so much time spent exhorting HR people to 'be strategic', is there still such a gap between rhetoric and reality? And what is needed for those carrying L&D responsibilities in particular to become strategic players?

To find answers to these questions, I believe that we cannot move straight into an analysis of L&D strategy-making. First, we need to understand the strategy process itself, and then the HR framework (whether formal or informal) within which all HR processes in an organisation have to operate. These, then, are the main themes of this chapter. It ends with some guidelines for a strategic and value-adding L&D process – guidelines that can act as a bridge into the detailed study of that process which follows in Chapter 4.

The strategy process

Terminology

Vision   is the picture that people hold in their minds about what kind of organisation theirs should be. Some believe vision should be clear and shared across the organisation in order to be an effective guide to action. Others see value in a vision that, while being compelling, also has sufficient ambiguity to cause searching questions to be asked about the organisation's direction, and to stimulate creativity in finding ways forward.

Mission   is routinely explained as the written and detailed articulation of vision. However, sometimes a mission statement represents only a minority view, and lacks widespread commitment. Mission statements also fall out of date. For both those reasons, many now view such statements as valueless. Yet the process that produces them does have value if it brings together organisational members in ways that encourage informed reflection on crucial issues, and that generate productive thinking.

Strategy   represents a route that has been chosen for a period of time and from a range of options in order to achieve organisational and business goals. But it is also a dynamic process in which that chosen route is frequently altered, sometimes abandoned, as changes occur in the organisation's external and internal environment.

Implementation concerns the execution of strategy. Considerable time is often spent generating strategic options and producing a formal strategy without paying sufficient attention to the factors – especially the human factors – which can signal that a particular option will not work in practice.

Nothing in this chapter contradicts these definitions, because they offer no more than a distillation of theory and practice drawn from many sources. They do not rest on any particular theoretical models and they are not prescriptive. Nonetheless, as we read the chapter we will come to look at them rather differently. We will see just why they are cautious in avoiding a prescriptive approach to strategy.

Strategy theory: some critical questions

Look again at that set of terms above – and now try the following task:

Task 1

Consider your own organisation, or one with which you are familiar. In respect of *either* its corporate level *or* of a particular business unit or divisional level (choose the level about which you are best informed) briefly identify its:

–   vision

–   strategy

–   mission

–   main processes for implementing strategy.

How many readers found this a difficult exercise – or simply gave up in the attempt? It should reassure you to know that it is unusual to find anyone who can supply quick answers to such questions. Many, even given a lot of time, can only come up with incomplete responses. Some cannot supply meaningful answers at all. And this points to the central dilemma for strategy students – the contrast between theory and real life. On the one hand there is the classic definition of strategy (Chandler, 1962; quoted by Whipp, 1999: 18) as:

the determination of the basic long-term goals of an enterprise, and the adoption of courses of action and the allocation of resources necessary for carrying out those goals.

On the other hand, there is the messy organisational reality in which, according to some (Clegg, Hardy and Nord, 1999: 7):

> *The concept of strategy has become a universal sign which is assumed to exist regardless of whether it does or not*

Now that is a startling statement. Put another way, it is claiming (*ibid.*) that:

> *What we know about strategy, we know only because we talk and write about it, and because some activities get talked about as strategy, whereas others do not.*

But the writers have a point. It is indeed the case that for many years 'strategy' has been the smart focus of debate whenever business performance is discussed. There must be few business leaders who would admit that in their organisations there is not (or will not shortly be) an inspirational and cohering vision and a clear corporate strategy to which all organisational members are or should be committed.

Some blame academics for the hype. Lyles (1990: 363) argues that '"Strategic" has become a buzzword for all disciplines trying to stress the importance of their work.' Inkpen and Choudhury (1995) agree. They speculate that the discovery of 'strategy' had more to do with academics theorising than with any certainty about how firms genuinely secure competitive advantage. They have reservations about the concept, even proposing that in certain conditions strategy can actually prevent progress.

Checkpoint

- In what kind of organisational scenario do you think an *absence* of strategy could be the best way forward – and why?

To explore such questioning further, turn to Chapter 22. Here, though, it is enough to say that smaller businesses in a period of fast initial growth, or organisations facing complex and turbulent environments, might well be advised to avoid the straitjacket of detailed formal strategy and plans, spending their time instead on ways of finding and implementing innovatory responses to unfamiliar external conditions.

Where, then, do all these concerns about strategy leave students who have struggled to master SWOT or PESTLE analysis, or the Boston matrix, and who diligently apply their theoretical frameworks to one case study after the next? These are the students accustomed to reciting the mantra:

> *First analyse, then diagnose, then set business goals, then produce a strategy to meet those goals, then draw up and execute plans for strategy's implementation, then monitor performance, then . . .*

And what of us, the tutors and writers? Have we too been mistaken in our belief in a strategic approach, logically derived and applied? The answer is the same as to so many questions about strategy: yes – and no.

Task 2

Assess the following statements from 1 to 6 in order of their accuracy as you see it.
Rate in an order from 1 = the least accurate statement to 6 = the most accurate.

a) Strategy should be designed for the organisation through a □ rational, analytical, top-down process in order to reach a good fit between internal organisational opportunities and external circumstances.

b) Strategy should be achieved by systematic forecasting, □ planning and control.

c) The sound economic positioning of the firm is the primary □ task of strategists, who should choose between generic strategies such as cost-leadership, differentiation or innovation.

d) Strategy is a matter of having a vision of the future and □ calculating how to manipulate and shape the environment.

e) Strategy is an incremental, adaptive process, shaped by □ bounded human rationality and by the dynamic interaction of people's changing mental maps, and learning.

f) Strategy is as much bottom-up as top-down, since it □ emerges from 'muddling through' as different kinds of learning and power-play occur across the organisation.

You may have had difficulty in rating these statements. It is not surprising if you did. In reality there is no right or wrong definition here. Each statement represents an influential school of thought, well grounded in research. Each school has its supporters and its opponents.

The schools of thought involved (Elfring and Volberda, 2001: 1–25), coupled with the names of the researchers who were first associated with them, are shown below, following the sequence of the statements as listed in Task 2:

a) the design school (Andrews, 1965)

b) the planning school (Ansoff, 1965)

c) the positioning school (Porter, 1980)

d) the entrepreneurial school (Schumpeter, 1934)

e) and f) the processual schools, including: cognitive (March and Simon, 1958; Simon, 1945); learning (Lindblom, 1959; Quinn, 1980); and political (Allison, 1971; Perrow, 1970; Pettigrew, 1973).

Every well-known strategy theory offers practitioners concepts and tools that, although they have no universal applicability, can prove relevant to use in different kinds of situation. We can conclude that:

- There is no one view of 'strategy'. The strategy field is fragmented by the number of schools of thought it contains and by the wide-ranging differences in their underlying theoretical dimensions and research methodologies (Elfring and Volberga, 2001: 8).

- At one end of the scale there are those who see strategy to be about the exercise of economic logic, formal planning and responding 'intelligently' to the market environment. In this view, that environment is the dominating force that shapes the actions of every organisation. Strategy is the product of good information-gathering and of top-down decision-making in the organisation, controlled ultimately by a single powerful individual or by a 'dominant coalition'.

- At the other (and increasingly popular) end of the scale, there are those who see strategy as a process more spontaneous than it is formalised. In this view, strategy represents a pattern in a stream of actions through time (Mintzberg and Waters, 1985). It continually changes as a result of ongoing learning and action across the organisation. It is powerfully influenced by individual and collective cognitions (often described as people's mental maps) and by the interplay of power and politics at every organisational level.

- Since there is no consensus about 'strategy', theory must be applied to practice selectively. The practitioner can gather from the many strategy schools a wide range of insightful ways of looking at different kinds of organisational situation, and many different analytical and diagnostic tools. It is for each practitioner to select those that appear to be most relevant for the given context. What works in one case can never be presumed to work in another.

Checkpoint

- If you were the owner/manager of a small firm operating in a turbulent environment, why might you be sceptical about the value of producing a formal strategy and detailed business plan?

- If you were explaining to students new to strategy theory your own view of the most realistic approach to the strategy process, which approach would you choose – and why?

Rationality and decision-making

One of the major themes in the literature of strategy is to do with 'bounded rationality'. The concept is based on the view that in organisational life (as more widely), decisions are not 'arrived at by a step-by-step process which is both logical and linear' (Miller, Hickson and Wilson, 1999: 44) but are reached by the exercise of a limited economic rationality. This is in sharp contrast to the classical view of the strategy process, which rests on two assumptions:

- that decision-makers share a common purpose when making strategic decisions: to maximise rewards and minimise costs for the business

- that in pursuit of this rational objective, they systematically 'collect and sort information about alternative potential solutions, compare each solution against predetermined criteria to assess the degree of fit, arrange solutions in order of preference, and make an optimizing choice which they then equally systematically draw up plans to implement' (Miller et al, 1999: 44).

Simon (1945) was the first organisational theorist to propose the concept of bounded rationality. Such writers observe that in reality strategy-makers pursue multiple aims that are to do with individual as well as with organisational interests. The organisation is not a unitary system, in which the players are united in pursuit of a common economic goal. It is a pluralist system, where 'rationality' repeatedly breaks down in the confusion caused by conflicting interests and by diverse perceptions as to 'what matters here' and how to tackle it.

All decision-making in organisations can be seen as limited in a similar way. The factors that explain this include ambiguous, excessive, incomplete or unreliable data, incompetent processing or communicating of information, pressures of time, and differences in individuals' cognitive processes, mental maps and reasoning capacity (Simon, 1955; Cyert and March, 1963). Decision-making is further limited by the complexity of modern organisations and the power-play that goes on within and around them.

In the face of so many limitations, it is impossible for people to achieve perfect knowledge of an issue, or share identical perceptions of it – particularly when it is one that arouses strong emotions or threatens established interests. As Miller et al (1999) observe, this does not mean that people behave irrationally. Quite the reverse: for most of the time most people are, by their own lights, very reasoned in their behaviour. What it means (runs the argument) is that the logic underpinning behaviour is always flawed by 'human frailties and demands from both within and outside the organization' (Miller et al, 1999: 45).

Task 3

Obtain information about *one* recent problematic situation in an organisation that you know about, and analyse how far the problem was resolved by a process of rational decision-making and how far by other means.

What 'human frailties and demands' do you think would have limited *you* in making decisions about that situation?

The concept of bounded rationality does not, of course, apply with equal strength to all types of decision-making. Many decisions that are made in organisations are straightforward and their logic is rarely questioned. They tend to be about familiar operational matters, usually of a routine nature. They are ordinarily made in accordance with well-tried procedures that ensure efficiency and consistency of decision-making across the organisation.

It is non-routine, complex and organisationally critical situations that make most demands on the exercise of human rationality. And it is in the strategic arena that this rationality is at its most bounded (Miller *et al*, 1999). This is because the big issues that arise in that arena are relatively unfamiliar, yet their resolution is vital for the organisation. They are to do with its future goals and direction, with new competitive pressures and opportunities, and with unexpected internal and external developments.

Big, unfamiliar issues pull decision-makers into territory where they have little if any direct knowledge or experience. There are usually few protocols to fall back on, and sometimes only one: that which brought them there. Some organisational members will have the automatic right to sit at the strategy table, but others will be excluded or, if there, will have little influence on discussion or outcomes. This returns us to the plurality of interests in organisations, and the increased likelihood in the strategic arena of 'multiple, competing interest groups vying for supremacy' (Miller *et al*, 1999: 47).

Task 4

Take the following list. Put a tick against those players you think are likely to influence strategic decisions in an organisation most, and a cross against those you think likely to influence strategic decisions least.

Sales and marketing
Chief executive officer (CEO)
External stakeholders

Personnel function
Accounting
Trade unions
The government
Production (or equivalent)
Purchasing dept

This enquiry was incorporated into a longitudinal research programme carried out over many years by a team at the University of Bradford (Miller *et al*, 1999). The researchers found that in the many types of organisation whose decision-making processes they tracked through time, those who overtly influenced critical organisational decisions *least* were unions, the personnel function, purchasing departments, and the government. Those who overtly influenced such decisions *most* were the CEO, the production department (or equivalent), sales and marketing, and accounting. Stakeholders 'do take part in the game' but 'the balance of power is held internally' (Miller *et al*, 1999).

These patterns of influence are predictable. Over the years, strategy has become so closely associated with business performance that those whose activities relate directly and measurably to that performance invariably carry most weight in the strategy process. Apparently recognising this, organisational actors who, like HR practitioners, have traditionally lacked that advantage now 'strive to make themselves more "strategic" by redefining their work as "performance-related" ' (Clegg *et al*, 1999: 8).

It is natural that in the strategic arena power and politics should assume heightened prominence. Where the stakes for the organisation are high, the stakes for key organisational players are high too. The strategy process has been likened to a game played out by influential actors who constantly seek to impose their understanding of the situation on others, each trying to protect old power-bases and secure their own, often widely differing, ends. As these actors 'jockey for position' amidst continuing negotiation and bargaining, the jockeying itself shapes subsequent actions and their outcomes (Miller *et al*, 1999: 51). Power begets more power; failure generates its own dismal further descent. In Chapter 6 issues of power and politics are explored in detail.

The strategy process: some conclusions

To conclude and to answer that disturbing question posed at its start: have we been wrong to place such faith in strategy? Yes, and no.

- It *is* important to analyse, to diagnose, to produce goals and plans that fit needs and context, and to work together in setting and trying to maintain a durable direction for the organisation. However, organisations are pluralist, not unitary, systems. Given the many and often opposing interests of the parties, there are limits to the extent to which continuously effective 'working together' can be achieved. Collaboration is a vital process, but whatever the skills of those who promote it, some failures will occur.

- Furthermore, nothing in strategy-making and its implementation is, or can be, set in stone: what occurs will never be exactly what was intended. The strategy process operates with bounded rationality only. It is dynamic and opportunistic. It is therefore, to a greater or lesser extent, unpredictable.

- Much of strategy emerges in an ongoing manner from individual and collective learning. As time goes on, new threats and opportunities – internal and external to the organisation – develop. These will call for adjustments, sometimes radical, to be made to the strategic route originally agreed.

- Finally, people's perceptions, actions and influence related to strategy change continually. These shifts have a strong influence on the strategic process as it unfolds.

For those interested, there is a more sophisticated discussion of themes related to strategic progress in Chapter 22. Here, it is important to turn our attention to the relationship between strategy and HR processes.

Checkpoint

- A colleague asks you what is meant by the term 'bounded rationality' and asks for a practical example. Outline your response.

- Your HR manager complains that although she carefully tailors HR strategy to support business goals, and supports all her HR plans with logical arguments, she still doesn't seem to be a strategic player in the organisation. 'Where am I failing?', she asks you. What will you reply?

Strategy and human resource management

It is helpful to think about HRM as a door. Open, it signifies the removal of human barriers to achieving the organisation's goals. Closed, it signifies the reinforcement of those barriers, and a consequent likelihood of failure to realise either organisational or individual potential.

Figure 4 (overleaf) shows the strategic and business context for HRM.

Figure 4 HRM and the business

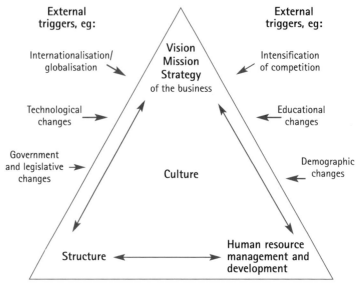

Many commentators believe that the HRM function repeatedly fails to prove its importance to the bottom line and to gain recognition from chief executives. Although it is admitted that sometimes failure springs from unrealistic expectations of HR at board level, blame is nevertheless regularly heaped on the shoulders of HR practitioners.

Guest and Baron (2000) suggest two reasons for HR processes' lacking strategic credibility:

- HR departments are not always seen to be effective in leading HR projects and initiatives.

- Many chief executives pay lip-service only to the idea that people are their organisation's most important assets.

But such explanations beg the question why it is that HR practitioners so often fail to impress on management the importance of their function to the organisation. The following comment (Baron, 2000: 31) typifies the views of many:

The findings from ... research projects ... will be relevant only if we place them firmly in a framework of practical action that is relevant to the business and rooted in its concerns. 〞

There is another perspective that is relevant here. It focuses on the need for top management to recognise what Hendry, Pettigrew and Sparrow (1988: 41) call the 'legitimacy' of HRM:

Putting capable personnel professionals into punishing environments is not a successful strategy. For this reason, the trend detectable in some firms towards putting line managers into the most senior positions to oversee the personnel function may represent a breakthrough in the acceptance of HRM issues at the highest level.

All these statements point to four conclusions:

- If HR practitioners lack credibility in their organisations, little that they do – regardless of its actual quality – will be perceived in a positive light.

- If they do not speak the language of the business, they will be unable to gain credibility.

- If they cannot propose initiatives that convincingly offer real value for the business, they will be unable to gain credibility.

- To speak the language of the business and to propose credible initiatives, HR professionals must form and maintain effective business partnerships across the organisation.

Task 5

Obtain information from an organisation with which you are familiar, and where HR professionals are employed, in order to enable you to answer the following questions:

What evidence could you find to indicate how successful those professionals are in demonstrating HRM's important to the business?

What seems to explain their success – or their failure?

Aligning HRM with the business

Consideration of business partnership issues leads naturally to one of the main themes in HRM strategy theory: alignment. Alignment here means two things:

- *functional alignment* (or 'horizontal integration') – the integration of all HR processes so that they are mutually supportive, and line up positively with overall HR strategy and its goals

- *strategic alignment* (or 'vertical integration') – the integration of HRM strategy and goals with business strategy at corporate and unit levels.

HRM: functional alignment

In Chapter 1 it was proposed that all HR processes are naturally interdependent, and Figure 3 (p14) was used to illustrate that interdependency. We should now look in rather more detail at the processes in the HRM wheel:

- *HR strategy and planning* determine how many people should be employed, how, when and where, and how they will be used. These processes provide the framework within which HR policies and practices becomes operational.

- *Recruitment and selection* determine what kind of people are employed and set the crucial parameters of human capability in the organisation. Ineffective recruitment and selection almost always defeat subsequent attempts to build competence and commitment, and to develop potential.

- *Learning and development* can in part be formally structured but are most powerfully influenced by daily operations in the workplace. The effective integration of learning and work drives the achievement of goals and ensures the development of knowledge and innovation in the organisation.

- *Career planning and development* provide the basis for the psychological contract between organisation and individual.

- *Incentive and reward systems* significantly influence people's motivation related to their performance and development. They either help to release the exercise of competence, learning and creativity in the organisation, or they act as barriers to human effort and energy.

- *Teambuilding and teamworking processes* exercise a powerful influence on the achievement of performance standards and on motivation, learning and adaptability within and between teams.

- *Performance appraisal* must strive to achieve an effective balance between focusing on current performance and developing people for the future. It goes to the heart of the performance management process.

- *Policies and processes related to the health, safety and welfare* of the workforce must be built into all HR processes if they are to have positive outcomes for individuals and for the organisation overall.

- *Redeployment and disengagement* policies require a strong developmental aspect if they are to facilitate and produce benefits from downsizing, restructuring, and other forms of organisational repositioning. They must also operate fairly across the work force.

HRM: strategic alignment

The command to 'align HRM with strategy' begs some awkward questions about the type of strategy in mind. Corporate or divisional? Short- or long-term? Feasible and relevant to organisational needs, or merely any strategy – good or bad – that is formally in place at the time? And how often in real life is such alignment actually achieved?

To take the last question first: most UK-based organisations now have HR representation at board level. A 1999 report by the Institute of Directors, for example, showed that such representation had jumped from 55 per cent to 72 per cent in only one year (Walsh, 1999). However, research continues to show that in many organisations there is still no meaningful link between corporate goals and HR activity. There is a widespread lack of HR strategies to tackle some of the areas most critical to the business, such as staff turnover, succession planning, and preparation for roles of company directors (Walsh, 1999).

It seems, then, that HR representation at board level is not doing enough to align HRM with business strategy. It has to be conceded, though, that there are external factors operating today that make that task uniquely difficult. As Purcell, Kinnie, Hutchinson and Rayton (2000: 32) observe:

> *One obvious area of tension is between getting things right inside the organisation while also coping with a competitive labour market for talented people, and responding to the changing demands of customers and clients.*

This quotation comes from an article about research being done at the Work and Employment Research Centre at Bath University, where a team is collecting data on a continuous basis on HR practices in 12 companies across a range of industries and sectors. In all those companies, HR strategy faces exceptional challenges:

- Each organisation is operating in an increasingly complex and often unpredictable external environment.

- Each is having to deal with multiple challenges which often conflict in terms of actions needed to meet them.

- Each is also encountering the pressures that come from increasing competition, fast-changing technology, tight labour markets and a growing requirement to respond to the needs of employees (as defined by Social Chapter and European human rights legislation).

Once again, partnership is the way forward. HR practitioners, including those on the board will only achieve a truly strategic impact when they work with managers and other stakeholders across the organisation to decide what combination of business and HR strategies offer the best way to make progress.

Lessons from theory and research

In such challenging times for HR strategists, many turn to theoretical models for help. It can be hard to find. This section includes some of the best-known approaches to HRM and strategy. It may be argued that those chosen are too unitary. However, my purpose is to enter the HR strategy field through a relatively straightforward gate. In that way I hope to capture the interest even of those who are quite unfamiliar with that field, encouraging them to reflect on and evaluate some of the important links between HR theory and practice. Such approaches to HRM and strategy tend to fall into two major categories: tight-coupled and loose-coupled. The prescriptions of the former – the 'grand models' – lack universal validity, containing too many internal contradictions to be reliable guides to practice in the particular organisation. It is the views of writers associated with the loose-coupled perspective that are proving more helpful – not because they offer prescriptions but because they emphasise the need for pragmatism, for achieving 'fit' with organisational *and* external contexts.

Tight-coupled approaches

Tight-coupled models advocate a close interconnection between different types of business strategy and organisational structure on the one hand, and different types of HR activity on the other. The type and content of selection, appraisal, reward and developmental policies should, in this view, follow the specific type of business strategy and organisational structure.

So-called 'hard' tight-coupled models come predominantly from the Michigan school of business management theory in the USA. They have been heavily influenced by the work of strategic management writers such as Galbraith and Nathanson (1978) and of HR specialists such as Fombrun, Tichy and Devanna (1984). The approach they advocate has a powerful appeal because of its surface rationality and its operational detail. In essence, however, it is highly engineered. For it to work, there must be a clear and detailed business strategy that is agreed by all the parties, that remains fairly stable through time, and that consistently guides action throughout the organisation. In real life this is asking for the impossible. Often there is no such strategy. Sometimes there is a strategy, but it is very different in its implementation from that intended by top management. Or, again, strategy may be clear and detailed – but it may also be of poor quality. Even when strategy is appropriate and has the commitment of most of the parties for much of the time, contingencies can occur that throw it out of line – together with any HR strategies that are tightly tied to its coat-tails.

For all these reasons the 'hard' approach to tight-coupling has been dismissed by some HR writers in the UK as 'a fantastically idealized picture: in reality achieving it is extremely rare' (Mabey and Salaman, 1995: 46).

The so-called 'soft' HR approach, typified by the Harvard school's 'mutuality' model, has many supporters. Its aim is to achieve a set of generic HR goals and elements that are strategic in their focus – because they are to do with building high performance, high commitment, flexibility, and long-term development of people and of the organisation – and that are to be applied regardless of organisational context. The claimed outcome of this universal prescription is to produce 'resourceful humans' who work together to ensure the achievement of organisational goals.

This high-commitment model (as it is also known) relies on its developmental drive to achieve the necessary 'mutuality of interest' on which its rationale is based. However, despite the attractiveness of its language, in reality the approach is riddled with internal contradictions. There is no need to go into these here (see Guest, 1990, and Harrison, 1993 [pages 58–63] for detailed criticisms). Suffice to say that the model is rooted in the work of mid-twentieth century American organisational psychologists like Herzberg and Likert (see Chapter 1) and is flawed by the same uneasy mix of scientific management and idealism about the 'perfectability-of-man' in the workplace (Butler, 1986: 119).

The loose-coupled approach

Chris Hendry (1995), one of the most respected UK academics in the HR field, urges HR practitioners to avoid any attempt to tie HRM strategy tightly to business strategy. Such 'tight coupling' can prevent HRM activity from being flexible enough to respond quickly to changing needs, stage of growth and strategic orientation of the business. Instead, practitioners should develop a deep knowledge of the business, its attributes and its environment, and should work with management on flexible HR strategies that best fit current needs and can be quickly adapted to meet new contingencies.

This approach is called 'loose coupling'. It relies on HR practitioners, working in business partnerships, to operate pragmatically and expertly. It has emerged as one of the most useful theories for those with HR strategic responsibilities. It is not prescriptive. Instead, it focuses on analysis, diagnosis and collaboration. It highlights the importance of processes of knowledge and learning (see Chapters 19 and 20) in building the organisation's adaptive capability.

Mark Huselid (1995), a US academic and consultant, takes the same line as Hendry. He believes that unless HR people are business as well as professional experts, they should not be allowed to make HR strategy decisions. The kind of qualities that he and Hendry have in mind here are similar to those listed some years earlier by another US writer (Ulrich, 1987):

- personal credibility
- ability to manage change and culture
- knowledge of HR practices
- understanding of the business.

Checkpoint

● Which would you recommend for your organisation – a tight-coupled or loose-coupled approach to HRM strategy – and why?

● Where loose-coupling is the chosen approach for HRM strategy, what kind of skills does it call for in HR practitioners, and why?

Organisational capacity and context

The firm's human resource base is a vital source of its distinctive capabilities, defined as 'what the firm is able to perform with excellence compared to its competitors' (Nordhaug and Grønhaug, 1994: 95). However, those distinctive capabilities depend for their effectiveness on the organisation's 'capacity to deploy resources, usually in combination, using organizational processes, to effect a desired end' (Amit and Schoemaker, 1993: 35). A strategic approach to HRM can help to build organisational capacity, and so add value to the organisation's capability to achieve its goals.

CASE STUDY: Terry and Purcell's 1997 research into 'leanness'

Organisational capacity is produced by organisational structure and culture, routines and procedures, budgetary controls and corrective actions, business processes and organisational networks. Many HR practices can enhance capacity. Two UK academics, Terry and Purcell, reported in 1997 on seven organisations restructuring in order to become more competitive. Their research showed that the HRM practices that most helped to expand organisational capacity in those organisations were:

● communication processes to explain the strategic purpose behind restructuring

● team structures and technology to spread knowledge across the organisation

● competency frameworks to identify and foster behaviour needed

● career structures to provide life-skills and employability

● reward systems, often group-based

● systems for monitoring and measuring performance, including appraisal

● training interventions, especially for team leaders, to equip them with the skills needed to manage team members as well as products.

All these practices were applied differently from one organisation to the next, in order to respond adequately to each organisation's unique needs and context. What mattered most was to choose and implement sets of practice that would work best in the particular context.

Worryingly, other research findings have indicated that most businesses are failing to make use of modern HR practices, and do not prioritise employee issues (Guest and Baron, 2000). Three factors have a unique significance here:

- top management's vision of the organisation

- the way that that vision is communicated and reinforced

- management style and actions across the organisation.

These factors significantly determine internal organisational context. In so doing they establish a workplace culture that influences the extent to which HRM can become a strategic process, and that determines how far HRM practices can make an impact on business performance (Hendry, 1995; Patterson, West, Lawthom and Nickell, 1997). Further information about these factors is included in the detailed examination of organisational context in Chapter 6.

The practice of 'bundling'

What Terry and Purcell (1997) were describing in the research outlined in the previous section is a 'bundling' approach to HRM. 'Bundling' is about choosing and integrating HR practices in different ways to suit different organisational configurations. It is a type of coupling process that aims to improve performance standards, quality, flexibility and commitment, since all these are essential to successful organisational performance. It involves the choice and use of groupings of HR practices that at a particular point in time best fit the needs, characteristics and core competences of the business and enable it to move forward in its environment.

A body of research studies in the USA and UK now indicates that the operation of mutually reinforcing systems of HR practice can directly improve company performance (Caulkin, 2001). Particularly significant findings have been reported by Patterson *et al* in their research for the IPD (1997), by Mark Huselid (1995) in the USA, and by David Guest in an ongoing research programme at Birkbeck College, London. Guest has surveyed more than 1,000 chief executives and HR directors and has found clear links between 18 key HR practices, employee attitudes and behaviour, and the financial performance of the business (Guest and Baron, 2000; Guest and King, 2001).

However, research also consistently shows that while the use of bundling is certainly spreading in the UK, only a tiny minority of organisations demonstrate all the key practices. The most frequently used bundles are to do with individuals 'working harder but not smarter' (Stevens and Ashton, 1999; Guest and King, 2001).

Bundles have to be chosen pragmatically, in order to fit internal and external context in the particular situation. They must be reviewed regularly, since the relevance, uniqueness and impact of any one type of bundle will inevitably change through time. Bundles quoted in research vary in their detail, but the kind that seem to have the most consistently powerful effects on organisational performance (Guest and King, 2001) have individual and collective learning at their core, being concerned with:

- skills acquisition and development

- knowledge management

- commitment

- job design

- employee involvement.

This conclusion is in line with the findings already noted above by Ulrich and by Terry and Purcell. They are also in line with those of the 1998 Workplace Employee Relations Survey (Cully, 1998) – the biggest survey of its kind in the world, and fourth in a series that began in 1980.

Guidelines for a strategic L&D process

In Part 4 of this book I examine in detail how to give the L&D process strategic thrust in order to achieve value-adding L&D initiatives. In this short section, we conclude by identifying some general principles to aid L&D's strategic orientation in an organisation.

Reflecting on the material covered in this chapter and applying it in an L&D context, it seems clear that for L&D to achieve its strategic potential:

- *The L&D process must be coherent and business-focused* – It should consist of a clear, durable set of practices and initiatives that interact positively with the employment system and HR policies of the organisation, and that support corporate goals and values.

- *L&D strategy should be 'loose-coupled'* – It should be of direct relevance to corporate and HR goals and strategies, but it should not be so tightly tied to specific business strategies that it rapidly becomes out of date or impossible to sustain.

- *The L&D process should be flexible and value-adding* – It must be able to respond to a variety of needs at different organisational levels and in different locations. (As an aside here, there is a whole literature now on HRD in international businesses, but this has become such a major area that most of it falls outside the scope of this book.)

- *L&D practitioners should form business partnerships* – As noted later in Chapter 6, these partnerships should be external as well as internal. L&D practitioners must be actively involved in external networks that enable them to increase their knowledge of the general business environment, and to gain various kinds of support for their L&D activity within their organisation.

Task 6

Reflecting on the content of this chapter, produce four or five recommendations that should enable L&D to make a more powerful strategic contribution to your own organisation, or to one with which you are familiar. Make sure that your recommendations have a convincing business rationale.

Finally, here is a case study to help you reflect on all the material in this chapter. You should think about the main HR issues that it raises and about the barriers to effective L&D at Pyrotem.

CASE STUDY: Linda, the disillusioned recruit

Pyrotem is a light-engineering company employing 1,000 people. It has been a very successful business for 25 years. However, it is now struggling to retain its market position. To do so, it has to continuously drive down costs while also achieving innovation and high quality in its products and excellence in its supplier and customer relationships. It boasts of its human resource management (HRM) policies and its refusal to recruit any but 'the best' to work there. Starting-pay, and terms and conditions for supervisors and managers are above the local average.

Linda has a good degree and an impressive school and university record. Two years ago, when she was a new graduate, she was recruited to a trainee HRM officer post at Pyrotem. At her interview, the HRM manager told her that he was looking for someone with the potential to become an 'excellent performer'. Linda would be encouraged to develop by using her initiative and by being given a significant amount of freedom in the way she carried out her tasks. She was attracted by the thought of working with what the HRM manager described as a high-quality HRM team managed with a concern to respond to individuals' learning needs and to develop their potential. She was delighted to be offered the traineeship and looked forward to an exciting career in the company.

Alas, Linda found that during her induction and basic training programme she was given little clarification of targets and little guidance, support or feedback on her performance. After six months she moved into a full HRM officer post, but the HRM manager expected her most of the time to perform her role in exact accordance with his instructions. She had little opportunity to exercise her own initiative.

Linda found the culture of the small HRM department backward-looking, and it soon became clear to her why, over the past few years, turnover of new young HR recruits like her had been high. She often wondered what exactly her contribution to the company's goals was – and quite what the HRM department was contributing, come to that. She also found that few promotion opportunities existed. When they did occur, the criteria for promotion were unclear and seemed to depend on the subjective views of a small group of senior managers. There was no effective performance review or staff development scheme. There was just an appraisal system that most managers treated as 'another routine job we have to do' and to which they gave minimal attention other than filling in annual forms in an arbitrary fashion. Linda's own most recent appraisal by the HRM manager did not clarify her forthcoming targets or give her meaningful feedback on her progress to date.

Being a bright girl with much to offer, Linda was easily able to get a job elsewhere. Half-way through her second year she left Pyrotem and went to a local competitor with a long-established reputation for skilful management and for getting, developing and keeping high-quality and enthusiastic people. Employees were proud to work there and could see the difference their particular job made to the business as a whole. It lived up to Linda's expectations, and she quickly became a big asset to the company.

CONCLUSION

Having read this chapter and completed its checkpoints and tasks, you should now:

- have an understanding of major theoretical approaches to strategy, and of their practical implications for the strategy process in organisations

- understand the factors that aid or inhibit human resource management (HRM) in gaining strategic status and credibility

- understand the general principles that aid L&D's strategic orientation in the organisation.

To test yourself against these objectives, what five-minute answers would you give to the following questions?

Review questions

A manager, chatting with you over coffee, asks why strategy is often described as 'a messy business'. Provide her with a brief explanation.

For a forthcoming talk to young human resource practitioners you have to identify and explain the common causes of HRM's failure to achieve a strong and sustained strategic thrust to its operations. Outline convincingly *three* causes you consider fundamental.

One of your L&D colleagues says to you, rather cynically, 'We're always being told "Get strategic with the L&D process." Just give me a few basic tips here.' Provide those tips.

Useful reference sources

CLEGG S. R., HARDY C. and NORD W. R. (eds) (1999) *Managing Organizations: Current issues*. London, Sage.

MCGOLDRICK A. (ed.) (1996) *Cases in Human Resource Management*. London, Pitman.

4 • Adding Value

CHAPTER OBJECTIVES

After reading this chapter you will:

- understand what is meant by the L&D process 'adding value'
- understand the importance of achieving strategic alignment in order for L&D to make a powerful 'added-value' impact on the organisation
- be able to identify any barriers and aids to such alignment in any particular situation
- know how to produce feasible and value-adding L&D goals and plans

Introduction

This second part of the book explores the practical ways in which, within the organisation, those who hold formal responsibility for the L&D process can achieve outcomes that are beneficial for the business and for individuals. The phrase 'L&D practitioners' is used throughout in its generic sense, since in organisations today those who have significant L&D tasks to perform can include HR specialists, senior and line managers/team leaders and external consultants.

The main themes of Part 2 relate to building L&D partnerships that will actively commit key stakeholders to the processes and outcomes of L&D activity; to ensuring ethical as well as professionally expert L&D practice; to the efficient and effective management of the L&D function however it is organised in the business; and to making the best use of new technology in L&D operations and processes. The scope of Part 2 extends to small and medium-sized as well as large enterprises.

The focus in this chapter is on 'adding value', the importance of which was noted in Chapter 1. To add value is one of the L&D practitioner's core responsibilities, yet some do not find the concept appealing. It smacks too much of a commercial approach, they feel. This is a mistaken understanding. To add value is to add to the organisation's capability to achieve its goals. It is to make a difference where it matters most. It involves the intelligent operation of a strategically focused L&D process, producing outcomes that enable the organisation to deal better than it could before with challenges and threats that face it, and generating returns that are over and above the cost of the L&D investment.

'Added value' should not be confused with 'best value'. The Audit Commission's 'Best Value' framework requires local authority services to be examined between 2000 and 2005 against four criteria, summarised (Gorman, 2000) as:

challenge   Why is the service carried out at all?

consult   What do customers think about our service and the level of performance?

compare   How does our performance compare against the best of the public and private sector?

compete   Can the service be delivered more effectively by alternative providers?

The personnel service is one of many to be reviewed using this framework, and many commentators – including Gorman – see this as a way of ensuring added value (see, for example, van Adelsberg and Trolley, 1999, and Spurling and Trolley, 2000). This is not necessarily the case. Adding value is about more than gaining feedback on current activity, comparisons with best practice or choice of good providers. It is about selecting L&D initiatives and processes of which the outcomes will significantly increase the organisation's capability to differentiate itself from other, similar organisations, and thereby enhance its progress.

It was in this sense that the managing director of a strategic HR consultancy criticised HR professionals' 'obsession with best practice'. He urged them to concentrate on adding value instead (Green, 1999). He was concerned at a common failure to sufficiently research the impact that specific interventions or tools can make in a given context. This failure results in an inadequate focus on the key drivers of organisational performance, and in a tendency to measure HR inputs rather than organisational outputs. He offered the following advice to ensure 'added value':

align   Point people in the right direction.

engage   Develop their belief and commitment to the organisation's purpose and direction.

measure   Provide the data that demonstrate the improved results you achieve.

This chapter first explores the ways in which L&D activity can be strategically aligned in order to ensure added value. In the second section, issues are examined that are related to developing vision, values and commitment. The third section deals with how to plan for added value at different organisational levels. And the fourth introduces issues concerning the assessment of valued added by L&D activity. The chapter ends with general principles and a case study illustrating the characteristics of a value-adding L&D function.

Achieving alignment

L&D: business-led or strategically aligned?

In discussing how L&D can achieve a strategic alignment in order to add value for the organisation, it is common to confuse two terms that are distinct although interrelated:

Business-led L&D is development aimed at the achievement of current business goals. It can also make possible a widening choice of business strategies as people at various levels of the organisation begin to achieve their full potential. Business-led L&D must be a dynamic process, continuously interacting with the cycle of business change.

Strategically aligned L&D is development that operates within the overall business strategy and human resource strategic framework of the organisation. Strategic L&D activity is intended to be durable, since it is focused on the longer term (Bratton and Gold, 1994: 226):

> *An organisation's investment in the learning of its people acts as a powerful signal of its intentions ... to take a longer-term view.*

To improve performance in the workplace and develop the competencies needed to meet future challenges – both important ways of adding value – L&D must be business-led but it must also be strategically focused. It will be business-led if it can justify itself in business terms. It will be strategically focused if it is also responsive to needs raised by the organisation's longer-term goals and can produce strategic initiatives that are 'built to last'.

Table 2 overleaf (although referring to 'training and development', whereas our preferred term is 'learning and development') shows how to identify the extent to which L&D activity in an organisation is business-led, strategically aligned – or merely peripheral to the business.

The formal roles of those holding L&D responsibilities have an influence on the extent to which strategic alignment can be achieved. However, roles and status do not automatically confer credibility or expertise. As we noted in Chapter 3, HR representation at board level in the UK is not

Table 2 Matrix to identify training and development role and contribution to the business

T&D activity	Alignment with business goals	T&D seen financially by management as	T&D formal responsibility of	Ownership of T&D felt mainly by	Focus and purpose of T&D mainly	Main mode of delivery
Peripheral to the business	Negligible	A cost to the business, one of the first that can be cut back in contingency	Specialist T&D/ personnel staff or some individual on full/part-time basis	Specialist staff of whoever holds formal T&D responsibility	No systematic focus, and *ad hoc* purposes	Formal and knowledge-based courses and/or picking up skills on the job from more experienced individuals
Business-led	Linked to current business goals and targets	An essential 'bottom-line' business cost	Specialist staff/ managers	Top and line managers, specialist staff, and to some extent workforce generally	Job-related, for individuals and teams, to improve current performance and prepare for specific changes in jobs, systems and workplace practices	Systematically designed internal learning events, and job-related external courses, skill and knowledge-based
Strategically focused	Linked to strategic goals at corporate and unit levels	A value-adding investment, essential to the future of the business	Member of board, specialists/ managers, teams and individuals	Shared by the parties	Continuous improvement of performance, and continuous development of organisation, teams and individuals. Purpose also to build a general climate of self-initiated learning and development	Planned and experiential learning to develop skills, knowledge and attitudes, and to aid development of learning skills

T&D = Training and Development
Source: Harrison R. (1999) *The Training and Development Audit*. Cambridge, Cambridge Strategy Publications, p8. Reproduced with kind permission of the publisher.

doing enough to prove the worth of the HR function. On current trends the HR board member is usually the official spokesperson for L&D at corporate level. If that spokesperson is ineffective, no amount of expertise and credibility of L&D practitioners lower down the organisation will be able to undo the damage this causes to the L&D function.

Of course there are more positive scenarios. There are HR directors who are held in high esteem at corporate level and whose L&D expertise is high. There are boards where there is no HR specialist, yet where there are knowledgeable board members who powerfully promote L&D as a strategic force in the business. In both such scenarios, there are many strategic opportunities for L&D.

Checkpoint

- What is the difference between L&D that is business-led and L&D that is strategically aligned?

- A colleague says to you, 'Our problem in L&D is that we don't have anyone on the board. Until that happens, L&D will never have strategic credibility.' How do you reply?

Developing a strategic focus

We must ask four questions in order to discover whether there is – or could be – a genuinely strategic focus to the L&D function in an organisation (the term 'function' is used here in its widest, not its specialist department, sense):

- Is there functional alignment (horizontal integration) of L&D?

- Can there be strategic alignment (vertical integration) of L&D?

- Are there major issues to indicate that the L&D function should become a strategic player?

- What critical indicators demonstrate that the L&D function is strategically focused?

Is there functional alignment of L&D?

We first discussed the principle of functional alignment in Chapter 3. Here, we have two issues to consider:

- the need to ensure that all L&D activity is sufficiently well internally integrated that no one L&D process or initiative fails to support, or be supported by, the rest. In the UK in the 1990s, although there was quite widespread developmental activity in relation to culture change, decentralisation, workforce competences and formal strategy planning skills, there was often little internal consistency in these initiatives (Storey, 1994), and this reduced their business impact.

- the need to ensure that all L&D activity is adequately integrated with other HR policies and practice across the organisation. For example, L&D strategy must be sensitive to the increasingly wide range of employment contracts in organisations. It must cater for diversity in all its forms, so that L&D policy and practice is fair, accessible and relevant to all individuals. Where the L&D process is 'out of line' with other HR processes, this can damage its credibility (Keep and Mayhew, 1994).

In attempting to achieve functional alignment, L&D practitioners can face conflicting demands:

- If there is an overall approach to HRM in the organisation that is in any important way unsatisfactory, the L&D process will be harmed, not helped, by seeking close integration with HRM strategy and practice.

- Yet if there is no attempt to integrate, one HR process (L&D) will be operating independently – and perhaps in opposition to – other HR processes. The dangers there are obvious.

Such difficulties are compounded when L&D is a stand-alone function in the business. Then, the L&D professional must convince the organisation's management of the need for highest priority to be given to establishing a framework of HR policy and action, must advise on what that framework might be, and must propose how it can best be implemented.

This issue of functional alignment is contentious. For example, a significant body of trainers in the UK is convinced that such alignment is unnecessary. The rationale here appears to be that 'training/HRD' (no clear distinction is made between the two) can be – and indeed often ought to be – quite separate from the human resource management (HRM) function in the organisation, rather than being incorporated within that function and required to report to it.

The ignorance that is displayed here helps to explain why many so-called HRD/L&D specialists fail to make a strategic impact. To those who support the 'integration' and 'alignment' of L&D with HRM, the crucial issue is *not* one of achieving a single HRM function within which L&D practitioners report to a HR director – often that does not or cannot happen, for whatever reason. The issue is of the need for L&D and other HR professionals to work in a business partnership that will ensure that L&D activity has all the support it needs from wider HR policies and practice in the workplace. Such collaboration is essential in order to effectively implement L&D strategy and plans.

It follows from this – as one contributor to the training debate on the UK *HRD Daily Digest* website (ukhrd@fenman.co.uk) pointed out early in 2002 – that trainers need to know about employee relations, employment law, people management, organisational behaviour, leadership issues, organisational culture, management styles and other contextual factors. Without that knowledge they cannot ensure that training gives due return on investment for the business both in monetary and in human performance terms.

Those who confuse 'functional alignment' with the formal reporting system operating between 'Personnel' and 'Training' have therefore missed the vital point – that if training is to add value for the business as well as for individuals, trainers must talk the language of the business and must work in collaboration with their other human resource colleagues. Such partnership is necessary no matter how their respective functions are structured in the organisation.

Can there be strategic alignment of L&D?

Organisational context
Surveys report wide variations in the extent to which training strategy in the UK is integrated with corporate strategy (Darling, Darling and Elliott, 1999). Training practitioners see such integration as problematic. They often point out that the fault does not lie with them but with weaknesses in the strategic process itself. That process in turn (as we noted in Chapter 3) depends ultimately on the quality of leadership, management and decision-making (Hendry, 1995). It is there, deep in the fabric of the organisation, that the biggest inhibitors to strategic alignment of L&D are to be found. In the view of many commentators (see, for example, Patterson, West, Lawthom and Nickell, 1997), the most common and serious inhibitors here are lack of stakeholder support and commitment – most of all from the top – and lack of competence and business credibility among L&D practitioners. We shall look more at these inhibitors shortly.

Corporate measures of performance
Organisations that are dominated by short-term financial measures of performance are unlikely to make any significant investment in L&D beyond job-related training and short-term competency development. It is in organisations' measuring performance by methods that incorporate long-term perspectives, and/or those to do with levels of employee as well as stakeholder satisfaction, that we can expect to find attitudes more supportive of a strategically focused L&D process. Two of the most powerful of such methods are:

- *the 'balanced scorecard' method* – This comprises measures clustered around four perspectives related to customers and to market share, to the financial dimensions of business performance, to internal business processes including those that promote long-term innovation, and to learning and growth. The latter are to do with 'identifying the structures an organisation must build to create long-term growth and improvement' (Kaplan and Norton, 2001: 54).

- *the economic value added (EVA) method* – This bridges the gaps between financial and strategic categories by focusing on 'all four ways wealth can be created in business': cost-cutting, release of unproductive capital, reduction in cost of capital, and investment in value-added activity (Stewart, 1996: 2.5). The questions raised by applying the EVA method are fundamental: what company-wide impact will this strategy or activity or innovation have, and what kind of value will it add?

HR practitioners, in promoting their vision and strategy, should reflect on the kind of value released or created by L&D activity in the organisation in the past, and on the value it could achieve in the future.

Task 1

Find out the main measures of corporate performance used in your own organisation (or one with which you are familiar). Then assess from the information you can gather how those measures affect the focus and scope of L&D activity in your organisation.

Are there major issues to indicate that the L&D function should become a strategic player?

The reasons for beginning to make a strategically focused investment in people's learning and development at work are never as simple as they seem, so any generalisation can mislead. However, there are three scenarios that should trigger a call for a closer alignment between L&D and business strategy:

- costly capability gaps

- changes in the competitive environment

- changes in the external labour market and/or technical base of the organisation.

Costly capability gaps

These are likely to have been caused by reliance in the past on *ad hoc* L&D activity. Lost opportunities in the marketplace and longer lead times when developing new projects are typical results of miscalculation related to the development of people (Prais and NIESR, 1990). The ability to react rapidly to changing external scenarios and reap the benefits they offer can be enhanced by a more strategic approach to the recruitment, retention and development of the right people. Unfortunately, it may take a crisis on several fronts to produce an awareness of the need to invest in L&D. L&D professionals can help to reduce the possibility of such skills gaps occurring by, for example, searching for relevant best practice outside the organisation and then alerting management to the value that could be obtained by applying some of that practice in their own organisation.

Changes in the competitive environment

These can require new business goals that in turn call for changes in performance, skills and organisational capacity. That will have clear implications for the L&D process, and should point to the need for a more strategic L&D approach.

Changes in the external labour market and/or technical base of the organisation

Where an organisation can no longer recruit suitable personnel from the external labour market, it will have to rely more on its own L&D process to provide the skills it needs. Major changes in the technical base of the organisation call for organisational restructuring, re-skilling of large sectors of the workforce, and changed patterns of management and decision-making. All this points to a need for a more strategically aligned L&D process.

Those carrying L&D responsibilities must work closely with stakeholders to identify the main strategies to which the organisation is committed at different levels, and the main strategic issues that it faces. When there is a clear need for L&D to become more strategically aligned, they must then agree on how to achieve that. For example, if a company is de-layering and downsizing but also wants an adaptive workforce, it will need L&D strategies related to teambuilding and multiskilling. Those who will have to manage that changed work system and workplace culture will need help to acquire the necessary skills and understanding. Organisations breaking into new markets will need L&D initiatives that can generate new knowledge and stimulate creativity and innovation in the workplace.

What critical indicators demonstrate that the L&D function is strategically focused?

The main indicators that demonstrate that there is a strategically focused L&D function are these:

- L&D has a vision and strategy – no matter how informally expressed – that support the organisation's corporate goals.

- All L&D activity also supports those goals.

- That activity supports and is supported by other HR policies and practice in the workplace.

- L&D as an organisational process is 'owned' by managers, who give it active commitment at all organisational levels.

- L&D specialists acknowledge that ownership through establishing effective business partnerships across the organisation.

- The outcomes of L&D operations help to drive down costs and to increase the value of the organisation's human assets.

Achieving commitment

Vision and values

Vision and values underlie crucial decisions relating to investment and the deployment of the organisation's resources, including its people. In Chapters 4 to 6 we will explore in detail ways in which L&D professionals can develop influence in their organisations and promote positive values about L&D at different organisational levels. In this chapter, only main themes are introduced.

First, L&D needs its vision – but it should be consistent with the overall organisational vision, not exist in some separate dimension.

CASE STUDY: My worst mistake

John Garnett, director of the Industrial Society from 1962 to 1986, admitted that his worst mistake was trying to sell ideas in relation to his own objectives rather than the objectives of the people to whom he was selling. He described how his passionate vision about the value of developing people's abilities and potential blinded him during his time as personnel manager of the plastics division of ICI to the equally important need to relate what he did to the objectives of the business. It led to the loss of his job because, he explained:

'My work, in the view of the board, was irrelevant and, more seriously, distracting. They were in the business of making profits in plastics, while I seemed to be in the business of developing people, which took their eyes off the main purpose.'

Source: John Garnett, *Independent on Sunday*, 8 March 1992

Typical attitudes that reflect a confused vision about L&D and do it no service include the following:

'L&D always matters in an organisation.' Some will see the development of employees as a crucial task for any organisation. They will argue for a heavy investment in it while at the same time showing no real concern to put it in the context of specific business needs or to measure and evaluate its outcomes. Like John Garnett, they are convinced that developing people is of such inherent value that it is bound to bring benefits to the organisation.

'L&D is essential to keep up with the competition.' Others may argue that L&D must be worthwhile because 'the best companies do it'. Again there will be no emphasis on clarity of purpose, responsiveness to specific needs or measurement of outcomes. Best practice is a useful tool for standard-setting in L&D – but only when L&D itself is relevant to the business.

'We believe in investing in people here – our employees deserve L&D.' Yet others may believe that investing in L&D is justified by a particular

organisation's general employment philosophy. They will tend to argue that *any* developmental activities are worthwhile that fit with that philosophy.

If the vision of L&D in an organisation rests on these kinds of assumption, L&D in practice will tend to be unsystematic, non-strategic and unconvincing to sceptical managers because they do not see its business relevance. The L&D process must add value if it is to achieve support in the organisation.

Support, however, is not achieved just by the introduction of initiatives that have a clear value-adding rationale. Appealing to that rationale is not always enough to convince those who have to carry out such initiatives and those who will be affected by them. For 'added value' to have a real meaning in the organisation, there has to be a shared system of beliefs, a culture that places that principle of added value at its heart. We will explore issues of vision, values and organisational culture in detail in Chapter 6. At this point it is sufficient to conclude that the L&D practitioner should help to build up a culture of 'adding value' across the organisation and should speak the language of 'added value', not just of 'value', in all that they do and seek to do. They must use that language in their interactions with their internal and external customers, in order to establish 'how to apply their technical solutions to customer problems'. They should define their function or role in terms of (Dougherty, 1999: 181):

> *how it contributes to the creation of the organization's value, strengthening the inside-outside thinking throughout the organization.*

Achieving external consistency

Research has repeatedly demonstrated that if corporate training interventions are to achieve a real impact in their organisations they must have external consistency (Kessels, 1996). This means that they must, from the outset, be perceived as valuable by the key L&D stakeholders, who themselves should be as actively involved as possible in the identification of needs, in the general operation or oversight of the interventions, and in the evaluation of L&D processes and strategy. This emphasises the importance of the 'relational' aspects of L&D (Kessels, 1996). It reinforces the view of those who regard L&D as a negotiated process in which political rather than purely rational analytical skills are of primary importance (Robinson and Robinson, 1989).

L&D's stakeholders are those who resource its operations, those who are actively involved in its processes, and those who are most affected by its outcomes. They can be any institution, agency or individual that has a direct interest in the operation and in the results achieved by the L&D process in the organisation. We will return to them in Chapter 6.

Planning to add value

The L&D planning process

Today, there is a preoccupation with ensuring that L&D aims and strategy are determined at the top of the organisation in order to achieve strategic alignment. At first sight this may seem a mechanistic approach and one that, because it is 'top-down', conflicts with the principles of a 'learning organisation'. Those principles emphasise the need for a continuous identification and responsiveness to individual and organisational learning needs, and for strategy to be recognised as an emergent as much as a planned process (see Chapter 3).

The conflict is apparent rather than real. A commitment to foster strategic thinking and action at all organisational levels, and to respond to ongoing learning related to emerging strategic issues, does not preclude a need to ensure also that there is a clear strategic framework for L&D in the organisation, and that L&D activity is aligned with business drivers. In that way, L&D can be sure to add value at all points in the value chain of the business.

Task 2

(You will find it helpful to keep the results of this activity for reference as you move through the rest of this section)

Research the concept of the 'value chain' in a business (see the end of this chapter for some helpful reading).

In respect of an organisation of your choice, identify ways in which L&D is aligned with corporate strategy, and outline (in general terms) how this has been achieved.

We now examine the cycle of L&D planning at different organisational levels that can help to produce such a framework.

Planning at corporate level

Fundamental business drivers in an organisation are:

- current business strategy and plans
- operational priorities
- major changes in the organisation's business environment and technical base.

Key decisions about L&D goals and strategy have to be made at board level so that they can be powerfully aligned to corporate goals. If such decisions are made at the stage when business strategy and other plans derived from it are being formally produced, L&D issues can influence as well as be influenced by strategic decision-making. However, the information to be taken into account when making those decisions should be gathered from across the organisation. It should then be presented to the board by whoever is formally responsible for L&D in the organisation.

The information must be presented in a form that, when discussed in relation to business strategy, should lead to sound decisions about the direction L&D strategy should take and the goals it should serve. The L&D manager from his or her vantage-point may perceive needs that no one at board level can as yet see. If that is the case, he or she must work hard to attract the board's attention and influence its judgement. Convincing the board – either directly or through an intermediary such as the personnel/HR director – is vital, since only the board can authorise L&D strategy and resource its implementation.

The outcomes of corporate decision-making should then be communicated back down and through the organisation. At each level, they provide the strategic framework within which L&D targets and plans relevant to those levels can be produced.

A postscript at this point. One important way in which the L&D process can add value is to introduce L&D initiatives that improve the strategic process itself. Such initiatives could be aimed at helping strategists to improve the quality of their decision-making and of their teamwork. They can provide insights and tools whereby to produce and continuously communicate a relevant vision of the organisation, generate challenging goals, and choose and implement the strategies that best support them. Such initiatives are to do with enhancing what may be called the 'strategic capability' of the organisation. However, enhancing strategic capability is a complex task, and brings into play issues of power, politics and collective learning that not all may have the knowledge or the influence to deal with. The task has been identified here, but will not be pursued at this point. It is explored more fully in Chapter 22 for interested readers.

Planning at the business unit level

Strategically focused but flexible and locally relevant L&D plans should be produced to cover each main unit or sector of the business. Whatever plans are made should operate on a rolling basis and be fast-responsive to emerging needs. Line managers and L&D professionals should collaborate to ensure their effective implementation. Major direct and indirect costs (such as lost opportunity time, lost production time, reduced quality and wastage during learning time, the cost of training and trainers, and so on) must be identified, as must those benefits that will outweigh the costs and bring added value for the business.

Many companies now include within their annual report business plans that have been produced by every business unit and that contain information about each unit's human resources and their performance and productivity levels. Where this is matched with information about the unit's investment in L&D, this will give clear recognition of L&D as a value-adding function.

Planning at the individual level

It is particularly important that personal development plans are agreed between individuals and those to whom they directly report in their business unit, are actioned and are regularly monitored by those individuals. Appraisals are one valuable source of information that should influence such plans. However, as is evident on examining this subject more deeply in Chapter 13, there are often tensions here. Some will arise because manager and individual disagree over what training and further development are needed, and why. Some will arise because certain developmental objectives urged by the manager as essential in relation to business needs will not seem equally important to the individual, or because the parties disagree on priorities for objectives. All these tensions have to be resolved if L&D at other organisational levels is to respond to business needs while also having the commitment of individuals.

These guidelines to planning L&D activity at different organisational levels should not be interpreted as inflexible rules. Achieving an added-value approach to the L&D process is a matter of working continuously to adapt L&D activity to current and emerging needs. This requires consideration of strategies to do with 'growing people' as much as of strategies to do with 'improving performance'.

A partnership approach is essential here. Line managers and their teams usually know best where L&D processes can make the most productive impact. It is they, too, whose co-operation is vital to the successful implementation of L&D strategies in the workplace. For both these reasons they must be actively involved in L&D planning. (There are other, less widely used approaches to establishing formal L&D strategy and plans. Information about two of the best-known – problem-centred and comprehensive – is given in Appendix 3 at the back of this book.)

It must be remembered, too, that as we saw in Chapter 3 the strategy process can be messy and unpredictable. HR practitioners must appreciate that there will always be a discrepancy between what is planned and what actually occurs. Flexibility and partnership are again the keywords here.

At this point, we can look again at Table 1 (seen previously in Chapter 1) to remind ourselves of the ways in which L&D can be integrated at every organisational level in order to ensure organisational relevance and added value in its operations (see page 92).

Table 1 Building learning and development into the business

Strategic level	L&D's strategic focus is on:	L&D must:	Crucial processes for L&D:	L&D specialist/manager needs to:
1 Corporate	• formulating L&D mission, goals and strategy to achieve corporate goals • influencing and developing strategic thinking and planning	• 'fit' with wider HR strategy • be aligned with corporate strategy • help to secure appropriate balance between corporate goals for survival and for advancement • produce L&D strategy that is capable of implementation at Level 2	• collaboratively developing mission and goals for L&D • strategic planning and thinking • influencing key stakeholders • adding value through L&D activity	• have board-level position/access and skills • be pro-active as well as reactive • have deep knowledge of competitive environment • fully understand the value chain and strategic assets of the business • speak the language and logic of the business • work in business partnerships
2 Business unit/managerial	• developing L&D policies and systems in line with strategic needs of the business unit • ensuring achievement of business targets • influencing and developing strategic thinking, organisational capacity and human capability	• 'fit' with wider HR policies and systems • be aligned with business unit policy • have a clear plan within the overall business plan, with agreed evaluation measures • ensure feedback on policies to Level 1	• working with HR and business unit managers to produce policies and plans for acquisition, retention, growth/redeployment of workforce • developing key performance indicators • strategic thinking and business planning • adding value through L&D activity	• work in business partnership with managers and others • have collaborative relationships with other HR specialists • have deep knowledge of competitive environment of company and of business units • fully understand how strategic assets can be developed • speak the language and logic of the business units
3 Operational	• ensuring individual and team performance targets are met • improving acquisition, quality and motivation of people for the business.	• adapt to needs of the business and needs and aspirations of people • ensure L&D activity is expertly carried out and appropriately evaluated • ensure feedback of outcomes to Level 2.	• working with teams and individuals to implement business plans for L&D • appraisal, personal development planning to achieve targets and improve core competencies and capabilities.	• working in partnership with internal and external stakeholders • have effective and efficient systems and procedures • have deep knowledge of culture of the workforce • be expert and continuously self-developing.

Assessing added value

In Chapter 5 we will look in some detail at ways of measuring the impact of L&D activity in an organisation. Here, it is helpful simply to make some introductory comments.

Assessing added value

As we shall see in Chapter 5, it is vital to set standards and targets, to monitor progress and to collaboratively assess the outcomes of L&D strategy and initiatives. However, it is the process followed rather than the measurement methods chosen that matters most. The critical issue is the nature of the true driving forces behind L&D strategy, and the extent to which that strategy has the support of key stakeholders. It is essential to agree with the stakeholders what L&D initiatives are likely to be the most valuable, how they can be implemented in the workplace, and what methods of measurement to apply to ensure that, through time, intended outcomes are being achieved.

Assessing the future investment

'Value for money' is usually assessed by a pay-back approach, with attempts to measure return on training investment in financial or analogous terms (Lee, 1996). A typical 'value for money' exercise would involve measuring the impact of past or current training outcomes on variables like turnover, profit, increase in sales, conversion of leads to sales – what accountants call the 'direct return' achieved.

To measure added value is different. It is not just about establishing 'Was it worth it?' It is also about 'Will it have been worth it?' It concerns what Lee (1996) called 'pay-forward' – the idea that any proposal to invest in future L&D activity must be assessed by reference to how that investment will enhance the capability of the whole organisation to make progress. This 'pay-forward' approach involves the generation of options, and the identification of which of those options are likely to have the most significant impact. Here, far more than financial considerations alone must be taken into account – as the following six crucial pay-forward questions show:

- *budgeting* – Which options are most affordable in terms of our L&D budgets?

- *L&D strategy* – Which of the options would be most consistent with the organisation's overall L&D strategy?

- *L&D needs* – How do options relate to needs? Have the needs been accurately identified, carefully analysed and correctly prioritised? Are any needs in tension with each other? If so, what do we do about that?

- *L&D outcomes* – Which of the options is/are most likely to produce outcomes that give the most added value for the organisation? What information can be obtained about the likely outcomes of each option, by reference both to past initiatives in the organisation and to external best practice?

- *transfer of learning* – Which options are likely to ensure the most effective transfer of learning for individuals and teams?

- *other options* – Are there any other ways in which the same kind and level of outcomes offered could be achieved but at less cost? What about team-briefings, quality circles, project groups? What would be the costs of doing nothing? Or might that lead to reduced motivation of the learners, to lack of development of their ability and potential, to longer learning-time for new techniques, or to poorer-quality work and higher rates of absenteeism or sickness?

The following checkpoint should help you to apply these questions to a realistic scenario. (It will be followed up in a slightly different form in Chapter 10.)

Checkpoint

- You are a training manager with the choice of improving supervisory performance in your organisation by sending supervisors away on an accredited course at a local college, or producing an in-house programme with the help of your capable and experienced training staff. What criteria do you use, and why, in order to choose the option that will bring most added value for the business?

The value-adding L&D function

There are four leading questions to test the extent to which a L&D function is likely to be able to make a value-adding contribution:

- Is there a positive fit between the vision and strategy of L&D and wider HR and organisational vision and goals?

- Is L&D activity focused on areas that will make a critical difference to the organisation's ability to achieve its goals?

- Does the way the function is organised enhance its ability to make that difference?

- Are the staff who carry L&D responsibilities expert in their tasks and knowledgeable about how to relate L&D activity to business needs?

The following case concerns a company where there were convincing responses to all these questions.

CASE STUDY: Aligning L&D to achieve added value at Cummins Engine Co. Ltd, Darlington, UK, 1979–1990

Business strategy

Cummins Engine Company Inc. is the world's largest independent manufacturer of diesel engines. Cummins Engine Co. Ltd is the UK subsidiary of the company, and has three manufacturing locations, one of which is at Darlington, in the north-east of England. In 1979 the workforce at Darlington numbered around 3,000.

By 1984 the company worldwide was suffering from overcapacity and new competition in a stagnant market. In the previous year the chairman had announced a new strategy, driven by restructuring, high investment in new technology, research and engineering, immediate price-cutting and a compensatory 30 per cent cost-reduction target. The strategy was to be achieved by mid-1986, with the long-term aim of growth in the 1990s and beyond.

HR strategy at Darlington, 1984

In 1984 Darlington's HR strategy had to be closely aligned with the new UK-wide HR strategy, which raised three priorities for L&D policy to tackle:

- *to achieve a lean, high-quality and efficient workforce*. Reducing materials costs would

make the most impact on the Cummins worldwide target of 30 per cent reduction in costs, since those costs accounted for 80 per cent of turnover, whereas labour costs accounted for only 20 per cent. The aim was to achieve a more efficient rather than a smaller labour force (although some downsizing was necessary). All unit labour costs had to be reduced, especially those related to production time, staff turnover and absenteeism, time-keeping, working methods and procedures, accidents, materials wastage, quality, and inefficiencies due to demarcation.

- *to ensure that the workforce had the skills needed to operate the new technology*. A new product, the 'B' series engine, was to be introduced at the Darlington site. Its smooth and fast installation was essential in order to achieve full operational efficiency quickly.

- *to develop a workforce with high added value*. With a target of growth in the 1990s, an immediate start had to be made on improving the company's skills base and

CASE STUDY: continued

employees' ability to learn fast and be flexible. The aim was to reduce labour costs and add value to the human resource.

L&D goals

Three L&D goals were established within the above strategic framework:

- to help people acquire and apply the new competencies needed to operate more efficiently, and to adapt to the new culture aimed at meeting the challenges of change

- to encourage and enable people to work effectively in teams

- to develop managers, especially supervisors, who could manage teams effectively.

L&D strategy and its implementation

The components of L&D strategy flowing from these goals were:

- *to build an enhanced quality of basic skills*, by providing training for those with the capacity and desire to acquire the skills needed to operate the new technology. For the others, there were favourable opportunities for early retirement.

- *to provide training for all, geared to business needs*, by giving all employees the opportunity to learn one new skill every year over the following few years, with a commensurate pay progression

- *to achieve effective teamworking*, by developing a new breed of supervisors who would operate quite differently from the way they had before, and who, given initial training, would adapt quickly. This proved to be one of the most challenging areas of L&D strategy to implement.

L&D strategy at Cummins in the 1980s focused on prioritising L&D activity around business drivers, in the belief that activity related to these would produce the biggest added value. These business drivers were:

- current business strategy and plans

- operational priorities

- major changes in the organisation's business environment and technical base.

L&D goals and strategy during this period had three defining characteristics:

- *They derived from the clear definition and measurement of 'productivity'* in different sectors of the workforce, and from agreement between stakeholders on where the introduction of L&D initiatives would produce the most added value for the organisation.

- *They were carefully aligned* with overall business strategy and with HR policy and practice – most crucially, HR policies to achieve integrated pay systems and harmonisation of the entire workforce (Pottinger, 1989).

- *They were in the hands of expert HR practitioners who worked as business partners* with managers, unions and workforce. They based all value-adding initiatives on data that were as sound and comprehensive as possible, and regularly monitored and adapted those initiatives.

(With acknowledgements to the company. An extended version of this case study appears in Harrison, 1996. There is a study of Cummins' more recent L&D practices in the next chapter.)

CONCLUSION

Having read this chapter and completed its checkpoints and tasks, you should now:

- understand what is meant by the L&D process 'adding value'

- understand the importance of achieving strategic alignment in order for L&D to make a powerful 'added value' impact on the organisation

- be able to identify any barriers and aids to such alignment in any particular situation

- know how to produce feasible and value-adding L&D goals and plans

To test yourself against these objectives, what five-minute answers would you give to the following questions?

Review questions

Respond as requested to the following e-mail just received from your personnel director: 'I note the L&D initiative you propose. It's interesting – but how can I decide whether it's going to add value for the organisation? Please outline a few criteria for me to use.'

Provide the requested reminder that has come up in a phone-call from a student to whom you have been teaching L&D at a local college: 'Really enjoyed your last lecture, but I'm stuck on how to explain the difference between L&D giving "value for money" and "adding value". Could you give me a quick reminder? Thanks!'

Identify L&D's main stakeholders in your own organisation and explain three ways in which you think that their commitment to an organisation's L&D goals can be obtained.

Useful reference sources

Harrison R. (1993b) 'Thorn Lighting Ltd, UK – a learning organization'. In R. Harrison (ed.) *Human Resource Management: Issues and strategies*. Wokingham, Addison Wesley, pp375-80. (Related feedback notes in Instructor's Manual.)

Kaplan R *and* Norton D. (2001a) *The Strategy-focused Organization*. Boston, Mass., Harvard Business School Press.

Mayo A. (1998) *Creating a Training and Development Strategy*. London, Institute of Personnel and Development.

Walton J. (1999) 'Outsourcing: what stays in and what goes out'. In J. Walton *Strategic Human Resource Development*. Harlow, Financial Times and Prentice Hall, pp279-99 (for its discussion of value chain analysis).

• Achieving Impact

CHAPTER OBJECTIVES

After reading this chapter you will:

- understand key principles associated with the setting and achievement of L&D standards and outcomes

- be able to set outcomes for L&D initiatives to achieve, and standards by which to achieve them

- know how to audit the impact of L&D in the organisation.

Introduction

In order to ensure that the L&D process produces outcomes that have a value-adding impact, we need to have a clear understanding of the factors that most directly affect that process, and the main elements involved in its operations.

As the starting-point of this chapter, I reproduce in Figure 5 (overleaf) my own model of training and development in the business (Harrison, 1999). The model identifies critical features relating to L&D in an organisation. Its eight components, with 19 associated performance indicators, should enable a reader to understand the drivers, vehicles, activity and outcomes of L&D activity.

The model is of course conditioned in its functioning by organisational context and external environment. There is no 'one best way' of ensuring that L&D achieves intended outcomes. The process is organised in different ways from one enterprise to another, and different L&D cultures operate across organisational and country boundaries. The terminology and performance indicators used in Figure 5 therefore do not fit every organisational context. They should be interpreted as common sense dictates.

This chapter first explores what is involved in setting intended outcomes for the L&D process. It then looks at the workplace environment in which that process operates, Approaches to measuring and auditing outcomes are then examined. The chapter concludes with an integrative case study.

Figure 5 A model of learning and development's impact on workplace performance

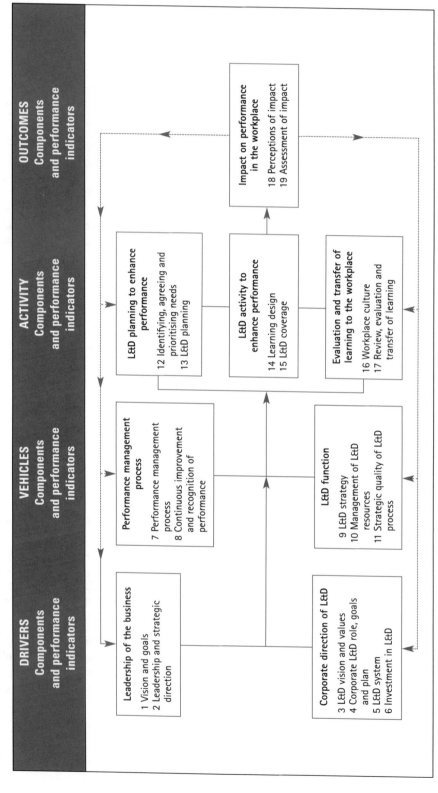

Source: Harrison R. (1999) *The Training and Development Audit.* Cambridge, Cambridge Strategy Publications. Reproduced (in adapted form) with kind permission of the publisher.

Setting outcomes and standards for L&D activity

Achieving a high-quality service

Those carrying L&D responsibilities in an organisation should always be asking themselves: how good a quality of service do we provide for our clients and customers? Are the outcomes that we aim for, and the performance standards that we set in order to achieve them, relevant and effective?

In the following task, try to assess the quality of your own L&D (or equivalent) function and its practitioners. If there is no specialist function, you could apply the questions to some other organisation with which you are familiar. If you are currently working in an L&D function, you could use the questionnaire to assess the service that you and your colleagues provide.

Task 1

Assessing the quality of L&D service in your organisation

Does your L&D (or equivalent) function collaborate in joint ventures with similar functions in other organisations to develop and offer value-added services? _____

Does your L&D function have its own business plans for developing its capability and performance, and are these plans related to the challenges facing your client businesses? _____

Does your L&D function use regular structured feedback and benchmarking in order to assess its performance? _____

Does it work to an explicit set of ethics and values that have been agreed at the highest level? _____

As an HR professional, are you clear about who your customers, suppliers and business partners are, and do you understand the people and organisational implications of the challenges they are facing? _____

Are you clear about the purpose of your job and the processes that you are responsible for managing? _____

Do you create and pursue your own development plan? _____

Do your assess your own performance with regard to: _____

- meeting standards _____
- satisfying your customers _____
- your contribution to your customers' performance _____
- finding more cost-effective ways to improve your contribution? _____

With acknowledgements to Fonda and Rowland, 1995

Processes and techniques to aid standard-setting

Among the many processes and techniques that can help the L&D practitioner to set meaningful standards to guide L&D performance are benchmarking, best practice and milestones. They can be defined in general terms as a continuous search for and implementation of best practices that lead to superior performance. Below, we look briefly at each.

Benchmarking
Benchmarking involves finding a particular standard, whether internal or external, and using that as a continuous marker for a particular strategy, process or initiative. There are three main types of benchmarking:

- *Internal benchmarking* looks at and compares similar processes within an organisation to achieve internal best practice. For L&D, examples might be the induction, appraisal or management development processes. The exercise of ascertaining how a process is carried out in different parts of the organisation offers two benefits: the highlighting of inconsistencies, and the identification of internal best practice that can then be used as a marker across the organisation.

- *Competitive benchmarking* is where organisations in the same sector – for example, a hospital trust and a community healthcare trust – agree to work together to compare best practice in key areas. In this example, two areas might be the matter of privacy and dignity, and the complaints process.

- *Functional benchmarking* takes place where a particular process is identified and then compared with best practice outside the organisation. An organisation that wishes to improve its measurements of customer satisfaction may thus take two or three external organisations of different types as comparators, and finally select one to use for benchmarking.

The benchmarking process should move through four stages:

- preliminary planning

- analysis, in which the gap between current performance and desired performance is identified as a result of benchmarking research

- action, in which changes are implemented and measured

- review and recycling stages in order to achieve continuous improvement.

To conclude: benchmarking is not merely a technique for copying, or picking up handy hints. It is a process concerned with planning comparisons in order to decide how to enhance performance. Organisations agree to being benchmarked because they acquire insight and information from the process too, and because it gives them a higher profile in the competitive environment. A particularly helpful benchmarking process is that involved in the Department of Trade and Industry's

Benchmark project. Its Index covers a wide range of businesses and is structured so that it is easy to compare your own business on a number of parameters (including spending on training) with those in your region, those of similar size, operations in the same industry, and so on (www.dti.gov.uk/business support).

Checkpoint

- Why might it be helpful for an organisation to benchmark some of its L&D practices and processes?

- You have been asked by your L&D manager to identify some key questions that would test the quality of service offered by the L&D unit to its organisational clients. Outline and justify *four* such questions.

Best practice

Best practice involves gathering information across the academic and practitioner fields in order to produce general principles to guide the implementation of a particular process or initiative. It is the search for best practice and new ideas that is most likely to change an organisation's collective mindset and so lead to radical change. This is illustrated in the following brief example.

CASE STUDY: English Nature's use of benchmarking and best practice

English Nature, the government's adviser on nature and conservation, aspired to be a learning organisation and so decided to benchmark approaches to training with a wide range of companies in order to achieve that transformation. The account produced by S. Dolan, its training manager, illustrates the many ways in which examining practice in other organisations can help an L&D department to set standards, decide on particular practical approaches, and monitor progress.

Twelve companies across all sectors were visited because they had adopted innovative approaches to learning and business development. Their beliefs, strategies and a range of key features were analysed and compared with those noted in the 'learning organisation' literature that had already been studied at English Nature. Common traits soon became evident, and it emerged that in a number of respects English Nature already had the elements needed. The company introduced many initiatives to develop the rest, at the heart of which was a range of programmes to strengthen the links between learning and action across the organisation. Company personnel also continued to develop external learning networks with other organisations in conservation and business.

Source: Dolan, 1995

Milestones

Milestones can be used to mark points at which progress towards planned outcomes are to be monitored and discussed. The case study overleaf is another example. It is a brief but useful illustration of the different kinds of value that can be obtained from the milestone process.

CASE STUDY: HRM strategic milestones in a British investment bank

During 1990–91 County NatWest, an investment bank, asked all its business units, including its personnel department, to establish strategic milestones for a five-year period. Their performance was to be measured against those milestones at specified target dates.

The requirement to produce strategic milestones as an input to the bank's five-year business plan 'marked an important watershed in defining the contribution of personnel to the business at a strategic level. It forced the department to reflect on the nature of that contribution.' The senior management of the bank duly authorised 18 separate strategic milestones. The milestones were consistent one with another and overall addressed issues that consultation within business units and across the three personnel teams had shown to be critical to business success.

Each milestone was assigned to a designated individual and was incorporated into his or her own targets of performance. Quarterly reviews on progress, involving the whole department, were subsequently held to ensure that the milestones were on target.

Source: Riley and Sloman, 1991

The workplace environment

Chapter 3 stresses the influence of organisational context on the L&D process and its operations. My own audit framework in Figure 5 (see p100) focuses especially on the primary shapers of that context: the vision and leadership of those who direct the business, management style and actions, and HR policies and practice.

A more detailed treatment of organisational context follows in Chapter 6, but at this point we should note the value of 'taking the temperature' of the workplace environment regularly. Some organisations use a 'health of the business' survey for this purpose. One example is an internal questionnaire focused on four areas to do with sharing the vision, integrating the effort, sustaining a healthy community and making intelligent decisions. Each area is broken down into a series of descriptive statements, with ratings listed against each statement. Such surveys can be carried out every year and the results then compared with previous norms in the company, external norms in comparable businesses (Cranfield holds manufacturing norms that offer competitive benchmarks) and UK norms. The results of all such surveys must be communicated quickly and fully as an aid to action-planning and to demonstrate a spirit of partnership and trust.

Commitment to achieving L&D's planned outcomes should be stimulated and supported in the workplace at team and at individual levels.

At team level, helpful processes include:

- regular team briefings, and emphasis on teamworking and flexibility of work and skills

- shop-floor-located continuous improvement teams

- accessible training rooms which also act as informal break-away areas for discussing quality issues and continuous improvement projects

- emphasis in the workplace on setting business-focused targets

- performance indicators and benchmarks used as business measures

- value analysis teams drawn from across the organisation to improve quality, reduce costs and ensure that products and services remain competitive

- learning networks involving customers, suppliers, producers and other key stakeholders.

At the individual level, helpful processes include:

- regular, voluntary appraisal of training needs of teams and individuals, from which development plans ensue

- high-quality, job-related training and personal development

- facilities for open learning and encouragement for individuals to take the initiative in their development

- good basic pay, and harmonised terms and conditions of work

- no financial incentives or reward schemes except those tied to the acquisition of qualifications and additional relevant skills

- high standards of health, safety and counselling services (usually off-site and always confidential and optional for the individual)

- accessibility of all company information to all company employees – contributing to the business requires understanding of the business; employees as business partners must be trusted to use access with discretion.

Checkpoint

- What ways of 'taking the temperature' of your workplace environment would you recommend, and why?

- Explain *two* team-level methods of building commitment to achieving L&D outcomes, and *two* individual-level methods.

Measuring the outcomes

Critical questions to ask

In determining how to measure the outcomes of L&D activity for the organisation, some critical questions must be answered at the outset:

Between what points in time should measurements be taken?
Too soon, and the outcomes of an initiative may have had no chance to become established. Too late, and too many other variables may have entered the picture, making it impossible to trace the specific impact made by the initiative.

Whose views should be sought?
People perceive change in different ways in an organisation. For example, what may at the time have been intended as a powerful value-adding initiative may be seen by some as nothing of the kind, yet by others as successful (this takes us back to concerns expressed in Chapter 1). It is important to obtain views from as wide a spectrum of organisational members as possible, in order to identify and reconcile such differing perspectives.

Whose views should be believed?
In Chapter 1 we saw that there is often a difference between what is claimed and what is actually occurring. What is described now as the implementation of a carefully designed L&D strategy may have been at the time little more than a series of trial-and-error reactions to various problems and opportunities.

Measurement methods

In an ideal world, measurement would involve the use of methods to precisely measure the rate of return on investment. For L&D this would mean:

- measuring identifiable costs (outflows) of direct and indirect L&D activity (see Chapter 10)

- measuring identifiable benefits (inflows) of that activity in financial or other quantitative terms. Performance measures can be categorised, starting with the most easily quantifiable and going on to more difficult qualitative indicators (Robinson and Robinson, 1989). They should identify the extent to which intended learning outcomes have been achieved and should take into account any deviation – whether planned or accidental – from the original learning objectives.

- analysis to produce a cost-benefit ratio or rate of return for capital employed. This involves assessing whether some other kind of L&D initiative would be more cost-beneficial than the one currently being considered (see Chapter 10 for a worked-out example).

In real life, it is impossible to precisely measure all the costs and benefits of L&D activity – nor should it be attempted. This is not only because of the difficulty of answering those three critical questions posed opposite. It is also because:

- sometimes the data required will simply not be available

- many of L&D's most valuable outcomes are to do with non-quantitative and long-term improvements

- such analyses are far too time-consuming and costly to merit constant repetition.

As we saw in Chapter 4, what matters most is that members of the L&D business partnership collaborate in planning and measuring activity to achieve added value. They should agree at the start on what learning objectives to set for that activity and should jointly determine the crucial milestones at which progress towards intended outcomes should be measured. Without this common-sense approach, L&D initiatives and processes are likely to 'drown in a sea of quantitative and qualitative measures' (Lorenz, 1994).

Taking all these considerations into account, L&D measurement methods should be appropriate to the kind of outcomes that an initiative or process is meant to achieve. They should:

- be broad and flexible enough to capture the essence of L&D activity without interfering overmuch in operations by imposing excessive and time-consuming checks and balances – 'measure everything' is not a natural law: it is a dangerous obsession

- be quantitative, for hard objectives

- take in a range of techniques to capture the essence of softer objectives – for example, behaviourally anchored rating-scales, surveys and benchmarking to ensure cross-checks on value and outcomes.

Checkpoint

- Senior management tells you that it wants you to measure 'rate of return on investment' in relation to L&D activity. What, theoretically, would be involved in doing this?

- In your reply to senior management, what will you advise about the approach you intend to use to measure L&D activity's impact on the business?

Achieving a sound measurement process

L&D practitioners can achieve a sound measurement process by ensuring that:

- when business partners are agreeing on L&D outcomes that they want to be achieved, they share a clear picture of the initial state of affairs and of how the outcomes should change that picture.

- they express desired outcomes in terms of clear and relevant goals. For example, a goal to do with 'improving managerial effectiveness' is too imprecise. In what ways is it necessary for managers to improve? How must they have changed once training and development has taken place? What will they know and be able to do, and how will they behave then, as distinct from now?

- they agree with partners on the path to follow in order to achieve those goals, and on how and when to measure progress along that path (using, for example, strategic milestones and performance indicators as in our earlier case-studies).

- there is agreement on what must happen in the workplace if that path is to be taken. For example, learning driven by new technology cannot achieve its aims in a workplace where there are no skills to use it, no infrastructure to support it, and no willingness on management's side to exploit its full potential. (For more on that topic, see Chapter 11.)

In Chapter 4 we looked at a case study on Cummins Engine. On page 109 we have the continuation of that story, showing how, in the late 1990s, outcomes and standards were set for all the company's people management and development activity.

Task 2

Choose an organisation known to you that has a specialist L&D (or equivalent) function. Collect information to enable you to answer the following questions convincingly:

What are the main standards of performance and specific performance indicators against which L&D activity is measured?

How far do those standards and performance indicators focus on the organisation's business goals?

CASE STUDY: Standards and indicators at Cummins Engine Co. Ltd, Darlington, UK

The Cummins story now moves forward to 1997. By then, 'customer-led quality' was the vision that drove Cummins' new production system, providing the focus for goals, standards, performance and recognition.

At the Darlington plant in 1997 human resource management and development (HRMD) was identified as one of seven 'functional excellence' functions. HRMD was regarded as a core function in the business because management believed that it was only through its processes that Cummins could achieve the human capability it needed to maintain its world-class competitive edge.

In 1997, the HRMD function at Darlington operated in relation to 11 policy areas where standards of performance were set and maintained:

- leadership
- environment
- health, safety and security
- administration
- staffing
- performance management
- training and development
- organisational design
- compensation and benefits
- employee relations
- community.

Standards to be achieved in each of these policy areas were expressed in terms of performance indicators with points allocated to each. Every year the HRMD function was rated by its internal and external customers against those indicators. A score was achieved in this way for the department's performance in each of the 11 policy areas. To take an example: 'Performance management' had seven performance indicators, which together carried a total possible score of 10.

The plant had five business goals to do with customer-led quality, and HRMD staff had to make a contribution each year to those goals. They also had to take lead responsibility for the goal related to 'Developing outstanding people'. They contributed to goals through projects that they managed and that also formed the basis for their appraisal as individuals. In 1996, for example, the training and development manager had a number of projects, each with its targets, time-scale and methods of measurement. Taken together, these constituted her individual responsibility for contributing to the business goal of 'Developing outstanding people'.

At Cummins in the 1990s, the presumption in the company was that if HRMD outcomes were agreed by business partners to be materialising, and if the function and its staff continued to have the confidence and support of management and workforce, then that was enough – the HRMD investment was clearly being justified. Only if planned outcomes failed to materialise, or poor ratings were received on the annual customer survey of the HRMD function, would there be a special exercise to measure the value of that investment.

(With acknowledgements to the company.)

Auditing L&D

The audit

The aim of an audit is to supply a snapshot of the current situation across the organisation in order to compare what is happening with what *should* be happening, and to identify any action needed. Audits enable trends to be identified and form part of a strategy to ensure continuous improvement of a function or of an area of activity.

How should the audit be constructed?

Every audit has its own focus. Once that has been determined, a framework for the audit can be devised and decisions taken on the areas of questioning that will produce the most relevant information. Examples of audit frameworks or approaches include:

- the Investors in People (IiP) Standard. This provides the most familiar audit framework in Britain for assessing links between training and development and the business. Its use involves working with external advisers and assessors, and so it is more costly than self-assessment audits, although some of the cost can be offset by IiP funding.

- the Quality Management Standards ISO 9001 and 9002 (1994). These are to be superseded in December 2003 by ISO 9001:2000, the requirements of which have several L&D implications, especially in relation to strategic focus (see Field, 2001; also website www.bsiglobal.com).

- the well-known US-based Malcolm Baldridge National Quality Award, of which the focus is on quality in the business. Looking into human resource management and development, it requires information to be gathered about five components, or standards, each of which is defined and to each of which performance indicators are attached. One of these areas is 'Employee development'.

- the European Foundation for Quality Management's 'Business Excellence' self-assessment model, which is based on best practice and regularly updated. It uses nine criteria, five of them 'enablers' and four 'results', and is based on the premise that excellence depends on partnerships, resource and processes.

Who should carry out the audit?

For the auditing of L&D in the workplace, a small team of L&D staff, line managers and an external consultant offers the best balance of internal expertise and external knowledge of best practice and credibility. Additional contributions can be invited on an *ad hoc* basis, but the core team is best restricted to around six members. In a smaller organisation, the audit may well be carried out by only one or two people.

Task 3

Your HR manager has asked you to recommend an audit framework or approach for assessing the impact of L&D activity in your organisation.

Find out what types of audit *other than* those mentioned so far in this chapter you might use.

Draw a comparison between those and the four outlined in this section.

Produce your recommendation for an audit framework or approach.

What comes next?

Once decisions have been made on an appropriate audit instrument and on who should carry out the audit, it is then useful to carry out a six-stage process:

1 Ensuring commitment
The first priority must be to ensure that top management and all senior managers are fully committed to the audit, to communicating its main findings to employees, and to taking action related to those findings. Then, all employees must have a clear understanding of the audit's purpose and intended outcomes, and be convinced that the audit has the full backing of all levels of management.

2 Planning the audit
This involves decisions on what data to collect, from whom, using what methods, and over what period of time. Table 3 (p112) provides some reference-points here. It also involves assessing all the resources needed to carry out and support the audit process, and gaining authority for those resources. A proper budget must be established and maintained.

Any audit should be broken down into parts in order to produce a systematic and comprehensive audit process. Mine, for example, falls into three parts (Harrison, 1999):

- Part 1: the first audit step, comprising a diagnostic survey to identify current perceptions across the organisation about the role, organisation and impact of L&D in the organisation

- Part 2: seven more audit steps to obtain information from all levels of management and from L&D specialist personnel about the drivers, vehicles and activity shown in Figure 5 (p100)

- Part 3: the stage at which Part 1 and Part 2 data are integrated in order to identify what management intends L&D to achieve, the reality as perceived by the workforce, and any gaps between them that have to be closed. Conclusions are then reached and recommendations produced.

Table 3 Rationale for involvement in the audit process

Involvement of	Rationale for involvement	Information to supply about
Top and senior management	Responsible for corporate vision and goals, and for overall direction and resourcing of T&D. Their active involvement is needed in order to ensure commitment of all management.	Corporation vision, leadership and direction. Business environment, corporate strategy. Performance management process. T&D function, plans and process. Internal image and impact of T&D.
Middle management	Responsibilities for T&D of their staff. Their active support is needed in order to ensure commitment of teams and individuals to T&D. They implement T&D strategy and control the structure within which it operates.	Corporate vision, leadership and direction. Business unit environment and strategy. Performance management process. T&D goals, strategy and plans. Image, coverage and impact of T&D activity at unit and operational levels.
Team leaders/ supervisors	They see the operation of T&D at operational levels and identify important performance-related needs. They must be committed to T&D activity intended to improve performance.	Corporate vision and goals. Workplace environment and performance management process. T&D activity and its impact in workplace.
Specialist staff	Where they are employed, they play a leading role in the planning, provision and evaluation of T&D, and operate the T&D systems.	Corporate and functional T&D role and goals. T&D function and process. Type, image and impact of T&D activity across the organisation.
Main body of employees	Their understanding of the role that T&D does and should play in the business, and of the purpose and relevance of T&D activity, together with the credibility they attach to T&D staff, all have a direct impact on their motivation to learn the skills, knowledge and attitudes needed for effective performance and development of future-related capabilities.	Type, image and impact of T&D activity across the organisation.
External individuals, agencies and institutions	Their view of T&D in the organisation can help to attract external resources and build external image. Some will be involved in strategic T&D alliances with the organisation.	External image of T&D activity. Best practice and benchmarks.

Source: Harrison R. (1999) *The Training and Development Audit.* Cambridge, Cambridge Strategy Publications. Reproduced with kind permission of the publisher.

3 Piloting the survey

Most audits of this kind involve a diagnostic survey to reveal the initial state of play. It is important to pilot the survey on a small group before carrying it out across the organisation. This will reveal any design weaknesses or other problems likely to be encountered in the administration of the survey. Any such can then be put right before proceeding further.

4 Collecting and analysing data

For every audit step it is important to obtain views and perceptions from a variety of sources. To supplement data obtained by questionnaires and/or face-to-face discussions (either individually or in focus groups), desk reviews must also be carried out. They involve the examination of current and historical documentation relating to L&D systems, processes, procedures, policies and operations. Desk reviews 'aid verification of policies, procedures and outcomes; the identification of trends; and assessment of the likelihood of those trends continuing or changing in the future' (Harrison, 1999: 33).

5 Establishing findings and conclusions

Comparisons should be made throughout the audit process between what people say or think is happening and what various kinds of written information – taken together – indicate to be the 'reality'. Historical data recording past intent, actions and their outcomes should supply the necessary backdrop to current trends and events. Auditors must always assess carefully the credibility they can place on their various information sources.

6 Producing the audit report

Any report should commence with a brief introduction to the organisation and its environment, to the L&D framework used for the audit, and to the audit process and information sources used. The report writer should then provide a concise, well-evidenced commentary on what has been audited. Recommendations should identify actions needed as a matter of urgency now, and those to take over the longer term.

Checkpoint

- What is meant by a learning and development 'audit'?

- You are asked to outline a sound audit process. What steps will you recommend in your outline, and why?

An organisational case study

In order to illustrate a central theme in this chapter – the importance of the measurement process – here is a real-life case study concerning management development at a time of radical organisational change.

CASE STUDY: Management development at a prescription pricing authority

During the late 1980s, the personnel department of a regional prescription pricing authority (PPA) in the National Health Service (NHS) organised a four-year management development programme for PPA staff, using both internal and external resources to design, deliver and evaluate the initiative. Its purpose was to develop managers to operate effectively in a new organisational structure and culture, spearheaded by a new chief executive officer (CEO).

Throughout the four-year period new technology was being introduced across all nine divisional offices of the PPA. This was a radical change, and PPA managers had to quickly acquire the competence and the social skills to ensure its success.

As an independent consultant with experience in such programmes and their evaluation, particularly in NHS organisations, I was invited by the CEO to evaluate the PPA's Management of Change programme. Throughout the evaluation process I had regular meetings with the CEO, involving frank discussion of information emerging from the process and its implications for the authority.

The first stage was to collect financial and non-financial data in order to assess the programme's true cost. In financial terms, it emerged that it had cost £47,400 over four years to put 210 officers through the programme and to provide some of them with the skills needed to facilitate the job-related training of a further 1,730 clerical officers. Part of that cost had been met by central NHS funding, the rest by the PPA itself. A great deal of the time and expertise of the PPA's small personnel department had been absorbed in the programme throughout its duration, and those costs were incorporated in my financial calculations.

The next stage was to carry out a desk review, a questionnaire survey, and follow-up discussions with staff drawn from each staff sector covered by the survey, some of whom had taken part in the training, some of whom had not. The data from this stage of the evaluation process cast vital light on the workplace environment over the four years of the programme. It became evident that in many ways there had been a favourable context for the programme, because of:

- changes in top management personnel and a consequent change to a more flexible, team-centred, open style and culture at the top of the organisation, which was gradually making itself felt throughout the authority's structure

- changes in roles and job content due to computerisation, which also provided aids to greater efficiency

- a greater recognition of, and focus on, individual rates of productivity because of new control systems

- more delegated responsibility with the innovations in budgetary systems.

However, the climate of the workplace had also been quite unsettling because of the number and scales of changes that had been taking place throughout the four-year period. The value of the programme here was to provide staff with a supportive learning environment in which they could express their concerns about these changes openly. The PPA's personnel director, advised by trainers about those concerns, was then able to outline major problem areas to top management and work in a business partnership to tackle them constructively. In my own discussions with the CEO, further weight was given to participants' concerns, the greatest of which were about:

- the threatening nature of change (not least technological) as perceived by long-serving staff (average length of service was between 25 and 35 years) who had worked for many years without any major alterations to their jobs or work environment

- the specialised nature of many people's jobs, which would make it hard for older staff, in particular, to get jobs outside the authority should that become necessary

CASE STUDY: continued

- the poor financial rewards available to most staff.

My evaluation report concluded that the programme had played a leading role in the successful and rapid introduction of radical change at the PPA. The evidence provided not only by participants but also by those who had been unable to take part indicated clearly that without the programme it would not have been possible to achieve the following outcomes:

- virtually no reduction in productivity during a time of fundamental change

- a positive approach to industrial relations issues

- increased motivation and commitment to organisational goals in the great majority of officers who went through the programme.

The programme was widely perceived to be constructive, motivating and energising. It helped newly promoted staff to establish themselves with more certainty in their managerial or supervisory roles. It helped longer-serving staff to sit back, away from their pressurised routine, and reflect on their own performance and approach to work, while learning from tutors and colleagues in a trusting and team-centred atmosphere. A comment by one supervisor represented the views of many about what the programme had achieved at her level:

All aspects of the course are in my mind daily. The week flies by, and I look forward to any further training.

These comments were particularly significant because they came from someone working in a PPA division that had a persistently poor industrial relations record. Her reactions were echoed by both the administrative assistants in that division. After the programme, weekly team meetings were introduced in that division at the initiative of those staff.

The evaluation report concluded that the programme had produced outcomes, quantitative and non-quantitative, that significantly exceeded both its financial cost and the non-financial costs related to specialist external and internal staff's time and expertise in designing and delivering it. I recommended further investment in order that the benefit of that 'added value' could be spread more widely across the authority and that the PPA's personnel function could be strengthened by the addition of a permanent training officer position.

Subsequently, further funding was obtained from the NHS at centre. The PPA's board implemented all the recommendations made in the report, thus demonstrating their commitment to a 'pay-forward' approach to investing in learning and development activity (see Chapter 4).

CONCLUSION

Having read this chapter and completed its checkpoints and tasks, you should now:

- understand the key principles associated with the setting and achievement of L&D standards and outcomes

- be able to set outcomes for L&D initiatives to achieve, and standards by which to achieve them

- know how to audit the impact of L&D in your organisation.

To test yourself against these objectives, what five-minute answers would you give to the following questions?

Review questions

National reports have publicised the damaging outcomes of irrelevant and poorly delivered training in many organisations. As the new training manager in one such organisation, what are the first steps you would take to improve the situation – and why?

What techniques and processes would you recommend to aid the setting of outcomes and standards for L&D activity, and why?

A line manager colleague says to you (a member of L&D staff), 'What can't be measured doesn't count.' Outline your reply

---

Useful reference sources

FONDA N. *and* BUCKTON K. (1995) *Reviewing the Personnel Function: A toolkit for development.* London, Institute of Personnel and Development. (Contains specially designed assessment tools to address key personnel and L&D issues, and builds on the frameworks of the Personnel Standards Lead Body and Management Charter Initiative.)

HARRISON R. (1999) *The Training and Development Audit: An eight-step audit to measure, assess and enhance the performance of your organisation's training and development.* Cambridge, Cambridge Strategy Publications.

INDUSTRIAL SOCIETY. *Managing Best Practice.* (Monthly reports on achieving excellence in the key areas of managing people.) Available by subscription or as single copies: 0121 410 3040.

www.sunday-times.co.uk/enterprisenetwork

www.dti.gov.uk/business support

• The Business Partnership

CHAPTER OBJECTIVES

After reading this chapter you will:

- be able to identify who the partners should be in an L&D 'business partnership', and the stakes they have in that partnership

- understand issues of power and politics raised by business partnerships and be able to identify conflict management styles appropriate to different kinds of learning and development (L&D) situation

- understand the meaning of 'organisational context' and the forces that shape that context through time

- be able to advise on how to build and maintain effective L&D business partnerships.

Introduction

We concluded in Chapter 3 that human resource (HR) practitioners must work with managers and others in the organisation to achieve business goals. In Chapter 4 we noted the importance of forming L&D business partnerships to achieve mutually valued ends. Working in collaboration with stakeholders is clearly another core responsibility of L&D practitioners.

The concept of business partnership as a collaborative process between interested parties has several dimensions, and to understand them we must go back to basics (Pearsall and Trumbull, 1996):

 Partner: *a person who shares or takes part with another or others, especially in a business firm with shared risks and profits.*

So a business partnership is not merely about working towards shared ends. It is about working with those who share in the risks and gains of an enterprise. Seen in this light, such partnerships must extend beyond the organisation. Who, for example, in a limited company takes some of the biggest risks in return for some of the biggest gains? Stockholders would say that they do – and even if the extent of their risk-taking may be arguable, the gains that they can achieve are certainly considerable. Either way, L&D practitioners cannot ignore their interests and power.

Already by January 1999, six corporate fund managers between them controlled £200 billion of British shares. They were beginning to force changes in boardrooms in order to enhance shareholder value, and during that one month alone a whole series of high-profile takeovers, mergers and boardroom sackings were initiated in this way. Shareholder influence over the performance measures by which the company's success is assessed can directly affect the extent to which the company itself invests in L&D processes – usually by forcing a focus on short-termism. This is where the politics of L&D's bottom line begin.

Looking inside the organisation, who, by the same kind of reasoning, are L&D's business partners there? Clearly the directors of the business, because they set the goals and strategy for the business and are held ultimately accountable for results. Clearly, too, managers. They carry the formal responsibility for ensuring that business targets are achieved at their organisational levels, and they receive rewards or penalties in line with the extent to which they discharge that responsibility effectively.

Our dictionary source, however, offers two further definitions of a partner:

- a player on the same side in a game

- a companion in dancing.

These definitions mean that we should expand our concept of the L&D business partnership to include other players. Externally, partners on the same side in the game include those agencies and individuals with whom L&D practitioners can collaborate to gain support – especially financial – for organisational L&D initiatives. Learning and Skills Councils are an obvious example here, providing not only funding but also a source of networking, local influence and support for L&D practitioners within that organisation. Educational institutions and consultancy firms are also frequently used as 'companions in dancing'.

Internally, other dancing partners include:

- team leaders

- teams and individuals with L&D needs

- those occupying and managing L&D specialist positions

- other human resource professionals in the organisation whose work impinges on L&D.

The implications of these varying interpretations of business partnership are wide-ranging. In this chapter, we relate them primarily to the internal L&D business partnership, taking as our major reference-points a partner as 'player on the same side', issues of power, politics, culture and structure, and the L&D practitioner as 'companion in dancing'.

Checkpoint

- What is the overall purpose of the L&D business partnership in an organisation?

- Identify key players in an L&D business partnership, and provide your rationale here.

A player on the same side

Playing the game

This dictionary definition suggests that those holding major L&D responsibilities in an organisation must always 'play on the same side' as their business partners. If we believe that those who invest most heavily in the business and/or those who carry the major burden of accountability for its results are the key partners here, then coming on side means working in the interests of the stockholders (if any), the directors and the managers in the organisation. To 'play on side' with them, an L&D partner must:

- aim for the same goals as those of the business. Setting up separate goalposts for L&D is a counterproductive exercise. There must be a clear even if loose-coupled alignment of L&D activity with business strategy – as we saw in Chapter 3.

- show that the L&D process is about adding value for the business. Chapter 4 focused on this theme.

- score wins for the business. Often, HR staff are regarded as losers. We explored possible reasons for that in Chapter 3. If L&D partners are to become major players, they must not just preach 'added value'. They must achieve notable results. In Chapters 4 and 5 we noted ways in which this can be done.

At this point, we should reflect. On the one hand it is surely fair to give the main consideration in a partnership to partners who carry most risk and invest a high proportion of the required resource. This, however, is to ignore the fact that often within their ranks there can be conflict and dispute about who *does* carry most risk. It ignores the fact that, in L&D, other players are involved and their needs too must be considered. Key here are those whose learning and development management wishes to shape to business ends. Learning is a property of the individual. It cannot be forced. It cannot be bent to the purposes of others without the consent of the owner/s. There are more sides than two in the L&D game. Learners must be convinced that they have something to win, here, if they are to invest their own learning, their own expertise, in a partnership with others whose interests many learners may not always feel that they share.

This view of the organisation as a pluralist, not a unitary, system – a system in which there are many and often conflicting interests, not one overriding goal or set of interests – gives a new dimension to our concept of partnership. L&D practitioners must continually focus on how best to make progress given the multiplicity of interests involved in the L&D game. From time to time, interests will clash, and personal preoccupations will begin to dominate. In such situations the L&D players will face a demanding test of their partnership skills.

Task 1

How do you deal with conflict in a particular task or area of work? *Be as self-critical as you can in circling each of the statements below as either 'Yes' (meaning 'Yes, I often act like this' or 'No' (meaning 'No, I rarely act like this').*

Conflict arises in many types of situation, so this exercise allows you to admit to more than one approach!

1 I try to avoid conflict, but when it arises I try to stifle   YES/NO
   or postpone it, or at least ensure that there is no
   direct confrontation.

2 I seek compromise by negotiation and by making   YES/NO
   deals.

3 I try to win, either by using rivalries to my   YES/NO
   advantage, or by using power to force submission.

4 I usually give way, either because I believe that   YES/NO
   conflict is counterproductive or because I see from
   the start that I cannot win.

5 I encourage the other party/parties to put the   YES/NO
   reasons for conflict on the table, then seek to work
   together to find solutions that build on our
   differences and help each of us to win something.

This task makes use of Morgan's classification of conflict-handling styles (Morgan, 1997: 205–9). He based his classification on a study of 28 chief executives carried out by Thomas (1976). The styles (in the same order as they are listed in the task) are to do with:

- avoidance
- compromise
- competition
- accommodation
- collaboration.

The first instinct of most HR professionals, especially those relatively new to organisational life, would probably be to favour the collaborative approach. Such professionals have been educated to espouse values of collaboration, of openness and of mutual benefit. These are the values that underpin the concept of 'business partnership'.

However, the more widely experienced and also the more senior HR professionals ought not to be blamed if they responded more cautiously. Collaboration is not easy to achieve in some organisational contexts – and the more powerful the players, the more politicised the game becomes. Politics has been described as 'the art of achieving the possible'. In politicised situations conflict management is about the exercise and control of power.

In the management of conflict, style cannot be prescribed. It must respond sensitively to the situation. Sometimes collaboration will not work; it may be better to go for compromise through negotiation in order to preserve all players' commitment and to move the game forward. Sometimes it may be wise to abandon a chosen course in the interests of making progress on another front.

Task 2

Take a conflict situation that arose in your own organisation (or in one with which you are familiar). It must be one that related to L&D issues.

In this situation, why and between whom did the conflict arise?

How was the conflict managed on the L&D side, and what were the outcomes?

Do you think that the conflict should have been handled differently? If so, how?

What have you learned about power and conflict from attempting this task?

Issues of power and politics

Throughout the previous section, issues of power and politics emerged. Let us look directly at these phenomena now. Torrington and Weightman (1985) declared that:

> *Power is a property that exists in any organisation . . . Politics is the way power is put into action.*

In Chapter 3 we noted that the strategy process has been likened to a game, dominated by power and politics. The game, however, goes further than the boardroom. Politics, or 'the art of achieving the possible', is what much of organisational life is about at any level.

It is not within the scope of this chapter to go deeply into theories of power. The aim in this section is simply to establish a starting-point for a brief discussion that informs on some of the basics while also stimulating interest in a phenomenon that is of great practical importance to all L&D practitioners.

My starting-point is some of the more obvious sources of power. Three are of particular importance:

- *resources* – the power that derives from control of resources valued by those you wish to influence. As Miller, Hickson and Wilson (1999: 46) point out, if an organisation is viewed as an open system that depends on its effective interaction with an external environment, then 'power accrues to those parts of the organization that can control the flow of resources, especially if these are scarce and critical for organizational functioning'.

- *position* – the power derived from formal position, its accompanying status and the knowledge and information to which it gives access. Since knowledge is vital to decision-making at all levels, positions that act as gateways to information and to knowledge networks constitute a formidable power source.

- *expertise* – the power derived from a uniquely valued area of knowledge or competence. Miller *et al* (1999) noted Crozier's 1964 study of a French tobacco company in which maintenance workers, despite their lowly position, had exclusive possession of expert and essential knowledge. Through this power source they were able to gain and maintain control over production processes and thereby negotiate to their advantage.

Yet no matter how many sources of power we identify, it remains 'difficult to tie down what the phenomenon is' (Morgan, 1997: 199). One of the most compelling accounts of how power is exercised in organisations is the social action analysis contained in Silverman's complex but fascinating book (1970). Another account that has particular value for management and HR students is provided by Miller *et al* (1999), who focus on the political complexity of decision-making in today's organisational settings.

Morgan provides a masterly discussion of power in Chapters 6 and 9 of his 1997 book. Although he admits to being unable to provide definitive answers to many of the questions he raises, he concludes that there is real value simply in discussing them because we thereby develop 'an inventory of ideas through which we can begin to decode power-plays and political dynamics in organizational contexts' (Morgan, 1997: 199). He concludes:

> *The manager must be able to analyze interests, understand conflicts, and explore power relations so that situations can be brought under a measure of control . . . In general, the manager can intervene to change perceptions, behaviors and structures in ways that will help redefine or redirect conflicts to serve constructive ends.*

This is a particularly interesting passage. In referring to 'control' and to interventions to change behaviour, it introduces a dimension of business partnership not mentioned so far – that of ethics. It is at this point that the metaphor of the L&D business partnership as 'a game' breaks down. Professionals work to a code of conduct that applies to all situations in which they become involved. There is no context in which an L&D professional should behave in ways that seek to exploit or undermine any of the players. Vulnerabilities in individuals or groups must never be used by L&D partners to gain advantage for themselves or for more powerful players. As we shall see shortly, the metaphor that is more appropriate to encompass ethical considerations is that of the dance.

Checkpoint

- Identify and explain *three* sources of power in an organisation.

- Give *three* reasons why it is important for the L&D professional to seek an understanding of power and politics in organisations.

Organisational context

What is organisational context?

Any analysis of power in organisations leads to at least one clear conclusion – that power is indeed a property, not an absolute. It is not just important to identify its sources, uses and outcomes. It is vital to understand the context in which it is embedded.

At this point, we reach a theme that is of central importance in this book and that will recur regularly hereafter. One of the most common weaknesses of L&D practitioners is to ignore or insufficiently understand the context within which they have to operate. One of the most basic skills that they require is that of effectively relating all that they do to the characteristics and needs of the particular organisation within and for which they work. They must be able to identify and assess the barriers and facilitators to L&D that exist in the workplace, and the external pressures and opportunities that face the organisation as it struggles to achieve its goals. They must then promote the kind of L&D activity most likely to be feasible, ethical and value-adding, given that context.

Although in all HR textbooks there are frequent references to 'organisational context', students are often uncertain about the meaning of the term. I define it as:

the internal and external organisational circumstances that directly influence, help to explain, or have any other clear bearing on, the organisational situation being examined.

Often, organisational context is summarised by reference to culture and structure. Although this is a useful shorthand, it is not sufficient, because culture and structure are themselves outcomes of something more fundamental – the interplay of at least three primary factors, all noted in Chapter 3:

- top management's vision and the way it is communicated and reinforced

- management's style and actions at different organisational levels

- HRM policy and practice and the employment system of the organisation.

To illustrate the interrelatedness of these three factors and the impact they have on the cultural and structure of the workplace, we can return to the brief account in Chapter 3 of Terry and Purcell's 1997 study of seven organisations seeking 'leanness', and expand on it here.

CASE STUDY: Seven organisations seeking 'leanness'

In the organisations studied by the research team, 'leanness' and 'responsiveness' were key elements of an organisational vision that it was essential for all employees to share if the organisations were to make progress in increasingly challenging business environments. However, the style and actions of some of the line managers and team leaders were inconsistent with that vision. In some cases this was because they were inadequately trained for their new responsibilities, in others because those responsibilities were not clearly identified.

To resolve this problem, seven key HRM practices had to be put in place (see Chapter 3). They made new responsibilities and structure transparent, and provided appropriate support mechanisms.

It was through an interaction between leadership's vision, management's style and actions, and HR policies and practice that the seven organisations were able to 'invent responsiveness for themselves – from within the history and culture of the organisation' (Terry and Purcell, 1997). That interaction produced a cultural and structural context in the workplace which influenced people's attitudes, performance and learning there through time.

In each firm, organisational context manifested itself structurally through human resource policies and the employment system – for example, through job descriptions, through planning and information systems and networks, and through performance and reward management, training and development processes. It manifested itself culturally in a set of developing norms, values, narratives (see Chapter 1) and practices that through time began to typify the daily work environment.

Source: Terry and Purcell, 1997

Culture-structure theory

As this case study demonstrates, structure and culture are not tangible entities. They are states of being. They develop from the actions of people and their interactions with systems and practices, and they are continually being changed by those actions and interactions. They provide an ongoing setting within which people perform their tasks, conduct their relationships (both formal and informal), and learn and develop from day to day.

Culture

At its simplest, we can understand the culture of an organisation as a set of human norms, practices, ideas and beliefs about 'how things ought to be done' in the organisation or in a particular part of it. Sometimes the word 'climate' is used instead, but culture is more than that. Essentially, it is an expression of identity – the identity of people and of the organisation that, collectively, they produce and perpetuate through their actions.

As we saw both in the case study above and in the case of the photocopier technicians in Chapter 1, culture affects behaviour by providing people with a 'toolkit' of material such as symbols, stories, procedures, habits and skills which become a set of general cultural 'capacities'. They draw on these 'capacities' when making choices about which actions to take, which initiatives to support (Swidler, 1986; discussed by Dougherty, 1999: 182). Culture is thus dynamic. It is also different at different levels and locations, and indeed some claim that 'all cultures are local ... [being] created by the behaviour of local managers and their teams' (Buckingham, 2001: 40). Certainly the culture of the boardroom may bear little apparent resemblance to the culture of the workplace. The culture of an L&D department may contrast sharply with that, say, of the accounts department, even though both functions are located in the same organisation. Yet running through boardroom and departments there will be some common thread, some generalised sense of a common history and identity. What matters is the strength and extent of that commonality.

In some organisations the thread is fragile because the organisation is divided by more forces than those that unite it. There is then insufficient 'shared understanding of what the company stands for, where it is going, what kind of world it wants to live in, and... how to make that world a reality' to stimulate productive learning (Nonaka, 1996: 19). In such scenarios it is indeed the case that local cultures are far stronger than corporate culture. The crucial issue then is that managers should understand how to engage their employees 'under existing conditions' (Buckingham, 2001).

This returns us to those three fundamental factors of leadership vision, management style and actions, and HR policies and employment system. In their type and interaction they can produce a strong sense of collective identity, and ensure that it is maintained through time. Equally, if they are inappropriate, or imperfectly aligned with each other, then they can achieve quite the opposite results.

Structure

Culture is reinforced or weakened by organisational structure – the network of roles and relationships by which responsibilities and activities are allocated across the organisation. Structure is both designed and accidental. We see designed structure in formal organisation charts. We see accidental, or emergent, structure in the systems, procedures and networks that actually regulate activity in an organisation.

Checkpoint

- Explain *three* of the major factors that produce organisational context.

- In what ways does context manifest itself culturally?

- In what ways does context manifest itself structurally?

Culture-structure analysis

Roger Harrison developed the first version of his 'culture-structure' model in 1972. Commenting on it, Charles Handy (1985, 1989) argued that although every organisation has its own distinctive culture and associated structure, there can yet be a number of different cultures and structures, especially in larger organisations. His views on this point contrast with those of commentators like Buckingham (2001), who roundly asserts that 'most large organisations actually look very similar to one another: they are all equally varied and equally incoherent'.

Yet Harrison's and Handy's models continue to be widely used by practitioners, who find that they make otherwise clouded notions of culture accessible. They can yield valuable insights into 'how we do things here' – whether the 'here' is the organisation at large or a particular local workplace within it. I have drawn particularly from those models in the following culture-structure summary.

The power culture and web structure

This is the culture of centralised power. It is most often found in small entrepreneurial firms and at the top of large organisations. Control is exercised by one person, or by a small set of people, from whom rays of power and influence spread out, connected by functional or specialist strings. The structure to which such a culture gives rise is therefore web-like.

Organisations dominated by centralised power move fast and react quickly to threats – they 'think on their feet'. People who succeed tend to be the politically skilled risk-takers. Success is a matter of achieving the ends desired by the point of central power; means tend to count for relatively little. Organisational life is competitive, and those with L&D responsibilities have to relate their activity to ends that are valued by the central power source.

This kind of 'business partnership' requires of the L&D practitioner political skills of a high order and a strong sense of what 'professionalism' really means. Power can be – and often is – used in benign ways that seek to ensure that all rather than just the powerful few share the gains achieved from shared endeavour. On the other hand, power can also be abused in organisations. That is where ethics becomes an issue, as we shall see in the next chapter.

The role culture and pyramid structure

This is the culture of bureaucracy, sustained by the belief that an organisation should have its purpose and overall plan defined at the top, and then rest for its strength on a clearly defined hierarchy of functions or specialisms. Rules and procedures govern this pyramid, as they also govern communications and the conduct of disputes. Precedents dominate decision-making, and the whole organisation tends to be security-oriented, with a tendency to rigidity rather than to innovation. Change is difficult when job descriptions, rules, established working practices and routines all pull people back rather than forwards.

The formal position allocated to whoever carries special responsibility for L&D in such a system will be a key determinant of their influence over their business partners. The higher the position, the more formal power they posses. However, even if formal position is fairly low, knowing ways round and through the rules can often aid achievement of desired ends. The greatest danger is that in this inward-looking world professional vision can become 'departmentalised'. How many HR managers have you met who have become absorbed in the goals and interests of their little empire, bending the rules to its advantage rather than striving for a common benefit?

The person culture and galaxy structure

This is not so much a type of organisation (although some professional partnerships operate on this basis) but more a way of describing clusters of individuals who have unique contributions to make on the basis of specialist skills or knowledge. These are the 'stars' who dominate the organisational galaxy.

Those with L&D responsibilities can find it difficult to forge any 'business partnerships' with 'stars'. Many need development but do not acknowledge it (may indeed be unaware of it). They refuse to play the game because they cannot acknowledge any expertise as greater or more compelling than their own. Stars can also be disinterested in aiding the development of others. Sometimes they actively block it.

On the other hand, many stars shine a bright light on L&D processes. They demonstrate their belief in the development of people's potential by opening doors that others would keep closed, by giving considerable autonomy to individuals and teams, and by acting as coaches, mentors and positive role models in the developmental process. Creativity and innovation thrive in such cultures.

The human investment culture and network structure

In 1995 two strategic management writers, Miles and Snow, drew attention to a spherical or network structure that they believed would soon typify many businesses. Such systems focus on 'core competences' – those things that the business can do uniquely well and that bring it competitive advantage. Firms with a spherical structure 'rotate competent, self-managing teams and other resources around a common knowledge base', use strategic alliances and outsourcing to enhance core competences, and in so doing often link together in a multifirm network (Miles and Snow, 1995).

Today, in the UK alone, businesses as diverse as Boots the Chemist and Abbey National come far closer to this model than to more traditional forms. Moynagh and Worsley (2001) described how, in a move to transform itself from a UK retailer into a global 'well-being' company, Boots:

> *has established a string of new centres to offer customers private health and fitness services alongside its traditional pharmaceutical offerings. These new services will come from outsourced and freelance providers, putting extra demands on store managers.*

At Abbey National, 'outsourcing has become almost passé as the company gets to grips with new forms of partnership' that include franchises and joint ventures (Pickard, 2001).

Such network structures are to a large extent clusters of separate small businesses, held together by a company brand (Pickard). Dominant features are knowledge as an intangible asset, employees who are expert in their work and can operate with minimal supervision, and management through performance measurements, targets and financial incentives rather than through more direct forms of control. Keywords are partnership, trust and mutual dependency. Yet, as we shall see in Chapter 7, although network structures represent a type of 'post-Fordist' workplace, they can be stressful environments, depending on how stable or fragile the networks themselves are and the communities working in or for them (Moynagh and Worsley, 2001).

L&D practitioners in such organisations must have high-level professional expertise and be particularly effective at 'relationship management' (Miles and Snow, 1995). They must continuously develop themselves and focus on developing in others the capability to produce the organisation's core competences. They must be able to do all this outside the protective walls of a specialist function.

Task 3

Consider an organisation with which you are familiar, or a division of it. Your task is to carry out an analysis of its primary structure and culture.

Start your analysis with a brief explanation of the 'organisation' and whether your chosen frame of reference is the whole organisation or a particular part of it. Explain, too, how far your organisation, or your chosen part of it, is considered to be 'successful', and any major problems and/or opportunities it faces in operating.

Then analyse each of the following issues, illustrating your analysis with practical examples and explanations wherever possible:

- the kind of culture and structure you think top management intends and believes to exist, and the kind of culture and structure you feel actually exists

- the kind of people who 'get on' in the system, and the typical reasons for their success

- the kind of people who are unsuccessful in the system, and the typical reasons for their failure

- the main kinds of pressures and opportunities facing L&D practitioners in the organisation.

A companion in dancing

The dancing partners

The metaphor of 'the game' led us quickly into an examination of power, politics and conflict management. By contrast, the metaphor of 'the dance' highlights themes of collaboration, diversity, and trust.

First, the reference to companionship makes it clear that a business partnership is not just a matter of sharing risks and gains. It is also about sensitivity to needs. In the dance in its simplest form, individual differences enrich the process. Each dancer can express himself or herself in a unique way, while responding with other dancers to the basic rhythm of the dance. There is thus a marriage of diversity and unity. In responding both to the music and to each other, the dancers are companions in the dance. So too in the L&D business partnership, seen in its widest sense, diversity should be welcomed and built upon – as we shall see in Chapter 7.

Second, dancing means adjusting one's step to a partner's in order to move forward harmoniously together. We have already referred in

Chapter 4 to the need to ensure 'external consistency' in L&D activity, gaining the active involvement of all the partners at each stage of the L&D process in order to achieve powerful business impact. The partners must be companions in the dance, from its beginning to its conclusion.

Dancing across boundaries

Extending the scope of the L&D dance beyond an organisation's boundaries is important for two reasons. First, it ensures that more of those on whom the organisation depends for the ultimate quality of its products and services become part of a mutually productive learning partnership. Second, it brings into the organisation skills, knowledge, networks and ways of perceiving and understanding the business environment that can add value for the business.

The customer–supplier relationship is a case in point (see, for example, Batchelor, Donnelly and Morris, 1995). Supplier development programmes tend to be driven by a training rationale. Most focus on issues of task, process and skill development. However, a few seek to achieve a more radical approach by which those from inside and outside the organisation 'dance in partnership' to improve their strategic thinking and creativity. The aim is to produce double-loop learning – the kind of learning that involves questioning why certain problems occur in the first place and identifying underlying causes instead of only their surface symptoms. This contrasts with single-loop learning, where the aim is simply to take the problem as given, and train to achieve improved performance. It is when double-loop learning occurs that things begin to change radically, and new, more appropriate, ways of thinking and behaving develop. We return to the concepts of single- and double-loop learning in Chapters 13 and 19.

There are other kinds of boundaries across which L&D partnerships should extend, including the contractual. Take, for example, the non-employee who is a voluntary worker. Adapting an organisation's L&D policies to meet volunteers' special learning needs is in some organisations becoming a necessary part of recruitment and retention strategy. These personnel offer knowledge, skills, commitment and a network of contacts that are of unique value to the business. Competition for their services is intensifying as, for a variety of reasons, their supply diminishes and essential services suffer (Welch, 1997). The National Health Service in the UK places great reliance on volunteers in areas of hospital and community care work. The management committees of housing association trusts too rely heavily on voluntary members who work with chief executives in developing and maintaining the strategic direction of those associations. In charitable bodies, likewise, voluntary staff carry a heavy burden of responsibility.

Practising the steps

We can summarise the various elements of establishing and maintaining effective business partnerships in L&D by identifying the major steps in the process (see below). It is important to understand that in real life these steps are rarely taken one after the other. They constitute a complex set of movements partners may have to perform almost simultaneously in order to achieve progress.

● Establish and maintain effective working relationships with L&D business partners in and outside the organisation, so that you gain external and internal support for the L&D process and its specific initiatives.

● Demonstrate a professional, ethical approach in all partnerships you form.

● Do what you can to ensure understanding of key L&D issues facing the organisation, from the top level downwards.

● Move around the organisation regularly, establishing a proactive L&D presence in the business.

● Carry out continuous L&D data-gathering and planning, identifying ways in which L&D initiatives are producing, and can produce, added value for the business.

● Work with partners to ensure shared planning, monitoring and feedback of results. Take joint action on outcomes.

● Be up to date. Keep informed about internal or external changes that are affecting the organisation, or may do so in future, and identify their L&D implications.

Finally, overleaf is a case study that incorporates many of the principles discussed in this chapter. It is about a programme called (appropriately) 'Stepping Out', intended to reflect a philosophy of what one of the key partners, Egg plc, calls 'dancing with the customer'.

CASE STUDY: The dancing companions

The dance

In 1999 Egg plc, Britain's first Internet bank, formed a business partnership with Harris Associates, a Birmingham-based training and organisational development company, to design a framework of training and development activity to complement current training provision at Egg. The aim was to recognise and accredit competence to national standards, without compromising the overriding purpose of the programme. A pilot was designed to cover around 500 call-centre staff (called 'Associates') working across two of Egg's UK sites, at Dudley and Derby.

The rationale

When Egg was launched in October 1998, much thought had been given to how best to train and develop its people. Retention of staff was from the start a major target for the company, and a strong training programme was considered to be vital in achieving this. By April 1999 there was already internal training in place, and national vocational qualifications (NVQs) were an additional option for staff. Egg now sought an external partner who could work closely with Egg's training staff to devise such a programme – a dancing companion sensitive to the organisation's needs. Harris Associates were chosen.

The development process

Harris Associates developed a programme framework over three months designed to address some of the human resource challenges faced by Egg. These included the provision of adequate personal and professional support for sales-centre staff working in a high-pressure environment. During that period, three processes were involved:

Research: Harris's staff collected data to enable them to understand Egg's values and culture, its people and the pressures on them, and the competitive environment in which Egg operates.

Design and develop: Harris' staff drafted a programme, delivery processes and materials to meet agreed objectives. Based on the outcomes of the research and analysis of the challenges facing Egg staff, they proposed a framework that was designed as a competency-based training programme. Through on-the-job training linked directly to customer service requirements, it would provide staff with the competencies they needed, and would provide them with the opportunity to gain national vocational qualifications. The programme was titled 'Stepping Out'. Its purpose was to provide staff with the skills, competencies and confidence to be able to deliver outstanding customer-led servicing.

The Stepping Out programme linked in to current training at Egg and was designed to overcome the challenges facing the business in promoting skills development. Its business improvement projects developed participants' understanding of the challenges facing Egg and encouraged their proactive involvement with their teams and within the company. Internal champions were identified to act as coaches (who later became NVQ-accredited) and mentors.

The programme (including NVQ work) was designed to take 12 to 16 months to complete, in order to fit in with Egg's business cycle. It was pitched at NVQ level 3 because that best reflected Associates' job levels and incorporated a more developmental process than levels below. For Egg, that process was one of the most important features of the programme.

Implement: Once the programme had been approved, the partnership of Egg and Harris Associates agreed on a structured project plan to ensure achievement, ongoing evaluation, quality assurance and performance review. The review focused on the achievement of quality standards, business benefits, and key performance indicators.

The outcomes

During the first stage of the pilot programme, which came to an end in June 2001, 504 Egg Associates participated in the programme, includ-

CASE STUDY: continued

ing nearly the entire workforce of 300 at the Dudley site. 250 Associates completed the initial programme, and 18 months on, 212 were still with the company – an exceptional retention rate for call-centre staff in any organisation.

Specific results included the following:

- 77 per cent of Associates recorded improvement in customer service through the use of proactive techniques and a focus on national customer service training standards.

- 72 per cent noticed an improvement in their confidence and ability to handle difficult calls.

- 74 per cent experienced an improvement in morale and motivation within teams.

- 66 per cent showed an improved relationship between colleagues/team.

- 57 per cent of managers/team leaders noted improvements within their teams.

- 30 per cent had already achieved promotion or identified a new opportunity for development.

- In each group, the top performers in the team had all completed the Stepping Out programme.

- All training being undertaken was accredited.

- Over 180 business improvement projects had been successfully implemented, producing significant savings in terms of costs and time. Many of these had a direct impact on customers, thereby also improving customer retention rates.

Harris Associates were then asked to extend the framework to cover seven more areas of the business. The (now renamed) Stepping Up framework that has been developed for this purpose also stretches to support organisational competencies. Again, it identifies recommended internal training programmes to support staff development within the business.

Sue Savage, people manager at Egg plc, commented:

> One of the key benefits of working with Harris Associates was their ability to adapt the programme to reflect the Egg culture and, through its project management, to avoid the bureaucracy usually associated with such a large internal qualifications framework. Egg is now looking at widening the programme to incorporate managers within the company as well as Associates and team leaders.

(With acknowledgements to Egg plc and to Harris Associates, Birmingham.)

CONCLUSION

Having read this chapter and completed its checkpoints and tasks, you should now:

- be able to identify who the partners should be in an L&D 'business partnership', and the stakes they have in that partnership

- understand issues of power and politics raised by business partnerships, and be able to identify conflict management styles appropriate to different kinds of learning and development (L&D) situation

- understand the meaning of 'organisational context' and the forces that shape that context through time

- be able to advise on how to build and maintain effective L&D business partnerships.

To test yourself against these objectives, what five-minute answers would you give to the following questions?

Review questions

Someone has said to you that much of the skill of being a 'business partner' lies in game-playing. What do you think they mean – and how would you reply?

You are preparing a talk to give to some HR students on organisational cultures and structures. Outline how you will illustrate the two concepts.

Produce a short practical example drawn from an organisation with which you are familiar to illustrate the key principles of L&D business partnership.

Useful reference sources

JOHNSTON R. (1996) 'Power and influence and the L&D function', in J. Stewart and J. McGoldrick (eds), *Human Resource Development: Perspectives, strategies and practice*. London, Pitman. pp180–95.

MOYNAGH M. *and* WORSLEY R. (2001a) *Tomorrow's Workplace: Fulfilment or stress?* The Tomorrow Project, tel. 0115 925 1114. Website www.tomorrowproject.net

MORGAN G. (1997) *Images of Organization*. 2nd edn. London, Sage (Chapters 6, 9).

• Issues of Professionalism and Ethics

Introduction

L&D professionals have a responsibility to raise awareness in their organisations of ethical issues related to the learning process. They should also strive to develop across those organisations a real commitment to tackle those issues rather than just achieve legal compliance.

It is important to distinguish between professionalism and ethics, since although they are related, they have discrete meanings. Going to our usual source, the *Oxford English Reference Dictionary* (Pearsall and Trumbull, 1996), it is interesting to find that none of the definitions of 'profession', 'professional' or 'professionalism' there make implicit or explicit reference to ethics. Throughout, 'being professional' is a state most closely associated with the word 'competence':

> **Professionalism**: *the qualities or typical features of a profession or of professionals, esp. competence, skill, etc.*

To be a 'professional' therefore does not necessarily imply ethical practice. (Dickens, with whose words this book began, would certainly agree with that, demonstrating as he did such a profound distrust of at least one group of professionals – lawyers!) However, the link between professionalism and ethics is made clear in the same dictionary's definition of ethics:

> **Ethics**: *the rules of conduct recognized as appropriate to a particular profession or area of life.*

In the UK there are various 'codes' providing moral guidelines for HR professionals. These include codes of conduct established by professional bodies, and UK and European legislation and codes of practice (see later in this chapter). However, in some situations legal prescriptions and codes of conduct are not enough. There remains a gap that only individuals can close, using as their reference point their own reasoning, core values and beliefs. Here again, though, there is a difficulty, because although our dictionary source defines 'ethical' as 'morally correct; honourable', we still have to ask – morally correct by whose standards? Honourable in whose eyes? Whose values do we have in mind here?

In this chapter we will explore issues of professionalism and ethics by reference to theoretical approaches, common types of ethical dilemma that confront L&D practitioners, the legislative framework that relates to the L&D field, and the debate surrounding the treatment of 'difference' in that field.

Checkpoint

- What is meant by being a 'professional'?

- Outline and explain a generalised definition of 'ethics'.

- What kind of guidelines help HR professionals in dealing with ethical issues?

Theoretical approaches to ethics

It is impossible in the scope of a chapter such as this to do more than outline some ethical considerations of which any L&D practitioner should be aware. Ethics is a minefield of theory and practice – the very word is fraught with ambiguity – yet ethical practice lies at the heart of true professionalism, so we must confront at least some of the basic issues.

It is necessary to be selective here. We have already referred to that helpful layperson's guide, the *Oxford English Reference Dictionary* (Pearson and Trumble, 1996). But I will also make reference to Karen Legge's masterly discussion of ethics in the human resource management field (1998). The dictionary identifies three main schools of thought in ethics, and Legge covers their ground in depth. Here are some key points.

Respect for others is a duty 'central to morality', owed by all rational human beings to one another. This is a concept of ethics that condemns as immoral any action performed out of self-interest and assumes morality to be a matter of the exercise of reason. It holds that people should be treated 'with respect and as ends in their own right, not solely as means to others' ends' (Legge, 1998, p23). This is an absolutist approach to ethics, which can encourage a flight to the moral high ground, as Godfrey Hodgson noted in *The Independent Weekend Review*, 15 September 2001, p4, discussing Henry Kissinger's book *Does America Need a Foreign Policy?* (Simon & Schuster, 2001):

 When the claim of moral superiority is made on one's own behalf, it should always be met either by rage or laughter.

Ethical behaviour is the hallmark of any civilised society. Such behaviour is characterised by the virtues of justice, charity and generosity, and its exercise brings mutual benefit to society and to all of its members. As Legge observes, this approach to ethics raises questions of how best to manage an organisation so that the rights of all its members are protected and that all stakeholders participate in decisions relating to their welfare.

Ethics is a matter of ensuring the 'greatest happiness or benefit of the greatest number' in society. This approach (utilitarianism) defines 'ethical' by reference to the consequences of behaviour (Legge, 1998), whereas the other two schools of thought view ethical behaviour as a duty or a virtue in its own right. This approach is often the implicit basis of ethics in a professional context.

Most HRM practice in Western society today probably represents a mix of all three approaches, with the stakeholder approach dominating. Such pragmatism is strongly shaped by legislative pressures, by best practice studies, and by the increasingly popular 'business partnership' model. For L&D practitioners, all of this emphasises the importance of seeking continuously to ensure that:

- no person or group is treated in an unjustifiably less favourable way than another is, or would be, treated in the same circumstance (we will look in detail at this legal framework for ethics later in the chapter)

- although specific L&D initiatives and activity may not bring equal benefits to all, no one should be the loser because of them, and over time their cumulative outcomes should bring some advantage, some 'added value', to all members of the L&D partnership.

To conclude this section and lead us into the next, it is helpful to reflect on the various ways in which the L&D partnership was presented in Chapter 6 – as a matter of balancing risks and gains, as a type of game, and as a dance. Now try to answer the following questions arising from that reflection. Keep your answers by you to refer to as you read through the rest of the chapter.

> **Task 1**
>
> Reply 'Yes' or 'No' to each of the following questions, in each case giving brief reasons for your reply:
>
> Is it the right of every group of 'players in the game' to be accorded equal consideration and respect in relation to their needs, interests and goals?
>
> Is it reasonable to expect that every partner should play for the whole partnership, not just for one group or individual within it?
>
> Is it the responsibility of those who are in positions of power to 'play fair by' those, no matter how lowly their own organisational positions, from whose learning and development the organisation as a whole stands to gain?

Identifying and tackling ethical issues

If you tackled the above task, it probably gave you considerable pause for thought. That was the intention. Identifying what is and is not an 'ethical issue' can be difficult – tackling ethical issues embedded in some L&D situations more difficult still. Disturbing failures in developmental provision across the public and private sectors continue to haunt L&D practitioners. In 1999–2000 alone there were damaging reports on training in the prison service, the Metropolitan Police, the care sector, and in hotel, catering, rail and agricultural workforces. The Health and Safety Commission's report on the 1997 Southall train crash in which seven people died was highly critical of training procedures in rail companies across the country. The criticism related to failure to focus on key areas of skill and knowledge needed by drivers, to a lack of consistency of practice between drivers, to an absence of any centralised core training programme, and to a lack of a unified training record system (Cooper, 2000). What kind of failures are we looking at here? Of professionalism? Of competence? Of ethics?

Let us look again at the story of the Paddington rail crash, this time from an ethical viewpoint.

> **Task 2**
>
> Re-read the case of the Paddington rail crash in Chapter 1 (p21). Then, on the basis of the information provided in that account, answer the following questions:
>
> Can you identify any L&D ethical issues in the situation revealed by the Cullen Report – and if so, why do you see them to be 'ethical issues'?
>
> Why do L&D practitioners sometimes appear to ignore or be unaware of ethical issues?

To follow that task, look now at the following case – and identify any similarities you can with that of the Paddington tragedy:

CASE STUDY: Training at Metropolitan Police

In 2000, a 'damning report' was published by Her Majesty's Inspectorate of Constabulary on the Metropolitan Police's efforts to erase racism (Cooper, 2000a). The race awareness training introduced since the MacPherson report on the Stephen Lawrence murder investigation was found to be particularly inadequate.

The report also criticised the Met's previous record of training, on the grounds that 'from 1989 to 1998 it wasted £780,000 on training community race relations trainers whom it then failed to use' (Cooper, 2000a).

Why was there failure on such a scale? Three main reasons emerged:

- Senior personnel chiefs did not exercise enough influence in the decision and delegation process.

- Those chiefs lacked the necessary power and credibility to give them the influence they needed.

- There was a fundamental lack of training and training management expertise, and this led to:

  - lack of clarity about where responsibility lay for training at a senior level

  - lack of clarity on overall training strategy and how it fitted with wider HR functions

  - lack of understanding as to who would be trained to what standard, and when

  - lack of rigorous training needs analysis

  - lack of an effective and long-term evaluation process.

    Source: Cooper, 2000a

Comparing these two cases, what may at first sight appear to be an ethical issue can on closer examination seem to be a failure in expertise or awareness. Yet further reflection should confirm that ethics remains an issue in both, if we accept that every professional has a duty of care to their colleagues, clients, and ultimate as well as immediate customers. One definition of the essence of professionalism is (Jenkins, 1999):

> *to give advice on the basis of a body of training and experience, and to stand by the integrity of that advice irrespective of financial reward.*

That interpretation, with its implicit emphasis on ethics as well as expertise, is echoed in the CIPD's professional standards and in its Code of Conduct (see Appendix 4). In most cases of bad or negligent practice in the L&D field, the failures of L&D practitioners are due in part to others – usually those who plan and provide the practitioners' education and training, and those who manage and are ultimately accountable for their performance. But the individual cannot entirely pass the ethical buck. No professional, HR or otherwise, should venture into areas of work where they are uncertain of their own competence if, in so doing, they are likely to jeopardise the duty of care they have for others. Nor should they stand silently by in situations where that duty of care is jeopardised by the incompetence of others.

Tackling ethical issues can require considerable courage. For example:

- It is hard to admit to one's own incompetence, and in some cultures the outcomes of such admission may endanger one's career progression, perhaps one's position.

- It is hard to speak out about incompetence that one perceives in others. There is a risk of damaging one's opportunities for advancement by alienating influential colleagues or superiors.

- It is hard to go to a senior manager and report errors or gaps in the oversight and evaluation of one's own or others' learning and development, which only that senior manager's actions can rectify.

Perhaps in the Paddington rail crash and Metropolitan Police Force cases some L&D practitioners took such hard courses of action. If they did so, they were not successful, and it may be that they suffered for speaking out. Yet even if that was the case, it does not detract from the professional appropriateness of those actions.

With the increasing transparency of complaints processes, and media hunger for cases of professional negligence, a harsh light often shines now on ethical issues. At the time, such issues might not have been so clear, as you may find when you tackle the following task. It highlights one of the most familiar types of ethical problem – whistle-blowing – but in so doing it also illustrates some of the less obvious ethical tensions involved in a mentoring role. There are no black-and-white answers to such cases, and often it can be difficult to respond to them because of insufficient data. But that is life – when is the HR practitioner ever able to obtain all the data ideally needed to resolve or advise on complex organisational problems? So please tackle this task as best you can, in the realisation that its main purpose is to stimulate discussion. As Morgan pointed out in his writings on power and politics (Chapter 6), such discussion is in itself is a worthy exercise. It can yield invaluable insights, even if no certain prescriptions.

Task 3

On an internal management course for clinicians at a big acute hospital, you (a CIPD-qualified member of L&D staff) are acting as mentor to a young doctor, Karen. She has just confided in you some personal information that could be damaging to her if passed on to management.

In brief, the doctor has serious concerns about the competence of one of the most senior medical staff in the unit in which she works. She has tried unsuccessfully on a number of occasions to persuade her colleagues to take her concerns seriously, but although some have let slip comments that suggest they too feel something may be amiss, no one will give her open support. She has considered going to management, but feels that this would be unlikely to achieve anything more than a 'warning off' (as she puts it). She is probably right. The hospital has not performed well in the latest 'league tables' and is under pressure to improve against a number of key indicators. The last thing management wants at present is trouble on yet another front.

Karen feels increasingly that she has only two options: to blow the whistle, or to keep quiet. In her confusion, she has turned to you for advice.

Karen's dilemma is real. The consultant in question is long-serving, powerful in the medical profession at large as well as in the hospital, and is surrounded by a group of loyal staff and grateful patients. Although Karen's concerns seem well-founded, she lacks concrete evidence, and she believes that only a systematic and detailed enquiry by a properly constituted authority would take them further in any meaningful way. The outcome of such an enquiry might or might not prove that her concerns are justified. Although she has only been at the hospital for a year she already has a promising career ahead of her; however, she is at the stage where losing the support of senior medical staff and of colleagues would undoubtedly damage that career.

What advice should you give to Karen?

As a 'business partner' in this organisation, what are your own responsibilities here?

The framework of law and good practice

One of the most publicised area of ethics, with which all HR professionals should be familiar (if only because of the impact of the law here), is to do with equality at work.

In the UK it is currently unlawful to treat any person less favourably than other people for a reason related to their race, ethnic origin, gender or disability. Under various European Directives it will by 2003/2006 also become unlawful to discriminate against any person on grounds of their religion or belief, age or sexual orientation. Details of UK and European legislation and codes of practice relating to equality in employment can be obtained from various professional and government websites and publications (see the end of this chapter for key sources).

It is not the purpose of this section to deal expertly with the law, but simply to explore ways in which L&D professionals can fulfil their professional and ethical responsibilities by helping to achieve equality of treatment and opportunity for all employees in the workplace. There are three main tasks here: to raise awareness and develop skills, to ensure equality of access to training and development opportunities, and to promote affirmative action.

Raising awareness

Those with L&D responsibilities need to ensure that training and guidance are given to everyone who makes policies and procedures, administers, or is in any way actively involved in the management and development of people across the organisation. Such personnel include top management, supervisory and managerial staff, team leaders, HR specialists and reception staff. (The latter are important because they are the organisation's public face, and the first point of contact for those visiting or working in the organisation.)

Poor communication and lack of awareness often cause or increase discriminatory attitudes and behaviour at work. Training to raise awareness of how these problems can arise, and also to draw attention to the special needs of minority groups in the workplace, can make a significant contribution to reducing these problems. Such training and guidance should help everyone to:

- acquire a sound and practical understanding of what inequality and direct or indirect discrimination mean

- understand their organisation's equal opportunities policy and have the competence to carry out the responsibilities and tasks that it involves

- be able to identify and alert relevant personnel to any discriminatory attitudes that may affect decision-making at various organisational levels

- understand the need to keep records of how recruitment, selection, promotion and reward processes are handled, and of their outcomes. Claims of unlawful treatment can be won on a failure by the employer to provide records demonstrating that all reasonable practical steps have been taken to avoid discrimination. This particularly applies in the case of claims of sex discrimination, because under the Sex Discrimination Regulations 2001 the burden of proof has shifted from the complainant to the respondent, who must show that no discrimination has occurred.

Checkpoint

- What forms of discrimination are currently illegal in the UK?

- Identify *three* tasks for the L&D manager (or equivalent) in relation to promoting equality of treatment in the workplace.

Achieving equal access

We saw in Chapter 2 that there are great inequalities in access to training and workforce development. It is easy to state that everyone in an organisation should have equal access to training and development related to their and the organisation's needs. It is far more difficult to achieve that aim. In the face of such a deep training divide, it is a particular responsibility of L&D professionals to ensure that:

- L&D specialist staff, managers, and all others with L&D responsibilities clearly understand the law relating to ensuring access to opportunities for training, promotion and other forms of development.

- all employees know how to access information about training, educational and other developmental opportunities, and how to apply for them. Such opportunities must not be communicated to employees in ways that could exclude or disproportionately reduce the numbers of applicants from a particular minority or racial group or gender.

- there is no direct or indirect discrimination in selecting people for training and development. Those with L&D responsibilities should check regularly to see whether, through time, people from a particular group or gender are failing to apply for certain kinds of training or assessment for promotion; are not trained, assessed or promoted at all; or are trained, assessed or promoted, but in significantly lower proportions than their rate of application or their representation in the workforce. If such checks show that problems are occurring, the L&D manager (or equivalent) must then find out why and take remedial action.

The following task is intended to test your practical understanding of some principles discussed in this section.

Task 4

Read through the following case, and then decide what should be done:

1 *to ensure that in future no direct or indirect discrimination of the kind indicated in the case recurs*
2 *to help those current members of the ethnic group who have been disadvantaged up to this point because of the unequal treatment they have received.*

[*Note: 'training' is used here to mean training courses and educational programmes.*]

In organisation Y, checks by training staff of records going back over the past three years have revealed that members of one particular ethnic group in the workforce consistently lack the training and

---

qualifications that would enable them to apply for promotion to certain posts in the organisation. They have thus been regularly disadvantaged in their attempts at career progression.

The training staff have talked to a representative sample of present members of the group and to their supervisors or managers. They have also obtained from them information about their own experiences and the experiences of others from the group who have left the organisation. It has emerged that some past and present group members applied to enter various relevant internal or external courses but were not accepted. There was no single reason for this: sometimes they did not get the support of their manager; sometimes they were told that the course was at the wrong level for their particular needs; sometimes they were advised that the course was 'full'. In only a small minority of cases did the records provide clear evidence that the reasons given to them for rejecting their applications were valid.

Others were accepted onto internal or external courses, but then found that the language used, or the delivery methods or style adopted, or the methods of assessment, posed unique problems for them. No account was taken of the linguistic and cultural difficulties that they encountered, and their rate of success in achieving course outcomes was significantly less than the success rate of other employees on the same or similar courses.

The training staff examined the process used over the past three years to select employees to go on training courses. They also looked at the design and delivery of courses mentioned by ethnic group members whom they had interviewed. They concluded that in most of these cases this ethnic group had suffered either direct or indirect discrimination in relation to access to training, and in training itself. This seemed to be due in most cases to a lack of awareness or understanding by managers and some training staff of the law and of good practice, lack of due monitoring of training, and poor training records.

Taking affirmative action

It is unlawful to discriminate against some groups in order to improve the position of others previously disadvantaged. However, it is lawful to take affirmative action to help those in the latter category. Thus in the case of the ethnic group members in the task you have just been invited to attempt, since there have been no or proportionately few employees of a particular sex or racial group in certain jobs, areas, or levels of work in the previous 12-month period, then it is lawful for:

- the employer to provide access to training facilities that will help to equip those ethnic group members for such work or responsibilities

- the employer to encourage them to apply for training or education, whether it is provided internally or externally

- the training manager to design training schemes for school-leavers designed to reach members of such ethnic groups; and to arrange training for promotion or skills training for those who lack particular expertise but show potential (supervisory training may include language training).

Another case illustrates good practice to help minority groups with special needs in respect of education or training.

CASE STUDY: Taking affirmative action

A workforce includes employees whose English is limited. Such employees are disadvantaged because of this, particularly in relation to attempting to undertake educational qualification courses that would help their chances of promotion.

The organisation's L&D manager therefore organises the following affirmative action to help remedy the situation for these employees:

- training in English and communication skills

- training for managers and team leaders in the background and culture of the ethnic minority groups concerned

- interpretation and translation facilities for grievance and other procedures and terms of employment.

Opening up access for women

The access of women to training and promotion opportunities is now an area of even greater concern than in the past for employers. The European Directives' Sex Discrimination (Indirect Discrimination and Burden of Proof) Regulations 2001 'widen the definition of indirect discrimination under the Sex Discrimination Act of 1975' and 'shift the burden of proof towards the employer' (Aikin, 2001). These changes make it vital to check selection criteria for promotion and training, to ensure adequate investigatory procedures are in place, and to advise employees of their expanded rights.

Employers and L&D managers who seek to reduce the barriers that face many women who strive for promotion in male-dominated sectors or organisations often focus on management training. However, women in non-managerial jobs have career development needs too. Programmes like the BBC's pioneering and award-winning *Springboard* (see overleaf) have led the way in opening up opportunities for such women.

CASE STUDY: The *Springboard* programme

Springboard evolved from a 'Women's development programme' launched by the BBC in 1989 that won the Lady Platt Award for the best equal opportunities training initiative.

The programme arose out of a perceived need that although the BBC had done much to open up opportunities for women managers, it was essential to widen these initiatives, extending personal and career development opportunities to women (between 8,000 and 9,000) employed in non-managerial positions at the BBC. Better utilisation and motivation of such a huge organisational resource was clearly in the interests of the business as well as being of benefit to those individuals.

Consideration of the kind of learning media and methods to be used indicated at first sight that distance-learning would be the most appropriate medium, given the extremely large size of the learning population. However, analysis of the profile of that population highlighted the importance to the learners of support and encouragement from other women, and this led to the decision to design a programme which involved a good deal of face-to-face learning. Its components were:

- three one-day workshops held over three months

- a workbook involving about three hours' work a week for participants, and involving a range of self-assessment and personal learning plan activities

- the formation of formal and informal networks

- a mentoring system in the workplace

- the involvement of senior women in the organisation.

The programme, designed by the BBC's management training unit working with Biographic Management consultancy, became so highly regarded that it was renamed *Springboard* and tailored for the use of other organisations, including Grand Metropolitan Foods, Europe, which incorporated it within a much larger initiative called the 'Learning Edge', designed to create a learning environment in which all employees could develop their full potential.

Source: Arkin, 1991

Difference and diversity in learning

Patterns of difference

So far, we have looked at ways in which to achieve compliance with the law relating to equality and build good practice through affirmative action. I will now explore some wider ethical dimensions of 'differences' in the workplace as they relate to L&D practice. In this section I draw particulary on the ideas of two writers: Barbara Walker (1994) and Nicky Solomon (1999).

There is an increasing interest in the workplace as a source of organisationally valuable learning (I explore this in more detail in Chapter 20). This is partly due to an emphasis on 'ongoing skills development in the context of the rapidly changing demands of work' (Solomon, 1999: 122). As the same writer points out, it is also a consequence of national vocational training systems that use competency-based training frameworks (as do the UK National Vocational Qualifications). In the UK, another and major stimulus has come from the present government's preoccupation with lifelong learning (see Chapter 2), which is resulting in many opportunities for organisations to secure funding for workplace learning projects.

All workplaces are characterised by differences between those who work there. The obvious differences include those we have already noted: of gender, race, ethnic origin, religion, disability, age, and occupational or professional grouping. But there are other differences, and they have a direct bearing on the L&D process. They include:

- differences in individuals' learning style, skills and preferences

- differences in their attitudes to change

- differences in their ability or disposition to fit into the culture of the workplace.

These last three types of difference are subtle, but they can result in some individuals' feeling (or in fact being) isolated from the majority, being under pressure to conform to values they do not share, or experiencing stress and confusion in situations where they cannot 'play to their strengths'. Take, for example, the type of culture that was developed in those seven organisations reported in 1997 by Terry and Purcell (see Chapter 3). It featured HR practices that included:

- team structures

- competency frameworks to identify and foster behaviour needed

- group-based reward systems

- appraisal systems to monitor and measure performance.

The benefits that such a culture brings to the business, and the ability of many employees to adjust relatively easily to such practices, can lead those who feel disadvantaged in such a workplace to be sidelined or dismissed as 'difficult' because of their difference from the majority. Yet that kind of 'difference' should be treated with consideration. Not everyone is able to work well in teams, particularly those who are self-managing by disposition. The stress on those who fail to fully conform to group norms is likely to be reinforced by group-based reward systems. Likewise, while competency frameworks have much to commend them (see Chapters 8 and 20), in prescribing certain types of performance and behaviour they tend to exclude others. New patterns of difference are thus created. Appraisal systems, too, can become divisive if they aim to achieve strict conformity of all employees to centralised norms relating to performance and learning.

In such scenarios, equity becomes a real issue because we can obtain no ethically satisfactory answer to the question 'Who benefits here, and at what cost to others?' In the so-called post-Fordist workplace, the emphasis is on collaboration, trust, self-managing teams, the abolition of hierarchy, self-development and visions of the 'learning organisation'. Yet despite this appearance of escape from the harsh controls of the scientifically managed Fordist workplace, many commentators argue that new forms of control have simply replaced the old, and that new inequalities have emerged as a 'hierarchical organising logic' has been replaced by a 'productive logic of quality, service, teams and learning' (Butler, 1999: 144–5). This explains the claim by Zuboff (1988), quoted in Chapter 1, that learning is 'the new form of labour', and the concerns of Bratton and Gold (1994) and of Solomon (1999) quoted in the same chapter.

Checkpoint

● What are typical features of the 'post-Fordist workplace', and why do you think that workplace is so called?

● In what ways can membership of a 'self-managing team' prove stressful?

While it is important not to underplay the many benefits offered by modern industrial society, it is important also that L&D practitioners recognise factors in today's workplace that intensify old patterns of difference between people and create new. These factors, if ignored, can foster in many individuals and groups attitudes that lead to alienation from workplace learning. A dispiriting downward spiral can then occur, as Figure 6 shows.

Building on diversity

There are many ways in which L&D staff can reverse this kind of spiral, so that diversity becomes a valuable source of reflection and learning for everyone. As one example, Barbara Walker (1994) has produced a unique 'Valuing Differences' model whose use by Digital Equipment Corporation – a Fortune 100 computer manufacturer – proved a powerful adjunct to the company's Affirmative Action and Equal Employment Opportunity work. The model's five steps are to do with:

● stripping away stereotypes

● learning to listen to and probe for the differences in people's assumptions

● building strong relationships with people one regards as 'different'

● empowering oneself in order to become more open to learning from 'differences'

● exploring and identifying group differences.

The most usual examples given of such diversity relate to ethnicity or

Figure 6 The downward spiral of 'difference' in workplace learning

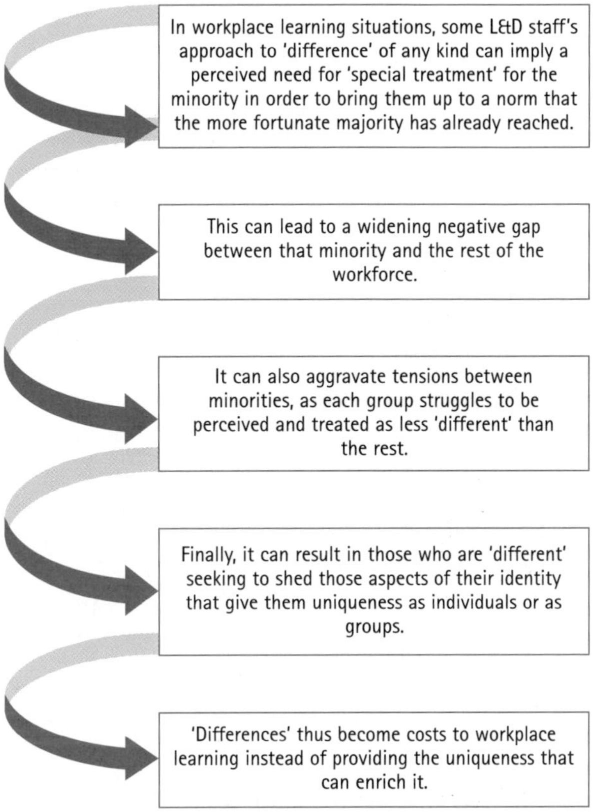

In workplace learning situations, some L&D staff's approach to 'difference' of any kind can imply a perceived need for 'special treatment' for the minority in order to bring them up to a norm that the more fortunate majority has already reached.

This can lead to a widening negative gap between that minority and the rest of the workforce.

It can also aggravate tensions between minorities, as each group struggles to be perceived and treated as less 'different' than the rest.

Finally, it can result in those who are 'different' seeking to shed those aspects of their identity that give them uniqueness as individuals or as groups.

'Differences' thus become costs to workplace learning instead of providing the uniqueness that can enrich it.

gender, but this is to think too narrowly. Consider the case of diversified contracts. The contribution of part-time and temporary workers can be crucial to the success and growth of a business. Research by the Policy Studies Institute (1993) indicated that flexible workers are an under-performing resource. Failure to integrate part-time and temporary workers into organisations' employee development systems sub-sequently gave rise to concern at government level (White, 1996). Often, such workers have less access than permanent full-time workers to four key areas of L&D practice:

- upskilling through training, growth in the job and increased responsibility

- performance management processes that combine appraisal reviews, target-setting, performance feedback and merit pay

- increasing personal discretion in tasks

- decentralised decision-making.

White (1996) noted that although the lowest skill categories of part-time and temporary workers fared worst, part-timers in management were particularly excluded from the performance management process, and temporary workers (expecting less than one year's employment) suffered disproportionately in every area except that of initial training. Contract workers, on the other hand, did well.

In the 1990s the catering company Beeton Rumford provided a model of good practice related to diversity in the workforce. This final case study exemplifies the kind of business-focused and also ethical treatment of differences that enriches the learning process for everyone involved in it.

CASE STUDY: Developing a flexible workforce at Beeton Rumford

In the late 1990s the Earl's Court Olympia catering company, Beeton Rumford, employed around 200 temporary workers. It was unusual in the catering trade in its promise of a good benefits package and equal commitment to the development of all its workers, not only those occupying full-time positions. The determination of the managing director, Richard Tate, to have an integrated workforce was so great that he banned the term 'casual'. He first developed his philosophy in an earlier career with Trust House Forte.

At Beeton Rumford the role of temporary employees was crucial but had in the past been undervalued. After 1991 the aim had been to ensure that through focused recruitment aimed at attracting and retaining high-calibre staff, and through eradicating from the company the casual ethos, temporary staff would be recognised by themselves and others as the backbone of the organisation, supported by rather than supporting full-time staff. After 1991 the company had been restructured from a functional to a customer-focused business, and a separate staff department had been established to recruit, train and manage temporary personnel.

At first, a large and relatively unproductive effort went into improving the status and training of temporary staff. Operational managers found it hard to support such a change in focus, given the stop-start nature of the business. Despite their efforts, the sizeable pool of expensively recruited and trained temporary talent would disappear at the end of every catering event.

Further human resource policy change took place, and this brought the improvements sought. By the late 1990s, temporary staff were no longer laid off at 24 hours' notice but were treated as full-time in terms of the focus of their jobs, being given information about events scheduled over the coming year in order to aid their own planning activity. At the heart of the development strategy was a six-tier career structure based on core competencies, with appraisals carried out regularly.

Source: Pickard, 1995

CONCLUSION

Having read this chapter and completed its checkpoints and tasks, you should now:

- be able to identify the link between professionalism and ethics
- understand the ethical implications involved in L&D partnerships, and the professional responsibilities that such partnerships also involve
- be able to identify and advise on core tasks of L&D professionals related to achieving equality of access and opportunity in the L&D field and to promoting good practice
- be able to identify and understand how to tackle various ethical issues central to L&D practice in the workplace.

To test yourself against these objectives, what five-minute answers would you give to the following questions?

Review questions

E-mail from the personnel director: 'I need some input from you for that paper I'm putting together on ethics. Can you please jot down for me *one* kind of ethical issue that can arise in a learning/training situation, explain why you regard it as an "ethical issue", and tell me very briefly how you'd tackle it.' Produce the input your personnel director has requested.

Identify and explain *three* tasks of L&D professionals related to achieving equality of access and opportunity in training and development.

A young and inexperienced training practitioner asks you for advice on sources of information that will keep her up to date on the law, good practice and ethical behaviour relating to L&D work. What advice will you give her?

Useful reference sources

ARAGON S. R., HATCHER T. *and* SWANSON. R. A. (eds) (2001) 'Ethics and integrity in HRD: Case studies in research and practice'. *Advances in Developing Human Resource.* Vol. 3, No. 1. February (quarterly journal of the Academy of Human Resource Development, USA).

INSTITUTE OF PERSONNEL AND DEVELOPMENT (1999) *Managing Diversity: Evidence from case studies*. London, IPD.

LE CARRÉ J. (2001) *The Constant Gardener*. London, Hodder & Stoughton. (For a layperson's introduction to the field of business ethics: a novel that provides a powerful and gripping condemnation of unethical practice in large corporations and governments, the more telling for drawing on a wealth of factual data.)

MARCHINGTON M. *and* WILKINSON A. (1996) *People Management and Development*. London, Chartered Institute of Personnel and Development (for their treatment of ethics across the whole field of human resource management and development).

STEWART J. (1999) 'Policy and ethics in employee development', in J. Stewart, *Employee Development Practice*. London, Financial Times and Pitman, pp240–260.

Websites

For CIPD students and members: www.cipd.co.uk homepage, links to CIPD Code of Conduct and to:

- information about the CIPD's Legal Advisory Service (tel. 0870 5561251)

- CIPD Employment Law online, with its own links to legislation and guidance, European law, UK government and other sources of advice

- FAQs (frequently asked questions) on all aspects of employment law

- information about CIPD 'Legal Essentials' books and about CIPD training courses on legal matters; also about other CIPD resources, including summaries of current news and *People Management* articles on employment law, access to the CIPD's library and information services, and Infosource documents giving examples of best practice.

General: www.hmso.gov.uk for details of all UK and European employment legislation and codes of practice. This website also includes answers to FAQs on employment law.

www.eoc.org.uk – the Equal Opportunities Commission website, whose links page connects to specialist equal opportunities sites.

In 1999 the American Academy of Human Resource Development published *HRD Standards on Ethics and Integrity*, a detailed and uniquely important document, which can be downloaded from www.ahrd.org. The e-mail address is office@ahrd.org.

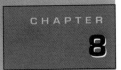

• Establishing Roles and Standards

CHAPTER OBJECTIVES

After reading this chapter you will:

- be able to assess the practical value of different models of L&D roles

- have a critical understanding of the basis and scope of L&D occupational and professional standards

- be able to advise on the implications of those standards for L&D values and tasks in the workplace

Introduction

If the L&D function in an organisation is to be well managed and appropriately staffed there must be a shared understanding of what the purpose of that function is to be, of the roles that it will involve across the organisation, and of the standards that are to govern performance in those roles.

What do we mean by 'role'? One dictionary definition (Allen, 1990) is:

> **role**: an actor's part . . . a person's or thing's characteristic or expected function.

This is a useful way of thinking about 'role' because of the emphasis on playing a part, on interacting in a particular way with others, as well as on functions to be performed. It also highlights the concept of dynamism. Every actor differs in his or her interpretation of a given part, and makes of it something unique, as well as fulfilling its formal requirements. These related ideas of a given and a developed element are emphasised in much of the published research about training roles.

L&D roles have changed considerably over the past two decades, and with that has come a change in the standards of performance associated with them. With so much emphasis in today's public- and private-sector organisations on targets of performance and measurement of outcomes, it is inevitable that there should be an increased concern on the part of government, professional and other awarding bodies to:

- produce for all occupations and professions standards of competency that specify clear performance outcomes expected at different organisational or functional levels

- produce qualification and assessment structures related to those standards.

Under the Bologna Declaration, made by 29 countries including the UK in June 1999, by 2009 all qualification standards and structures must be linked into a national and into a European qualifications structure. To this end, by 2003 all UK educational programmes must be part of the UK's National Qualifications Framework and comply with the Qualifications and Curriculum Authority's (QCA) criteria.

It can be argued that to emphasise 'standards' is to become a slave to compliance and to stifle innovation and challenges to 'the norm'. However, in a field like L&D where poor practice is widespread, it can also be argued that the provision of clear and relevant standards is essential in order to improve levels of competence. If those standards encourage rather than discourage the development of new knowledge, then they can also help to ensure that managers and practitioners examine critically both what they do and how they do it.

Other benefits that can be achieved by the sensible use of national or professional standards in L&D include:

- clarification of what is involved in the exercise of L&D roles at different levels

- the provision of job descriptions of L&D staff to guide their recruitment and selection

- improved organisational and individual development, career-planning and progression

- benchmarks for good practice

- effective evaluation of L&D both at individual and at organisational level and as a basis for appraisal

- greater organisational and individual flexibility and responsiveness to changing demands.

This chapter looks at a variety of ways to classify L&D roles in the workplace before exploring the standards associated with those roles that have been produced by the Employment National Training Organisation (EmpNTO) and the CIPD in 2001, following a two-year consultative process in each case.

Two things should be stressed at this point. First, from the start of the CIPD's two-year consultative process to revise its 1996 Professional Standards, I was closely associated with the development of the generalist and specialist standards in Learning and Development (CIPD, 2001). I have striven particularly hard for objectivity throughout this chapter, but readers must judge for themselves whether I have achieved that. Second, unless stated otherwise, the comments that follow, like all the comments that I make in this book, are my own personal views, and must not be taken to represent the views of any other individual or institution.

Checkpoint

Identify and explain *three* kinds of benefit that the application of occupational or professional standards in L&D could bring in your own organisation, or in one with which you are familiar.

Classifying L&D roles

As we saw in Chapter 1, there have been considerable changes in the conceptual and practical base of L&D over recent years. We look briefly now at some of the classification systems (otherwise known as 'typologies') that have been produced to identify and describe L&D roles over the past two decades. I shall then suggest a typology of my own.

The Pettigrew typology (1982)

For at least a decade after it was first developed in 1982, the typology produced by Pettigrew, Jones and Reason (1982) provided a meaningful description of the range of activity in which training staff were involved across different organisational settings. It was based on role analysis, using views collected from training practitioners at that time about the roles that they played and observed were being played in a variety of organisations.

The research identified five main types of role:

- *the change agent* – This role is concerned with the definition of organisational problems and with helping others to resolve them through changing the organisational culture.

- *the provider* – 'The provider offers training services and systems that are primarily oriented to the maintenance and improvement of organisational performance rather than to changing the organisation in any major ways' (Pettigrew *et al*, 1982). This is the operational delivery role that reinforces the organisational status quo.

- *the passive provider* – Again, this is a role concerned with maintaining, not with changing, the organisation. It differs from the 'provider' role because of the lack of expertise implied (especially of political skills) in putting across and developing even that role with conviction. It operates at a low level of activity and influence. Anyone adopting this kind of role is clearly at risk in organisations looking for professional expertise and impact on business performance.

- *the training manager* – In this role the focus is on the managerial aspect of training. It is primarily concerned with the planning, organisation, direction and control of training operations. The training manager may have responsibility for a group of training staff, or may simply be responsible for co-ordinating the provision of training courses and operations.

- *the role in transition* – This describes a role that is in the process of changing from that of 'provider' to that of 'change agent', and therefore includes elements of both kinds of activity.

The Pettigrew typology still has value to contribute to contemporary discussion of L&D roles. However, it cannot at this distance of time reflect the profoundly changed environment in which many practitioners now work, or the changed focus from 'training' to 'learning' that characterises the field today.

Checkpoint

- Identify the *five* roles in Pettigrew's 1982 typology and outline the meaning of each.

- Why should a 'passive provider' role give rise to concern in an organisation, and what outcomes are likely to be typical of that concern?

The IPD typology (1999)

Martin Sloman claimed in the mid-1990s that the world of training could no longer be adequately managed as the orderly, sequential series of planned learning interventions envisaged by the systematic training model (Sloman, 1994). He proposed a twofold typology of roles for the training professional – as internal consultant and as strategic facilitator. Equivalents to both these roles emerged too in subsequent research into the changing role of the trainer in the late 1990s, sponsored by the Institute of Personnel and Development (now Chartered). The report of the research team (Darling, Darling and Elliott, 1999) rested on the views of a wide-ranging sample of those practising in workplaces, many of which had changed greatly in their employment and work systems since the early 1980s.

According to those practitioners, their training roles fell into a fourfold typology (Darling *et al*, 1999):

- *managerial* – those working as managers or equivalent in training organisations such as TECs/LECS and National Training Organisations (see Chapter 2)

- *service* – those providing a service function in organisations

- *external* – external training providers and consultants

- *line manager* – those holding primary responsibility for training within their units.

The emergence of these roles was strongly influenced by the increasing importance of outsourcing, training consultancy, line-managed development, work-based developmental approaches, and a wish for more strategically-focused training.

The National Occupational Standards typology (2001)

At the time of writing, National Occupational Standards in L&D that were produced in 2001 have been related through the National Vocational Qualification structure to six types of L&D role, operating at three qualification levels:

- L&D director

- L&D manager

- manager of L&D provision

- co-ordinator of L&D provision

- training officer

- direct trainer

Level 5, Learning and Development
This qualification level, for which there is one National Vocational Qualification/Scottish National Vocational Qualification (S/NVQ), relates to what can be described as the role of *learning and development director*.

This kind of role is carried out by those who hold a senior level of responsibility for L&D in an organisation, and also by consultants operating at strategic level. The main tasks it involves concern identifying L&D needs across the organisation, developing an organisational strategy and plans for L&D, and securing and managing the financial resources needed to implement those plans.

Level 4, Learning and Development
This level relates to three types of role, each incorporated in an S/NVQ: *learning and development manager* (generalised organisation and management of L&D), *manager of L&D provision*, and *co-ordinator of L&D provision*.

The main tasks involved at this level concern designing, agreeing, supporting and evaluating learning and development programmes in the workplace, managing the contribution of others to the learning process, and creating a workplace climate conducive to learning and responsive to changes in learning and development. They also concern identifying organisational training and development needs, and planning the implementation of training and development objectives. Those who occupy roles at this level are likely to be responsible for the improvement of a range of programmes, and for the delivery and/or facilitation of a broader range of learning opportunities than those characterising level 3.

Level 3, Learning and Development

This level relates to two types of role, each incorporated in an S/NVQ: *training officer* and *direct trainer*.

The main tasks these roles involve are identifying individual learning aims and programmes, agreeing learning programmes with learners, developing and reviewing the progress of those programmes, and facilitating and supporting other work-based learning activity. They are also to do with delivering such activity.

National Occupational Standards in L&D are examined in more detail later in this chapter.

The CIPD typology (2001)

The CIPD's 1999–2000 standards review process identified two generic roles for those with personnel and development responsibilities – those of *business partner* and of *thinking performer*. These have already been mentioned in Chapter 1. It was clear from the views of L&D stakeholders that these two roles are of overriding importance in L&D work as in personnel work more widely.

The review also suggested that there is no single functional role at any organisational level that those with L&D responsibilities tend to perform. L&D roles vary from smaller to larger organisations and from one organisational level to the next. These variations are due far less to functional differentiation than to differing contextual demands, stemming particularly from:

- vision, goals and corporate leadership related to L&D as an organisational process
- L&D's business purpose
- workplace settings and HR practices
- the type of financial and staffing base available to support L&D activity.

The review did, however, identify five major fields of activity in which L&D professionals have central roles:

- learning and development as a generalist field
- managing the training and development function
- managing organisational learning and knowledge
- designing and delivering training
- management development.

The CIPD's 2001 Professional Standards cover these fields (CIPD, 2001). A specialist standard for career management and development

– another L&D-related field – has been produced as part of the Employee Resourcing stream of standards (CIPD, 2001).

The CIPD's L&D standards are also examined later in this chapter.

Task 1

A training officer in mid-career aims ultimately to become an L&D professional operating at corporate level. She has just completed a learning styles inventory (LSI) and has scored high as an activist and pragmatist but low as a reflector and theorist. [If you are unfamiliar with LSIs, or need to refresh your memory, read (eg) Marchington and Wilkinson 2002, pp389–92 before doing this task.]

You are about to discuss her career aspirations with her. Draft a memo for yourself covering the points you intend to make in that discussion and the advice you will offer her.

An integrative typology of L&D roles

The various approaches to classifying L&D roles in organisations described so far cannot be fully reconciled, nor is it important that they

Table 4   The author's typology of L&D roles

Role	National Occupational Standards level at which it is commonly practised	Major focus of role
Strategic change agent	4 and 5	Promotion and facilitation of strategically focused L&D process, particularly at divisional and corporate levels
Consultant	3, 4 and 5	Business partnership, to ensure L&D advice, planning, provision and assessment at any organisational level achieve added value
Manager	4 and 5	Management of the L&D function across the organisation, whether through L&D specialists, line managers or internal/external partnerships
Trainer/ learning facilitator	3 and 4	Design, delivery/facilitation and evaluation of training events, learning processes and workplace learning
Administrator	3	Support for L&D operations at all organisational levels

should be. Each has something of value to offer, and it is for users to decide which best suit their individual and organisational needs. Building on insights that they contain, and reflecting too on other factors that relate to L&D roles, I have produced in Table 4 a typology of my own.

This typology emphasises the diversity of situations in which L&D practitioners have to operate. Many carry more demanding responsibilities than their titles, qualifications and hierarchical level might suggest. Often, for example, the role of strategic change agent has to be performed by a middle-level practitioner who is an HR generalist. In some organisations, the person in managerial charge of L&D in the business may be located at S/NVQ level 4 yet may be fulfilling elements of all the roles in the table. That person may be an L&D specialist, a line manager, or an HR generalist.

The consultant role in Table 4 deserves special comment. The L&D consultant, whether internally based or brought in by the organisation, is there to provide a service, and must work in business partnerships to ensure that the service is relevant and of high quality. Consultants have to be 'professional', to be clear about targets, costs, the activities to be carried out, and about ways of establishing what outcomes have been achieved. (For practical techniques to help internal consultants improve their effectiveness, see Thomas and Elbeik, 1996.) They must ensure that the projects for which they are responsible are delivered on time and to specification.

L&D practitioners who are internal consultants must remember that potentially they are in competition with external consultants. Competition may sharpen their efforts, but it may also lead to their operations' being outsourced. As we shall see in Chapter 9, outsourcing should be viewed as a healthy challenge that can bring benefits to HR personnel as well as to their organisations.

Checkpoint

- Outline and explain the types of L&D role identified in *one* typology with which you are familiar.

- What competencies underpin the roles of the L&D practitioner as business partner?

- How is the 'thinking performer' role associated with a strategic approach to the L&D process?

Assessing national occupational and professional standards

Criteria for assessing any L&D standards

Any set of occupational or professional standards intended to guide L&D practice in the field should be up to date in relation to that practice and should also be forward-looking. Such standards should therefore:

- adequately reflect the many changes in workforce composition, in work practices and workplace organisation, and in approaches to workplace learning that have taken place over recent years

- recognise the changes in focus and content of L&D activity that are needed in organisations, given the impact of an increasingly knowledge-based, technologised and globalised economy

- provide clear guidelines to the practice of tasks and the conduct of processes by which to achieve effective L&D practice in an organisation and to ensure that it is adaptive to emergent issues

- provide clear guidelines to help practitioners identify and tackle any inequities associated with the operation of L&D policies and processes

- stimulate critical thinking, strategic vision and innovation in the L&D field.

National Occupational and Professional Standards in learning and development, 2001

In 1994 the IPD was formed from the merger between the Institute of Personnel Management (IPM) and the Institute of Training and Development (ITD). In 1996, it produced Professional Standards relevant for all personnel and development practitioners and for those studying to achieve professional qualification. In July 2001, following a two-year consultative process, the Institute (now Chartered, and so titled CIPD) published revised standards that incorporated new performance guidelines for those in the L&D field (CIPD, 2001).

In a parallel process, National Occupational Standards produced in 1996 had also been revised. In 1995 the Employment Occupational Standards Council (a body formed by the merger in 1994 of the employer-led Training and Development Lead Body, the Personnel Standards Lead Body and the Trade Union Sector Development Body) published Training and Development (T&D) standards at levels 3 and 4, following these with level 5 standards in 1996. At that time they were stand-alone standards reflecting different functional traditions.

The publication of the Beaumont Report in 1996 (see Chapter 2) led in 1999 to a two-year cross-UK review of all National Occupational Standards. The review was funded by the Qualifications and Curriculum

Authority (QCA) and Scottish Qualifications Authority (SCA), with involvement also of the Qualifications Curriculum and Assessment Authority for Wales. National Training Organisations became the Standard Setting Body for all National Occupational Standards.

In 1997, during the review period, employment-related standards were brought together under one cross-sector grouping under the Employment National Training Organisation (EmpNTO). The aim of EmpNTO's review process was to tackle inconsistencies and provide a structure to support a suite of standards that would be integrated while retaining functional distinctiveness. EmpNTO worked with a consultancy firm, HOST, on the revision task. The extensive consultation included use of a website, focus groups, newsletters and other briefings.

The new EmpNTO L&D standards and a set of six related S/NVQs were approved in December 2001 by QCA and SQA. Awarding bodies have been able to offer the new vocational L&D qualifications since June 2002.

The CIPD standards provide the basis for CIPD professional qualifying examinations and the EmpNTO standards provide the basis for National Vocational Qualifications. The two sets of standards are being cross-mapped at the time of writing. They will then be used to guide assessment of the performance of all personnel and development practitioners currently working in the field, as well as the performance of those seeking entry to that field.

In the following two sections the L&D standards produced in 2001 by EmpNTO and by the CIPD are compared, using six parameters:

- the primary analytical approach
- the conceptual base
- the qualification structure
- the view of the organisation
- the approach to practice
- the core values.

National Occupational Standards in Learning and Development

The primary analytical approach

In any discussion of a particular set of national standards it is important to stress that the development and review of National Occupational Standards is subject to a unique set of rules and criteria defined by QCA and SCA. A functional analysis approach was applied to the revision of all the 1996 standards, not simply of those in Training and Development (T&D). This helps to explain the extent to which the 2001 L&D

Standards and their related qualifications are dominated by the concept of learning and development as a set of discrete functional tasks and competencies that operate at different organisational levels.

The most worrying outcomes of the in-depth functional analysis approach applied to the development of 2001 national L&D Standards were an insufficient emphasis on the need for a holistic and integrative approach to L&D as an organisational process, and inadequate attention to the need for planning and management of interactive L&D processes that often cross functional boundaries and organisational levels. The higher-level skills involved here cannot adequately be derived from functional analysis, but they are central to effective L&D practice in any organisation.

The conceptual base

The 2001 national L&D Standards make a much clearer distinction between operational and strategic activity than did the 1996 Training and Development Standards. They also refer repeatedly to 'learning' as well as to 'training'. However, no explicit distinction is made between these two terms, nor does one emerge with conviction at the two levels where the term is used most: level 3 and level 4 in Learning and Development.

Despite the new 'Learning and Development' terminology of the standards, they are underpinned by the same systematic training cycle concept that was used to frame the 1996 T&D Standards. The cycle involves identifying and analysing training needs, planning and designing training, delivering training events, monitoring and evaluating their outcomes and effectiveness, and feeding the results of that evaluation into ongoing identification of needs.

The systematic training framework is familiar across the training community and embodies a concept of L&D with which a large body of practitioners can readily identify. However, that does not mean that the framework is the most appropriate to use. The image that the training cycle presents is one of an orderly sequence of functional tasks that relate primarily to planned training activity. This falls far short of adequately representing the messy world of practice or of focusing adequately on learning, rather than primarily on training. There should be an emphasis on L&D as a *process* also, if any standards are to capture some of the most demanding dimensions of L&D activity.

As we saw in Chapter 3, decision-making and practice in L&D (as in other fields) are not simply a matter of a systematic approach to functional tasks. They require careful attention to the processes used to integrate and pursue those tasks in the specific organisational context.

It is particularly important to appreciate what major constraints the bounded rationality of the parties places on the workings of the strategy process and on the implementation of strategy in the workplace. Take corporate strategy. In the matters of setting goals and priorities for the business and passing final judgement on the success of any L&D strategy, the ultimate say lies with top management, not with HR professionals, no matter how senior. It is upon the exercise of top management's power that the ultimate direction of L&D strategy depends. At board level, the language of functional logic has little chance if it is at odds with the established views and values of the main actors. That baseline never alters, and unless L&D practitioners fully grasp its implications it will be impossible for them to achieve credibility and impact.

The qualification structure

The EmpNTO Standards in L&D are delivered through a revised S/NVQ qualification structure that is at three levels, as outlined above. The standards can be found in:

- the catalogue of Personnel Standards produced by EmpNTO
- the catalogue of Learning and Development Standards produced by EmpNTO.

Each L&D qualification, like all S/NVQs, follows a core-plus-options model by which candidates must achieve all the named mandatory core units plus a specified number of optional units to be selected from a larger pool. The rationale for making certain units mandatory is twofold:

- to ensure that there is parity of value between S/NVQs obtained in different circumstances
- to ensure that the S/NVQs thereby make common demands of every candidate regardless of his or her working role.

The concern to achieve a high degree of consistency in the treatment and formatting of national standards in order to make them applicable and assessable across all sectors of employment is understandable, and the scale of the national standards review has to be appreciated here. The EmpNTO process alone involved the review and revision of around 200 units. However, such a drive for consistency – coupled with an underpinning functional analysis approach – is bound to focus more on what is common than on what is idiosyncratic, and to be preoccupied with that which can be generalised rather than also giving emphasis to that which must be contextualised.

The view of the organisation

The 2001 national L&D Standards are based on a view of the organisation as a largely unitary system. Although the standards stress the need for the collaboration and involvement of stakeholders, there is the implicit assumption that such an approach, if expertly handled, will and should achieve consensus. Such a view underplays the importance of the plurality of interests that exists in any organisation, and the roles played by power, politics and conflict in organisational life. Furthermore, to treat conflict as an avoidable mishap instead of an inevitable feature of organisational life is to ignore the vital part that conflict plays in the generation of new knowledge. Conflict can break old mindsets, spark challenges to various established norms, and thereby promote the innovation that comes from new ways of thinking. None of these implications of a pluralist view of the organisation are given significant attention in the national L&D Standards.

The approach to practice

In EmpNTO's two-year consultative process, the development of new occupational standards was informed by a wide range of stakeholder views and by benchmarking good practice. However, standards should also take worst practice fully into account. They should identify and provide clear statements and guidance on known problem areas in the field. In EmpNTO's 2001 L&D Standards there was a major effort to achieve this in relation to work-based learning. This was because large amounts of government funding were to be tied up in that area, and extensive poor practice there was a major cause for concern (see Chapter 20). Elsewhere in the L&D Standards it is far less clear where the predominating problems lie, or what kinds of skill are of most relevance in tackling them.

The core values

EmpNTO's L&D Standards, like its other standards in the employment sector, are informed by core values of functional competence, flexibility in the face of changing organisational and external challenges and demands, legal compliance, and problem-solving expertise. Reference is made in the Standards to values of professionalism and ethics. However, the degree to which these last two values are given clear and practical expression is open to question.

Checkpoint

- A colleague asks you to explain to him some of the main features of EmpNTO's 2001 L&D Standards. Comment on *three* of those features.

- What are the advantages and disadvantages of focusing strongly on best practice as a guide to competence? (You may wish to look back on some of the content of Chapter 5 when answering this question.)

CIPD Professional Standards in Learning and Development

The primary analytical approach

The 2001 CIPD Professional Standards were not derived from functional analysis. They emerged from a type of role analysis based on identifying and discussing with stakeholders their views and experience. They were also informed by the Institute's own extensive research into good practice in the management and development of people. They place a central emphasise on context, especially in the following respects:

- the context of the national and international environment

- the context of the business and its needs

- the context of the workplace and its practices

- the context of the professional standards and ethics that should influence the values, behaviour and work of practitioners in whatever organisation they are currently located.

The L&D Generalist and Specialist Standards reflect the same emphasis on context.

The conceptual base

The conceptual base of the L&D Standards is of L&D as an organisational process that should be understood and treated in a holistic, integrative way in order to add value for the organisation and for individuals. The emphasis is on L&D as a process rather than a function, and the ten performance indicators covered in the L&D Generalist Standard relate to areas of responsibility, pursued in an interactive and often non-linear fashion, not to discrete tasks (see Appendix 1).

The conceptual base for the Specialist L&D Standards is of the same kind, and also mirrors that for the CIPD standards overall. Those standards place a unique emphasis on the need for vertical integration across human resource (HR) and business activity in the organisation as well as for horizontal integration of all L&D activity.

The fundamental conceptual differences between the CIPD and the national L&D Standards are particularly evident in the broader and deeper knowledge base required by those who choose to be assessed against the CIPD's L&D Standards. The latter, like all the Institute's 2001 standards, are set at master's level (see below), and this is another reason for the demanding knowledge as well as operational base.

The qualification structure

The CIPD's revised Professional Standards are delivered through a new Professional Development Scheme at master's level that conforms with the QCA's M-level descriptors. The M-level practitioner standards for the L&D field can be found in:

- the core People Management and Development (PMD) Standard against which all seeking CIPD qualification through the Professional Qualification Scheme must be assessed (CIPD, 2001)

- the Learning and Development Generalist Standard (Appendix 2), and its associated specialist standards (CIPD 2001).

Standards incorporated into the CIPD Certificate in Training Practice cover those skills required by proficient trainers, whether specialists or line managers. These Support Standards underpin the new level 3 S/NVQs in L&D (CIPD, 2001).

In requiring all those wishing to qualify as professionals to achieve its Core Management Standard (or an equivalent qualification), the Institute is emphasising the need for HR professionals to take a wide-ranging and informed view of the business issues and to take fully into account the context shaping HR policies and practice in an organisation. In making the 2001 People Management and Development Standard likewise 'mandatory', the Institute has provided a spine for the key generalist standards on People Resourcing, Development, Relations and Reward. It believes this to be essential in order to address the issue of ensuring internal consistency and coherence across all HR fields, including L&D.

Applying the same principle of horizontal 'fit' to the specific fields that derive from each main HR process, each set of generalist standards has attached to it an evolving 'string' of specialist standards. The CIPD standards cover in depth not only the generalist L&D field but also four closely related specialist fields (see p158) that have no comparable emphasis, let alone coverage, in the National L&D Standards. CIPD candidates can obtain professional status by moving through an L&D route, or by going across various areas of HR activity in order to emerge with a more generalised grounding in personnel and development work. Whatever the chosen route, however, they must also qualify in the two core areas of the CIPD's standards.

This latter requirement is hotly disputed by that body of trainers already discussed in Chapter 4, whose argument appears to be twofold – that in order to 'put training on the business agenda' it must be recognised that 'training' can, and often should, be a separate function from 'personnel', with the same formal status; and that therefore trainers should not be required to study 'personnel management' in order to gain the CIPD's professional qualification.

As was earlier explained in Chapter 4 (p82), this stance is a fundamental misreading of the principle of 'integration' of L&D and wider HR policy and practice. It is this principle that informs and explains the integrative nature of the CIPD's qualification structure. It has also been confirmed in much recent research, including that on the 'bundling' of HR practices in order to enhance organisational performance (see Chapter 3).

Cross-mapping of the National L&D Occupational Standards and the CIPD's L&D Professional Standards (Generalist and associated Specialist Standards) was achieved in 2002 after lengthy discussions between the EmpNTO and the Institute. The cross-mapping reflects the CIPD's view that the National Occupational Standards (not only for L&D but also for Personnel) do not reach m-level at level 4 and only partly reach it at level 5.

The view of the organisation

The CIPD's L&D Generalist and Specialist Standards place central emphasis on the need for collaboration and for seeking consensus. However, they differ from the National Standards in the greater emphasis that they give to the plurality of stakeholder interests, the importance of identifying and knowing how to respond to issues of power and politics, and the positive role that conflict can play in the operation of the L&D process (especially in relation to knowledge development).

The approach to practice

The CIPD's L&D Standards directly address the some of the most complex and troubled areas of practice that are reported regularly in national surveys and research studies. This is in recognition of the need to ensure that students and practitioners understand their responsibility to query such practices, uncover their fundamental causes, and achieve commitment to tackling them.

The areas of practice that are emphasised in this way in the L&D Standards but have no similar prominence in the EmpNTO's L&D Standards are:

- the vertical and horizontal integration of L&D activity
- the bounded rationality of the strategy process and of strategic implementation in organisations, and the implications for L&D policy and practice
- the design, implementation and delivery of e-based learning, training and assessment systems, and the ability to challenge and build on current learning processes in order to take advantage of innovation offered by new technologies
- the audit and evaluation of L&D as an organisational process
- the evaluation of learning events and processes (as distinct from simply learning programmes) at different organisational levels, including those delivered by external partners
- the facilitation of the knowledge process at individual and collective levels, and the need for learning and development activity to challenge and expand the organisation's knowledge-base
- the need to go beyond legal compliance in ensuring good practice

related to equality of access and opportunity for L&D in the organisation at all levels, to the treatment of diversity, and to promoting ethical practice across the whole L&D field.

The core values

The CIPD's 2001 Professional Standards are underpinned by three core values that are embedded in the L&D Generalist and associated Specialist Standards. All were discussed in Chapter 1. Two relate to *business partnerships* and *adding value*, and are self-explanatory. The third relates to being a *thinking performer*. This involves an essentially proactive and strategically focused perspective, which CIPD-qualified professionals are expected to demonstrate no matter at what organisational level they operate. In the performance of their roles they must show their ability to move beyond 'compliance' to providing a critique of organisational policies and procedures. In the L&D context, such professionals must therefore be able to identify and explain from their perspective where and how organisational policies and practices should be improved, and how the organisation can be developed for the future.

In the CIPD Standards, the HR practitioner is also viewed as a citizen of a wider professional community, who must be able to take a lead in identifying and tackling ethical issues related to HR practice as part of his or her professional responsibility. In its L&D Generalist Standard, one of the ten performance indicators is explicitly focused on professionalism and ethics.

Checkpoint

● Why do the CIPD's L&D Standards focus so strongly on the need to build up and regenerate the organisation's knowledge-base?

● What core values inform the CIPD's 2001 L&D Standards?

Implications for practice in the workplace

This chapter has had as its main concern the implications of evolving L&D roles and standards for practice in the workplace and for the education of human resource professionals. Necessarily, therefore, the greater part of its coverage has focused on the relationship – and the many differences – between the 2001 National Occupational and CIPD L&D Standards that are intended to guide that practice and education.

A different approach would have been to give the chapter a strong sociological dimension, expanding on issues of social interaction, power and politics that are hinted at at the beginning of the chapter and are implicit in much of the examination of L&D role typologies on subsequent pages. However, other writers offer important insights here. Gareth Morgan (1997, p169), for example, illuminates the ways in which roles can be affected by role-holders' attempts to maintain or increase their own status, self-respect and political influence at the expense of those of others. He describes how people can identify with and protect the responsibilities and objectives associated with their specific role, work group, department, or project team, to the point where they 'value achievement of these responsibilities and objectives over and above the achievement of wider organizational goals'. He concludes (Morgan, 1997) that 'the potential complexity of organizational politics is mind-boggling, even before we take account of the personalities and personality clashes that usually bring roles and their conflict to life', and that:

> *Many organizational conflicts often become institutionalized in the attitudes, stereotypes, values, beliefs, rituals and other aspects of organizational culture. ... History can shape the present in subtle ways.*

Such observations return us to the discussion in Chapter 6 regarding power, politics and organisational culture. This kind of sociological perspective could fruitfully be applied to analysing the concerns expressed by that group of trainers mentioned earlier in this chapter, relating to the CIPD's new professional qualification structure. That debate has many echoes of the complex negotiations that led up to the merger of the Institute of Training and Development and the then Institute of Personnel Management in 1994 – a merger that some ex-ITD members still feel did 'the training profession' a disservice, while others disagree and wish to move forward within an integrated personnel and development profession.

Turning once more to the impact of National Standards on workplace practice, the final task in this chapter aims to encourage readers to integrate and update its material while also relating it to a real-life context.

Task 2

First, please study the EmpNTO National Standards in L&D and the CIPD's L&D Generalist and related Specialist Standards (you can obtain them either by accessing the relevant websites or by requesting copies from the two bodies).

Then explain:

- what you see to be the most important similarities and differences between the two sets of standards

- which set of standards seems to you to offer the best guide to the practice of L&D in your organisation – and why.

CONCLUSION

Having read this chapter and completed its checkpoints and tasks, you should now:

- be able to assess the practical value of different models of L&D roles

- have a critical understanding of the basis and scope of L&D occupational and professional standards

- be able to advise on the implications of those standards for L&D values and tasks in the workplace.

To test yourself against these objectives, what five-minute answers would you give to the following questions?

Review questions

What would be the most appropriate role for an L&D professional who is responsible for the L&D function in an organisation operating in an unpredictable environment – and why?

In what important ways do you think the adoption of a functional analysis approach to the production of revised national occupational standards in L&D has influenced those standards?

Your L&D director asks you to outline for her *three* of the major differences between the National Occupational L&D Standards and the CIPD's L&D Standards in order to help her decide which to use for assessing the competence of her L&D staff. Draft your reply.

Useful reference sources

DARLING J., DARLING P. and ELLIOTT J. (1999) *The Changing Role of the Trainer*. London, Institute of Personnel and Development.

GILLEY J. W. and EGGLAND S. A. (1989) *Principles of Human Resource Development*. New York, Addison Wesley. Chapter 5.

HAMLIN B. and DAVIES G. (1996) 'The trainer as change agent: issues for practice', in J. Stewart and J. McGoldrick (eds), *Human Resource Development: Perspectives, strategies and practice*. London, Pitman, pp199–219.

Websites and other sources for National Occupational Standards and qualification structures:

www.empnto.co.uk

www.thelearningnetworkonline.com

(You can also phone the Learning Network on 011 6251 8138, and EmpNTO on 0116 251 7979 or e-mail: info@empnto.co.uk.)

www.dfes.gov.uk (with links to many other sites, including those relating to Scotland, Wales and Northern Ireland)

www.qca.org.uk (this website of the Qualification and Curriculum Authority provides up-to-date information on all approved S/NVQs and explains the whole national qualification framework).

Websites and other sources for CIPD professional standards and qualification structure:

www.cipd.co.uk (This lists all the CIPD's free information sources on professional standards and practice, and enables downloading of the relevant publications, including:

- 2001 Professional Standards at Support, Practitioner (M) and Advanced Practitioner levels

- Infosource documents on different aspects of human resource management and development that are available free on the CIPD's website at www.cipd.co.uk/infosource

- position papers, surveys and reports, which clarify the CIPD's official position on a wide range of current issues. These are available through the Institute's library information service.

The CIPD's website also provides members with access to its Online Training Digest, which provides up-to-date information on all training and development matters and offers a network of contacts for members to tap into.)

• Organising the L&D Function

CHAPTER OBJECTIVES

After reading this chapter you will:

- understand the scope of the L&D manager's role

- understand different organisational approaches to L&D in the business

- be able to draw up an action plan to organise and develop those with L&D responsibilities

- be able to analyse different organisational scenarios in order to decide on appropriate management and action for the L&D function.

Introduction

Conventional definitions of the L&D manager's role relate it to a specialist training/L&D section or department. This, however, is a mistake, since there is a trend now for L&D responsibilities to be primarily located with line managers. Throughout this chapter, the word 'function' therefore refers (unless otherwise specified) to the way in which the whole body of L&D activity is managed in an enterprise.

Towards the end of Chapter 7 we examined the L&D needs of part-time and temporary workers. The L&D (or equivalent) manager in many organisations now has to organise and manage a function expanded to respond to needs of such 'flexible' workers. Any outsourcing of L&D operations also carries special challenges for L&D managers, as does the extension of learning network across the boundary of the organisation to encompass external partners such as suppliers, customers, distributors, purchasers, franchisees and volunteers.

Finally, L&D managers must also be leaders. They must develop and share an appropriate vision of the L&D process in the business with all those who have to carry out major L&D responsibilities in the organisation, not just specialist staff. They must continually demonstrate by their style and actions that they understand and support in meaningful ways the needs of all these personnel.

The purpose of this chapter is not to provide a detailed prescription for managing an L&D function, but to give guidelines under a number of critical headings. Even relatively inexperienced HR generalists may find themselves working in an organisation or unit where they are expected, effectively, to 'manage' L&D for the business. The guidelines presented in this chapter have been produced with their needs especially in mind.

Before reading on, it is helpful to look at the existing state of the leadership and management of L&D in your own organisation. Your answers to the following questionnaire can then provide you with a checklist of points to think about as you go through the rest of the chapter.

Task 1

How is L&D valued and managed in your organisation?
Take each of the following statements and give it a mark of 0 to 3 according to the extent to which you agree or disagree with each:
0 = disagree   1 = unsure/don't know
2 = agree more than I disagree   3 = strongly agree

In this organisation the vision and goals for L&D are set at the very top, and there is strong commitment to L&D across the organisation.   _____

In this organisation L&D is seen to have a vital role to play in supporting and improving people's performance. Managers have been given the main role to play in relation to the training and development of their staff.   _____

In this organisation all L&D plans are business-focused, well understood and effectively implemented in the workplace. _____

In this organisation all L&D plans to improve performance arise out of business goals and targets, and are regularly reviewed to take account of changes.   _____

In this organisation L&D makes a major contribution to the overall performance management process. L&D activities are regularly shown to have added real value to the performance of individuals and teams.   _____

In this organisation L&D operations and resources are well managed. Those with L&D responsibilities are fully competent and have high credibility in the workplace.   _____

In this organisation L&D staff are always looking for better and innovative ways to design and deliver training programmes and other learning experiences.   _____

In this organisation all employees have a personal responsibility for the continuous improvement of their performance, and are expected to play an active part in identifying, and thinking of how best to meet, their own L&D needs.   _____

                                                        TOTAL _____

A **score above 15** indicates that L&D operations to improve per-formance in your organisation are strongly led by the needs of the business, well aligned with business goals, and well managed.

A **total score between 12 and 15** indicates that improvements must be made if L&D is to make a powerful contribution to performance.

Anything below 12 indicates either that the present state of L&D gives rise to serious concern or that there is inadequate information for any assessment to be made about its impact in the workplace. In either case, urgent action is needed.

Source: Harrison R. (1999) *The Training and Development Audit*. Cambridge, Cambridge Strategy Publications. Reproduced (slightly adapted) by kind permission of the publisher.

Organising the L&D function

Let us first look at three models in common use for organising the L&D function: the decentralised model, the line-managed model, and the out-sourced model.

The decentralised function

Decentralisation is a feature of public-sector organisations as well as of those in the private sector. By the early 1990s local government decen-tralisation had already resulted in between 60 and 80 authorities' de-layering management at the expense of the personnel function, pushing personnel off the top management team and 'absorbing' it lower down. Such decentralisation is a typical response to a need to be 'lean', focused, efficient, and fast-responsive

In organisations where there is a push to decentralisation, the L&D specialist function is often vulnerable and is sometimes stripped of its strategic influence. Typical approaches to L&D decentralisation include:

- organising most of the specialist staff to work permanently in or with the units, retaining only a small core staff at headquarters to make and co-ordinate L&D policy and strategy

- passing most of the responsibility for L&D activity to line man-agers who have been trained and developed to carry out that responsibility (as noted below)

- contracting the function out, whether in whole or in part (as noted below).

Often decentralisation is accompanied by a counter-pull to centralise policy, strategy and control functions. For L&D, the key question then becomes 'Who holds the strategic L&D role in that situation?' Basically, this an issue of 'fit' – how best to strike a balance between corporate goals and needs, and localised strategies of divisions and units. If L&D strategy has to adapt to meet local needs, the result may be that every unit will pursue its own L&D policies at the expense of any overall integrative L&D strategy. One way this problem is tackled in some organisations is for top management to make business units more accountable to each other and more guided by a set of strong overall corporate goals, yet allow them to retain sufficient autonomy to enable them to respond to local contingencies.

L&D staff who are permanently seconded to business units or who need to work collaboratively with those units from the base of a central L&D function should have:

- good 'boundary management' skills in order to work effectively with business partners across units and levels in the organisation

- a wide-ranging knowledge of the business to give them credibility in the units, and to enable them to fully understand the units' training and development needs

- skills, motivation and professional commitment to ensure that they neither identify so closely with business units as to 'view the central function as an influence to be kept at bay' (Fowler, 1992) nor identify so closely with the central function as to lose credibility at unit level and become inflexible in their approach.

Checkpoint

- In an organisation with which you are familiar, top management is considering the possibility of decentralising the L&D function:

  - What advantages or dangers do you think might follow such a decision?
  - If the decision is made, what approach to decentralisation would you recommend, and why?

The line-managed function

Where line managers carry the main responsibility for the L&D function in their units, there may still be a small central L&D unit. If there is, its role will usually be one of ensuring overall strategic direction and of monitoring and co-ordinating the L&D process across the organisation.

There are four principles that should always be observed when handing over primary responsibility for the L&D process to line managers.

- Have a clear L&D corporate vision and strategy that is in line with overall HR and business goals and strategy.

- Have strategic L&D objectives that are carried through by

divisional and unit managers into detailed. practical plans for implementation of the policies that serve those objectives.

- Have an organisational structure and company-wide systems and procedures to ensure that all who carry L&D roles and responsibilities have a clear understanding of their tasks.

- Have a system of training, guidance, monitoring, appraisal and rewards related to performance development and recognition of all those who carry L&D roles and responsibilities.

The following case study shows how one company puts these principles into practice. The case is anonymous, but is based on a real-life organisation. It will be concluded later in the chapter.

CASE STUDY: Company X, Part 1: handing over L&D to the line

The company

Company X is UK-owned and operates across the world. It has a long history of investment in the development of its workforce and has a creative capability that has led over the years to a stream of innovative products.

Organisation of L&D in the business

At corporate level HR strategy is owned by the board. A small headquarters HR team is responsible for maintaining strategic direction for human resource management and development across the organisation. HR policy, agreed between the HR director and other board members, is built into corporate business strategy, and sets the strategic goals and direction for all HR activity (including that related to L&D) in the company.

Each strategic operating unit is responsible for its own HR (including L&D) policy and arrangements. These must be in line with group policy but must also respond to the unit's local needs. Specialist L&D staff, usually brought in as short-term consultants from outside, work within business units, helping managers to produce and implement a set of policies at unit level that will support corporate goals but also respond to local needs. Each unit has its own L&D budget, and L&D activity is supported by other HR policies. There is a small corporate L&D budget, held at centre, to cover the cost of certain core training across the company.

Integrating L&D with HR and business policies

Company-wide HR systems provide support for local HR (including L&D) processes and initiatives. There is a world-wide framework for performance management and development, and this is instrumental in ensuring that there is a good fit between corporate and local HR policies.

Leadership responsibility for L&D

At Company X, leadership must be in deed as well as in word. There are high-priority, in-house training programmes for the most senior staff that reinforce the cultural, strategic and organisational developments needed. Strong leadership and commitment are expected from the chief executive of each business unit in the following areas of the company's HR policy:

- a focus on customer-led quality, on understanding and responding to customer needs

- effective development of the company's people at all levels of the organisation — corporate, business unit and operational

- a substantial investment in familiarising every employee with the company's and the unit's strategic objectives, and in ensuring that each individual has performance targets and longer-term development related to those objectives

CASE STUDY: continued

- appropriate and timely training of staff involved in all planned change in the company

- a competency-based approach to training for excellent performance, and equality of access to this training by every employee

- financial rewards for those employees who achieve relevant vocational qualifications.

Line management responsibility for L&D

The effective implementation of L&D strategy across the business depends on line managers' performance in their L&D role. At Company X, managers have the primary responsibility for the learning and development of their staff. A group training manual, issued throughout the worldwide group, clarifies how those responsibilities should be carried out (further details follow in Part 2 of this case study).

Individuals' responsibility for L&D

Company X relies on individual employees taking responsibility for their own development throughout their careers by:

- learning and applying the knowledge, understanding and skills necessary for the performance of their jobs

- working with their managers to identify their learning, training and development needs and opportunities.

Line managers must encourage and support employees in this self-development process. They must focus planned learning on the job, where it can directly feed into the individual's development, the achievement of business targets, and the longer-term growth of the organisation. Each unit and every manager must have documented plans, reviews, reports, records, and performance evaluations as evidence that the wider principles of performance management and development are actively supported at this level.

Here is a task to give you the opportunity to explain how you would put the principles outlined in this section on 'handing over to the line' into practice.

Task 2

You are a L&D consultant asked to advise the top management team of an organisation on how to establish L&D as a line-managed function. Produce a paper for that team which identifies and explains
- the major tasks that you will advise the team to carry out
- what the team's leadership responsibilities will be in this new organisational situation.

The outsourced function

Two considerations immediately occur in relation to L&D outsourcing:

- whether and which L&D activities or processes should be outsourced

- whether the time is coming when the whole function should be outsourced.

Should we outsource anything?

The key issues here are to do with cost-efficiency, added value and control. Often an external party can provide at least some L&D operations at a lower cost than is possible internally. Provided that the L&D manager can be assured that the organisation will retain control over targets and standards, and has good evidence that value will accrue to the organisation by outsourcing – whether on an occasional or permanent basis – then there can be many benefits. Hardingham (1996) notes three:

- 'The combination of internal clout and external credibility is a winning card to play in designing and delivering the most challenging types of training' – that is, training of major importance to the organisation, but which also involves major tensions, difficulties or fundamental behavioural changes.

- External training designers and deliverers can represent a source of best practice for internal L&D practitioners.

- The internal practitioners' own approach and values can be transformed through partnership with external agents. This, in turn, can help to change values within the organisation.

Specific questions for those calculating possible costs and benefits of L&D outsourcing include:

- What if there were no specialist L&D function in this organisation? Where and how does it currently add value?

- If it is essential to the business, does it need to be carried out internally or could it be outsourced – in whole or in part?

- Should it be market-tested (a process involving tendering of certain operations to external agencies)?

CASE STUDY: Forming an L&D agency

At Northumbria Water (NW), the privatised water company located in the north-east of England, training and development operations were re-organised on an agency basis in the late 1980s, around the time of privatisation.

Training specialists were able to choose either to work in the agency or to stay in the parent organisation, where they would be developed for any new roles it might be more appropriate for them to take on. In its early years the agency was assured of a full workload from NW, but thereafter was expected to achieve commercial viability in its own right. In the event the agency, CPCR, rapidly became a successful business and achieved full autonomy, with NW only one of its many clients.

CPCR in recent years has expanded its market and gained a strong national profile. Meanwhile, L&D remains a core function of NW's business, but is mainly in the hands of line managers. There is an umbrella of HR company goals and policy, and supporting administrative and personnel systems. There is also training of managers for their L&D roles, and monitoring of L&D across the company.

- Is it sufficiently large to be made into an agency and floated out of the organisation? This particular solution, if well managed, can benefit all the stakeholders, as the case study on p179 shows.

What about the future?

At the 1996 Conference of the American Society of Training and Development, attention was paid to a number of trends in the USA that could lead in the future to a significantly increased pace of outsourcing training activities. Such trends are prevalent too in the UK, but currently there is no strong pattern of complete L&D outsourcing here. These trends include:

- the learner-centred approaches necessitated by the drive to develop 'learning organisations'

- the tendency to hand over L&D to line managers, especially in downsized and de-layered organisations

- the powerful and efficient electronically based learning routes now available, which often need little support from a specialist function

- the dissatisfaction often expressed by senior executives about the returns being offered to them by their training functions.

The L&D manager should always keep in mind the possibility of future outsourcing. However, what is essential is that when a decision is made to outsource part or all of an organisation's L&D operations, a strategic L&D role is retained in the organisation. Unless that happens, there is a very real possibility that the whole L&D process will lose its alignment with business goals and corporate strategy. Much of the L&D activity that then takes place is unlikely to achieve added value or to support the strategic direction of the business.

Managing specialist L&D staff

Key aspects

Unless any specialist L&D staff are well managed, committed and expert in their jobs, and flexible in skills and outlook, the whole function can decline into the role of 'passive provider' (see Chapter 8). There are seven key aspects to the management and development of such staff:

- employee resource planning
- job analysis
- recruitment and selection
- induction and basic training
- appraisal
- continuous development
- career development.

Employee resource (ER) planning

There must be an ER plan for the function, no matter how small in size it may be. The L&D manager should calculate the kind, number and level of staff currently required, and identify what is likely to be needed through time. An informed assessment of the current staffing situation can then be carried out, new responsibilities can be allocated, and job and career development plans for L&D staff can be agreed.

Job analysis

L&D roles and tasks should be analysed in order to identify their relevance to the business, and the skills, knowledge and attitudes they require. Analysis should also take into account any need for L&D staff to acquire National Occupational Standards or professional standards related to L&D.

Recruitment and selection

Job descriptions and personnel specifications should aid the recruitment and selection of those who are to hold L&D responsibilities. They will also aid the planning and allocation of L&D work. With some appointments it will be more important for the person to make the job than the reverse, and this should be carefully considered when deciding how tight or loose the job description and personnel specification should be. Recruitment, short-listing and selection for L&D positions must be carried out competently. It is particularly important to recruit staff with the appropriate *disposition* as well as *skills*, and this is a crucial factor when considering the suitability of any line managers in an organisation to take on major L&D roles. Ability means nothing if there is not the will to exercise it.

Induction and basic training

Effective induction of all staff new to L&D roles will clarify the different contexts in which they will have to operate, and the work and organisation of the L&D function. Basic training may also be required. Most positions are likely to need a probationary period, during which new staff can be regularly appraised and receive coaching, guidance and other forms of support and development. Mentors for new members of staff can be invaluable counsellors, friends and facilitators of learning during this period. It is as important for the job-holder to be given this period to learn what the job and the organisation is really like, as it is for the organisation to be sure that the selection decision was a wise one. More detail on these processes is given in Chapter 13.

Appraisal

There is a detailed treatment of appraisal in Chapter 13. Here, we can note the need for L&D staff, like others, to receive regular feedback on performance, to have clear work plans, and to agree on their personal development plans. In decentralised organisations where L&D staff work for most of their time in business units, the appraisal discussion is a particularly important source of feedback and forward planning for them.

Retraining, continuous learning and self-development

When the management and orientation of the L&D function are changing, retraining is vital for L&D personnel. A focus on the 'learning organisation', for example, creates a need in many L&D staff to learn how to take on a more facilitative and also more strategically focused role in their organisation. That role will call for new skills and new ways of looking at the world.

Pressures of time and financial resource sometimes mean that self-development is the only way for L&D staff to remain expert. Self-development is also a process that L&D staff should encourage throughout their organisation. They should therefore themselves be role models for that process. Sadly not all are, even if they are CIPD-qualified staff (the Institute has built into its professional qualification the need for continuous updating, and has produced a Continuous Professional Development pack). It is a dangerous omission. Most professionals' livelihoods depend on keeping up to date, on looking ahead, on constantly sharpening their learning skills, and the HR profession is no exception to this. Those who survive and flourish in the L&D field will be those who have a convincing vision of L&D and who can provide clear, practical processes and policies to meet unfolding needs. They will have an up-to-date understanding of trends and best practice. They will also be well-informed about the changing business environment, and about how to operate in it. Without continuous learning and self-development, these kinds of capability cannot be achieved.

Career development

Chapter 17 covers the career development process fully, but at this point we should note the importance of paying attention to the needs of all L&D staff, not just those likely to be moving up or moving on. Career planning for all makes a statement about the many ways in which career development can be achieved within as well as beyond the boundaries of present positions. It will give impetus to 'growing' a learning culture in the L&D function. Since achieving relevant qualifications is a crucial part of the career development of professional L&D staff, their manager must consider the kind of workplace experience and formal education and training that will help them gain those qualifications.

Task 3

As L&D manager in an organisation with which you are familiar, out-line a plan
- to establish or improve the management of staff in the L&D (or equivalent) unit
- to ensure the self-development of those staff .

Include in your plan some estimate of any barriers you expect to encounter in its implementation, and how these should be tackled.

Organising and developing line managers with L&D responsibilities

The principles that apply to the organisation of specialist L&D staff apply equally to line managers who carry the main responsibility for L&D in their units. Attention must be paid to establishing clear roles and tasks, to assessing the competencies and disposition that are needed in L&D work, to adequately guiding and monitoring performance, and to ensuring that such managers have appropriate training and development.

For this section, a case study illustrates the crucial factors that help to prepare and equip line managers for their L&D responsibilities. It is a continuation of the Company X story (see p184).

The principles embedded in this case study are applicable to any organisation in which line managers are required to carry the main responsibility for the L&D process. Once you have read the study, please tackle this check point.

Checkpoint

- Identify and explain *four* ways in which an organisation can 'hand over L&D to the line'.

- What are some of the key L&D responsibilities for line managers in any organisation where L&D is primarily a line management function?

- Explain *three* ways in which line managers can be helped to perform their L&D tasks effectively.

CASE STUDY: Company X, Part 2: developing managers to carry L&D responsibilities

Supporting the line manager's L&D role

At Company X, L&D is a key area of every manager's job. Managers are appraised and rewarded for their performance here, because it is recognised that they will not take their L&D roles seriously unless they perceive that these are treated by the company as a key area of business activity.

Clarifying line managers' L&D responsibilities

Line managers' L&D responsibilities are clarified in the company's Group training manual. They are to do with:

- ensuring that employees are equipped with the necessary knowledge, understanding and skills to do their current jobs competently

- determining L&D needs, both present and future, setting priorities, allocating resources and reviewing results

- ensuring that L&D activity is reinforced as an aspect of the company's performance management process

- providing a work environment in which individuals can take responsibility for their own training and development.

Equipping line managers with L&D skills

The philosophy at Company X about 'handing over L&D to the line' is that managers who are well trained themselves are the ones most likely to take training seriously and guarantee that their own staff are also trained and continuously developed in their work performance. Corporate L&D policy has four objectives to ensure that line managers are well equipped to carry out their L&D roles:

- to raise line managers' awareness of their responsibility for staff training and development

- to enable line managers to own training and development

- to develop line managers' skills in leading and managing people for performance

- to enable line managers to adapt to a continuously changing business environment.

Many procedures, initiatives and formal programmes have been designed to help line managers here, including the following:

- appointing line managers in key functions or departments to overview training and development

- running workshops about current major business topics with line managers and encouraging advocates among them for training and development implications of emerging plans

- selecting influential middle managers and training and developing them to achieve NVQs in training and development at levels 3 and 4 (hundreds of managers have become certified trainers with NVQs at level 3)

- encouraging committed managers to raise the profile of training and development as part of the core responsibilities of line management through the agenda of management meetings

- establishing a mentoring system and training managers as mentors

- creating more flexible and accessible methods for delivering training and learning

- requiring all managers to have personal development plans, and ensuring that their staff have such plans also.

Continuous learning and improvement in the L&D role

Managers are encouraged to achieve NVQs at level 4 related to 'learning and development' as a way of achieving added personal value in the work they do to develop a culture of continuous learning and development in the workplace.

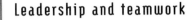

Leadership and teamwork

Those holding L&D responsibilities must be skilled leaders as well as managers, and must be able to build and sustain an effective L&D team. Whoever is responsible for managing the L&D function in an organisation has two crucial issues to consider here:

- *leadership style* – What should be his or her leadership style? Tight or loose, controlling or developmental, task-centred or person-centred?

- *teamwork* – How should L&D specialist and line management staff be organised in relation to their L&D responsibilities and to the L&D manager? As a close-knit team, as a loose collection of individuals, or in some other way?

When specialist L&D staff are working away from the L&D centre in business units, there is a danger that they will become professionally isolated. They may also lose their identity as members of an L&D team. The L&D manager in that situation must act as 'head of profession', retaining functional responsibility for the staff's professional and career development, and holding regular meetings with them (Fowler, 1992).

The L&D manager must also consider his or her own preferred leadership style. It is pointless trying to adopt a style that runs quite counter to your personality, but you should be sensitive to the impact of your style and actions on the group, and the extent to which they 'fit' with group members' expectations, and with their individual, occupational and professional characteristics. The matter of 'fit' is so important as to be a critical factor at selection stage. However, 'fit' must be seen in a wider perspective. Adapting to better meet the preferences and expectations of a group is not productive if the group's behaviour and performance is at odds with what is needed in the organisation, or if currently the members of that group are prejudicing the effectiveness and credibility of L&D in the organisation.

More follows on the operation of teamwork in Chapter 19.

Analysing organisational scenarios

Analysis, diagnosis and action planning

When deciding how best to manage L&D operations for the business, a new L&D manager has a great deal of initial analysis to carry out. He or she must:

- analyse the external environment and internal strategic framework for L&D (examined in Chapters 1 to 3)

- identify where the L&D process can add most value for the organisation (examined in Chapter 4)

- decide how to achieve impact with L&D activity (examined in Chapter 5)

- analyse the internal organisational context and its implications for that activity (examined in Chapter 6)

- identify those inside and outside the organisation with whom the L&D function should create business partnerships (examined in Chapter 6).

It is a depressing fact that many HR students (not just on CIPD programmes, but on other master's level courses) demonstrate poor analytical, diagnostic and action planning skills when confronted with an L&D case study. The regular criticisms made of L&D practice referred to in Chapter 1 suggest that these skills also need considerable improvement in the field.

There are many ways of gaining a practical understanding of an organisational scenario in order to respond to it appropriately. In the Vitex case (below), the L&D manager uses a straightforward but thorough approach that draws on principles established in earlier chapters of this book. The case acts as a conclusion to this chapter by drawing together its major themes and issues. It has another purpose, which explains its length – it provides a way of integrating key material at a halfway point in the book so far. Relevant reference points are indicated in the text.

CASE STUDY: Vitex Ltd

The scenario

Vitex is a well-known and successful engineering firm. Five years ago it had a workforce of 2,000 and was operating in many home and overseas markets. It had a large, centralised training department. Training tasks tended to be predictable and repetitive, and members of the 'team' operated mainly as individuals who specialised in particular types of training activity. Training policy and the annual company training plan were established and monitored by the training manager working in partnership with the personnel director. A central training budget covered all training activity.

Vitex, up against very severe competition in its markets, is now a much leaner and flatter firm, with a workforce of around 800 working on three sites all within five or so miles of each other. It is project-driven, makes maximum use of new tech-

nology and has a reputation for innovation and high-quality products.

The Learning and Development Group

The old training department has been retitled the 'Learning and Development Group' (LDG) and has been reduced to only three positions: manager of the department, one L&D specialist, and an administrator. The L&D specialist, Maria, is the only one left out of the department's original six training officers. She is 35, has a training diploma and a good record as a training administrator and instructor. The administrator, Josef, is 23, with a diploma in management studies. He was transferred from the sales department to training when sales was downsized.

Fernando has just been recruited from outside as the new LDG manager. His brief is to make the whole organisational process of L&D more business-led, and to achieve greater ownership of it by

CASE STUDY: continued

line managers. Top management will support L&D activity that convinces them it can add value for the business. External L&D resources can be used where the expense can be justified by sound business proposals. Each business unit now holds its own L&D budget, and unit managers are responsible for deciding on their units' L&D needs. The new LDG has a small central budget to meet core organisational needs.

The LDG manager's analysis

Fernando spends time immediately after his arrival at Vitex in analysing factors that will help him to decide how best to manage his staff and to lead the L&D function throughout the organisation. To carry out this analysis, he uses an approach that involves exploring five factors:

The business environment – In the challenging environment in which it now operates, Vitex has to be lean, fast-adaptive and innovative if it is to maintain its leading edge. Fernando is concerned to build an LDG of similar kind, and is especially anxious to avoid the poor practice that characterises a number of training functions he has known in the past. He realises that the LDG must have a flexible structure, and that he and his staff must be multi-skilled and adaptable, expert in the use of new technology as it relates to L&D operations. Knowledge development must be a central plank in L&D activity, in order to stimulate and support creativity across the organisation, and new technology will have a particularly important role to play here [Chapter 1].

The internal strategic framework – At Vitex, corporate vision and goals have been clearly defined and are well understood generally in the organisation. Femando is clear that he and his staff must work to four basic principles in seeking strategic alignment for the L&D process [Chapter 3]:

- The L&D process must be coherent.

- L&D strategy should be 'loose-coupled'.

- The L&D process should be flexible.

- L&D practitioners should form external as well as internal business partnerships.

Adding value – The LDG staff must strive constantly to add value through their operations. They must also be clear about the specific outcomes that each L&D process and initiative is intended to achieve, and they must set relevant standards against which to measure their performance as they work with others to achieve those outcomes [Chapters 4 and 5].

Workplace environment and organisational context – Fernando is anxious to create strong links with a new, small HR team at Vitex alongside which the LDG must work in future. He understands the need to operate within an umbrella of supportive HR policies and practice, and to take due account of the employment system at Vitex. He also appreciates that Vitex now has a team-based, project-driven structure and a human investment culture, and that he must build an entrepreneurial LDG, whose culture and structure achieves 'best fit' with the rest of the organisation [Chapter 6].

The L&D function and staffing issues – One of Fernando's main tasks is to help the organisation 'pass L&D over to the line', and he spends a lot of time reflecting on his responsibilities there (following in this the principles outlined in the Company X case study earlier in this chapter).

In parallel, he reflects on some of the issues that he must resolve as he builds up his own specialist team – himself, Maria and Josef. Maria is not used to operating as a member of a close-knit professional team or as a business partner, but in future she will have to do both. She has valuable expertise to offer, but its base needs broadening and she must acquire consultancy skills. Fernando decides to start by giving her the task of visiting each business unit in turn, discovering L&D needs and priorities, assessing what help units need from the LDG, and producing a report and recommendations for Fernando. He is going to have

CASE STUDY: continued

an early meeting with her to brief her, agree on a time-scale and a few milestones, and give her whatever help she needs in order to perform the task capably.

He is also going to spend time soon with Josef, whose contribution, and the image he gives of the department, will be so important. If Josef proves capable and willing, his role and type of work could change through time to incorporate other responsibilities – particularly in the IT area. It is important to explore his potential. Fernando decides to give him two immediate projects: designing a basic L&D records system, working closely as he does so with Maria, feeding in information she gathers in her visits to business units; and collecting information on 'best practice' learning systems and funding sources to pilot new training technology initiatives. The LDG must be innovative in its approaches to learning, and may be well advised to use external consultants to design and pilot certain initiatives. Those consultants will have to be carefully selected, managed and monitored, and drawn into a partnership with internal staff. Josef will be asked to provide some recommendations for Fernando on this aspect too.

Another priority for Fernando is to ensure that both Maria and Josef agree with him their personal development plans for the next 12 months. He intends that their routes for development (like NVQs, or gaining part or full membership of the CIPD) will be integrated into a career plan for each of them.

L&D leadership

Finally, Fernando considers his own style as someone who has overall accountability to top management for the L&D process and its outcomes, and who must also be a role model for a business part-ner and leader of a largely self-managing professional team. He sees the importance of quickly gaining the confidence and commitment of his staff and of line managers, and of ensuring that they share with him a clear vision of the L&D process and of how it should operate across the organisation. In initial team meetings with his two staff, he plans to strike a balance between pursuing a collaborative approach, and demonstrating leadership through providing a clear, appropriate and powerful vision for the LDG, and the processes and systems to support it. Through time, he will work with them and with business partners across the organisation to produce a strategy that can translate this vision into reality.

Diagnosis

At Vitex, Fernando has rightly seen the need to build with his two specialist staff a basically self-managing but also cohesive, flexible, project-driven team. Throughout his start-up work, he focuses on four critical issues [Chapter 4]:

- the need to achieve a positive fit between the vision and strategy of L&D and wider HR and organisational vision and goals

- the need for L&D activity to be focused on areas that will make a critical difference to the organisation's ability to achieve its goals

- the need to organise the LDG in such a way as to enhance its ability to make that difference

- the need for all those with major L&D responsibilities (specialists, line managers and team leaders) to be expert and knowledgeable about how to relate L&D activity to business needs.

CONCLUSION

Having read this chapter and completed its checkpoints and tasks, you should now:

- understand the scope of the L&D manager's role
- understand different organisational approaches to L&D in the business
- be able to draw up an action plan to organise and develop those with L&D responsibilities
- be able to analyse different organisational scenarios in order to decide on appropriate management and action for the L&D function.

To test yourself against these objectives, what five-minute answers would you give to the following questions?

Review questions

Why would a decentralised L&D function be appropriate for a fast-moving, fairly large organisation, operating in a tough business environment?

If, as a line manager, you are told that, regardless of any specialist HR function, you have the basic responsibility for the development of your staff, what are the main activities you would have to carry out – and why?

An organisation advertises for an L&D manager post and refers to the need for applicants with team management skills and 'the ability to lead, train and motivate staff'. Identify and briefly justify some key tasks that such a post is likely to involve.

Useful reference sources

HACKETT P. (1997) 'Getting organised'. In P. Hackett, *Introduction to Training*. London, Institute of Personnel and Development. pp20–33.

WALTON J. (1999) 'Outsourcing: what stays in and what goes out'. In J. Walton, *Strategic Human Resource Development*. Harlow, Financial Times and Prentice Hall. pp279–99.

WALTON J. (1999a) 'The emerging role of managers and staff in strategic human resource development'. In J. Walton, *Strategic Human Resource Development*. Harlow, Financial Times and Prentice Hall, pp181–209.

Managing Finance, Marketing and Records

CHAPTER OBJECTIVES

After reading this chapter you will:

- be able to advise on principles to guide the financial management of an L&D function

- understand the purpose of marketing L&D in an organisation, and how to achieve an effective marketing process

- be able to advise on the needs that an L&D records system must serve.

Introduction

The responsibility of L&D professionals to esure a well-managed L&D function incorporates not only matters covered in Chapter 9 but three further aspects of L&D resource management:

- financial management

- managing marketing

- managing records.

In de-layered organisations in which line managers carry out the majority of L&D operational tasks, there is a danger of resource management's becoming fragmented – a danger that has particular implications, as we shall see, for records systems. However the L&D function is organised, there has to be a balance between any decentralisation of resource management to local level and adequate central monitoring and co-ordination of L&D's resource base. That base must be cost-efficient, well-integrated, and fast-responsive to changing organisational context and needs. New, electronically based technology can greatly improve the efficiency of resource management, but that is not the subject of this chapter. The purpose here is to aid understanding of key principles, not to build financial or technological expertise.

The chapter begins by outlining key features associated with managing of L&D resources, both tangible and intangible. In a report on training activity across the UK in the late 1990s, Darling, Darling and Elliott (1999) identified considerable problems in accounting for training. In the central sections of the chapter, detailed attention is paid to this area – not in any attempt to develop specialist skills in readers, but to increase their understanding of an area that holds many traps for the unwary. The chapter continues with a discussion of the role played by marketing in building and maintaining L&D business partnerships, and concludes with an examination of the characteristics of a well-designed and effectively managed L&D records system.

L&D resource management

There are two main categories of L&D resources: the tangible and the intangible.

The main tangible resources are:

- personnel who are available within and outside the organisation to help with the planning, design, delivery and evaluation of L&D activity and processes

- physical resources: accommodation, equipment, training materials, L&D databases and IT-based information systems – both those available within the organisation and those available externally. This is becoming an increasingly complex area, especially as many organisations now outsource some or all of their L&D operations, and a number develop (often in partnership with other organisations) such facilities as learning resource centres and corporate universities (see, for example, Stewart, 1999a, pp261–279, and Walton, 1999b, pp412–437)

- finance available within the organisation for the L&D of the workforce, whether allocated to a central budget, to unit budgets, or to a mix of both; also funding available from external sources such as Learning and Skills Councils.

The main intangible resources are:

- *time* – the time available to carry out L&D activity, including the management and development of resources, will have a crucial effect on L&D strategy, often putting constraints in the way of what could, ideally, be achieved

- *the past image and reputation of L&D* within the organisation, which can be used to promote future L&D operations

- *employees' competence, learning capability, potential commitment*, which provide the human resource base for achieving current work targets, and for building for the future

- *external learning networks*, which can offer a potential source of knowledge and expertise to improve learning in the organisation

- *natural learning opportunities* available in the normal course of work, which are the most powerful source of L&D in any organisation.

Figure 7 The cycle of L&D resource management

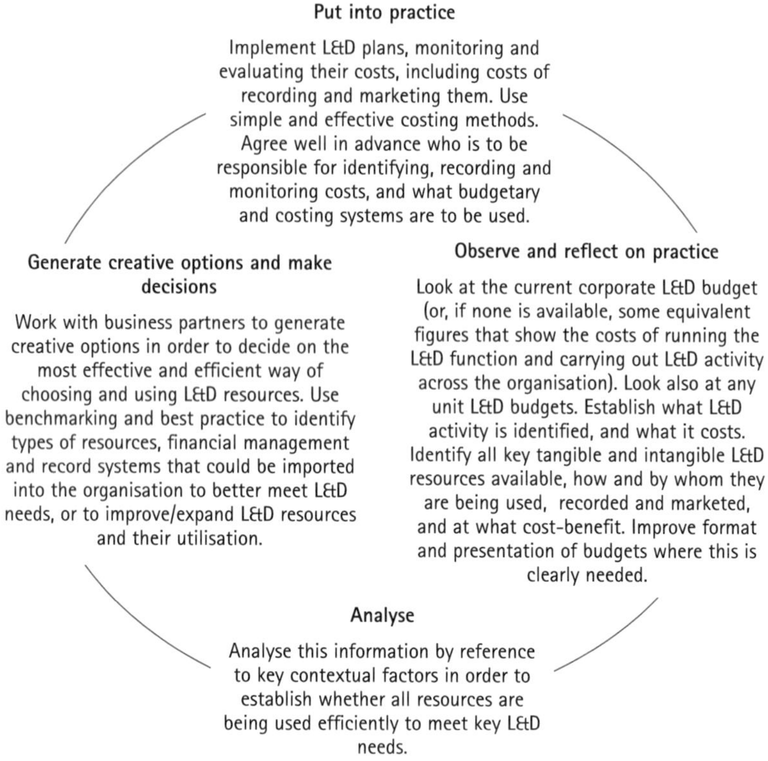

Put into practice

Implement L&D plans, monitoring and evaluating their costs, including costs of recording and marketing them. Use simple and effective costing methods. Agree well in advance who is to be responsible for identifying, recording and monitoring costs, and what budgetary and costing systems are to be used.

Generate creative options and make decisions

Work with business partners to generate creative options in order to decide on the most effective and efficient way of choosing and using L&D resources. Use benchmarking and best practice to identify types of resources, financial management and record systems that could be imported into the organisation to better meet L&D needs, or to improve/expand L&D resources and their utilisation.

Observe and reflect on practice

Look at the current corporate L&D budget (or, if none is available, some equivalent figures that show the costs of running the L&D function and carrying out L&D activity across the organisation). Look also at any unit L&D budgets. Establish what L&D activity is identified, and what it costs. Identify all key tangible and intangible L&D resources available, how and by whom they are being used, recorded and marketed, and at what cost-benefit. Improve format and presentation of budgets where this is clearly needed.

Analyse

Analyse this information by reference to key contextual factors in order to establish whether all resources are being used efficiently to meet key L&D needs.

(Several of these intangible resources are examined further in Chapter 20.)

We can adapt the learning cycle first produced by Kolb, Rubin and McIntyre (1974) to produce a resource-management cycle for the L&D function (see Figure 7). This emphasises the importance of those interlinked skills of observation and reflection, analysis, creativity, decision-making and problem-solving, and evaluation.

Checkpoint

- Identify and briefly explain *three* tangible resources that are used for L&D activity in an organisation.

- A colleague in your own organisation asks you to explain to her what you see to be the most important intangible resources that L&D can use in your organisation. Outline your reply.

Financial structure for the L&D function

Where an organisation has a specialist L&D department or centre, there are options about how to structure that centre financially. The most common choice is between running it as a cost centre and running it as a profit centre.

- In lay terms, a cost centre has its costs paid by the organisation, and its key task is to provide cost-efficient as well as cost-effective L&D activity for the organisation. It is not uncommon to find a cost-centre approach in hierarchically designed organisations and/or those where L&D operations are managed centrally and their range is relatively predictable through time.

- A profit centre, on the other hand, has to generate and sustain its own financial base (although in reality there is usually some form of financial support from the organisation, often at the centre's start-up stage – as was the case with the Northumbria Water agency described in Chapter 9). Profit centres require their personnel to have well-developed entrepreneurial and marketing skills. They must establish a strong profile for the centre and find sufficient internal (and usually also external) clients to ensure the centre's profitability while enabling it to operate in markets that best suit its unique vision and competencies. In de-layered organisations operating in challenging competitive environments, it would be natural to organise L&D operations using the profit centre approach.

It should by now be evident that there is no one best way of financially structuring the L&D function in or for an organisation. A profit centre is not 'better' than a cost centre – both approaches can be strategically focused and cost-efficient, collaborative and value-adding. The choice of one or the other has to do mainly with the overall vision, business philosophy and financial process of the organisation, and with its existing L&D expertise.

Consultancy-oriented texts like those of Moorby (1991) and Bentley (1990) give detailed guidance on how to financially structure the L&D function. They also advise on financial management techniques for those with L&D resource management responsibilities.

Checkpoint

- What are the main differences between an L&D function organised as a cost centre and one organised as a profit centre?

- Your organisation's senior management has decided that from now on the L&D function must be organised as a profit centre, not as a cost centre. Outline your advice on the main implications management ought to consider, following on from this decision.

Managing the budget

The budgetary process

However the L&D function is structured financially, budgeting is always a key process. L&D budgeting can take various forms, but in larger and especially multi-divisional organisations it is common to use a mix of:

- a budget for the specialist L&D department (provided from corporate funds for a cost centre, or self-generated in the case of a profit centre)

- L&D budgets devolved to operational managers. This is a distinct trend, but sometimes leads to uneven development, with 'some units struggling more than others' (Darling *et al*, 1999). The issues here are to do with managers' skills to manage the budgets and their capacity to make the best decisions about the L&D investment. Also 'maintaining the appropriate balance between long- and short-term development needs must inevitably become a problem'.

- a corporate L&D budget to cover the cost of core, organisation-wide activity and of various contingency-based L&D initiatives.

In the public sector, funding is a particularly complex issue because funds come from a variety of sources, including the European Social Fund, and are combined with high expectations of accountability.

Presentation of the budget

Overall, there is considerable evidence to indicate that 'accounting for training is an area where there is a lack of clear thinking'. One of the problems is responding effectively to accounting conventions. The type of format to be used in the presentation of L&D-related financial information depends on four factors:

- why the information is needed – this determines what information is to be collected, and what focus to give the costings

- for whom the information is needed – this determines the way the information is expressed and the specific format to be used. If financial information is needed by the accounts department, it should follow the format and language used in their accounting system. If data on costs and benefits of one L&D option compared with another is needed by line managers to help them decide which to choose, the data must be expressed in language that they will have no difficulty in understanding.

- when the information is needed, and what is available – for if a request comes in today for information needed tomorrow, it may prove impossible to obtain all the data you ideally need. The format must be tailored to match whatever data can be produced in time so that the overall presentation makes its proper impact even if it cannot fully cover the ground.

- the availability of time and expertise – extending the previous point, budgeting is a time-consuming activity involving a variety of skills. It is essential to put the task into perspective, calculating how much time and expertise should be devoted to it in the light of other L&D tasks that also have to be done.

The central purpose of any budget is to identify and cost the main categories of an activity across all divisions of the organisation, with subheadings that clarify which groupings of personnel that activity covers. An L&D budget's format and coverage should make it possible to quickly identify changing trends in L&D activity from one financial period to the next, and to highlight areas of activity that, cost-wise, are problematic. Where priority needs cannot be met within current budgetary limits, a business case must be put forward for obtaining more money, or for meeting needs by the use of a changed pattern of L&D activity.

In a report on workplace training published in April 1999, the (then) Institute of Personnel and Development revealed that many firms failed to take the total costs of training into account in their budgets, thereby seriously underestimating the real amount of training taking place. The major items of expense most frequently omitted from budgets were:

- costs of the continuous development and training of the organisation's training staff

- the cost of outside consultants' advising on training

- costs of on-the-job training whether formal or informal

- the cost of technology and support materials.

A good L&D budget ensures that such crucial omissions cannot occur. It identifies all the main areas of activity and cost, with headings focused on personnel, overhead and administration costs:

Personnel costs
These are the costs associated with personnel who plan, design, deliver, evaluate and support L&D activity. 'Activity' must include personnel costs associated with informal as well as formal L&D, with L&D activity that is externally or internally delivered, and with L&D activity whether in the form of processes (such as mentoring) or of specific events (such as a customer care training course). Personnel costs should also cover provision for any training or development of L&D staff. In the IPD's 'omitted' list, the first two, and personnel-related aspects of the third, items would be included under this heading.

Personnel costs can be broken down under two sub-headings related to:

- those who spend only some of their time on L&D activity (for example, line managers and external consultants). For internal personnel, these 'variable' costs can be calculated by identifying the number of days each individual is likely to be spending in carrying out L&D-related activities, expressed as a proportion of his or her annual salary and employment costs. A more sophisticated calculation would include lost opportunity costs – for example, the estimated cost to the organisation of deploying line managers on L&D work when they could have been doing something else.

- those employed by the organisation to work in a specialist L&D function or centre, including any support staff. Their 'fixed costs' relate to their salaries, National Insurance contributions, and any employee benefit packages they receive.

Overhead costs

These are the costs associated with the provision and maintenance of L&D accommodation such as staff offices, training rooms, and learning resource centres. Like the cost of L&D specialist staff's annual salaries, they are often described as 'fixed costs' because they have to be paid regardless of the L&D activity that takes place during the financial period covered by the budget.

Administration costs

These costs, usually annualised, cover such items as travel and subsistence expenses related to employees' attendance on formal training and educational programmes and to trainers' own activity, and the costs of technology and support materials for L&D operations (including those related to learning resource centres or similar within the organisation or operated on an intra-organisational basis). The fourth item on the IPD's 'omitted' list would therefore be included here.

Administration costs are often described as 'variable' because they depend on the L&D activities that take place or are planned to do so. When making projections for the coming financial period, administration costs can be estimated in one of three ways:

- If there is no annual L&D plan for the organisation, but the pattern of past activity has been quite similar to that of the activity proposed, a reliable enough figure can be reached by taking an average of total administration costs incurred during, say, the last two years' training activities and adding on an amount for inflation.

- If there is an annual L&D plan for the organisation, the L&D manager can look at the administration costs actually incurred by the activities involved in last year's plan and, knowing the kind of activities planned for the forthcoming year, assess how much more or less the related administration costs are likely to be. Again, an inflation cost will have to be built in.

- If there is no specialist L&D department, or any overheads, and there is no relationship between past and planned provision, then administration costs have to be calculated from scratch.

Throughout this section, I have referred to 'fixed' and 'variable' costs. Another way of classifying costs is to divide them into *direct* – to do with the variable costs associated with the provision of L&D activity – and *indirect* – to do with the fixed costs of running an L&D department. Each organisation has its own budgetary conventions, and the terminology to accompany them. (Sometimes, for example, 'indirect' means 'hidden'.)

Task 1

Study the paper presentation of *either* an organisation's annual training budget *or* of its L&D departmental budget, looking carefully at format and content.

How comprehensive is the information that has been produced?

To what extent does it clearly identify all critical costs?

Accounting for L&D operations

In this section I wish to acknowledge the help of Alan Rutter, of the University of Northumbria Business School, in compiling financial data for the tables and case studies.

Whatever the accounting conventions, it is essential to use a sound, reliable approach to identify the costs of running a L&D department or centre (for shorthand purposes, we refer simply to the 'L&D centre' throughout most of this section). Here, we need to find three pieces of information:

- the annual running cost of the L&D centre

- how to recover that cost

- how to cost and compare various L&D options.

Calculating the annual running cost

There are many ways of calculating a centre's running costs. The approach used in this section is basic, since its purpose is to illustrate principles, not to develop any detailed financial expertise. It should, however, enable readers to acquire a reasonably accurate picture of an L&D centre's fixed and variable costs.

First, the (relatively) fixed costs. Table 5 (overleaf) illustrates one way of identifying the basic costs of running a small specialist L&D centre – a training department belonging to a fictional organisation called Mintech. The table uses the three budget headings that we identified in the previous section: Personnel, Overheads and Administration. It does not include capital expenditure (which is often dealt with separately) or the

Table 5   Basic annual running costs of Mintech's training department

	Cost (£)
Personnel (two training officers and a secretary)	
Training staff salaries plus, say, 25 per cent for employment costs	
(pension, NI and other payments)	40,000
Support staff (administrative and clerical) plus 25 per cent	12,000
Overheads	
Annual rent and rates (or some approximate calculation of these)	
related to training accommodation (one training room; two offices);	
to heating, lighting and cleaning; and to other maintenance costs	
of training accommodation	6,000
Administration	
Estimate/actual:	
telephone and postal costs	
printing, photocopying etc costs	
computer costs (eg cost of computer time, software)	4,000
Total basic annual running costs	**62,000**

costs of planned L&D activity (which we will come to shortly). It does, however, include administration costs. To do that, it uses a calculation based on costs incurred over the past two years because the coming year's training activity is not expected to differ significantly from that provided during that past period.

Recovering basic annual running costs

Having calculated the Mintech training department's basic annual running costs, it is possible to calculate how much the department needs to make in order to balance its budget at this basic level.

One way of doing this is to calculate two types of cost: trainer day costs and training day costs. To produce the *trainer day cost*, we can use a simple equation:

$$\frac{\text{Annual running cost of the training department}}{\text{Number of days worked by each trainer}} = \text{the } \textit{trainer day cost}$$

This approach can be used to calculate the trainer day costs of anyone who carries out L&D activities. Table 6 provides our practical example.

Table 6 Cost of the Mintech training department's trainer day

Days actually to be worked by the two training staff (once all holiday entitlement has been taken)	= 250 each = total of 500 days
Annual running cost of the training dept (see Table 5)	£62,000
So the cost of each day the training staff are actually working is	£62,000 ÷ 500
The cost of one trainer day is therefore	£124.00

During their working days, Mintech's two trainers will be occupied, of course, on tasks that run across the whole L&D process – planning, designing, delivering or organising delivery of L&D events and processes, and evaluating them.

Next, we need to look at variable costs associated with the coming year's planned L&D activity. We can expand the Mintech example to demonstrate how this may be done (see Table 7).

Table 7 Calculating Mintech Ltd's training day figures

Trainer day cost at Mintech (see Table 6) = £124

In the coming financial year the department will be involved in two sorts of training activity, the *direct* costs of which are shown below.

Training employees	*Organising external training for employees*
Number of days trainers will spend on direct training (all their other training-related activity has already been identified when calculating the department's annual running cost):	Number of days trainers will spend with chosen external providers, from planning programmes to evaluating their results:
Mike – 30 days John – 20 days	Mike – 220 days John – 230 days
Total: 50 trainer days Trainer day cost: 50 × £124 = £6,200	Total: 450 trainer days Trainer day cost: 450 × £124 = £55,800
Number of days employees will spend attending these courses: 300	Number of days employees will spend attending these courses: 3,000

Amount to be recovered for internal training activities:
  £6,200 to pay for 300 training days
	Amount to be recovered for external training activities:
	  £55,800 to pay for 3,000 training days

Total cost of 1 internal training day thus £21	**Total cost of 1 external training day thus £19**

Note: These figures exclude additional costs such as fees, travel, subsistence, accommodation, course materials, per employee and per trainer, and consultancy charges to the organisation for work associated with external provision. Those costs will have to be added on once they are known, in order to arrive at final costs incurred in the provision of training activity by Mintech's training department in the coming year.

Table 7 shows us that in order to decide what costs must be recovered in running a L&D centre and in carrying out planned L&D activity, we must identify how many internal and external training days the centre's staff plan to organise, and then what the cost of those training days will be. Note that these calculations do *not* identify how many employees will be trained – they simply identify how many days per year of trainers' time will be spent on internal and on external training activity.

By using two basic sets of calculations we can thus gain a reasonably sound grasp of three financial parameters:

- how much it is costing us to run our L&D centre per year (the trainer day cost enables us to work this out)

- how much it is costing us to provide the amount of training activity, internally and externally delivered, that we plan to provide for employees in the coming year (the training day cost is the figure we need to discover here)

- what we need to charge for our internally and externally provided activity in the coming year, if the L&D centre is to recover its running and activity costs on a strict financial basis. (If it is run as a profit centre, and/or has to also have a contingency fund, then clearly the training day charge would have to increase.)

I must emphasise again that in this section basic approaches have been deliberately chosen in order to illustrate some crucial points about costing L&D activity. Such costing is in reality very complicated, and anyone responsible for the financial management of an L&D centre would of course need much more detailed financial expertise than can be gleaned from this chapter. They would also be helped by using appropriate computer software packages.

Checkpoint

- What are *three* areas of cost on which the manager of an L&D centre must be clear, if he or she is to carry out the task of financially managing that centre effectively?

- Explain in simple terms how to calculate the 'trainer day cost' of a centre, and why that information is important.

Costing and comparing L&D options

The generation of options is essential in order to achieve the best balance of activity. It should be done on a collaborative basis. As noted in Chapter 9, options should be carefully assessed in order to identify that mix of L&D activity which, in the coming period, will:

- add value for the business where it counts the most

- have the commitment of business partners
- achieve active participation by learners
- be adequately aligned with organisational context
- provide the financial base needed by the L&D centre.

Managing marketing

The L&D marketing process

In the CIPD's professional standards, the need for competent 'marketing' of training operations and other learning and developmental activity has always been stressed. However, the new 2001 L&D Generalist Standard places more emphasis on the need for collaborative working with stakeholders and less emphasis on 'branding' and other public relations aspects of the marketing process than did the 1996 Employee Development Standards. Marketing in this sense means 'that L&D practitioners will aim all their efforts at satisfying their clients' (Gilley and Eggland, 1989). It is not to do with glossy brochures or expensive selling efforts. It is to do with developing the right kind of products for a particular organisation.

Marketing is an integral element in L&D business partnerships. To quote again from Gilley and Eggland's illuminating chapter (1989), L&D professionals must become 'skilled at understanding, planning and managing exchanges'. A business partner approach to marketing should raise awareness of the centrality of the L&D process to the organisation, and of the need for all key stakeholders to be actively involved in L&D operations from first to last. An L&D marketing plan must therefore clarify:

- how the L&D function fits into the organisation's value chain and serves the organisation's vision and goals

- how L&D specialists will work with internal customers in order to identify their L&D needs, relate them to overall business needs, and agree on how best to respond to them

- how the L&D function will offer the most appropriate and cost-effective L&D products, services and processes for the organisation

- how L&D plans will be collaboratively implemented, monitored and evaluated across the organisation.

Task 2

How is the L&D function marketed in your organisation (or one with which you are familiar)?

Analyse the effectiveness of that marketing, and identify any changes you think should be made.

Managing records

The success of marketing depends to a large extent on having and maintaining a records system that provides an accurate, up-to-date and comprehensive database. However, records are important for far more than marketing purposes alone. The database contained in a good records system aids the identification of training needs, supplies evidence of L&D activity, provides details of when, where, why, for whom and for what purposes that activity has been undertaken, and constitutes a centralised source of up-to-date knowledge, experience, practices and ideas. The following two cases illustrate what can happen when an organisation lacks a unified L&D record system.

CASE STUDY: The Southall train crash

In its report into the 1997 rail crash in Southall in which seven people lost their lives, the Health and Safety Commission extensively criticised the training function. One of the most disturbing deficiencies that the report highlighted was a failure to maintain and pass on drivers' records, so that key performance errors which training should have remedied were not always identified.

Another was a 'surprising' absence of any unified record system (Cooper, 2000). One of the recommendations was that Railtrack and the Association of Train Operating Companies set up a national qualification and accreditation system for drivers. This would enable centrally held records to be made available to the current employer.

Source: Cooper, 2000

CASE STUDY: The new police force database

The National Police Training body (NPT) announced early in 2000, in the wake of the Macpherson report into the Stephen Lawrence murder investigation, that it was setting up a database to ensure that there is a central outlet 'for the extensive reserves of knowledge and information held by the UK's regional police forces' (Pawsey, 2000). The database will enable quick access to information about best practice. More importantly, it will enable those with L&D responsibilities in the police force to provide the most relevant and effective training for all personnel.

The database will focus on equal opportunities and performance management issues, since these are critical areas for the police force. By concentrating attention on them the record system will be able to provide added value and help the police to become more competitive with the private sector. The establishment of the new record system was timed to coincide with the introduction of mandatory audit of police services in April 2000, and was the result of 'a wide-ranging shake-up of training methods' (Pawsey, 2000).

Source: Pawsey, 2000

In both the cases we have just looked at, there was a lack of a unified centralised training records system. Such a system is essential in some form in any organisation, since without it there is the danger that:

- L&D activity across the organisation will not be adequately identified and monitored, leading to the possibility of irrelevant, costly, or needlessly duplicated initiatives

- the organisation will lack adequate evidence to show that all its L&D activity is legally compliant and ethical

- there will be no central store of knowledge to show outcomes of L&D activity initiatives across the organisation, and this will impair the quality of the L&D planning process

- there will be no integration of L&D and personnel records held in different parts of the organisation, thus making consistency difficult to achieve in overall human resource policy-making

- there will be insufficient attention to core organisation-wide L&D needs

- individuals' records of training (and associated data on any problems in their performance during or after training) may get lost when they move from one part of the organisation to another, or from one organisational level to another

- there will be a lack of coherent organisational policies on qualification structures, and on career and succession planning.

We are not talking here about the importance of having a computerised record system, although certainly that is a common way of achieving centralisation. We are talking about the need to strike an effective balance between retaining the benefits of unit-based systems and achieving sufficient central unification of databases to avoid the various changes identified above.

Any L&D record system must achieve eight outcomes:

- *Activities are identified and monitored* – It should be possible at any time to check on how far, in what ways, at what cost, and with what results L&D activity is being carried out in every part of the organisation. The more collaborative the approach to the L&D process is, the easier it will be to obtain and record that information. Records must also be comprehensive, up to date and accurate.

- *L&D needs, learner profiles and the consequent training and development of individuals are recorded* – Personal records must be kept showing the numbers and identities of those who are trained and developed through time, the reasons for that L&D, and the learning outcomes. They must also facilitate monitoring to ensure non-discrimination.

- *Knowledge is accessible for dissemination across the organisation* – Knowledge, especially in the form of good practice, ideas and experiences arising from various learning processes, should be stored on a centralised database, where it is centrally accessible to stimulate continuous improvement, creativity and innovation.

- *There is legal compliance* – It must be possible at any time to identify how far, and in what ways, the law relating to employment is being observed. As we saw in Chapter 7, failure to ensure that all employees are aware of their rights and responsibilities in this respect can mean that they and the employer are liable for breaches of the relevant legislation. As we also saw in Chapter 7, there must be up-to-date information to show exactly what steps have been taken to prevent discrimination in the workplace and to take any affirmative action.

- *The records system itself adheres to the law* – The records system must meet legal requirements in the way it is designed and operated, and in its accessibility. Fundamental legislation is contained in the Data Protection Act 1998 and also in the less widely known European Union Data Protection Directive 1995, Stage 2 of which came into effect in October 2001 (Aikin, 2001). Basically, employees have the right to access all their files, whether in manual or computerised systems. Employers must also have instructions listing the purposes for which information is collected, clarifying access and security arrangements and guaranteeing that no additional use will be made of the information without first obtaining the consent of the person in overall charge of employee records.

- *The records system is cost-beneficial* – The records system should be as simple as possible, using sophisticated methods and processes only when the ensuing benefits can be shown fully to justify the human, physical and financial resources and costs. Particular attention must be paid to how detailed particular records should be, for how long records should be kept, who should keep records, how often records should be updated, and what use to make of electronically based information systems and tools.

- *L&D records are linked to, and consistent with, other HR records* – Training and development records should have a positive relationship with records maintained in any other areas of human resource management in the organisation (a highly relevant factor in the Southall case reported above). Whenever possible they should therefore be drawn up using a format and technology that complement rather than confuse other HR record-keeping and data analysis.

- *Confidentiality is observed* – Particular attention must be paid to confidentiality and accordingly to what information goes on record, to who should have access to various records, and to how access can be protected.

Taking a holistic view

To conclude, here is a case revolving around staff requests for training. It illustrates how a sound understanding of L&D's resource base can enhance the quality of L&D decision-making overall. (This case expands on the kind of scenario outlined in the checkpoint in Chapter 4, under *Assessing the future investment.*)

CASE STUDY: Mintech Ltd: identifying and assessing L&D options

Three supervisors from different departments have applied to Mintech's training department to go on a day-release supervisory studies course at the local college. It lasts for a year, involves absence of half a day plus an evening (same day) over three terms, and ends with an examination leading to a national supervisory skills qualification.

Mike, one of the two training officers working in Mintech's training department, first identifies the costs involved in sending the three supervisors away on the day-release course. He must charge £19 per day for every member of the organisation who attends an external training course, and £21 per day for every member who attends an internal training course (see Table 7 p199). He must now identify additional trainee-related costs.

Option A

Sending supervisors on external training course leading to national supervisory qualification:

	Cost (£)
Fees (£1,000 per person per year): £1,000 × 3	3,000
Travel and subsistence (£5 per person per day at college): £5 × 3 × 30 days	450
Materials (books and other items used by trainees) on the course: £60 × 3	180
Administrative overhead cost: external training day cost × number of days × number of trainees £19 (already calculated) × 30 × 3	1,710
Total cost of sending three people on course	£5,340

Mike could have made out a more complicated list that would have included indirect as well as direct costs. In practice, though, such costs are rarely taken into account unless direct costs are occasioned by the supervisors' absence (for example,

---

CASE STUDY: continued

overtime payments because their work has to be done by others). Of course, if Mike had needed to make a particularly powerful case against sending people away on an external course, he would have done well to draw attention to these 'hidden' costs!

The next step is for Mike to think carefully about the external course. Sending three supervisors on it will be an expensive undertaking, and it may not be possible to offer the same opportunity this year to any further applicants. So what are the other options? He and his colleagues identify some. They then agree that three one-week courses run internally by the training department would cover the necessary material well, and would be a real benefit to at least 12, instead of only three, supervisors. The department has a good reputation for running tailor-made programmes, and so it is unlikely that this would be viewed as inferior by the supervisors. It would not lead to National Vocational Qualifications (NVQs), because the company is not yet tied into the NVQ system but, should that become an important consideration in the future, then this particular option can be reconsidered then. What will this Option B cost?

Option B

Internal supervisory training course run by training staff: there would be three one-week courses, each led by one tutor and involving a total membership of 12 supervisors, four attending each course.

	Cost (£)
Fees	N/A
Subsistence (mid-morning and mid-afternoon refreshments for four participants and one trainer @ £1.50 per head per day): £7.50 × 5 days × 3 weeks	112.50
Materials (£50 per trainee plus 3 trainers' copies)	750.00
Administrative overhead cost: internal training day × number of days per trainee × number of trainees £21 (previously calculated) × 5 × 12	1,260.00
Total cost of training 12 supervisors internally	£2,122.50

Mike noted the much greater cost of Option A, but realised that in Option B he had not included the cost of identifying the training needs of the supervisors, designing the one-week programmes for them, and producing the necessary training materials. This was because he was confident that they could be substantially offset by repeat runs of the programmes for further groups of supervisors. However, adding on those costs did substantially increase the initial bottom line for Option B.

Mike decided to seek discussions with the supervisors' managers and with the personnel director in order to ensure that a sound choice was made between Option A and Option B.

The case study has deliberately been ended at this point. Each option has much in its favour, and the final decision has to be the one that best meets our original criteria, and will:

- add value for the business where it counts the most
- have the commitment of business partners
- achieve active participation by learners
- be adequately aligned with organisational context
- provide the financial base needed by the L&D centre.

CONCLUSION

Having read this chapter and completed its checkpoints and tasks, you should now:

- be able to advise on principles to guide the financial management of an L&D function

- understand the purpose of marketing L&D in an organisation, and how to achieve an effective marketing process

- be able to advise on the needs that an L&D records system must serve.

To test yourself against these objectives, what five-minute answers would you give to the following questions?

Review questions

Accounting for training has been heavily criticised. As a training manager, identify and justify the steps you would take to ensure good accounting.

Justify major items that you would include in an organisation's annual training budget.

You are drafting a plan to market the L&D function in your organisation. What *main* points should your plan cover, and why?

Useful reference sources

GILLEY J. W. *and* EGGLAND S. A. (1989) 'Marketing and positioning the L&D program within the organization'. In J. W. Gilley and S. A. Eggland, *Principles of Human Resource Development*. Wokingham, Addison Wesley and University Associates Inc. pp243–65.

STEWART J. (1999a) 'Resourcing the ED function'. In J. Stewart, *Employee Development Practice*. London, Financial Times and Pitman, pp261–79.

WALTON J (1999b) 'Human resource development and the corporate university'. In J. Walton, *Strategic Human Resource Development*. Harlow, Financial Times and Prentice Hall, pp412–37.

11 • Harnessing New Technology

CHAPTER

CHAPTER OBJECTIVES

After reading this chapter you will:

- understand what is meant by 'e-learning' and its importance in the knowledge economy

- be able to explain why harnessing new technology to the learning and knowledge processes is increasingly essential for organisations

- understand the tasks and challenges that it involves for L&D practitioners

- know how to find sources of information on new technology applied to L&D activity.

Introduction

E-learning essentially means learning via electronically based technology. It offers exciting opportunities for those engaged in L&D activity, yet its potential in that respect is far from being achieved. Ralph Houston, joint UK managing director of training consultancy Fielden-Cegos, once said (quoted by Rana, 1999c):

> *We have made a real mess of technology-based training by allowing the technologist to define and develop the methodology for training, while trainers appear to have run away from it.* 💬

In 1999, research by the International Data Corporation predicted that new technology-based training would increase by more than 50 per cent by 2002 and would become the largest delivery vehicle for corporate training (Rana, 1999d). Yet in 2001 the CIPD's third annual training survey revealed a disappointing level of impact. The survey covered 502 respondents who were interviewed by telephone; they were either training managers/directors or others who could speak on their organisation's behalf at the establishment level. The data gathered is therefore of considerable interest to those seeking insights into what is happening in the L&D field.

Overall, the survey presented a picture of UK establishments making extensive use of structured workplace learning but of few using new technology as a primary means of delivering that learning (CIPD,

Table 8 Use of different training methods, by percentage of respondents

Training method	Regularly	Sometimes	Never
On-the-job	87.3	11.4	1.4
Classroom	84.3	14.7	1.0
Intranets	23.7	34.5	41.8
Internet	16.5	38.0	45.4

Source: CIPD Survey Report, 2001 (summarised from Table 5)

2001a). Certainly since the first survey in 1999 there has been a rapid increase in the use of computer-based training, but it seems from the 2001 responses that although the use is spreading rapidly, in most establishments that use is not intensive (see Table 8).

The survey team tentatively concluded that new technology did not have much innate appeal for organisations. It tended rather to accompany the introduction of high-performance working practices such as self-managed work groups and Total Quality Management (CIPD, 2001a). It seemed to be used fairly extensively only in general tasks such as induction (38 per cent of respondents), health and safety (47 per cent), and communications training (50 per cent).

The word 'technology' is itself an ambiguous one, and in the first section of this chapter we look at how to interpret it. That section also contains an outline of the possibilities offered by e-learning for businesses and for individuals. In the second section, e-learning is placed in the context of the knowledge economy, in order to clarify how that learning has the potential to transform employees into 'knowledge workers'. The third section explores some reasons for the relatively slow rate of take-up by L&D practitioners, and some factors critical to the success of e-learning. The chapter concludes with a brief survey of information sources related to e-learning technology.

E-based learning technology

Consider the following scenarios:

Scenario 1: harnessing new technology to education
On 7 March 2000 the UK Prime Minister announced in a speech that he was committing the country to a goal of universal access to the Internet by 2005. By 2002 all schools in Britain were to be linked to the Internet (Michael Wills, Learning and Technology Minister, 2000).

Meanwhile, David Blunkett, Minister for Education and Employment, was heralding the arrival of Universitas 21, sponsored by the Department for Education and Employment, and linking Massachusetts Institute of

Technology, Cambridge University, and the Institute of Enterprise. What would the link do? It would enable the institutions involved to (Blunkett, 2000a):

> *share resourcing, facilitate staff and student mobility and use new technology to spread excellence... [By such means, the government intends to] harness globalisation as a force for progressive change. ... In a knowledge economy, expansion in high-quality higher education is critical to social justice.*

Scenario 2: learndirect – *e-learning for you and me*

The University for Industry (UfI), through its operating arm *learndirect*, offers online training packages, accessible to all, backed up by paper-based induction courses to help individuals to learn how to use the packages, and supported by online and face-to-face mentoring and group discussions over the Internet. The aim is that anyone, anywhere, using a computer, will be able to identify courses to meet their interests. They can enrol, pay for courses, receive learning materials and support – all electronically. Delivery methods will include interactive digital TV, video, CD-ROM and Internet. You don't own a computer? Then you can go to a local *learndirect* centre and use one of theirs ...

Scenario 3: *company training goes online*

In August 1999 ICL launched *KnowledgePool* in order to maintain its lead in the IT training sector. By amalgamating its six European training businesses, it established a new company that provides training services 'ranging from multi-site programmes tailored for global companies to distance-learning for individuals via the Internet, intranet or CD-ROM' (Rana, 1999d). By 2001 IBM expected to deliver half of its internal training online, not to completely replace traditional learning but to integrate it with new learning technology.

Scenario 4: *in the near future* ...

You are watching a factual programme on the BBC. You switch to interactive online packages that provide you with more information about the subject matter. You want to learn even more. You link into tailor-made online short courses, their content built around research carried out to develop the programme that originally sparked off your interest. The course gains you accreditation from a British university (Ewington, 2000).

Checkpoint

- What is meant by 'e-learning'?

- You are asked by a colleague who is ignorant of new technology to outline for him some ways in which e-learning can operate. Provide a convincing response.

'Technology' and 'e-learning'

The scenarios just outlined show how new technology can be applied to learning processes in novel ways. Before going further, it is worth thinking about that word 'technology'. It has many meanings, and indeed for more than half a century it has been the subject of learned if somewhat inconclusive debate by writers in the management and organisational behaviour fields. What should be stressed here is that 'technology' is a generalised term. It does not of itself imply electronically based information systems. It simply refers to:

> the particular way in which, in a workplace, technical systems, machinery and processes are designed to interact with human skill and knowledge in order to convert inputs into outputs.

In the old 'Fordist' workplace that dominated throughout most of the 20th century, the basic technology was that of the mass-production line. Scientifically designed machines required little more of workers than a repetitive pattern of physical actions. Training was the critical learning vehicle. It enabled the individual to acquire the needed skills and to reach the required standards of performance.

That 'old' technology became more sophisticated with scientific and engineering advances. It was revolutionised with the advent of the computer. As more and more routine tasks became fully automated, there was a greater dependence at all organisational levels on human knowledge and judgement in order to solve the tasks that were left – the non-routine (Roberts and Grabowski, 1999). As environments became more turbulent, bringing with them new, unfamiliar and unpredictable challenges, that dependency increased. Now, in the so-called 'post-Fordist' workplace, new information technology is bringing together computer-based hardware, human skills and knowledge in unique ways that are capable of changing yesterday's production line workers into today's knowledge workers.

I will shortly be exploring the relationship between the emerging 'knowledge economy' and knowledge workers, and the part played by e-learning in linking the two. Here, the task is to clarify the relationship between 'technology' and e-learning. This is not easy, because 'the vocabulary of training and learning is confused. It is in a state of transition and no agreed terminology has yet emerged' (CIPD, 2001a: 9):

> E-learning is emerging as the term referring to ... training or learning delivered or received mainly through the Internet, intranets, extranets or the Web. [Thus] for example, the use of CD-ROMs should not properly be described as 'e-learning'.

A wider term, and one that covers both e-based learning and such computerised learning tools as CD-ROMs, is 'computer-based training'.

Throughout this chapter I use those two terms in the way they are defined here.

Checkpoint

- Your training manager quickly corrects you when, in a reference to training delivered by new technology, you use the term 'technology based training'. She says: 'That doesn't mean anything!' Why is she right?

- Distinguish the term 'e-learning' from 'computer-based training'.

E-learning: benefits for the business and for the learners

E-learning offers many benefits to business and to individual learners. The most common claims made include:

- *There will be an increasing alignment of e-learning and e-commerce.* 'Information collected on the world-wide Web about product knowledge, for example, can be accessed in the same way for someone else to learn from' (Masie, 1999). Without the intervention of any third party, the learner can access the Web and quickly build up a comprehensive store of product information, some of which includes self-teaching aids. (For instance, you can learn how to use Norton Ghost, a computer hard-drive back-up system, by going into the Web and accessing an interactive tutorial session).

- *Effective e-learning is fast learning.* 'Organisations train online for competitive advantage: to deliver knowledge to all of their employees between 1 and 10 per cent faster or better – or both' (Masie, 1999).

- *E-learning can be highly efficient.* It can deliver exactly what the learner needs, at the time when he or she needs it, and in the form that he or she prefers.

- *E-based technology connects to the knowledge process.* It enables not only rapid learning but also the rapid development and sharing of new knowledge. Such knowledge can stimulate the creativity and innovation needed to produce new strategic assets for the organisation. Learning aids knowledge management.

- *Online training networks can help the organisation to build intellectual capital.* They can enable the efficient gathering of information about learners in order to produce skills profiles of individuals and jobs. The Internet and intranets (in-company websites) can enable the tracking of learners and the use they make of training courses, capturing information about their prior knowledge and how they interact with online material. They can combine learning material with competency profiles and personal learning plans, producing information that can be recorded for analysis and accreditation (Hills, 2000).

- *Computer-based assessment (CBA) allows instant scoring and feedback of results to learners* (Hills, 2000). Many are sceptical about the use of CBA, especially where the purpose is not to test learners on accuracy related to facts, or on choice of a 'right' response, but to assess their ability to produce their own solutions to problems where there are no black-and-white answers. Nonetheless, used in an appropriate context – for example, to test ongoing (formative) rather than final (summative) learning – there is no doubt about the aid that CBA can offer to learners and to those administering the learning process.

Task 1

Produce a discussion paper for your L&D/personnel manager containing well-justified recommendations to stimulate enthusiasm for e-learning among employees in a part of your organisation with which you are particularly familiar. The recommendations should be specific and feasible. They should also suggest responsibilities for implementation.

Cost-cutting and changing attitudes and expectations in students, together with rapid technological advance, have all had an explosive effect on most educational institutions. The development of multimedia products is becoming widespread, and the implications of the global Internet network in particular cannot sensibly be ignored. The World-Wide Web is 'not just a tool to provide access to existing data in more flexible, user-friendly, timely ways' but is changing the way new information is generated by offering users 'a new medium through which to exchange ideas, formulate proposals and generate solutions in ways not previously possible' (Lymer, 1996).

Overleaf is a case study showing how the benefits of e-learning were harnessed across an educational institution in the 1990s.

A case such as this demonstrates how new technology applied to learning can flourish, given the right conditions. It demonstrates the added value to be achieved when a creative approach to learning is allied to the vision and strategy of the organisation – that which benefits the learners can also become a unique source of competitive capability for the business.

CASE STUDY: Thames Valley University: the 'whole organisation' approach to learning technology

Thames Valley University (TVU), chosen in 1997 by the (then) Institute of Personnel and Development as a key provider of learning materials for its professional qualification flexible learning scheme, was already at that time in the forefront of innovation both in educational and in learning technology. It had not just expanded its open learning operations, using the term to mean 'any scheme of education or training that seeks systematically to remove barriers to learning whether [of] time, place or space': it had transformed itself into a 'flexible learning environment' that enabled its 27,000 students – 65 per cent of whom were part-time and therefore not eligible for state subsidies – to obtain an affordable, fully accessible and self-paced education (Nicholls, 1997).

'Transformation' is the appropriate term. The whole university had been radically reorganised, with 40 per cent of its campuses turned into technologically sophisticated learning resource centres. At the Ealing centre, for example, each of its 12 floors housed books, videos and CD-ROMs relating to a different subject group, and each contained study and seminar areas, and teaching and learning support facilities, including a shop where computers could be purchased or hired.

The most significant change at TVU was its 'strategic approach to printed resources', comprising free course folders and books for all students, made possible by economies of scale and by a reduction of course modules from eight to six. 'Everything at TVU is a heavily managed process designed to give the student as much support as possible while encouraging self-directed learning' (Nicholls, 1997a).

Source: Nicholls, 1997, 1997a

The knowledge economy

Throughout the previous section, the relationship between e-learning and the development of knowledge was referred to in various ways. This introduces another claim: that e-learning offers people a unique route by which to operate effectively in the emerging knowledge economy. But what exactly does this mean?

The knowledge economy is a way of describing a world in which 'knowledge' has become the key to wealth. In this world, the application of knowledge adds more value than the traditional factors of capital, raw materials and labour, and the 'knowledge worker' has unique status. Peter Drucker (1993) claimed to originate that term, describing (in Scarbrough, Swan and Preston, 1999: 6) knowledge workers as:

> *individuals who have high levels of education and specialist skills combined with the ability to apply these skills to identify and solve problems.*

We have already seen earlier in the chapter that with the advent of highly automated workplaces and more turbulent organisational environments, there is pressure on all employees to become, in a sense, knowledge workers. Their unique value for the organisation lies in their ability to rapidly acquire and share new knowledge, and apply it to the identification and solution of new challenges, opportunities and problems.

To the extent that e-based learning becomes an integral part of L&D activity in organisations, learning and knowledge processes will increasingly merge. It is not simply a matter of the opportunities that e-learning offers for people to learn for themselves. It is that this self-directed learning is taking place in a context where more and more people are performing tasks that are facilitated by electronic means. Their workplaces, dominated by computer-based information technology, can provide an environment for thinking and problem-solving. This combination of circumstances means that the employee's role can become transformed, so that it is (Schuck, 1996: 199):

> not only to push buttons to control processes, but also to use the information generated by the technology to 'push the business' – to redefine process variables, to improve quality, and to reduce costs.

In such an environment, the intelligence of employees can expand until it exceeds the intelligence of the software with which they interact. Employees can thus become 'smart' (Schuck, 1996) – smarter, finally, than the machine that they have for so long served. They become knowledge workers in the sense of continually using knowledge that they have developed to improve operating procedures, products, services and processes, and to innovate. We discussed this theme first in generalised terms in Chapter 1. Here, we begin to see its real significance. Later in the book, in Chapter 20, we take the whole discussion about knowledge further by looking at ways of making organisations 'knowledge-productive' (Kessels, 1996).

Traditional training methods teach people what to think rather than how to think. They stimulate the learning process, but only with the purpose of ensuring that learners acquire predetermined skills, knowledge, even attitudes. E-learning, like computer-based training, can do that. But it can do much more. In opening up access to the information that the learners want, when and in the form that they want it, it can not only help them to quickly acquire targeted learning outcomes – it can also offer to them a voyage of discovery that can transform the way they see the world. It can enable them to generate knowledge and then use it in ways that they could not have predicted when they started out. E-learning can speed up the acquisition of skills; but it can also fuel the development of knowledge. This is how learning and knowledge become fused in an integrated process.

Checkpoint

● What is meant by a 'knowledge economy', and why do you think it is emerging?

● It has been claimed that e-learning can transform employees from button-pushers to smart workers. What is the basis for this claim?

The organisational context

In previous chapters (see, for example, Chapter 6) we have seen the impact of organisational context on L&D activity. So far in this section the emphasis has been on e-learning's transformational potential. Yet we must be cautious here. As we saw in the introduction to this chapter, there is a long way to go in most organisations before any such transformation occurs. As yet, e-learning seems to be used as a training tool rather than as a knowledge process. For e-learning to turn employees from mere learners into 'smart people' (Schuck, 1996), the context must be right. There must be the leadership and management, the workplace environment and culture that is conducive to the installation of e-learning systems. There must be the capital expenditure, the human expertise and the operational infrastructure to support it.

However, if a substantial investment is to be made in e-learning, management at all levels must understand the likely outcomes for learners, as well as for the business. If the workplace is of the traditional kind, in which the given role of some is to think, to make decisions and to pass on instructions, and the role of others is to perform the tasks that those instructions involve, then the true potential of e-learning cannot be realised. It is pointless for individuals to participate in a learning process through which they develop operational competence and 'the intellective skill required for original, independent problem-solving' (Schuck, 1996: 205), only to return to a workplace where that skill cannot be used, and where their capability as knowledge workers is not recognised. In such a situation, expectations will be disappointed and motivation will decline. In such a workplace, new technology can be harnessed to training, but its use will be restricted to speeding up traditional learning and instructional methods, making them more accurate, quicker and more accessible. Its most powerful value-adding impact will not be achieved.

Harnessing new technology: the right time

Concerns of L&D practitioners

There are regular warnings to employers and trainers of the dangers of failing to jump aboard the computer-based learning bandwagon. Rana

(1999d) referred to a number of reports, developments and predictions all pointing to the same critical issue: 'Employers that fail to ensure that their training providers are able to cope with rapid changes in delivery will find their competitiveness reduced.'

In one way or another – whether to help produce new knowledge workers or to continue to perform their more familiar role of developing the competence of individuals and teams – L&D practitioners are under pressure to integrate online learning into their curriculum. They need 'to understand the strengths and weaknesses of new technologies and be able to identify when and where they can offer cost-effective solutions' (Cannell, 1999). Yet those who express a need for caution before making what can be a costly investment are right to do so. Legitimate concerns include the following:

- *Online training must be focused on the learner, or it risks failure.* Online packages and support systems will not work unless they are carefully tailored to the organisation's specific needs, to the individuals' learning styles, capabilities and expectations, and to the workplace environment. Multimedia education also works 'only if it mimics the human learning process. It must induce failure and allow explanation' (Schank, 1999). So a learning package or process, delivered electronically, must be capable of 'allowing many choices and stimulating realistic responses to all of these' (Schank, 1999).

- *E-learning material must be of high quality.* One of the concerns about the University for Industry's claims about e-based learning (see Chapter 2) is whether there will be the expertise to ensure that e-learning materials are well-designed, given the dearth of high-level design skills currently. (See texts like Christian-Carter, 2001, Cannell, 1998 and Tucker, 1997 for guidance.)

- *There must be an effective infrastructure to support it.* This means not only technical but human, so that there is accessible face-to-face guidance and support for learners at critical points of the e-learning process.

- *Motivation is crucial.* There must also be a way 'of motivating and rewarding the learner through human contact'. Unless it is well planned, e-learning can be an isolating process (Hills, 2000).

Criteria for choice

New technology is not always the best solution. It is expensive in terms of capital investment, specialist expertise needed, and the costs to the organisation if its introduction does not bring the benefits expected. There are certain situations in which it is unlikely to be as effective as more traditional methods. These include:

- when other, cheaper and equally effective modes are available
- when learners dislike computer-based training

- where lead-time is short and software has to be custom-made yet may only be used infrequently by learners

- where senior decision-makers and line managers are not committed to its use

- where trainers fear its introduction and do not have the skills that it requires

- where support of IT professionals is not available and there is no appropriate infrastructure for the technology (Cannell, 1998)

- where the cost of installing and training for technology-based training and learning is unlikely to be offset by the advantages that they will produce.

Achieving cost-benefit

When is it most likely that investment in technology-based learning will bring returns over and above its costs for an organisation? Cannell (1998) suggests the following:

- situations in which the learning content will not change much through time

- courses which are significantly knowledge-based

- where the learners are geographically scattered – ie over many sites, up and down the country or across the world

- unusual, expensive or dangerous situations where simulation is vital in order to learn in a safe environment how to deal with the problems involved. For example, the Health and Safety Commission's report on the Southall train crash of 1997 made clear the need for simulated training to improve drivers' reactions and performance in confused signalling conditions and when confronting potential crash situations. The Cullen Report on the Paddington Rail Crash identified exactly the same need (Marston, 2001).

Checkpoint

- You are a trainer in an organisation where little use has so far been made of new technology in training courses or other planned learning initiatives. Management is urging you to jump onto the technological bandwagon. You have done quite a lot of thinking and research on the applications of new technology to learning, but you still have some concerns. Identify and justify *three* of these.

The need for integration

A few years ago the (then) IPD produced a guide for those interested in new technology applied to learning (Cannell, 1998). In it, the point is made that trainers 'need to be able to work with IT specialists to develop solutions that make the best use of available technology and which can be married to more traditional learning approaches' (Cannell, 1998). It is that integrative approach that is so important in any technology-based approach to learning – not the avoidance of the exclusive use of either the traditional or the IT-based modes and methods, but rather the bringing together of the two in imaginative, stimulating and cost-effective ways. The real issue for trainers and developers is not (as they often think it is) how far new technology is more, or less, effective than traditional approaches. It is integration (Carnall, 1999: 54):

> *While technology can create or remove barriers to learning, it cannot by itself create the motivation to learn. So there is a need to plan learning and development in an integrated way.*

Critical success factors

E-learning depends for its success on factors that distinguish any effective learning situation (Schank, 1999):

- having a clear goal
- taking learners' needs fully into account, especially by helping them play a role in realistic situations during which they can accomplish the goal
- providing access to the knowledge needed to achieve the goal
- providing instruction from experts when needed
- ensuring continuing motivation of learners.

People tend 'to see using technology for training as a solitary experience which takes place away from the real job' (Hills and Francis, 1999). E-learning must be organised in ways that promote a positive image of the learning process.

It is vital to the success of e-learning that its facilitators have relevant skills. For example, online learning involves accessing much wider groups of people than is customary in traditional training situations. E-learning facilitators should therefore be particularly competent in working cross-culturally and in building on diversity.

The importance of skilled facilitators emerges in studies like that carried out across Lloyds TSB's 450 learning centres in the UK in the late 1990s. Hills and Francis (1999) found some regions to be significantly better than others in achieving enthusiasm among employees for computer-based training. This was mainly because local training administrators and line managers were supportive, proactive and imaginative in their approach to learners and the learning experience.

Salmon (2001) outlines a popular five-stage model by which organisations can structure their online learning processes. Facilitators should possess skills in line with each of those stages (see http://oubs.open.ac.uk/e-moderating/fivestep.htm).

The responsibilities of those who have to harness new technology to learning should now be clear. They should study best practice, calculate costs in relation to anticipated benefits, and ensure the effective design, facilitation and evaluation of any computer-based learning and training processes and initiatives that they introduce.

Task 2

You have decided to incorporate e-learning into a programme that you are currently planning. You intend to integrate it carefully with more traditional learning approaches in order to achieve a good balance. Produce a brief discussion paper for your L&D director in which you:

- set out the outcomes that you want e-learning to achieve on the programme
- identify some of the difficulties you expect to encounter initially in promoting the programme and in motivating those who will be coming onto it. Suggest how to tackle those difficulties.

Getting started: information and services

There are many sources of information to help those with L&D responsibilities make decisions about how to harness and use new technology in the most appropriate and cost-efficient ways. Here are some of the most widely used. Each will take you into further information sources.

Sources of immediate knowledge for those seeking self-development

- BBC Online, Europe's most popular website: www.bbc.co.uk/education/home
- Open University: www/open.ac.uk
- University for Industry: www.ufiltd.co.uk

Information sources for trainers/learning facilitators

- Technologies for Training, a DfES-backed national consortium: www.tft.co.uk. It helps on all facets of IT-based training and sends out e-mails on new developments. It plans to link into more than 350 information points and demonstration centres across the country.

- A classroom of the future website has been set up on the National Grid for Learning: www.futureclass.ngfl.gov.uk

- The CIPD's website (www.cipd.co.uk) gives CIPD members access to its Online Training Digest, featuring a wide range of topics grouped in categories. An online training and development network offers among other facilities bulletin boards for exchange of views.

CASE STUDY: Training in the call-centre industry

There are an estimated 203,000 call-centre employees around Britain. The figure is likely to rise to 270,000 by 2003, thereby exceeding the combined workforce of coal mining, steel and vehicle production. Almost two-fifths of these employees work at the heart of the knowledge economy, in financial services and insurance. They provide the human infrastructure for the knowledge workers who dominate those industries. Their jobs are pressured, fast-moving and rapidly changing. They may spend 80 per cent of their time on the phone and 'sales teams have systems which can start dialling the next number when a call is nearly over'. There are big challenges for those in charge of planning and delivering training in the call-centre industry, as a glance at the nature of that industry makes clear (Brown, 2000).

As the call-centre industry grows it is embracing Internet technology. Call-centres link customers to information sources direct, whether by telephone (the most familiar aspect to the public), by postal communication, by e-mail or by other web-related communications. It is the latter mode that is increasing most rapidly (Warman, 2000).

Many companies are establishing websites without understanding the implications. Warman (2000) referred to a survey of call-centres carried out for Merchants Limited, one of Europe's largest call-centre and customer management organisations. It surveyed 269 companies in the UK and overseas. Growth in call-centre companies' setting up a website was about 15 per cent a year, and by 2000 had covered about 90 per cent of large companies and 75 per cent of small. For many, the learning curve was steep. As soon as a company goes live as a 24-hour operation, e-mails are immediately generated. In the survey, e-mail was used by 61 per cent for inbound communications and by 44 per cent for outbound, but many companies were not ready to deal with this escalation from 29 per cent and 19 per cent respectively in 1999. This kind of problem becomes acute when, as is often the case, 'technical staff add "call me" buttons to websites without talking to the operatives first' (chairman of the Call-Centre Management Association, quoted in Warman, 2000).

Call-centres have been widely criticised for employing 'armies of sweating teleworkers' (Brown, 2000), and although this description cannot be applied to all, it is the case that many are inadequately trained and poorly prepared to handle their stressful jobs. In the worst cases, new workers are thrown in with just a few days' training. Unsurprisingly, some companies lose a third of their employees every year. In training-aware companies, however, training is well-designed, with the use of multimedia software and the capacity for learners to practise at their own pace. Soon, it is predicted, call-centres will become a focal point for customer interaction – with interactive TV – and that has big training implications.

In training staff the focus will move from the transaction to the agent as an adviser to the customer. To that end, work is under way to design NVQ programmes for the call-centre industry (Warman, 2000).

Sources: Brown, 2000; Warman, 2000

Sources of services (Masie, 1999)

- Learning Service Providers (LSPs) offer learning delivery systems customised to an organisation's needs. They distribute the systems to organisations' staff and monitor their use. Training can thus become a variable expense for the organisation, not a capital expense tied to a single system. This can therefore break the stranglehold of the IT department over online learning plans of trainers, reducing the organisation's requirements for IT resource.

- Publicly accessible systems such as *learndirect*. Some offer access to learning materials, some to catalogues of learning materials that can be searched, purchased and downloaded by the user.

To conclude, the case study on the previous page brings together a number of themes explored in this chapter.

CONCLUSION

Having read this chapter and completed its checkpoints and tasks, you should now:

- **understand what is meant by 'e-learning' and its importance to the knowledge economy**

- **be able to explain why harnessing new technology to the learning and knowledge processes is increasingly essential for organisations**

- **understand the tasks and challenges that it involves for L&D practitioners**

- **know how to find sources of information on new technology applied to L&D activity.**

To test yourself against these objectives, what five-minute answers would you give to the following questions?

Review questions

As training manager in an organisation with around 250 employees, many of whom are only familiar with traditional learning methods, what *three* things would you do in order to ensure that e-learning technology can begin to make a real contribution to learning?

You are about to design electronically based learning packages for use in your organisation's Learning Resource Centre. Identify and justify *four* factors to which you will give particular attention in your design work.

Customer service must improve across a national chain of high-street stores. Take *one* of the following aims, and explain *three* electronically based methods that could help to achieve it:
- to motivate staff to improve their customer service skills
- to develop staff's customer service skills
- to improve staff's ability to apply and sustain their customer service skills.

Useful reference sources

SLOMAN M. (2001) *The E-learning Revolution*. London, Chartered Institute of Personnel and Development.

WALTON J. (1999c) 'Working in the virtual organisation'. In J. Walton, *Strategic Human Resource Development*. Harlow, Financial Times and Prentice Hall. pp536–57.

In addition to the information sources referred to throughout this chapter, local public libraries, universities and other learning centres, journals and the press all offer information and advice on new technology and its educational, training and learning applications.

To give only a few examples:

- The Technologies for Training website at www.tft.co.uk is a major source of information. It is supported by the DfES's Innovation in Training initiative.

- Cambridge University has a virtual classroom open to all (www.english.cam.ac.uk/vclass/virtclas.htm).

- www.uhi.ac.uk is a pioneering university for north-west Scotland.

- Coventry University has 2,600 course modules online for distance-learning.

- *The Sunday Times*, the Saturday *Telegraph*, The *Guardian* Education and The *Independent* all provide regular features and inserts that keep readers up to date with developments in new technology.

• Learning and Development in the Smaller Organisation

CHAPTER OBJECTIVES

After reading this chapter you will:

● be familiar with the context in which human resource management (HRM) and the L&D process operate in the smaller organisation

● understand the main issues related to the practice and provision of training in the smaller organisation

● be able to identify an appropriate approach to L&D activity for the smaller organisation.

Introduction

HR professionals with L&D responsibilities must be able to work effectively in a variety of organisational settings. Because smaller organisations are major employers, it is important for such professionals to understand L&D in the small-firm context.

Becket (1996) – generalising from a wide range of research findings – observed that:

● 96 per cent of all companies in Britain employ fewer than 20 people, and that 91 per cent have fewer than 10

● around one-third of all jobs are in firms with fewer than 20 employees, and half of all jobs are in firms with fewer than 100.

Small to medium-sized enterprises (SMEs) are those independent organisations that employ a workforce of up to around 500 people. Some argue that there is a case for also including in this category divisions and establishments of large groups that employ no more than 500 people, are in most respects autonomous, and operate in an insecure environment. SME definitions vary, but all involve dimensions of workforce size, ownership and annual turnover. The following classification system is widely used:

● *micro* – up to nine people

● *small* – 10 to 99 people

● *medium* – 100 to 499 people.

Often, the L&D process in SMEs is better aligned with the business and with other HR processes than it is in many large-scale organisations. This is unsurprising, since those providing L&D advice to small enterprises can only make their impact if they demonstrate a sound grasp of the business and its competitive environment, communicate in a language that stakeholders understand, forge effective business partnerships, and show that they are expert in relating L&D operations to the small-business context.

Many SMEs come close to being natural 'learning organisations'. They are fast-reactive, well informed about their external and internal environments, and foster a climate of continuous learning leading to the development of knowledge that fosters innovation. They operate like this not necessarily because there has been any conscious decision to do so, or even because there is an awareness that this is what is happening, but simply because that is how these organisations thrive.

In this chapter we will look at general issues related to the management and development of people in smaller organisations, then at factors affecting training as the most common form of organised learning process in those organisations. External support is particularly important for the smaller enterprise, so an examination of this is the basis for the third section. The chapter closes with an outline of how to assess outcomes of L&D activity in the smaller enterprise, and an integrative case study.

[The term 'owner-manager' is used in this chapter as shorthand for those who run small firms as a single owner, a partnership, a franchisee, or similar.]

Managing and developing people in the smaller organisation

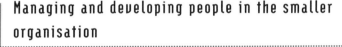

The employment relationship

Most of the literature concerning HRM in the UK derives from its observation in larger organisations, but there is no evidence that the conclusions reached in that context apply to managing people in smaller organisations (see Ritchie, 1993). Life in SMEs can be very different. Keasey and Watson (1993) explained some of the reasons:

- *Costs* – not least the cost of time spent dealing with paperwork – are a major preoccupation. Relatively high transaction costs typify the smaller firm, which has to deal with a complex set of regulatory requirements and negotiation, financing, monitory and bonding activities.

- *Face-to-face conflict* is endemic in smaller firms because the owner-manager is so intimately involved in managing employee relations and carries a high burden of financial risk.

- *Major uncertainties* surround SMEs' continued viability and survival:

  - They have a limited customer and product base and are vulnerable in the market, especially when they operate in areas in which competition is fierce or they are struggling for a new market where there are many obstacles to entry.

  - Capabilities of owner-managers vary widely and directly affect a firm's chances of survival. Some have little knowledge of basic management practice. Many see no need to acquire any, priding themselves on 'gut feel' for the business they are in.

  - Opportunities for growth may be passed over, the owner-manager often fearing that they threaten his or her desire for independence and for doing a good job. Many small firm owner-managers do not have substantial growth as their goal. Their financial strategy centres on survival and stability, and they see loss of their personal control over the business as the greatest threat posed by growth.

These interacting factors exert pressures on areas of HRM such as recruitment, rewards, training and employee relations. They differentially affect the way each SME is structured, its decision-making processes, how much the owner-manager is paid, and the extent of profit retention.

Task 1

Consider any SME with which you are familiar. This might be a business, a charitable undertaking, a professional partnership, even a franchise.

Analyse the organisation by reference to the factors just listed and identify the problems it typically experiences.

Then comment on the ways in which those factors appear to influence human resource (HR) practices in the organisation.

Clearly, employment relationships in SMEs are not simple. Not all small-firm employees share the aspirations and outlook of the owner, so that the concept of employee protection through collective organisation can be highly relevant in some cases. Conditions in SMEs can be harsh and exploitative, far from the 'small is beautiful' image (Ritchie, 1993). Nonetheless, the exercise of managerial control tends to be easier in the smaller than in the larger organisation, even if it is not necessarily more effective. Marlow and Patton (1992) identified common characteristics of the employment relationship in small owner-manager firms compared with those in larger enterprises:

- *domination of the owner-manager* – In the formative years especially, management style and tactics exercise a dominating influence on the culture of the firm. Every employee is directly exposed to the owner's managerial style and knows it well. SMEs are less likely to have a union presence, and owner-managers are unlikely to consider trade union issues relevant to their organisation. This gives the owner considerable power over the contractual relationship, work conditions and the management of performance.

- *a more shared and clearer perception of the primary goal* – Whatever their conditions of employment and work, employees will tend to identify strongly with the owner's strategies and business goals because their jobs and security are so directly tied up in them. However, goal conflict and the need for bargaining to resolve it are likely to develop once ownership spreads to more than one or two individuals, and once salaried managers are introduced.

- *more individualised employment relationships* – Recruitment and selection techniques will be biased towards identifying individuals who 'fit' the culture rather than those who possess formal professional managerial qualifications.

- *a more adaptable workforce* – SMEs are flexible and small enough to change their management practices and training initiatives as the organisation fluctuates in size. The necessity for and results of such change can also become quickly apparent.

HRM as a planned process in SMEs

There is little evidence of a planned approach to HRM in SMEs in the UK. Research has indicated that a number of dynamic forces interact to condition and explain a smaller organisation's employment practices. Hendry, Jones, Arthur and Pettigrew (1991) found that to understand those practices it is necessary to:

- understand the history of the firm, that has shaped those practices.

- examine its survival and growth strategies, that will significantly determine the kind of employees it needs.

- identify its strategies to obtain skills, and the external factors and internal organisational context that influence those strategies.

- examine its approach to training and development, that will tend to focus either on 'topping up' imported skills or on building an internal labour market.

In 1990 Price Waterhouse looked at SMEs throughout Europe and concluded that in the UK, although management and production skill shortages are critical barriers to growth, SMEs are less likely to have employment management strategies or training schemes to overcome these barriers. It seems that HRM in these organisations is not widely held to 'matter' in any formal, strategic sense.

This apparent failure to take HRM seriously in smaller businesses is, on reflection, not surprising. Managers will always focus their attention on those factors that they see as most likely to bring success, and only rarely do management skills and the administration of the employment relationship come under scrutiny here. Financial factors are the most frequently quoted in studies of SME failure. The most widely used measures of success relate to increased sales, employment growth and crude profit levels (Kelmar, 1990). HRM factors receive little attention, despite their importance. As Marlow and Patton (1992: 4) said:

> *Effective and efficient use of human resources can make the relatively small differences which allow some firms to make step function increases in performance while others struggle to make marginal gains.*

Many owner-managers in the UK also have had little if any formalised management/HR education or training, and so are often unaware of HRM's relevance to their organisations. In a study of how best to implement Investors in People (IiP) programmes in smaller organisations, researchers observed that owner-managers are unlikely to be able to relate their fragmented and unfocused experience of managing people to the formal systems and procedures involved in such programmes. They are otherwise preoccupied in the early growth years of the business. In transitional and terminal stages of the firm's growth they have to cope with demanding financial and market pressures. One way or another they (Harrison and Lord, 1992: 6):

> *are unlikely to have the time, knowledge or experience to make appropriate policies [or] to make the shift from task to people orientation. They have a strong need to appreciate the relevance of any initiative that may eat into their business time.*

Task 2

You are a consultant advising a small enterprise on its business strategy. (Choose any kind of small organisation you wish for this exercise, but preferably one with which you are familiar because that will make the task more convincing.) In discussion with the owner-manager you realise that you must convince him or her of the need for a more effective use of the enterprise's people. Your reasons are to do with

---

business growth, complexity and change, and with the associated need to move into longer-term planning in order to advance in a competitive market.

What should you do to help the owner-manager understand the issues and appreciate the need to develop some kind of planned approach towards the recruitment, retention and development of the kind of people the business now needs?

How should you do this?

Training in the smaller organisation

The organisational context

Training is the most common form of planned L&D activity in the smaller organisation. Four of the factors that, interacting together, provide the organisational context for training in the SME are its size, its sector, the stage reached in its lifecycle and its skill supply strategy (Hendry *et al*, 1991).

Size
Increasing size usually brings a more complex occupational structure into the firm, and that structure has a direct impact on training needs and practice. Larger firms tend to employ staff in all recognised skill categories, indicating that they have a high proportion of clearly defined jobs, whereas about 70 per cent of micro firms do not employ any workers in most recognised skill categories (Cambridge University Small Business Research Centre, 1992). They are more dependent on their local market and are less likely to need or to undertake formal training (Pettigrew, Arthur and Hendry, 1990). Their owner-managers also tend to have a low regard for the standards and quality of external training – often through ignorance.

Sector
Most SMEs (except micro firms) in manufacturing and service sectors have problems in recruiting the skills mix needed to maximise their competitive potential, even at times of high unemployment. Such needs become complex for SMEs at times of technological change and when they try to survive in increasingly segmented markets (Cambridge University Small Business Research Centre, 1992). There is thus an emphasis on internal training in firms in these sectors. Even here, however, easy conclusions cannot be drawn – service firms, for example, tend to recruit more trained staff.

Looking at subsectorial differences, it is skills in the technological and science areas that have grown most, especially in manufacturing firms.

This directly affects the recruitment and training strategies of such firms, although much depends on the existing availability of skills within and outside the individual firm.

The stage reached in the firm's lifecycle

Human resource needs in most SMEs change as the firm itself moves from start-up, through growth, to either a period of stability or further growth, or to failure and close-down.

- In start-up ventures there is often a need for labour flexibility and loosely defined tasks. This influences recruitment policy and training tends to be informal and on-the-job, restricted to teaching or showing people how to reach required performance levels (Hendry *et al*, 1991).

- During the period of initial growth, other pressures make it inevitable that any except the most obviously necessary training tends to receive little attention. In the early stages of the SME's lifecycle the factors most likely to influence the ways in which people are attracted, retained, rewarded or disengaged are the values and style of the entrepreneur, and an interacting range of product market structure and industry structure factors. In so far as HRM processes are recognised as being important, most attention is paid to recruitment, pay and termination.

- As the firm becomes more mature, it often undergoes change of ownership, organisational structure and managerial style. At this point, the need to develop people for the future is likely to become more apparent. However, this is not always the case, especially because at the time no one may be aware of what stage of development a firm is entering or leaving – such stages are easier to identify in retrospect

Progression through stages of the lifecycle is not a neat linear process. A deliberate choice may be taken not to 'go for growth'. An owner-manager may decide to close the firm down prematurely, or for no apparent reason let it be acquired at some stage. A poll commissioned in 1996 for the *Sunday Times* (Oldfield, 1996) indicated that as many as a quarter of owner-managers would like to sell their businesses. Most of the firms were not in financial difficulty. Quite simply, and for various personal reasons, most owner-managers wanted to 'retire'. In the smaller firm the quirks of human behaviour are more visible than in the larger. Often, too, they have a more direct impact on the management and development of people.

Skill supply strategy

All firms have some kind of skill supply strategy, no matter how intuitive or disorganised. Keasey and Watson (1993) observed that although in the early days the entrepreneur is likely to favour the internal market, as growth becomes apparent, so does a need for new managerial skills and new levels of sophistication in existing skills. There then appear to be three types of skill supply strategy:

- The owner may develop new skills or implement new procedures.

- There may be internal promotion and development.

- New people may be recruited from outside.

Checkpoint

- If you were analysing the organisational context for training in an SME, what major factors would you examine, and why?

- Outline the key stages in the lifecycle of an SME and the main HR processes that are most important at each of those stages.

The importance of informal training in SMEs

In official SME returns, the term 'training provision' simply means that training activity is actually taking place, no matter how or by whom it is being provided. Abbott (1994) found that in 350 owner-managed firms employing a maximum of 25 people a number of constraining factors – including lack of financial resources and time – made the provision of training extremely difficult. However, this did not necessarily mean that training was either absent or low. In some sectors where there seemed at first to be uniformly low levels of training, he found on closer examination less use of public provision and more of informal training. Some owners, however, did not think of it as 'training provision' and so did not enter it as such in their official returns.

In assessing the provision of training in smaller organisations, some commentators tend to regard 'high' (planned, strategic) training as superior to 'low' (informal, fragmented) training. This is misleading. It is not that 'high' is better than 'low', but that these two forms of training are different. The critical issue is whether the training carried out, high or low, most effectively raises the skill base of the labour force. There is a good deal of informal training in SMEs, and it makes a vital contribution to the business (Jones and Goss, 1991) since it can be highly effective and efficient. The sector of the firm is important here. In an enterprise such as a free house, restaurant or wine bar, informal training is widely prevalent for obvious reasons to do with the nature of the job, the small workforces and the wide geographical dispersion of the sites.

Tacit skills in smaller organisations

There is another aspect to informal training. It is to do with the type of skills needed in smaller businesses. 'Tacit' skills are crucial (Manwaring and Wood, 1985). These are skills that are not taught or acquired by formal processes. They are largely instinctive, part of the individual's repertoire of natural talent or skills mastered so long ago that they have now become habitual and are practised without the need to think about them. They are typified in the way in which someone develops a unique 'knack' of tackling a job and always does it to a high standard of performance and quality. The worker may not be able to explain quite what the key is to this consistent success, but as others watch, copy and listen to him or her as he or she works, they too can begin to achieve similar outcomes. (We saw an example of this in the case of the photocopier technicians, Chapter 1.)

There is more about tacit skills and knowledge in Chapter 20. Suffice to stress here that for a small firm, tacit skills can represent vital strategic assets. This is because, since it is impossible to discover exactly how they have been acquired, they are hard to copy. It is also because they explain much of the performance achieved by the business. Their uniqueness and value give competitive advantage. Their development in the smaller firm in many complex ways illustrates powerfully that the informal development of people in those enterprises is often superior to a formal approach to training.

Hendry and his colleagues found that there was a high proportion of genuinely unique jobs in many smaller firms, and noted the 'desire of SMEs to hang on to and keep hidden specific skills and competences developed within the firm' (Hendry *et al*, 1991: 84). Once a skill becomes explicit, and once systematically based training can be provided to develop it, the skill can be poached or copied by other organisations. Loss of valuable tacit skills represents a loss of strategic assets.

Triggers to a more formalised L&D process in SMEs

Hendry *et al* (1991) found in their research that although the growth of formal business planning in the firm did not tend of itself to act as a trigger, the managing director often had a view of where the company should be in the future and would broadly support educational initiatives in line with that. It is in this way that a focus on development rather than just on immediate training can emerge. Harrison and Lord (1992: 10) found that training and development activities in small firms became more managerially oriented and time-consuming with growth, many being 'related to new staff or potential "stars" who were identified to take the weight from the owner-manager in terms of administrative help or staff training'.

Hendry *et al* (1991) identified a number of common triggers for a more formalised and systematic approach to training in the smaller enterprise. Their interactions are unique to the particular firm, so it is important to identify how they operate in the particular organisational context, what outcomes training aims to achieve, and what strategies are selected to achieve them.

Seven key triggers are (Hendry *et al*, 1991: 69–82):

- *the skill supply strategy of the firm* – Inability to achieve the kind of skill supply it needs often directs a firm's attention to the value of a longer-term, planned and systematic approach to training within the firm. One typical outcome is a decision to introduce a recognised structure of skills and vocational qualifications for the whole workforce. Another, often associated with this, is to introduce a pay structure that defines skill requirements and specifies how these can be acquired through training and education.

● *the acquisition of new technology* – The introduction of new technology may in some firms lead to a drive for training or retraining, in others to a drive for recruitment, or to a reorganisation of the workforce – everything depends on the specifics of the situation.

● *customer relations* – Attempts to improve quality systematically can lead to formal training initiatives, but they can also, or alternatively, generate a changed environment in which L&D emerges from changed ways of working – project teams, worker involvement and participation, improved work systems, re-education in the workplace, and so on. Such attempts can also prompt the workforce to raise issues such as personal career advancement, demands for a job-grading structure and clearer pay progression.

● *growth* – With rapid growth, and especially with pressure of production, training may be influenced adversely or positively. Adverse effects will occur, for example, if management has a short-term perspective with no forward planning or vision. Too much will then be likely to happen at once, defeating attempts to produce an ordered training and development strategy. What is needed is 'a strategic vision – backed by market projections but not necessarily embodied in a formal plan'.

● *management culture related to training* – The values and perceptions of whoever owns or controls the SME have a dominating influence on all aspects of the business. If they become convinced of the need for a planned, systematic investment, then that conviction will be a major trigger for HRD.

● *workforce expectations and desire for betterment* – Although these are strongly affected by management's stance towards training, employee attitudes can be ambivalent. Employees' background and qualifications will be as important as stance of top managers in setting the climate for training in the firm.

● *the advent of a large cohort of new recruits* – The sudden entry of a relatively large cohort into a smaller firm can radically disrupt planned training and distort patterns of growth. For SMEs it is particularly important to provide a 'natural life-cycle of training which matches the cohort progression of employees'.

Whatever the triggers, constrained resources can still inhibit the development of a more systematic and formalised approach to training in the smaller firm. Money is an obvious issue here, but so too is the difficulty of releasing people for off-the-job training. In these circumstances, the cost of any formalised training has to be balanced carefully against the extent to which it can give fast pay-back. For the smaller organisation, time-scale is crucial. Longer-term advantages offered by L&D initiatives may be clear, but there must be sufficient immediate cost-benefit too (Cambridge University Small Business Research Centre, 1992).

Checkpoint

● In what ways can a smaller organisation be a type of 'learning organisation'?

● The owner-manager of a small firm feels that the time is coming when he will need to take a more systematic, planned approach to training. Identify and justify *three or four* of the factors you would advise him to look at in order to be sure about this.

External support for training in SMEs

Raising awareness of external provision

The most common reasons such organisations do not make a more significant investment in training and development are:

● scepticism about value, often coming from history – 'a bad training experience can be damaging to training provision' (Kirby, 1990): repetition of such experiences reinforces the scepticism

● a perception of inability to pay, of lack of time, and of the likelihood of lost opportunity costs

● failure to recognise skills shortages and areas of lack of managerial capability

● lack of awareness of, and some scepticism about, sources of external provision and expertise.

Group training schemes and facilities, external funding, and cheap but good-quality external educational provision can all help to minimise formal training costs for SMEs. However, many government initiatives in the past have been launched and delivered without real evaluation (Jennings, Richardson and Beaver, 1992) and government agencies are often perceived much less favourably in terms of standards and quality than further-education institutions. Smaller firms give considerable support to external vocational education, but generally SMEs tend to have little certainty that external training provision will meet their needs.

Renewed efforts are now being made to spread awareness of important initiatives. Amongst these, a new programme from Investors in

People was produced in 1997, with help from Scottish Enterprise, the Confederation of British Industry and the Federation of Small Businesses. The aim was to make the package practical, allowing businesses to gauge how well they are doing compared with similar enterprises. It was aimed at the bottom end of the size scale, with eight elements instead of the 23 that, at that time, larger organisations were measured against for IiP accreditation. This represented a real advance in thinking, making IiP more attractive, meaningful and accessible for smaller organisations, whatever their type and sector.

In 2001 the Department for Trade and Industry introduced a new Small Business Service to allow small firms to be given higher priority and greater influence within the government. The 1992 Business Link system was retained, and now delivers all the government support services on offer to small firms. This means that provision is more accessible and coherent than in the past. Similar systems operate through Business Shops in Scotland, Business Connect in Wales, and the Economic Development Network for Northern Ireland.

Externally provided information and expertise can often clarify misapprehensions that many smaller organisations have about the cost and value of training and development. Through such help, outcomes like the following can be achieved:

- The organisation can be helped to identify a particular area of need with a clear impact not only on the current bottom line but on future capability. The provider should work closely with key parties in the firm to provide a cost-efficient learning experience targeted to achieve one or two clear objectives, and should agree at the start on measures to indicate the success of the initiative. A progression of such carefully planned and targeted learning initiatives should slowly begin to change the culture to one that sees 'value' (rather than 'cost') in planned learning (rather than 'training') in the firm. This is the aim of the IiP process.

- The use of benchmarking and good practice can reduce scepticism, promote interest and stimulate change.

- Training costs can be reduced. Good consultants can help a smaller firm to become more aware of funding sources and of relevant, affordable training provision. They can explore with the firm ways to facilitate learning relatively cheaply – for example, by mentoring and work-shadowing instead of formal induction; by project teams rather than expensive outdoor development programmes; by team briefings rather than externally provided 'team-building' courses. Many external consultants lack experience and understanding of SMEs (Jennings et al, 1992), so using the local network to find out about consultants and their track record is crucial.

- External and intra-organisational learning networks can be developed. They provide access to many sources of HRD aid for the firm and also stimulate interest and boost confidence. There are now many websites that act as a gateway to information for small firms. Some are listed at the end of this chapter.

Checkpoint

- Working as a consultant to a small organisation, you want to raise the owner-manager's awareness of the value of external training and development provision. What kind of advice will you give her?

- The same owner-manager says to you, 'By the way, if you're thinking about IiP, forget it. Far too bureaucratic for our needs.' She clearly doesn't know about the revised IIP programme. Identify and explain to her *three* of the ways in which that programme offers help for smaller organisations.

Outcomes of training and development in the smaller enterprise

There is little evidence in smaller organisations of training in training needs analysis or training planning (Harrison and Lord, 1992). Failure to document either needs or plans can give the impression either that no training is being done or that any that is taking place must be unplanned and therefore invalid. Such conclusions can be mistaken, but lack of relevant paperwork does create some evaluation difficulties. However, Pettigrew *et al* (1990) showed that the outcomes of HRM and training in SMEs can be assessed:

- *in terms of impact on current performance goals*, as indicated by a range of measures (performance will be the dominating criterion at an early stage of the firm's lifecycle)

- *in terms of development*, as indicated by impact on prospective medium-term outcomes associated with planned changes in products or services, or adjustments to environmental forces

- *in terms of learning related to prospective long-term outcomes* that are impossible to specify but can be assured only by the growth of strategic capabilities 'so that the firm can cope with crisis or make the big strategic leap forward which unexpected opportunities may present'.

It is important to achieve strategic awareness and thinking across the workforce in smaller organisations, and forms of development and work experience that can enhance those abilities are therefore of particular value.

What follows is a case study to review and consolidate learning in this chapter. It draws on many real-life small-business scenarios.

CASE STUDY: Triggers to training and development in the small firm

Rob Jones, now 47, is the owner-manager of a small manufacturing firm which he founded eight years ago. It has secured a solid place in the market and is now expanding as demand for the product increases. Turnover has increased from £1 million in the early years to nearly £5 million in the current year.

Rob set up the firm after working for some years as a marketing executive in a multinational firm. In a major restructuring and de-layering exercise, he was one of several to take a golden handshake. Having benefited from a good university education, he is a believer in the education system and therefore invested some of his severance pay in a 'small-business growth course' at a local university business school. He formed many useful academic and small-business contacts while on the course, and at its end he established his own firm, which has prospered.

Rob has a team of three key people who, with him, carry the responsibility for the management of the firm. All are around his age and were recruited at start-up. They are hard-working and dedicated to the success of the firm, but are not yet agreed on future strategy. Rob and Mark, the production manager, see an international future as the ultimate goal to go for. On the other hand, Bill, the finance manager, is concerned about the implications of that and feels that an expansion within the national market, clearly targeted, would be desirable: it should generate sufficient profit and investment revenue without ultimately leading to the likelihood of merger or takeover. Tony (sales and marketing) is keen to expand the customer base but has concerns about the fast-growing firm's ability to maintain its quality, delivery and sales standards.

The team is shortly to go away for a three-day hotel break in order to hammer out their future goals and strategy. Rob uses this technique regularly, but in this case he and his colleagues face a particularly challenging task because of the grow-ing complexity of the business and of the strategic choices it faces.

There are three watchwords in the firm: quality, service and best-in-class. Managers and team leaders attend external learning events regularly in order to keep up to date and to develop strong networks; Rob's business school and other external links are productive here.

Rob sees 'development' as getting and keeping a high-calibre management group and workforce team, and enhancing their capabilities for the future. Training means, for him, a combination of informal on the job learning and skills-based formal interventions.

Rob has always believed that management development in a small firm must mainly be achieved by natural learning processes. Their low cost and direct relationship to the work situation bring unique benefits. He also believes that the structure of the firm, like the jobs within it, powerfully affect the workforce's flexibility, quality and commitment. The flat, matrix structure he and his small team have carefully developed has so far produced the kind of adaptable labour force that the firm has needed to ensure its survival and growth.

As issues of management succession, organisational restructuring and skills change bite deeper, Rob realises the need for a longer-term and planned approach to training and development – and indeed to all human resource issues – but he is unsure how to deal with this. He has always spent a large proportion of his time on people-related activities – about 75 per cent, he estimates. Now he has major decisions to make. These are not only about future direction and investment in the business but about the management, development and reward of an increasingly diversified workforce. He can see that the influx of people at different levels, all bringing with them different histories and work experiences, has

CASE STUDY: continued

implications for skill and pay levels, for management succession, and for expectations, culture and behaviour in the workplace.

Rob has so far used a consultant with whom he has worked since start-up to help him sort out HR matters. However, he is now seriously considering establishing an HRM post in the firm. He recognises the need to adopt a more coherent approach to the workforce. He has a clear view of where he wants the firm to be in the future, and sees the value of well-chosen and flexible initiatives that are in line with that. He also feels that there ought to be a move in emphasis from 'training' to 'learning and development' but sees this to be particularly complex territory where a HR professional should be able to be a source of real added value for the firm.

CONCLUSION

Having read this chapter and completed its checkpoints and tasks, you should now:

- be familiar with the context in which human resource management (HRM) and the L&D process operate in the smaller organisation

- understand the main issues related to the practice and provision of training

- be able to identify an appropriate approach to L&D activity for a smaller organisation.

To test yourself against these objectives, what five-minute answers would you give to the following questions?

Review questions

You are a human resource consultant, asked by the owner-manager of a small but growing firm to advise her on how best to organise training and development in the firm. What *three or four* contextual factors do you examine before giving her your advice – and why?

A general practitioners' (GP) practice is recruiting a practice manager for the first time. The job-holder will be responsible, among other managerial tasks, for employee development related to the practice's 10 reception, nursing and GP staff. What purpose and core tasks would you expect the practice manager's employee development responsibility to entail, and why?

Explain the main steps that you would recommend the owner-manager of a small, rapidly growing firm to take in order to provide it with high-calibre managers for the future.

Useful reference sources

HARRISON R. (1993b) 'Strategic human resource management at HMH Sheetmetal Fabrications Ltd, 1993'. In R. Harrison (ed.) *Human Resource Management: Issues and strategies*. Wokingham, Addison Wesley, pp335–9.

HILL R. *and* STEWART J. (1999) 'Human resource development in small organizations'. *Human Resource Development International*. Vol. 2, No. 2. pp103–23.

WALTON J. (1999d) 'Small and medium-sized enterprises and human resource development', in J. Walton, *Strategic Human Resource Development*. Harlow, Financial Times and Prentice Hall. pp324–51.

There are many websites that offer helpful information for smaller organisations, including the following:

- the Department of Trade and Industry's website, www.dti.gov.uk, and www.businesslink.org

- the Small Business Service or its equivalent in Scotland, Wales and Northern Ireland (see www.businesslink.co.uk; www.scotnet.co.uk/sb/bsu.htm; www.cbc.org.uk; and www.ednet.ni.com)

- the Enterprise Zone, run by the DTI, which provides links to wide-ranging functional information for smaller enterprises, including human resources (www.enterprisezone.org.uk)

Information about training can be found through *learndirect*'s drop-in centres, and through www.ufiltd.co.uk

DEVELOPING PERFORMANCE AND POTENTIAL

• Achieving a Developmental Performance Management Process

CHAPTER OBJECTIVES

After reading this chapter you will:

- understand the importance of achieving a developmental performance management process

- know at what stages of the performance management process planned L&D activity can make its best contribution

- be able to advise on principles to guide the planning and operation of induction, skills training, appraisal and personal development within the performance management process.

(Note: throughout this chapter the term 'individual needs' may be taken to refer also to group/team needs.)

Introduction

Part 3 of this book focuses on ways in which effective L&D activity can enhance the performance management process (PMP), can build competence, and can expand the organisation's capacity to perform current tasks better and do new things in new ways. These are challenging tasks, and from now on some more complex activities are incorporated into the text. The aims of these are twofold – to encourage readers to apply an increasingly holistic and integrative approach to L&D situations, and to develop their L&D consultancy skills.

Building competence and capacity can encompass a good deal of specialised activity, including, for example:

- the training and development of specific groups such as clerical and administrative staff, apprentices, supervisors and team leaders

- the training and development of part-time and temporary employees and of voluntary workers, including non-executive directors of the business

- continuous learning and development for professional staff

- training and development programmes for management at all organisational levels

- the training of those with special needs, such as ethnic minorities, the unemployed, or those returning to work after a career break.

The scope of this book does not allow detailed coverage of all these fields. Its purpose is rather to identify and explore the conceptual and practical frameworks within which all L&D activity should be located. This chapter is concerned to relate L&D to the organisation's PMP, and in the three following chapters we examine ways of planning, designing, delivering and evaluating effective learning initiatives and processes, whatever their specific focus.

Why start with the PMP? Because at the heart of all business activity in an organisation is a concern to discover what 'teams, managers, team leaders and individuals do (and could do better) to manage their performance in order to achieve success' (Armstrong and Baron, 1998: Introduction). Performance management is an ongoing process, not a product or technique. It has been described (CIPD, 2001) as:

a strategic approach to managing the business ... largely concerned with the continuous development of the organisation's broad strategic capabilities and the specific capabilities of individuals and teams.

One of the most important tasks of L&D practitioners is to contribute to achieving an effective performance management process. In an IPD report on a survey of performance management in a sample of UK-based organisations (Armstrong and Baron, 1998), the authors observed that:

Overwhelmingly, performance management processes in the organisations covered by our survey focused on employee development as the route to improved organisational performance.

The survey had a limited database but produced significant findings when its results were compared with those of previous, similarly based IPD surveys. The researchers found that 'the philosophy of planned personal development as part of the overall process has now become firmly embedded in the policies and practices of a large proportion of the organisations covered' (Armstrong and Baron, 1998: 387). They observed a shift from a directive to a supportive approach to the management and development of performance in 'best practice' organisations. They also found a learning-focused rather than a training-focused approach to development, with frequent use of coaching, counselling, guidance, and redesigning roles or redefining team responsibilities.

Writers vary in the way they describe the operation of the PMP. Torrington and Hall (1995) identified four stages, and Armstrong and Baron detailed nine, including two final stages of 'rating' and 'reward'.

Figure 8 The performance management process and related L&D activity

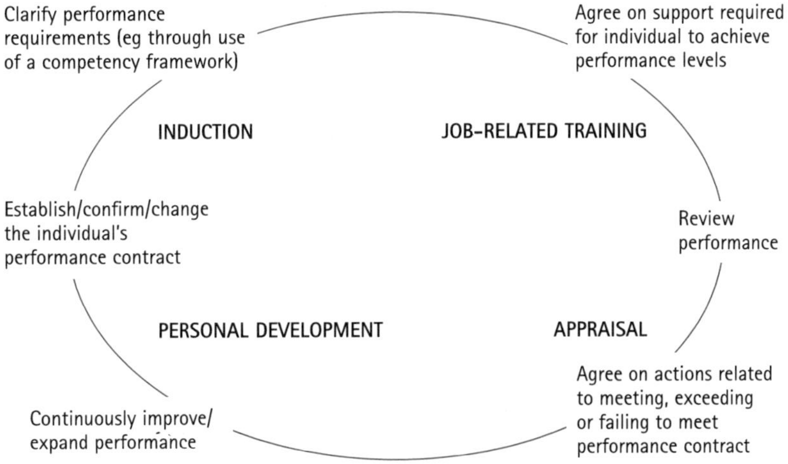

Clarify performance
requirements (eg through use
of a competency framework)

Agree on support required
for individual to achieve
performance levels

INDUCTION   JOB-RELATED TRAINING

Establish/confirm/change
the individual's
performance contract

Review
performance

PERSONAL DEVELOPMENT   APPRAISAL

Agree on actions related
to meeting, exceeding
or failing to meet
performance contract

Continuously improve/
expand performance

Adapted from Lockett J. (1992) *Effective Performance Management: A strategic guide to getting the best from people.* London, Kogan Page, p38.

Lockett (1992) identified seven and I have drawn primarily on his approach in Figure 8. All such descriptions are variations on a common theme – that the PMP involves an interaction of elements and activity along the lines shown in Figure 8. This Figure also shows the developmental activity that can support the PMP. In the context of L&D, the key elements of a PMP are those to do with:

- setting targets and establishing desired performance levels

- appraising and improving performance

- ensuring continuous learning and development

- giving recognition and rewards.

The first part of the chapter explores ways in which the learning process appears to operate at the individual level. In the second, it identifies factors that can inhibit individual performance and those that can stimulate it. The third part of the chapter examines how, at each of four stages of the performance management cycle, L&D strategies can help to achieve a developmental process. The chapter concludes with a case study on one of the most problematic elements of any PMP – appraisal.

Checkpoint

- What kind of performance management process is evident in your own organisation?

- What, if anything, do you think should be done to make that process more developmental?

Understanding learning

Many definitions focus on learning as an outcome, this well-known one (Bass and Vaughan, 1967: 8) amongst them:

> *Learning is a relatively permanent change in behaviour that occurs as a result of practice or experience.*

However, in Chapter 1 we concluded that learning is a process – one that enables the development of the organisation and of individuals, and that leads to the acquisition of knowledge.

In fact, learning is both a noun and a verb. It can be an outcome ('I now have knowledge') but it is also a process ('I am learning'). In this chapter, I emphasise its meaning as a process, because unless we have some understanding of the dynamics of learning we shall not be able to choose the most relevant actions to take in pursuit of desired learning outcomes.

There are many theories about the learning process (see Marchington and Wilkinson, 2002, pp385–92 for a helpful summary). We examine two here. They are explained in basic terms, but even at that level they can help us to understand the learning process in the organisational as well as the individual context. Later in the book, in Chapter 20, I will look more closely at learning and knowledge processes particularly as they appear to operate in the workplace. Here, the focus is on individual learning in relation to the PMP.

The experiential learning cycle

Learning can be viewed as a circular process to do with continuously undergoing and learning from experience, as we saw in Figure 2, Chapter 1. Honey and Mumford (1992) expanded on this kind of theory to produce their inventory of learning styles, in which four main types of learning style are associated with key stages of the learning cycle. Figure 9 outlines the way in which they do this.

Figure 9   A model of learning styles and skills

The activist
Learns best from doing things, from
practical experience. Is stimulated by
learning on the job and, in a planned
learning event, by interactive learning
and training methods. Tends to act
first, think later

The pragmatist
Will accept anything that 'works' in the
real-life situation. Is stimulated by the
challenge of new ideas or approaches
and the opportunity to be creative,
applying what is learned to problem-
solving and decision-making. Likes to
'get on with things'.

The reflector
Learns best by observing others'
experience and by reflecting on own
past experience. Is stimulated by
learning situations in which he/she can
take an observer role and has time to
think everything through. Tends to
think first, act later.

The theorist
Learns best by being presented with
models or conceptual frameworks and
by analysing and building on them in
order to develop a body of theory. Is
stimulated by a systematic, well-
structured approach to learning, with
strong theoretical elements. Tends to
be good at all analytical activity.

(Adapted from Honey and Mumford, 1992.)

Marchington and Wilkinson (2002) produced a valuable critique of the Honey and Mumford and other learning-style inventories. Such inventories are useful aids in identifying the kinds of learning situation in which individuals feel most comfortable and most able to learn effectively. They lack clear scientific validity, but this is unsurprising when we consider that there is no consensus amongst experts on exactly how the learning process operates in individuals and in groups. Theories of learning abound, all based on different assumptions. As your response to the following task may well show, the learning process is not as easily explained as learning inventories might suggest, but such inventories do offer significant clues about the reasons for difficulty or success in an individual's learning process.

Task 1

Identify a recent occasion during which you felt that you were learning very effectively *or* very ineffectively.

Reflect on that occasion, relating it to the cycle of learning and the types of learning style outlined in Figure 2 (Chapter 1) and Figure 10.

What does your analysis *explain* and *fail to explain* about reasons for your effective/ineffective learning on that occasion?

It can be as important to challenge learners' preferred learning styles as to work with those styles. Given the purpose of a learning event, the designer must ensure that there is the most appropriate kind of stimulation, practice and feedback at crucial stages of learning. Those overseeing learning in the workplace should also 'manage' everyday work situations in ways that foster in individuals and teams learning styles and skills that can be applied to an ever-widening range of job-related problems and organisational issues. This will lead to the enhancement of organisational as well as individual performance.

Stimulus-response theory

Our second theory identifies four principles of learning (see Bass and Vaughan, 1967; Stammers and Patrick, 1975; and Gagne, 1977 for classic explanations of this framework) that provide a framework for the learning process:

- *drive* – For learning to occur there must be an underlying need to which it relates. Once the individual realises that entering a particular learning situation will enable him or her to satisfy that need, this will provide him or her with the motivation to learn.

- *stimulus* – A stimulus corresponds to a message that makes an impact on our senses because it relates to one or more of our primary or secondary drives. A stimulus is a trigger that 'switches on' and maintains the learner's attention and interest during the learning process.

- *response* and *reinforcement* – In every learning situation the learner must acquire appropriate responses – skills, knowledge, attitudes – that will lead to improved performance or to some other learning goal. These responses must be reinforced by practice, experience and feedback until they are fully learned. Unproductive responses must be corrected before they become habitual.

This is a simplistic outline of a major body of theory about human learning. It is based on the so-called 'law of effect' in classical conditioning theory. Pictures come to mind of the dog, cat or pigeon being 'trained' to perform in desired ways by a process of instruction, reward and punishment. Such a mechanical approach seems at odds with Kolb's naturalistic concept. Yet four principles underpin both theories, and they point clearly to the ways in which barriers to learning can so easily arise in planned learning events, and to how those barriers can be tackled:

- *Clarify the purpose of learning.* Clarity about the purpose of any learning event or process is essential in order to communicate its relevance to organisational and individual needs. Kolb, Rubin and McIntyre (1974) stressed the need to identify the purpose of the whole learning process for the organisation. They believed that learning should be an explicit organisational objective, 'pursued as consciously and deliberately as profit or productivity'. They stressed that there must be 'a climate seeing the value of such an approach ... developed in the organisation'.

CASE STUDY: The uninterested learners

Management is convinced that a particular training course is essential for a group of employees. The employees themselves, however, disagree. How can management convince them? Exhortations or commands will not be enough: people can be driven into a training-room but, once there, they cannot be forced to learn.

Management tries to convince the employees by outlining a clear purpose for the training and by demonstrating that the specific outcomes it promises will bring mutual benefits. Some are convinced by this, but some are not. To change the attitudes of those who are uninterested, the trainers who are planning the course design it in such a way that from the start the methods and content will quickly arouse and sustain the learners' attention. They know that once that stimulation has been achieved – and given the fact that this course is in fact of real relevance to all the learners involved, even though some as yet do not realise that – it is increasingly likely that the initially sceptical participants will begin to see the importance of acquiring the skills, knowledge and attitudes that the course develops in them through time.

The trainers know that individuals cannot be made to learn but that the learning process will begin to work effectively once learners can identify with its purpose, enjoy learning experiences that help them achieve successful and relevant outcomes, and respect the expertise and knowledge of those who are delivering the course and working with them for its duration.

- *Ensure stimulation during learning.* The learning process must be designed to attract and maintain the interest and energy of the learners. The case study above illustrates this.

- *Ensure adequate feedback and practice during learning.* Learning has to be regularly reinforced if learners are to acquire new knowledge quickly and confidently apply it to practical situations. Kolb's theory emphasises this when it shows the stage of experimentation leading into further experience, which then generates the possibility of review, analysis and modification or repetition of the new learning. Appraisal is an important – although of course not sufficient – way of ensuring reinforcement of learning that has occurred during everyday work experience as well as in formal learning events and processes.

- *Ensure effective transfer and retention of learning.* The way in which learning is transferred into, as well as out of, the new learning situation has a direct impact on the ultimate outcomes of the learning process. Sometimes knowledge, skills and attitudes acquired before a learner enters a new learning situation will exercise a negative influence on that situation. Those barriers have to be tackled if the learning event can go ahead with hope of success. In the same way, learning that has been newly acquired may prove difficult to transfer to the workplace and to use effectively there. Due thought must be given at the planning stage to what learning will be most relevant, given workplace context, and to how best to ensure its effective transfer to that context.

Chapters 14 to 16 deal in detail with how to plan, design, deliver and evaluate learning events. What is presented here is no more than an outline of some general guidelines that have emerged from considering two basic theories about the learning process.

Checkpoint

● Explain the basis of stimulus-response theory, and identify some of its practical implications for those designing learning events.

● You are enthusiastic about learning style inventories, and plan to use one in a forthcoming training course that you are running. Explain and justify *one* way in which you intend to use it.

Types of learning process

Three types of learning process can aid individual performance (Mezirow, 1985):

● instrumental

● dialogic

● self-reflective.

Instrumental learning
This means learning how to do the job better once the basic standard of performance has been attained. A key strategy to achieve instrumental learning is learning on the job. This can involve an interaction of formal and informal processes and can be highly effective, provided there is someone to encourage learners in the course of their daily tasks to identify problems, formulate appropriate action, try it out, observe the effects and learn from them. That 'someone' may be a trained member of the work team. For example, new entrants at McDonald's go through a three-hour induction and are then partnered with a 'buddy' who comes from a 'training squad' of specially trained employees belonging to their work team. 'In a typical restaurant employing a crew of 50, about five will be members of the training squad' (Cannell, 1997). The on-the-job learning for which 'buddies' are responsible is rigorously organised and very effective. On the other hand, the 'someone' may be a high-performing member of a workgroup who has proven training skills and the disposition to foster job-related learning in others.

Managers have to be good at helping – or training and encouraging others to help – new recruits to learn from their mistakes as well as successes, and to focus on continuous improvement of work processes rather than simply on the achievement of task targets. They also need to set the recruits new challenges from time to time in order to stretch their abilities. Such managers should be recognised for their achievement in developing effective performance-related learning in the workplace.

Dialogic learning

Dialogic learning involves interacting with others in ways that produce a growing understanding of the culture of the organisation, and of how it typically achieves its goals. As we shall shortly see, dialogic learning is particularly valuable at the stage when newcomers enter the organisation, or when people are promoted into parts of the organisation with which they are unfamiliar. It can help individuals to quickly make sense of the organisational world they have entered, and develop the confidence to operate competently in it.

Self-reflective learning

This is the kind of learning that leads individuals to redefine their current perspective in order to develop new patterns of understanding, thinking and behaving. It is needed when people have to operate in roles or situations that are very different from those to which they have become accustomed in the past. Because self-reflective learning involves challenging, and breaking out of, old mindsets it requires unlearning as well as new learning. As Argyris (1982) pointed out, that is possible only in an environment that 'enables and empowers individuals to be responsible, productive and creative' and to see error as a positive learning vehicle.

Educational and training programmes have an obvious part to play in generating self-reflective learning. So too have work-based learning processes like quality circles, briefing groups, benchmarking and best-practice exercises, secondments, new project work and action-learning sets. Such processes all expose people to new ways of thinking and new situations, making them question familiar prescriptions, operations and routines.

Single- and double-loop learning

Clearly self-reflective learning involves a different approach from that required by instrumental and dialogic learning. The difference is to do with the stance of the learner. Instrumental and dialogic learning enable continuous improvement of skills, behaviour or attitudes so that they fall in line with existing standards and norms. Self-reflective learning can involve questioning those standards and norms themselves.

In Chapter 6 we noted one of the best-known – yet quite often poorly understood – ways of classifying approaches to learning: the concept of single- and double-loop learning. Chris Argyris first formulated the concept (1977) and developed it with Donald Schon in 1978. In essence it is about the difference between simply tackling 'surface symptoms of a problem' (single-loop learning) and questioning 'why the problem arose in the first place and . . . [tackling] its root causes' (double-loop learning) (Pickard, 1997).

Not all researchers in the field of individual and organisational learning believe that the concept of single- and double-loop learning is valid. Some see it as too simplistic, ignoring the possibility of discontinuous, non-linear learning to explain the sudden leaps in understanding that result in people breaking out of customary ways of thinking and perceiving. However, the concept is undeniably powerful and exercises an enduring appeal. I return to it in Chapter 19.

Checkpoint

- Identify *three* types of learning process, and for each, outline and justify a situation for which it would be well suited.

- Why is double-loop learning claimed to be essential for radical innovation to occur?

A warning note on theories of learning

In concluding this section on learning, I must again emphasise that I have had no space to focus on more than a handful of the best-known theories. The primary focus and the scope of the chapter mean that my examination of the learning process has had to be selective. It has therefore omitted much evolving but highly complex theory that is currently influencing the debate on individual and collective learning in organisations. In particular, I have not explored the relationship between learning and the different ways in which individuals organise and process information. Reference to cognitive theory and the decision-making process, however, was made in Chapter 3, and those interested in a further examination of individual cognitions in a strategic context will find it in Chapter 22 (pp436–7). For more detailed treatment, readers are referred to specialist articles and texts (Harrison, 2000; Hodgkinson and Johnson, 1994).

Understanding performance

The motivation calculus

Performance is the result of the interaction between an individual's needs, perception of the results required and rewards being offered, and the amount of effort, energy and expertise that the individual has or wishes to apply to the task in hand. Handy (1985) called this interactive process the 'motivation calculus'. He explained that performance can be understood by reference to four factors, which revolve around the learner, his or her manager and his or her workplace – needs, results, rewards and 'E' factors. We can see links here with learning theory discussed earlier in this chapter.

- *needs* – How far, in individuals' minds, do their jobs or tasks relate in any positive way to the needs that those individuals bring to work? What we should try to discover is not all their needs, but those which influence them at work. If a particular task or job relates to those needs only in a minor way, clearly we cannot expect more than minimal performance from the jobholder. We must be careful about the labels we attach to people. An individual may be regarded as 'ambitious' – but ambition can take many forms. Trying to motivate such an individual to take on extra work by dangling the carrot of 'enhanced chances of promotion' will be ineffective if in fact he or she is driven by the need not for the increased responsibilities or high level of skill that promotion would involve but for some form of professional or workgroup status. Taking on another task when already expending maximum effort on an existing workload could mean a reduction in that individual's overall effectiveness, and a consequent loss of status.

- *results* – How far do individuals appreciate what is wanted from them? Do they fully understand what their jobs involve, the results they are supposed to achieve, and the opportunities, constraints and challenges that surround those jobs? Have they had any opportunity to set work targets jointly with their managers, rather than simply have these imposed on them? Do individuals know when they are achieving good results, and why? Do managers help them by acting as good role models, reinforcing effective performance and discouraging poor performance?

- *rewards* – Does the task or job offer valued rewards to the individual? Rewards can take many different forms – not just money and position (which may have less impact than managers believe, or may not be within their power to offer) but also status and praise – non-financial recognition. It is essential to talk and listen to employees about all the rewards that they value, instead of simply acting on assumptions. It is important, furthermore, to understand how people view the promise of rewards. Promises are often treated with scepticism because they have been made before but, for whatever reason, not been fulfilled.

- *'E' factors* – How far do individuals see it as worthwhile to expend effort, energy, excitement and expertise in the task, given the results that are required, the rewards it appears to offer them, and the workloads they already carry? And what level of those 'E' factors do those individuals actually possess? Are assessments about this accurate, or is either less or more expected of jobholders than they are actually able to give?

Every individual's motivation calculus is unique. The records of a poorly-performing member of staff may show high levels of absenteeism, sickness and notes of continued refusals to take on new tasks. These records may cause unfavourable judgements to be made about him or her, so that training or development is considered inappropriate. In such cases the individual has been written off. Yet with more insights into the factors that lie behind performance, quite a different picture may emerge. That picture may lead to an awareness that changes should be made in the ways in which staff recruitment, work allocation, leadership functions or appraisal are carried out in a department. Once again, as so often before in this book, we see the importance of other human resource policies in framing L&D activity.

Learning difficulties in the workplace

Learning difficulties in the workplace typically arise in relation to:

- *task performance*, where they are connected with difficulty in carrying out one or more specific tasks related to the job

- *task management*, where they are connected with difficulty in general planning, problem-solving and decision-making in the job

- *boundary management*, where they are connected with difficulty in operating confidently and effectively in the role and job by reference to the social and political environment in which the job-holder must operate

- *motivation*, where they are connected typically with mistaken expectations about the job, or its level and content, or with unsatisfactory training, support and rewards, or with poor supervision and feedback on performance.

Such difficulties can be increased or reduced by:

- the learner, who needs the right level of competence, motivation, understanding, support and incentives in order to perform effectively

- the learner's workgroup, whose members will exercise a strong positive or negative influence on the attitudes, behaviour and performance of each new recruit

- the learner's manager, who should act as an effective role model, coach, stimulus and communicator related to performance

- the organisational context, which may produce barriers to performance (see Chapter 6). For example, there may be a lack of any compelling vision and leadership; there may be an ineffective or inappropriate structure and culture; there may be poor management, or a lack of motivating and supportive human resource policies and practice in the workplace.

Task 2

Identify an area of your organisation (or one with which you are familiar) where there are problems in performance – perhaps involving one or two individuals, or perhaps characterising the entire workplace.

Use some of the theory we have just covered to examine possible causes of that poor performance, and to suggest some ways in which it might be tackled.

A corporate learning programme to support the performance management process

Integrating the drives for direction and development

The PMP incorporates a natural drive to direct performance towards the achievement of specified targets, and to direct learning towards the closing of gaps between actual and desired performance. The popularity of competency-based frameworks in performance management systems must be treated with caution in this context. A robust competency framework focuses attention on key areas for performance in the organisation and on what is needed to ensure adequate or superior performance levels in those areas. It performs a helpful role in clarifying performance requirements. However, an obsessive preoccupation with competencies and an inexpert approach to competency-based analysis can be counterproductive (Healy, 1995; Sparrow, 1996). It can narrow the focus of the PMP to exclude the development of more generalised abilities needed to survive in an unpredictable future. (I examine competency frameworks further in Chapters 14 and 18.)

Carefully planned learning activity is needed at critical stages of the PMP in order to balance the drive for control with a drive for development. Figure 8 (p245) showed key L&D strategies to support the PMP – induction, skills training, appraisal, and personal and continuous development. Let us now look at an integrative approach to these in what we may call a 'corporate learning programme'.

Induction
The purpose of induction, whether for the newcomer to the organisation or for the employee who is moving into a new job or organisational level, is twofold:

● to introduce newcomers to the job

- to help them understand and adapt to the vision and goals of the organisation and the organisational context of the work-place.

Induction should therefore incorporate both dialogic and self-reflective learning processes, and should be planned so that it leads naturally into the next stage of the performance management cycle, where instru-mental learning becomes crucial. Time for self-reflection is crucial. Individuals at this initial stage need to understand more about their own and the organisation's values and belief systems in order to identify any tensions here and how to tackle them. They need to achieve self-assurance and self-esteem, and learn how to function confidently and in new ways in the organisation (or new level or part of it) that they have just joined.

Many larger organisations arrange regular induction programmes for groups of new recruits rather than on an individualised basis. All induc-tion processes should incorporate a balanced range of activities and experiences through which dialogic and self-reflective learning are pro-moted. Outdoor development courses, for example, are valuable when they focus on acclimatisation to company culture, on fostering skills relating to teamworking, problem-solving and creativity, and on personal development. Whatever the form and content of induction – and cost-benefit analysis is vital to achieve value for the organisation here – the process should lead to the production of personal development plans that will contribute to work performance and personal growth.

Important sources of information that aid induction planning include:

- *exit interview records or other data* indicating reasons for early departure from the organisation. These may have important messages for the induction process.

- *views of recent recruits*. If they went through an induction pro-gramme, what did they get out of it, both positive and negative, and have they any views on whether or not it should now have different aims, design, content or operation? If they did not have any kind of planned induction, what do they think should be offered to new-comers?

- *views of managers* for whom the recruits will be working, or who may need to be involved in the induction process for other reasons. What do they think induction should achieve, and what programme would they find useful?

- *surveys of internal and external best practice*. There may be approaches to induction in different parts of the organisation that are innovative, successful and could be adapted to suit the needs of this programme. Likewise contacts with external organisations and published or electronically accessed information can provide relevant information here.

- *up-to-date job descriptions and personnel specifications for new recruits.* These will offer important information about the recruits' main areas of work, about the organisational environment and culture, and about the kinds of personal profile required by different jobs and roles. This information will also be valuable when planning basic training for new recruits.

Task 3

Identify a group of new recruits in your own organisation (or one with which you are familiar) and design a programme for their induction.

Provide a convincing rationale for the programme and an indication of its structure, content, objectives and time-scale. Note also the sources of information you have used when designing your programme.

Mentoring is often used during induction periods. It is a process in which one person acts as counsellor and friend to another, usually to support them as they enter an organisation and have to familiarise themselves with its culture and processes, or as they take on new responsibilities in an unfamiliar part or level of an organisation. Mentors can facilitate not only dialogic and self-reflective but also instrumental learning, because, in the atmosphere of trust that effective mentoring creates, the new recruit feels able to admit openly to any performance problems, to reflect on and learn from them, and steadily to improve. To avoid conflict of interests and authority, mentoring should not be carried out by the mentee's manager.

Like any other L&D initiative, mentoring needs careful introduction and support if it is to be an effective process. Predictably, it will founder if there is:

- lack of active support and understanding by all levels of management for mentoring

- failure to set clear objectives for the mentoring process and to monitor and evaluate it

- lack of an up-to-date database of potential suitable mentors, and poor selection

- lack of support for mentors – for example, through insufficient training and ongoing counselling and guidance facilities, and through excessively heavy workloads that make mentoring too burdensome a task to take on in addition

- lack of adequate resource materials to support the mentoring process

- failure to pilot the introduction of mentoring effectively

- failure to highlight benefits of the mentoring process to mentors, mentees and the organisation more widely, and to identify and tackle any problem areas.

Skills training

Basic skills training for someone new to a job, role or organisational level can be achieved in many ways. Common approaches include:

- mentoring (again) to provide support and guidance

- short training events, special assignments and projects

- coaching by managers or other relevant parties

- flexible/computer-based learning packages

- visits to other organisations or departments

- educational programmes to achieve an enhanced level of professional knowledge or a broadening of business or functional awareness.

Sometimes basic training needs may be slight and can be met within the induction period, but more usually basic training follows on immediately after induction. If there is a probationary period, such training should normally fall within that period.

It is at the basic training stage that manager and individual should agree on clear, measurable targets for job performance, and use these as the framework for regular discussion, feedback and planning of ongoing work. Newcomers to a job or role should have personal development plans, and should be supported by their managers and mentors (the two should be different) to pursue the plans through time. There should be regular monitoring and support during probationary periods. This will identify any problems as they arise in order to ensure that they are corrected before becoming ingrained and habitual. Where new recruits are left to learn by trial and error on their own, neither they nor the organisation can judge their real capabilities. The result can be low morale, lack of confidence and increased labour turnover.

Objectives and programmes for basic training should be set out in an organisation's L&D strategy and plans. Where such training is to be provided in the form of a course or programme, much of the information needed to plan the details of that event will emerge from the selection process. It is important that whatever strategy for learning is chosen, it should be adaptable to individual learning styles, as well as being capable of developing skills, knowledge and attitudes that the personnel specification shows are unlikely to be present in new recruits, and yet are vital to effective performance in the job or role.

There are three primary planning principles for basic skills training:

- *Define the business objectives.* Objectives might be to attract and retain the calibre of people needed by the organisation; to provide training that is standards-based and related to National Vocational Qualifications (NVQs); to establish a cost-effective way of reinforcing company culture as well as ensuring good standards of job performance; and to build a base for flexibility of skills.

- *Ensure sufficient scope.* Such training should be available both to enable new recruits to move confidently and competently into their new posts and to support them throughout the early stages of job occupancy. It is at these two stages that performance problems are most likely to occur. Provided newcomers have the ability to achieve good job performance (ie that there has not been a selection error) and have appropriate basic training, such problems are not likely to endure – indeed, they can become valuable learning vehicles.

- *Identify ways in which employees currently acquire basic skills.* Be aware that sensitive political issues may be involved in proposing new training approaches related to the acquisition of new skills. The process of the audit as well as its operational design and implementation is therefore important if outcomes are to be achieved to which all parties are committed.

CASE STUDY: Basic training at SmithKline Beecham

At SmithKline Beecham in 1995 the company sought to achieve all four of the basic training objectives suggested above through promoting multiskilling of operators and craftsmen on a site where there were still strong traditional demarcation lines. The divide was particularly marked between these two groups, and working practices were deeply entrenched.

Given the importance of a partnership approach, working parties made up of white- and blue-collar workers set about identifying situations where it would be sensible for an operator to carry out basic engineering tasks. Outsiders, including a senior union official, were brought in to talk about multiskilling elsewhere in order to give insights into best practice and to show the positive outcomes of the process.

There were inevitable difficulties as current ways of learning were examined in order to identify how best to organise the training for new skills. However, helped especially by winning a substantial grant from the European Commission under the Force programme (later superseded by the Leonardo programme), which required employers to forge links with transnational partners, mindsets began to change. The internal and external partnership approach helped to build trust, and eventually a powerful basic skills training programme using a mix of National Occupational Standards and internal standards was developed.

Source: Arkin, 1995

Appraising performance

Appraisal is one of the most contentious areas of the PMP. Its practice suffers for a variety of reasons from one organisation to the next, but four factors consistently explain its course and outcomes: the organisational context, the relationship between the parties, the key features of the appraisal scheme, and the appraisal methods used.

- *the organisational context* – As always in L&D activity, context is all (see Chapter 6). For example, it is fruitless to try to introduce a developmental appraisal process into an organisation that has a rigid, divisive role structure, and a culture and a controlling management style that discourage openness, the use of initiative and the development of individuals' potential. The final case in this chapter focuses on issues to do with organisational context and appraisal.

- *the relationship between the parties* – This, which is itself fundamentally shaped by organisational context, is the single most powerful influence on the conduct and outcomes of an appraisal discussion, and constitutes one of the major areas of difficulty related to it. If the appraiser–appraisee relationship is not open and supportive, it is most unlikely that a formalised appraisal system can make it so.

- *the key features of the appraisal scheme* – Much has been written elsewhere about the characteristics of effective appraisal schemes. Suffice to say here that for a scheme to be developmental it must have objectives and a process that reflect that aim, active management commitment, the opportunity for mutual learning and understanding by appraisers and appraisees, and an emphasis on future-oriented action-planning as well as the enhancement of current performance.

- *appraisal methods* – Some methods used within the appraisal process are more likely to produce valid information than others. A popular appraisal method is 360-degree appraisal: it reduces reliance on the limited number of sources otherwise involved in reviewing the individual's performance. However, although the views of peers, customers, functional bosses and other parties must all carry weight, those of the line manager are still likely to be the most powerful in determining the outcomes of appraisal.

Newton and Findlay's survey of the literature (1998) led them to conclude that the basic problem in appraisal is an underpinning assumption that an organisation is a unitary system rather than one in which there is – and it is legitimate that there should be – a multiplicity of interests and power groups. This takes us back to ground that we covered in Chapters 3 and 6. Failure to understand the practical implications of viewing the organisation as a unitary system means that appraisers may be genuinely unable to appreciate some of the fundamental differences in interest, perceptions and expectations that they and their appraisees have in relation to the PMP. Such failure can produce a divisive appraisal discussion of which the outcomes bring little if any practical value either to the organisation or to the individual.

However, not all difficulties in appraisal are of this fundamental kind. The following observations assume that there is a will to find out what is really going wrong and an ability to tackle causes in a positive manner.

Barriers to an effective appraisal discussion

The appraisal discussion, whether or not part of any formal appraisal process, makes many demands on managers anxious both to ensure high standards of performance in their units and to help individuals develop over the longer term. Common problems that make it difficult to agree on learning needs include:

- Some appraisees do not admit to failings in their performance and become hostile and defensive at any attempt to discuss them. They may see no need for adjustments to work targets, or for training or development to achieve improvement.

- Some, lacking self-confidence, have too low an opinion of their performance and potential. Others have too high an opinion and are overconfident.

- Some managers are resistant to any discussion of their own shortcomings that may be obstructing their appraisee's learning and performance. They may even (knowingly or not) have been unfairly discriminating in relation to certain appraisees.

- Some managers lack the interpersonal skills needed to handle a difficult appraisal discussion.

- Some do not know enough detail about what the appraisee actually does in the job, or understand the technical aspects of it.

Such problems cannot always be resolved, but aids to prevent them from wrecking the appraisal discussion include:

- a genuinely collaborative approach to the setting of individuals' performance targets, in order to help them understand priorities and how their work fits in with the objectives of the organisation

- the appropriate use of competency frameworks and of 360-degree appraisal that can help individuals to understand their performance better, and to identify areas of strength even in a generally weak performance (see Chapters 14 and 18)

- the avoidance of the use of ratings or rankings in appraisal schemes of which the aim is to improve performance and develop potential

- training to tackle common problems and to build up those task and process skills essential for productive discussion of performance and development needs – Haringey Council's Housing Services, for example, trained all its housing managers over four years from 1990 in the skills of performance management, with a particular emphasis on how to tackle poor performance constructively (Harris, 1995)

- training appraisers in the avoidance of unfair discrimination in appraisal, and raising awareness about the potential outcomes of such discrimination

- adequate opportunities to help appraisers and others involved in the monitoring and improvement of individual performance try out their new skills and improve with practice.

In any appraisal discussion a strategy of self-appraisal is valuable. It gives the early initiative in the discussion to the appraisees, enabling their viewpoint on their performance and their needs to be the main driving force that opens up the discussion. The appraiser should focus on listening, because the need is to learn and understand, not to judge. Once immediate needs have been agreed, there should be a discussion as to what kind of longer-term perspective each appraisee has on his or her work and career, and the kind of developmental actions that might bring the best advantage to individual and organisation over the coming period.

Personal development planning and continuous learning
Just as there are barriers to an effective appraisal discussion, so too there are often problems to be overcome when agreeing personal development plans (whether or not within the context of the appraisal process). A manager, for example, may think that an individual needs interpersonal skills development, whereas the individual may think that this relates to only a very minor problem, and sees other training or development as much more important. A manager may want to focus all effort on training to reduce current gaps in performance, whereas the individual may be trying to achieve some discussion also of how his or her longer-term development, whether or not within the company, can be enhanced and how professional development (where relevant) in particular can be supported.

Once again, process is what matters most here. There must be a genuine collaboration between managers, any HR professionals and individuals in order to produce personal development plans that are feasible and that meet the needs of individuals in ways that also benefit the organisation. Good performance must be recognised and built upon, and any weaknesses be tackled.

All action that is agreed in a personal development plan (PDP) should be recorded, noting:

- a clear distinction between job-related training and development on the one hand and, on the other, learning experiences to support the individual's longer-term personal development plan (an aspect of career planning to be covered in detail in Chapter 17)

- the recommended training and development plan for the individual for the coming period

- timings for key elements of the plan

- resources needed and agreed for the plan

- the first date for appraiser and appraisee to meet in order to discuss progress with the plan.

The effective PDP promotes self-development and so develops skills of self-directed learning. We look again at self-development in Chapter 17. Here, we can note that continuous improvement and self-development can be powerfully aided through day-to-day work activity. However, for this to happen there usually has to be stimulation and support from managers and any specialists carrying L&D responsibilities. We saw in Chapter 9 how that might be done, in the case of Company X.

Task 4

Collect two or three examples of personal development plans from different organisations (including your own, if you wish), or from a variety of published/electronically delivered sources.

Compare the examples, and from this exercise produce a design of your own for a PDP that could be used in your organisation, justifying its format and content.

Critical indicators of a developmental performance management process

How can we be sure when there is a genuinely developmental performance management process (PMP) in an organisation? Critical indicators include the following:

- There is a distinctive, well-communicated and well-understood process for the management of performance in this organisation.

- It is based on the philosophy that everyone shares the responsibility for the effective management and development of performance, and that all are jointly accountable for results that will help to achieve the organisation's goals and purpose.

- There is a sound balance achieved in the PMP between the focus on performance needed to ensure achievement of work targets and the focus on development needed to ensure continuous improvement and adaptability.

- Appraisers and appraisees jointly set targets, review performance and produce work plans. Together, they agree on how best to meet L&D needs.

- Personal development plans that are the outcome of the PMP are regularly monitored to ensure their effective implementation.

- Effective performance of individuals and of teams is recog-

CASE STUDY: Trying to improve the appraisal process

Some years ago I had to carry out a consultancy assignment for a division of a large organisation whose appraisal process gave divisions flexibility in adapting the organisation's scheme to their own context and needs.

Formal appraisal in the division concerned had an unhappy history of failure to achieve improvements in the management of performance or development of its people. Its operational weaknesses had been compounded over recent years by lack of any clear, effective HR strategy or systems to support developmental appraisal, and by a business strategy for the division that, although convincing at design stage, repeatedly ran into problems of implementation. The division had long had an uneasy relationship with the wider organisation, which regarded it as something of a maverick, performing strongly in relation to some targets but poorly in relation to others, and with a generally capable workforce but unreliable direction and management.

The new approach to appraisal was welcomed by staff during a series of workshops attended by mixed appraiser/appraisee groups across the division. In conjunction with the workshops, it was seen by most to lend clarity to a confused process, and to identify ways in which appraisees could

exercise more control and initiative in the annual formal appraisal discussion.

In the short term, appraisal discussions appeared to proceed more effectively and to receive more commitment from staff. Top management of the division resourced the whole training and appraisal process generously and was actively involved in it. In the longer term, however, appraisal outcomes proved little different from those in the past. This was unsurprising, since the original barriers to the success of appraisal in the division, although identified and discussed with management on this occasion and apparently taken seriously at the time, subsequently remained. The expectations created by the improvements to the appraisal process were frustrated, which led to a further decline in staff morale. During the following year wider organisational and strategic changes occurred in the division that increased those barriers.

Reflecting later, I could see that the consultancy assignment had been a largely wasted exercise for all of us. Sadly, appraisal, like the performance management process of which it is simply one element, cannot resolve deep-rooted problems related to business strategy, organisational effectiveness and HRM policy. At best it can expose them, but at worst it will be destroyed by them.

nised and rewarded in ways that ensure a shared commitment to achieving the organisation's purpose and aims.

● The PMP ensures guidance and support when performance falls below required standards.

(Extracted from Harrison, 1999, by kind permission of Cambridge Strategy Publications.)

To conclude, the case study opposite illustrates the importance of organisational context in determining the course and outcomes of appraisal – one of the key processes in performance management.

CONCLUSION

Having read this chapter and completed its checkpoints and tasks, you should now:

● understand the importance of achieving a developmental performance management process

● know at what stages of the performance management process planned L&D activity can make its best contribution

● be able to advise on principles to guide the planning and operation of induction, skills training, appraisal and personal development within the performance management process.

To test yourself against these objectives, what five-minute answers would you give to the following questions?

Review questions

What can be done to achieve developmental appraisal in an organisation where appraisal in the past has been a token exercise with few, if any, meaningful outcomes?

Despite commitment from an organisation's top management to mentoring for new employees, the company's mentoring scheme is unsuccessful. What advice would you give top management?

In Organisation X, the form identifying an individual's training and development (T&D) plan produced as a result of an annual appraisal process has two sections. One section is to do with T&D related to his or her job in the coming year, and the other is to do with that individual's ongoing 'personal and professional development' (PPD). Outline and justify the kind of information that should be included in the PPD section.

Useful reference sources

ALRED G., GARVEY B. *and* SMITH R. (1998) *The Mentoring Pocket Book.* Alresford, UK, Management Pocket Books Series

ARMSTRONG M. *and* BARON A. (1998) *Performance Management: The new realities.* London, Institute of Personnel and Development.

FOWLER A. (1999) *Induction.* London, Institute of Personnel and Development.

REYNOLDS J., CALEY L. *and* MASON R. (2002) *How do People Learn? Research Report.* London, Chartered Institute of Personnel and Development.

14 • Facilitating Planned Learning Events: an Eight-Stage Process – Stage 1

CHAPTER OBJECTIVES

After reading this chapter you will:

- be able to outline an eight-stage process to facilitate the provision of effective learning events

- in relation to the first stage, be able to advise on the job training analysis process and on analytical methods appropriate to different contexts

- be able to advise on the production of job training specifications to aid programme design

- be able to produce a business case for a specific learning event.

Introduction

Anyone charged with responsibilities for L&D in an organisation must be able to perform a number of functional tasks related to facilitating learning events. The word 'events' is used throughout this and subsequent chapters as a generic term. It is intended to refer to a variety of learning activities and processes: those that have a formal design – such as training courses and educational programmes – and those that can be delivered informally in or away from the workplace – such as quality circles, mentoring and action learning. Common to all, however, is the fact that they have to be facilitated by careful planning, management, design, delivery and evaluation. That facilitation may need to be done with the lightest of touches – mentoring and action learning pose particular challenges here (see Harrison, 1996a for an explanation of the unique problems involved in 'managing' action learning). With formalised learning events, facilitation is time-consuming and must plot an effective course between systematisation and adaptability.

Facilitating planned learning events can never be effective by exercising functional expertise alone, since the tasks involved are not discrete but are dynamically interrelated. The challenge for the L&D practitioner is to successfully practise functional and process skills in order to achieve *internal* and *external consistency*. The latter term was mentioned in Chapter 4 and in Chapter 6 (pp87, 130). Internal consistency refers to the outcome achieved by the effective application of a systematic approach to planning, design, delivery and evaluation tasks. External

Figure 10 Eight-stage process to facilitate planned learning events – Stage 1

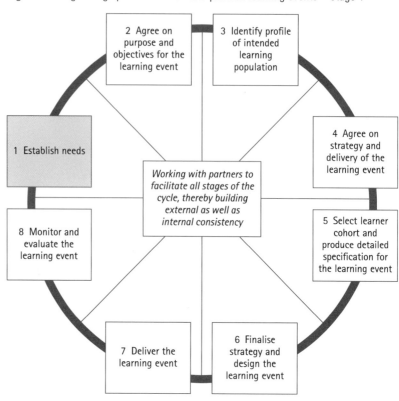

consistency refers to the commitment, shared purpose and perceptions of stakeholders gained through actively involving them in those tasks.

Figure 10 shows an eight-stage process for achieving internal and external consistency. Part of the first stage of the process – relating to identifying learning needs at organisational and individual levels – was covered in Chapters 3 and 13. The other part is covered in this chapter. Chapters 15 and 16 give details of Stages 2 to 8.

As with all processes, that shown in Figure 10 never in reality proceeds along clear-cut and sequential lines. Some stages may have to be pursued in parallel. Some will have to be revisited as new contingencies arise. Successful execution of the process requires a holistic and integrative approach to the functional tasks that have to be performed. It draws on the L&D practitioner's skills as a thinking performer and as a business partner.

An eight-stage process to facilitate learning events: Stage 1

Establishing needs: job training analysis

In addition to analysing individuals' learning needs it is also necessary to identify any important learning needs embedded within jobs. This information can be obtained through job training analysis, a process that can be summarised thus:

> *Job training analysis is a process of identifying the purpose of a job and its component parts, and specifying what must be learned in order for there to be effective work performance. A key outcome of job training analysis is usually a job training specification that enables learning objectives to be established and appropriate training to be designed.*

All jobs comprise three broad components: skills, knowledge and attitudes.

- *skills* – Skills may be, for example, manual, diagnostic, interpersonal or decision-making. They include any component of the job that involves 'doing' something.

- *knowledge* – Knowledge may be, for example, technical, procedural or concerned with company organisation. In this context, it represents 'a person's range of information' or sum of what he or she knows and understands about the job (Allen, 1990).

- *attitudes* – It may be important in a job that certain attitudes and types of behaviour are demonstrated at all times – for example, courtesy and sensitivity in dealing with customers or clients, flexibility and co-operation when working in a close-knit team, or calmness and patience in coping with various tensions. The training analyst must note any attitudes that are critical to job performance.

Each of these components has implications for learning design and methods. A programme focused on the development of skills is very different in its design and operation from a programme where the central focus is the promotion of certain attitudes or of particular areas of knowledge that the job-holder needs to acquire. With different combinations of these components occurring from one job to the next, it is essential to have an effective job training analysis process.

To lead into the next section, an initial task is given on page 270.

Task 1

Take a job in your organisation with which you are unfamiliar, and analyse it in order to produce a description of its skill, knowledge and attitudinal components.

Now identify the sources of information that you used to do this analysis, and any difficulties that you encountered in the analytical process. Check back on these as you read through this chapter.

The job training analysis process

Job training analysis (JTA) is a long-established process, described in many texts. Personally, I was particularly influenced by a framework first developed in a rather different form by Reid and Barrington (1997). My own approach, outlined immediately below, presents JTA as a six-stage process with which various methods and techniques are associated. I thereafter look at four JTA methods in common use.

JTA Stage 1: the initial investigation

Any request for training should always be met first with investigatory questions like the following:

- *Is training really the answer?* For example, poor performance may be due to ineffective supervision, lack of financial or other incentives, or lack of innate ability. If any of these is the primary cause, training is not going to improve performance, and job training analysis is pointless.

- *Is training the most cost-beneficial answer?* There may be other ways that knowledge, skills or attitudes can be developed without the expense of formal training. Would careful integration of work and learning be more cost-beneficial? Or would buying in the skills or some other non-training solution be more appropriate?

- *Are there sufficient incentives for training to succeed?* People will only want training, and be committed to it, if they see that it is important to their job performance and will be recognised in their workplace. The analyst should therefore establish how far effective job or task performance will be rewarded in ways that are meaningful to the job-holders (Fairbairn, 1991). For example, at Cummins Engine, Darlington (see Chapters 4 and 5), in the late 1980s and early 1990s employees were offered financial rewards for going through a series of modular skills training courses related to different areas of skill. However, that rebounded because it unintentionally conveyed to some the message that training was an end in itself instead of simply a means to an end. As a result, Cummins had to shift the emphasis from rewarding people for undergoing training to rewarding them for the skilled performance that was the outcome of training (see Harrison, 1996).

● *Is analysis necessary?* Perhaps reliable and up-to-date information already exists about the job. Perhaps there is already a job training specification.

● *Is the job likely to change?* If so, a new analysis will be needed when the change takes place, and that consideration has a bearing on the analytical approach to be chosen now. If change is likely, then why, how often, and over what period of time? Or is this a stable job that will alter little through time and will therefore repay the expense of detailed analysis now? Is it a job that many people do, or is it fairly unique?

● *Should the person be adapted to the job, or the job to the person?* With certain jobs – for example, those at senior management levels, those that are very specialised or those involving a high degree of innovative talent – it may be more important for the person to make the job than the job make the person. The job-holder's vision of how the role should be translated into reality, and the identity he or she gives to the job, may matter far more than any predetermined specification. In such a situation selection and reward, not training, are the critical processes.

JTA Stage 2: selecting the analyst

In many organisations it is specialist staff, whether internal or external, who carry out JTA. However, it is the line manager and the person who actually does the job who know most about the job, so whoever carries out the analysis must collaborate with those parties. A related point is that much of a sensitive nature can be uncovered during the process of job training analysis – motivation, discipline and supervision problems, misunderstandings caused by ill-defined responsibilities, and conflict and inefficiency arising from inappropriate organisation structures or cultures. The training analyst, having identified these issues, must know how to draw them to the attention of those who can deal with them, and how to influence those parties to take action. Until that happens, training cannot be effective.

JTA Stage 3: gaining co-operation

Before jobs are analysed everyone involved in, and likely to be significantly affected by, the process must be given a clear explanation of its purpose, how it will be carried out, by whom, over what period of time, and with what probable outcomes. If the analysis is likely to have outcomes tied to pay awards and/or gradings, then there must be an appeals procedure. Willing co-operation of all the parties is essential to the success of JTA.

JTA Stage 4: selecting analytical method/s

Information obtained in Stages 1 to 3 will enable the analyst to decide which method (or mix of methods) and techniques to choose. We look at four major methods in the next section.

JTA Stage 5: carrying out the analysis

Here the analyst needs to consider two factors: the sources of information to use and the depth of analysis required.

- *sources of information* – Written sources may have been produced on differing bases and may be out of date or not comprehensive. Care must therefore be taken when referring to technical manuals or to records of various kinds. Records should reveal essential information such as whether any performance problems are common in those doing the job or whether good standards of performance are the norm; and whether there are any trends in labour turnover, absenteeism, sickness or lateness that could relate to difficulties experienced in the job. Job descriptions will be particularly useful, provided they are up-to-date, accurate and comprehensive.

  Oral sources of information – eg the job-holder, the job-holder's manager, co-workers – are all liable to be biased, and may sometimes contradict one another in their perception both of the content and characteristics of the job and – very important – in its order of priorities. Handling such sources will require considerable sensitivity.

- *depth of analysis* – It is vital to decide how much detail is needed about a job and the skills, knowledge and attitudes required to do it. The analyst must also look for any problems in the workplace – either social or work-related – that could impede transfer of training by making it difficult for the trainee to apply learning acquired in a training programme. Annett, Duncan, Stammers and Gray (1979) suggested that every task in a job should continue to be broken down and described until the point is reached where the remainder of the task can be readily learned without training and does not in any case require flawless performance. This detailed method is not always feasible or relevant. What is necessary is to obtain sufficient information about the job, at an affordable cost in terms of time, money and expertise.

JTA Stage 6: producing the job training specification

When the process of analysing the job is finished and the information has been carefully checked, the analyst will in most cases have to produce a job training specification, to be agreed as accurate by the parties involved. What is a job training specification? My definition is:

> *The job training specification describes in overall terms the job for which training is to be given, or the key problem areas in a job which training will enable learners to tackle. It then specifies the kinds and levels of knowledge, skill and, where relevant, attitudes needed for effective performance, together with the performance standards for the job and the criteria for measuring the achievement of standards.*

To understand how to produce a job training specification, we need to look at some JTA methods, since each tends to be associated with a particular format of job training specification. First, though, it will be helpful to review some key learning points thus far.

Checkpoint

- Identify and briefly explain *three* of the key stages in the job training analysis process.

- A line manager says to you, 'I've got three people doing the same job, and none of them has the skill he or she needs to perform it to standard. Can you sort out some training for them?' Outline and justify your reply.

Job training analysis methods

There is a wide choice of methods and techniques to use in the JTA process. Useful sources of information about them are shown at the end of this chapter. One outstanding in the field is Mills, Pace and Peterson (1988).

For this section four of the most commonly used JTA methods have been selected:

- comprehensive analysis
- key task analysis
- problem-centred analysis
- competency-based analysis.

Comprehensive analysis

This involves a detailed examination in which every task in a job is broken down into KSA components (ie the knowledge, skills and attitudes involved in doing them). It must also be described by reference to its objectives, its frequency of performance, its standards of performance, and ways of measuring that performance. This is extremely time-consuming and requires considerable skill. The first question to ask, therefore, is 'In which circumstances should we use the comprehensive method?' Here are some criteria:

- when tasks are unfamiliar to learners, difficult, all more or less equally important, and must be learned quickly and to standard – In such a situation there is a need for a thorough approach that covers the full scope of the job.

- when change is unlikely and new recruits are fairly frequent – If these conditions apply, the expense involved in comprehensive analysis will soon be offset by the number of times training resulting from it can be carried out before it is necessary to do any fresh analysis. New recruits may be frequent because this is a category of job held by large numbers of people in the workplace, or perhaps because there are unavoidably high levels of turnover.

- when the job is closely prescribed – If little or nothing can be left to the initiative of the job-holders, it is essential that they learn the correct ways of performing virtually all tasks in the job.

- when resources are adequate – There must be the resources available (time, skill, numbers of staff) to carry out this rigorous approach.

Comprehensive analysis is therefore used most commonly for jobs consisting of simple, usually manual, repetitive and unchanging tasks. It leads to two typical outcomes:

- a job description for training purposes – This is a broad statement of the purpose, scope, responsibilities and tasks that constitute a particular job. It should contain an outline of the job by reference to such crucial parameters as title, purpose, unit, reporting relationships, main accountabilities and major tasks, social and physical environment of the job, and any difficulties that job-holders commonly experience that need attention in training.

- a job training specification – For every task of the job, divided as necessary into sub-tasks or elements, the job training specification should show the skill, knowledge and (if relevant) attitudes required; the standards of performance to be reached; and how performance will be measured. The way the specification is laid out and the kind of information it contains will depend on the analytical techniques used. However, the specification is a guide to action (because it leads to the design of a training programme) and must therefore have a simple, easily understood format and be clearly expressed.

Checkpoint

● Your senior management has introduced an organisation-wide drive to improve customer care. As part of this, you have to design and deliver within two months a training programme on 'Total Quality' philosophy and methods for 250 people in one of the business units where customer service is particularly poor. Why would you *not* use comprehensive analysis as your JTA method?

Key task analysis

This approach analyses only those tasks in which performance of a certain kind is critical to competency in the job overall. A brief job description needs to be produced, in exactly the same format as in comprehensive analysis. However, the job training specification must this time be selective, covering only those tasks crucial to competent job performance.

Key task analysis is appropriate for any type of job where:

● Tasks are varied, and not all are critical. Such a job usually consists of a large number of different tasks, not all of which are critical for competent performance. The job-holder requires training only in the key tasks.

● The job is changing in emphasis or in content, so that priority tasks, standards and identification of skills and knowledge may have to be identified and analysed regularly.

Problem-centred analysis

This approach focuses on defining problems that require a training solution. The analysis must uncover the nature and causes of each problem, and the skills, knowledge and attitudes (if relevant) needed to cope successfully with it. The analytical process actively involves job-holders.

Warr and Bird (1968) did pioneering work on this approach with their 'training by exception' technique. They developed it when their attempts to use first comprehensive and then key task analysis to identify supervisory training needs failed because of the diversity of supervisory tasks and the amount of time needed to analyse them.

The problem-centred approach is most appropriately used when:

● Training is urgent, but analytical resources are limited.

● The job-holder's work is satisfactory – except in one or two problem areas.

- It is important to involve learners in the analytical process.

It is relevant to combine problem-centred and key task analysis when designing training for people new to jobs for which they already have most of the skills and knowledge required, but where they must get to grips quickly with any problematic areas. The two approaches also work well together when it is important to ensure that the job-holders have a clear understanding of key tasks and difficulties commonly associated with them.

With the problem-centred approach there is no one way of gathering and collating the information. Whichever methods are used must ensure that the perspectives on the problems of job-holders, their supervisors, managers and any other key parties are obtained. This approach does not involve drawing up a job description or a job training specification because its outcome is simply a description of the problems and how they can be tackled in training. Problem-centred analysis will reveal:

- common training needs – Needs will emerge that are common to all or most of the group. These can form the basis of a core training programme or other kind of learning event.

- individualised training needs – There will also be needs specific to individuals that will have to be met using personal learning plans.

- training/learning strategies suggested by job-holders – These will be the learning approaches and methods that job-holders are confident will best help them to overcome identified problems.

- learners' commitment – Because of the methodology it involves, the approach is likely to obtain the commitment of those who will be participants in the ensuing planned learning events. They have to take a leading role in the diagnosis and analysis of their problems and needs and in suggesting training solutions, and so the objectives and relevance of the learning events do not need to be explained to them. From the start of the analytical process they begin to 'own' those events, and the drive to learn is a natural outcome.

Checkpoint

- Go back to the situation described in the previous checkpoint. What method or methods would you now use in order to carry out analysis needed to design the Total Quality training programme – and why?

Competency-based analysis

There is another method that you could have used in relation to the last checkpoint. It is competency-based analysis.

Woodruffe (1991) observed that the word 'competency' carries two different meanings:

- Used in a job-related sense, it refers to areas of work at which a person is competent. Here he recommended the use of an alternative term: *areas of competence*.

- Used in a person-related sense, it refers to dimensions of behaviour that lie behind competent performance. Here he recommended the use of the term *competency*.

For a thorough explanation of competencies and the applications to which competency frameworks have been put, read Whiddett and Hollyforde (1999). Other useful texts and articles are shown at the end of the chapter. Here, the aim is simply to provide an overview of the method.

Like problem-centred analysis, competency analysis is both job- and person-related. It tends to be used when:

- there is a need to develop clearly defined standards of performance relating to one or more groups in the organisation, or to the whole workforce. This is usually because lack of such standards is impeding attempts to measure and improve performance and to establish clear guidelines for selection, training, development, rewards, and succession and career-planning.

and/or when

- there is a need to relate training within the organisation to national vocational L&D standards and qualifications. Competencies identified in a particular organisation as necessary to performance of jobs at different levels can be related to lists of competencies required at each of four or five levels in order to achieve National Vocational Qualifications (NVQs) across different occupations. Appropriate learning, development and assessment in the workplace can then enable individuals to acquire NVQs at the necessary level.

and/or when

- the main concern is to identify the core behavioural attributes needed in order to perform effectively across a job sector (usually, but not necessarily, management) and the extent to which those attributes are, or are not, possessed by all job-holders in that sector.

As we saw in Chapter 8, National Occupational and Professional Standards are based on competency frameworks. In Chapter 13 we noted the use of competency frameworks in relation to the performance management process. Many organisations now base training and development programmes on competency frameworks, whether their own or imported from elsewhere.

Competency-based analysis results in the production of:

- a statement of the role or purpose of the general category of job being studied (for example, managerial jobs, or managerial jobs at a particular level) in the organisation

- a breakdown of that role into its discrete areas of competence

- statements of the competencies needed to perform satisfactorily in each of those areas

- criteria for measuring competency in each area.

Checkpoint

- Returning again to the situation you dealt with in the two previous checkpoints, why might you now decide to use a competency framework for your Quality Management training programme for the business unit's 250 employees?

Some techniques used in competency-based analysis

Although it is not the aim of this chapter to develop specialist expertise, competency frameworks are now so common that it is important to understand at a general level what their design can involve. All such frameworks involve a great deal of time and expertise. They can also be controversial, and so the possible price of conflict has to be taken into account too when deciding whether or not to go down the competency route. At the end of the chapter we look at a major organisation that did so and was well satisfied with the outcomes. In Chapter 18 we explore issues relating specifically to competency frameworks for developing managers.

The strategy behind any competency framework is to define the core competencies needed by all members of a role set, or organisational sector or level, to use them in order to define L&D needs, and to assess individual performance or potential for promotion.

Competencies can be identified in different ways. One technique is to start by analysing the current performance of a sample of job- or role-holders. Usually the sample is chosen by senior managers, although sometimes the views of peers and subordinates may also be used. The aim is to select a mix of those agreed to be excellent in their performance and those who are rated as adequate but no more than that. Following interviews and rigorous cross-checks on data gathered, analysts produce a 'competency profile' of each individual, and compare it with previously obtained rankings of their job performance. In this way, the characteristics and behavioural patterns unique to those who are high-achievers emerge. Core competencies required for excellent performance are then identified and are described in appropriate behavioural terms. A similar technique aims to identify the characteristics of effective rather than excellent performers. It involves widening the sample group to include some who are generally agreed to be less than satisfactory in their job performance.

Another technique involves selecting an existing core competencies framework such as the well-known US McBer model (used by Manchester Airport in the case at the end of this chapter). To make sure that the framework chosen is indeed valid for the organisation, it is carefully checked against job definitions in the organisation. Analysts then define the clusters of attributes needed to reach a satisfactory standard in each of the core competencies in the framework, and individuals are assessed to find how much or little of each attribute they possess. Finally, L&D plans are agreed.

Making a business case for learning events

In this chapter we have so far reviewed four approaches to job training analysis. Now it is important to understand how to use information from analysis when drawing up a business case for a particular learning event.

The business case

A proposal making out a business case for a learning event – and indeed for informal as well as formal L&D activity or processes of any kind – should be as brief as possible. It must be expressed in 'business' language and should cover the following:

- the aim of the learning event – why it is needed, what it will cost (financial and non-financial)

- the outcomes that the event should achieve, and the added value that it can offer to the business

- the learners who will be involved, by reference to number, types and levels of job in the organisation, and any other relevant information

- the time-scale proposed for the event

- how and by whom the event will be monitored and evaluated

- a brief outline of the proposed event, showing the design, main content areas, learning strategy and key personnel who will be involved in its delivery

- any prior training of those personnel that may be needed (for example, competency assessment for NVQ purposes involves the use of trained expertise).

Information needed

When producing a business case, you will need access to:

- *job training specification/s* – If there are none, you will need to draw these up yourself.

- *evaluations of previous training* – Have training programmes been run for this job before? If so, are there any evaluations, formal or informal?

- *job changes* – Have there been any changes in the job (its purpose, key tasks, etc) since the job training specification and personnel specification, if any, were drawn up? If so, do those changes have training or development implications?

- *performance levels to be attained, and the type of learners who will be involved* – What type of learners will be involved in this learning event, and what are the performance levels to be achieved? For example, if this is to be a basic skills training course for new recruits, then will it need to take those new recruits up to an above-average or only to an essential standard of performance? A good personnel specification should list qualities/competencies needed to perform a job at two levels, not one: 'desirable' and 'essential'. This will enable differentiation at selection stage between applicants likely to perform the job to a high standard immediately, and those likely to be able to perform to only an adequate level. The basic skills training course must take those different performance levels of new recruits into account.

- *timing of the learning event* – When and for how long is the event to run? How will its timing relate to work schedules of the departments concerned, and to the time-scale for achieving the performance goals with which the event is concerned?

For further advice on how to make out an effective business case, see Bee and Bee (1994).

Putting the job training analysis process to work

Here is a task that requires you to integrate knowledge that you have acquired in this and the previous chapter. It should enable you to feel confident that you can advise on and collaborate in the JTA process. You will find it helpful to read Bee and Bee (1994), chapters 12 and 13 before attempting this task.

Task 2

Using the seven bullet points under 'The business case' above as your headings, produce a business case for a training programme you wish to run in your own organisation.

Supply a job training specification with your proposal (either one that you can obtain or one that you have devised yourself).

Finally, here is a case study to demonstrate the value of a thorough analysis of learning and training needs. Although I first used it in my 1992 text, since when management development approaches have moved on, the case remains valid in illustrating how to tailor the job training analysis process and its methods to organisational context.

CASE STUDY: Competency-based management development at Manchester Airport plc

A competency-based approach to management development was used at Manchester Airport in the late 1980s in order to achieve a systematic approach to the selection, training and development of senior managers at a time of fast growth and major changes when the airport had just (1986) become a public limited company (plc).

The first stage in the design of a programme was to develop a template for superior performance at senior management level. In 1988 the directors met to agree the attributes that the company expected from its managers at this level. They were based on 15 of the defined (US) McBer list of managerial competencies, which have been found quite widely to predict success in performing managerial jobs. The role of the group had to be examined, since it was clear that in assessing what was needed for future performance, reliance could not be placed on past types of competency.

The profile that emerged identified clusters of behaviours associated with the three core competencies needed by all senior managers at Manchester Airport plc, whatever their specific jobs:

- understanding what needs to be done – critical reasoning; strategic visioning; business know-how

- getting the job done – achievement drive; proactivity; confidence; control; flexibility; concern for effectiveness; direction

- taking people with you – motivation; interpersonal skills; concern for impact; persuasion; influence.

This profile was checked against job analysis information already in existence at the airport to ensure its validity. It was also agreed that the new criteria for successful performance of the job would be used for subsequent selection and promotion decisions within the group. Performance review and reward decisions would be based on the criteria agreed as underpinning superior performance (Jackson, 1989).

All managers then had to go through a two-day assessment centre. They were assessed by the directors (who had received special training) and the consultants, who had helped internal personnel staff design the whole project. Each manager was rated against every attribute. Attributes associated with core competencies were defined in behavioural terms at four levels, from 'low' to 'outstanding'. Thus, for example:

CASE STUDY: continued

Attribute involved in 'getting the job done': direction.

Definition: being able to tell others what they must do and confront performance problems; to plan, organise, schedule, delegate and follow up.

Low: unable to confront others about performance problems, to enforce rules, or to insist that subordinates comply with directives. Insufficient experience, or unwillingness, to delegate to subordinates the responsibility for doing anything other than less significant tasks.

Outstanding: confronts staff when they fail to meet standards. Has contingency plans for all objectives. Sets demanding objectives for staff. Demonstrates the ability to organise large numbers of people.

After the assessment process individual profiles were drawn up, summarising the assessed level for each competence. Written reports were produced, and each manager had feedback sessions first with a consultant, then with personnel and top management staff. Personal Improvement Plans were produced by each individual and were incorporated in annual targets for the forthcoming year.

Jackson detailed the positive results of the project and concluded that the model for superior performance was confirmed by the subsequent success of the selection, training and development processes.

Source: Jackson, 1989

CONCLUSION

Having read this chapter and completed its checkpoints and tasks, you should now:

- be able to outline an eight-stage process to facilitate the provision of effective learning events

- in relation to the first stage, be able to advise on the job training analysis process and on analytical methods appropriate to different contexts

- be able to advise on the production of job training specifications to aid programme design

- be able to produce a business case for a specific learning event.

To test yourself against these objectives, what five-minute answers would you give to the following questions?

Review questions

You are advising one of your less experienced members of training staff about the need to treat job training analysis as a process, not simply as a set of methods or techniques. What key aspects of that process do you stress to him, and why?

You are designing a training programme to prepare a small group of employees who have been selected for promotion. In two months they will move up into supervisory posts in different parts of their organisation. What job training analysis method/s will you use, and why?

As training manager, you are preparing to submit to management a business case for a new training course relating to a particular type of job in the organisation. Outline and justify essential points that you must cover in your proposal.

Useful reference sources

Bee F. and Bee R. (1994) *Training Needs Analysis and Evaluation.* London, Institute of Personnel and Development. (An excellent practical guide.)

Boydell T. and Leary M. (1996) *Identifying Training Needs.* London, Institute of Personnel and Development.

Thomas K. and Mellon T. (1995) *Planning for Training and Development: A guide to analysing needs.* London, Save the Children. (For those working in the voluntary sector on the identification of training needs, production of development plans and budgets, and training evaluation.)

Facilitating Planned Learning Events: Stages 2 to 4

CHAPTER OBJECTIVES

After reading this chapter you will:

- understand the importance of clear and appropriate purpose and objectives for a learning event
- know how to produce a profile of a learning population and relate this to a choice of learning strategies
- understand the practical issues affecting choice of learning strategies
- be able to draw up purpose, behavioural objectives and strategy for a learning event.

Introduction

Once learning needs have been agreed and prioritised, there must be agreement on the purpose and type of learning event that is being proposed to meet needs. In this chapter we look at the next three stages of the process, as shown in Figure 11: agreeing on the purpose of the learning event, identifying the profile of the learners, and planning the event.

Stage 2: Establishing purpose and objectives

The purpose of a learning event answers the question why the event is taking place, whereas its objectives define what attitudinal, behavioural or performance outcomes are to be achieved. It is essential to agree between the parties on the purpose and objectives of a planned learning event, since these provide the context of the event. If there are errors or misunderstandings at this stage, expensive resources are going to be wasted in carrying out irrelevant activities.

The interrelationship between purpose and objectives

In theory, the designer of the learning event should be involved in formulating the learning objectives in line with an overall purpose that has already been agreed with a 'client' in the organisation. In reality, the designer may have to work to objectives that have already been established by someone else. This can pose many problems if, even when it seems clear that objectives should be changed or modified in some way,

Figure 11 Eight-stage process to facilitate planned learning events – Stages 2 to 4

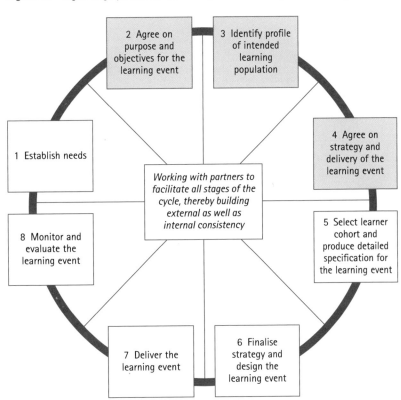

such change seems impossible. A case study-based on a real-life situation illustrates the point (p286). Certain details have been changed in order to ensure the anonymity of the institution.

In this case, note the influence exercised by the purpose and the learning objectives of the management programme. Discrepancies there started off a chain of difficulties which led, in the end, to unsatisfactory outcomes of the whole complex learning event. If, two years previously, the programme leader and her colleagues had looked more critically at the educational and practical implications of running the kind of revised programme the business school wanted them to deliver – in other words, if at the start of the change process they had queried the programme's overall purpose and objectives – then at least some of the problems would have been avoided and the resource issue would have been highlighted at a time when it could have been properly considered.

Note, too, that little is said in the study about contextual factors which, in real life, would be essential to examine in order to decide whether or not the programme itself should be continued. Perhaps it has outlived its purpose, and consideration should be given to other ways of improving the business school's ability to achieve its business goals. What is the nature of those goals, and the business and human resource (HR)

CASE STUDY: 'X' University and the programme review

The business school of X University had just gone through the external teaching review process, and one of its programmes – a two-year part-time post-experience management programme – had been singled out for critical comment. The programme had been running for many years, but in the last two had undergone a significant change of emphasis. The review panel made five main points about the programme:

1   The programme had in the past carried a clear educational purpose which had been reflected in its formalised and theoretically focused methods of assessment. Two years ago, however, the business school had decided that in order to reflect national trends, there had to be a change in focus to the development of managerial competencies (although it decided not to deliver a competency-based programme tied to National Occupational Standards – the focus was on competencies in the more generalised sense).

2   Consistent with this overall purpose, the learning objectives had become skills-oriented. However, the main method of assessment remained the formal examination. All subjects were assessed in that way, and the format of each paper remained what it had long been – a three-hour, closed-book paper, with a choice of four out of 10 or 12 questions.

3   Students who did well in the examinations and in the programme overall were consistently those with a proven record of high academic attainment, whether accompanied by practical competence or not. Those without such a record, however competent they were in the workplace and however well they did in the practical activities and assignments on the programme, did notably less well. Such students in fact made up the bulk of those who failed the programme – usually about 15 per cent.

4   The skills-oriented objectives of the programme called for a resource level that the programme leader, struggling with the large classes that she was obliged to recruit and with inadequate staffing ratios, could rarely obtain. Access to film, closed-circuit television, computers and library facilities was difficult because of the heavy demand on those resources made by other programmes. Technical support was also patchy and unreliable.

5   Students recruited on to the programme differed widely in the skills and knowledge that they possessed related to the programme content. This was unsurprising in such a large part-time programme, where the selection process was not very discriminating. They also entered the programme with widely varying levels and types of learning skill and style. Several had no ongoing experience of one or more of the core modules, and practical activities during class-time provided the only medium through which they could be helped to 'acquire' such experience. Visits to external organisations were rare because of the large numbers of students and timetabling problems. Good outside speakers were highly valued, but those charging fees were little used because of their cost. The performance of voluntary speakers was variable.

The review concluded that the examination failure rate was understandable in the circumstances but unacceptable, and noted the declining rate of recruitment on to the programme, coupled with decline in the quality of recruits. The business school was advised to reconsider the overall purpose of the programme, its learning objectives and its assessment methods, and to revise the cost and activity base of the programme in order to generate more resources if it could find no other way to resolve its resource problems.

The business school responded to the review by confirming the purpose and most of the overall objectives of the programme and by altering the structure and methods of assessment accordingly. A new emphasis was placed on assessing competencies at final as well as interim stages, mainly through the vehicle of work-based projects. Resourcing, however, remained a taxing problem not only in relation to this programme but more generally in the business school and the university.

strategies to achieve them? What role does the business school play in the wider university? What is the position of the university itself in what will undoubtedly have become a tough competitive environment?

The main lesson to be learned from such case-studies is that the designer of a learning event should always challenge its purpose or objectives if they seem inappropriate in some important way.

Levels of objective

Except in very simple learning situations, it is helpful to formulate learning objectives at two levels: final and intermediate.

- final behavioural objectives – Sometimes known as 'ultimate' or 'criterion' or 'overall' objectives, these, however they are titled, explain the kind of outcomes that the learner should have achieved once the learning event is completed.

- intermediate behavioural objectives – Sometimes known as 'interim' or 'specific' objectives, these, however they are titled, explain the kind of outcomes that the learner should have achieved at key stages of the learning process.

The reader may have noted the use of the phrase 'behavioural objectives' in the above definitions; also the reference to 'outcomes'. This is because the clearest guide to design can be obtained not so much by stating what the learning event aims to do in general terms but in closely specifying what the learner should be capable of by the end of parts or the whole of the event. By describing the kinds of behaviour and performance to be achieved at the end of a learning event, 'criterion' objectives give a clear focus to that event.

Another function of learning objectives is that they should be appropriate to the specific conditions in which learners will be expected to perform once they leave the learning event. Without this, transfer of learning will be difficult if not impossible. (For a detailed explanation of how to design learning objectives, see Mager, 1984.)

To illustrate all these points, consider the difference between two ways of defining one of the objectives of this chapter:

Chapter objectives

Example 1
One of the aims of this chapter is to explain the term 'learning objectives'.

Example 2
After reading this chapter and completing the various checks it contains, you should be able to understand what is meant by 'learning objectives' in order to be able to draw up objectives related to a learning event.

From the reader's point of view, Example 1 says what the chapter aims to do, but only in a very general way, with no explanation of intended outcomes. On the other hand, Example 2 gives concise information on what is intended. It should therefore act as a stimulus to readers by explaining what they will be able to do by the end of the chapter (provided, of course, that the learning outcome is something they want to achieve).

From my own point of view, if I had been given the kind of general brief set out in Example 1, it would have been hard to decide what to put into the chapter. However, with Example 2 it is clear that providing a simple explanation of 'learning objectives' will not be enough. I realise that I shall have to help the reader to understand the meaning of the term 'learning objectives', and then to apply it to his or her own organisational context. So I shall have to build in a variety of practical illustrations (especially case examples), checkpoints and tasks, as well as theory.

Checkpoint

● What is meant by 'behavioural objectives', and how should they be expressed?

● Outline and justify *two* behavioural objectives for a short (one- or two-day) customer care training course.

Stage 3: Identifying the profile of the learners

Information needed

Sometimes a learning event is designed for a specific cohort of learners. In that case, detailed analysis can be done at this early stage to establish the 'learner profile'. In other cases little may be known about individuals, because the selection process is to come at a later stage. What will always be known at the start, however, is the sort of numbers likely to be involved, the levels of the organisation from which they will be drawn (some, of course, may come from outside the organisation, perhaps from suppliers or purchasers) and the kinds of learning strategy likely to be most relevant to them.

To establish the 'learner profile' for a learning event, information is needed on four factors related to the learners. Once individuals have been selected for the learning event, this information will have to be expanded and the design of the event amended as necessary:

● numbers and location

● jobs and competencies

● learning styles and skills

● attitudes, expectations and motivation.

Numbers and location of learners

Numbers and location of the learners must be viewed in the context of the purpose and objectives of the learning event in order to help decide on an appropriate learning strategy.

Small numbers should enable quite individualised learning. However, location must be considered here. A small number spread over dispersed physical locations may suggest a need for some form of distance learning, with occasional workshops to bring the group together. On the other hand, it may be important to bring the learners together throughout a programme in order that they form a cohesive group and build a strong team identity. That involves a different learning design.

If the cohort is a small group from a single workplace, the best strategy may be to arrange the event around their work location or in proximity to it. Alternatively, the purpose of the event may make it desirable to take them away from the work environment and focus their attention on wider issues. That could argue for one or more external residential events.

Jobs and competencies of the learners

At this early stage it is important to acquire as much information as possible on the kind of jobs held by the learners and their general level of competence in them. Once individual learners have been selected, a more detailed analysis requires to be carried out.

Learning styles and skills

We first looked at learning styles in Chapter 13. We noted Honey and Mumford's (1992) fourfold classification. However, we should remember that people can usually develop learning skills in more than one mode, and that some learners can move – and may need because of the nature of their work to move – easily between the four modes, able to learn equally well in any of them.

Although little may be known at this stage about specific individuals, the type of jobs held by the proposed learners, together with their age and ability range, their length and type of experience, and other similar information will nonetheless give useful insights into the type of learning styles and skills they may possess. This information will indicate those learning situations and methods most likely to promote stimulating and effective learning for them.

In selecting a learning strategy – and later in designing the detail of learning events – it is important to consider not only how the event can build on the learners' primary learning styles and learning skills, but also to what extent the event should itself seek to change those styles and skills. Honey and Mumford's work, for example, has indicated that trainers as a profession tend to be activists rather than reflectors or theorists. If this is the case, then any 'training the trainers' course should aim to redress that imbalance by involving learning experiences that promote styles and skills in all four modes, rather than simply favouring the activist style.

When a learning event calls for learning styles and skills of quite a sophisticated order, and the type of learners envisaged are unlikely to have reached the required level, then an introductory input can serve a useful purpose before the main event begins. Useful too are 'access' or 'foundation' courses which introduce the main topics at a lower level than will be experienced in the main learning event, thus building a grounding of skills that will make entry to that event easier and progress more effective.

Attitudes, expectations and motivation

Even at this early stage enough will probably be known about key behavioural aspects of the intended learning population (rates of absenteeism and turnover, performance levels, reactions to earlier learning events and any conflict patterns) to assess their likely motivation related to proposed learning events being organised for them. Little useful learning can occur if an individual does not want to learn, so it is important to assess the motivation and expectations learners are likely to bring to the learning event and to take these into account when choosing learning strategy.

Motivation can be considered under two headings (Gagne, 1977): social motivation and motivation related to task mastery.

- *social motivation* – This relates to the social situation in which the learners are placed: their social needs, characteristics, problems and types of relationship with each other and with the training staff. All these factors will affect their motivation during the learning event. Take as an example the design of a programme in a new and difficult area of skills for a group of people who may come from different departments, levels or even organisations. If they are brought together into a cohesive group from the start, sharing expectations and concerns, this will help to build up an atmosphere of social supportiveness that will stand them in good stead as they try to master the various learning tasks. Many organisations hold outdoor development periods towards the start of training or educational programmes. The aim is to bind participants into a close-knit group, motivated to tackle a long-term learning experience as a team rather than as a heterogeneous collection of individuals, and to develop appropriate learning styles and skills. Outdoor development periods can also be used at key stages during a long learning event as a way of consolidating and progressing learning in major areas. In a sense they can act as strategic milestones in an extended programme.

- *motivation related to task mastery* – The issue here concerns what drives individuals to 'succeed' in a learning situation. Some may seem spurred on by a need to 'win', achieving most in a competitive learning situation; others may be stimulated by any opportunity to learn something new – a 'curiosity' motive. While classifying learners in such ways may prove to have considerable practical value in some situations (see, for example, Otto and Glaser, 1972), generalised assumptions must be avoided.

In Chapter 16 practical guidelines are presented to help the designer and trainer in the task of achieving and sustaining learner motivation, and of stimulating learners to master their tasks. Here, it should be noted that when selecting a learning strategy three points about motivation must be considered:

- unpredictability – Motivation will vary, often significantly, from one group of learners to the next, even with types of learning event that have often been run before.

- individual differences – There will be significant individual differences in motivation and expectations within any group of learners.

- dynamism – Motivation is dynamic, often changing during the course of a learning event.

Time should be spent before and during learning events in diagnosing the needs and expectations of the learners and in deciding how much flexibility should be built into the learning system in order to accommodate them adequately. This requires close collaboration between designer and trainer (if the two processes are carried out by different parties) especially during monitoring of the event. In that way any motivational problems that do arise can be carefully analysed, and the style, pace or content of the learning event adjusted accordingly.

The reader may wish to end this section by tackling a consultancy assignment that I once carried out (minor details have been changed to ensure anonymity of the client organisation). The main purpose of this Task is to reinforce the learning covered in this section. Because the assignment itself is about appraisal, you may find it helpful to read Chapter 13 again before starting, and to refer to its contents as you tackle the assignment.

This is the equivalent of a major case study, so expect it to take some time to complete. Some feedback notes are provided at the end, so that you can find out what occurred after the events described in the case.

Task 1

You are a learning and development consultant. You have just been invited to visit the managing director of a retail store with many branches across the region, in order to discuss the possibility of carrying out training in appraisal skills for about 15 managers and supervisors.

You arrive at 9.00 am and are met by the MD. He is 38, a high-flier with an impressive record of success behind him. He is already establishing himself as a man of action, committed to increasing the

---

store's turnover and full of ideas about how that can be done. He needs to make a major impact on the store, with results in 18 months at the latest.

You start by asking the MD to explain the assignment to you and to put it into organisational context. He replies that he wants you to train all the managers and supervisors [about 15] in appraisal 'so that I can find out what their performance really is, get a few standardised disciplinary procedures sorted out, diagnose training and development needs, assess potential, and get the managers working together as a team'. He wants the training done within the next two months.

He explains that the store – a long-established one – is profitable but that its turnover has declined in the last five years, and competition is increasingly severe. It has had a paternalistic role culture for some years, which has stifled the drive and initiative of its managers and supervisors, most of them long-serving employees in their forties and fifties. A few have become complacent because profits [due to cost increases and customer loyalty] are still good.

At the time the new MD arrived there were some redundancies (they had been initiated by the previous MD, but the new MD approved them) at all levels of the store, and a makeshift appraisal scheme was used to determine who should go. This caused quite a lot of trouble and has led to a belief in some quarters that the MD himself is a hatchet-man, with a list of those he intends to get rid of in the next year or so. It is, in fact, a mistaken belief. The MD is genuinely determined to build up a high-calibre, committed and enthusiastic team of people who will regain the store's hold on the market. He has already reduced the management hierarchy from five to three levels and, having given early retirement on advantageous terms to three directors, has reorganised their jobs and brought in two new directors in their early thirties who work closely with him and are fully committed to his way of doing things.

The MD's style is open and positive. He sets high standards and rewards those who achieve, while seeking to understand reasons for poor performance before passing any judgements. His views on appraisal can be summed up in the phrase 'I may not know much about the detail of assessment, but I know what I want it to achieve for me.'

He says that he wants to start off with closed appraisals, because he thinks anything else at this stage would be 'too threatening'. By closed appraisals he means that each appraiser should produce a written report on his or her staff. Those reports may or may not be followed up by an appraisal discussion with the staff concerned, but in any event, staff will not be able to see them. The reports will then 'be pushed through the system', to enable him to see what sort of skills and potential exist in his workforce and what kind of performance is being achieved, as well as examining needs for training and development. The MD adds that he does not want a complicated ranking system on the reports – just something simple and understandable.

The MD wants to be involved in the training. He himself is appraised by the chief executive of the chain of stores and appraises his two directors. He intends the appraisal system to stop at supervisory level, with supervisors appraised but not, at this stage, appraising levels below them.

You have broken off the discussion for lunch, and are due to resume in a couple of hours' time. What issues will you then raise with the MD, and what will you try to achieve during your discussion with him, in order to reach agreement on the task that you will help the organisation to carry out?

Feedback notes

The initial discussion between the consultant (myself) and the MD took almost a day. However, by the end of that time the crucial issues had been straightened out, leaving the way clear for agreed action to take place. You will have had all sorts of ideas about how to tackle the discussion. All that I can usefully do is to suggest the major issues that any similar discussion should confront, and to tell you how they were actually dealt with in this case.

The overall purpose of the learning
The first issue to clarify is the true reasons for the consultancy assignment. At present there is no clear overall purpose for the planned learning, and there is an inconsistency in objectives. There is also a confusion in terms – the MD refers at one point to 'appraisal' and at another to 'assessment' as if they are the same activity, whereas to the consultant they are quite different activities, the former related to examining current work performance, the latter to diagnosis of potential. Terms must be defined at the outset and a common language developed if any lasting agreement is to be reached between the parties.

Important points to establish centred round one key question – what is the MD really after? He mentions the need to find out people's abilities and performance, but also a need to develop fair disciplinary procedures. He refers to a need to discover people's potential, but also wants to find out their training and development requirements. He talks about a major need for teamwork, but then refers to closed appraisals. These are mutually contradictory needs. Too many of the results he wants to achieve from appraisal will appear threatening to his managers and supervisors, and will almost certainly result in their opposition to appraisal and any training related to it.

- Discussion of this issue did, in fact, lead to agreement that what he most wanted was to introduce appraisal as an aid to reviewing work performance, helping work-planning, and diagnosing training and development needs. If this could be achieved as a first step, then establishing effective disciplinary procedures, sorting out how to perform assessments of potential, and so on, could be tackled at a later date. By that time there should be more confidence in appraisal related to current work and to training and development, and the appraisal scheme would have had the chance to get over any teething problems and be working well.

- This part of the discussion also looked at what was meant by the terms 'appraisal' and 'assessment'. The MD realised he had been using the terms indiscriminately. Once the distinction between them had been clarified and agreed, many other things became clearer, and a shared frame of reference and language began to develop between us.

The learning objectives

The next issue is the learning objectives. The MD has referred to 'appraisal skills training', but what, specifically, are to be the outcomes of any training that takes place? Initially his one answer – that his managers should be able to operate a closed system of appraisal – presupposes three things: that there is an appraisal scheme already in existence to which training can be related; that it has the support of his managers and supervisors, so that they will welcome training; and that closed appraisal is consistent with his overall purpose of using appraisal as an aid to reviewing work performance, helping work-planning, and diagnosing training and development needs.

Discussion of this issue took a long time, but in the end significant progress was made. It emerged that:

- there was no appraisal scheme worthy of note; the one used for selection for redundancies was agreed to be unsuitable from every point of view. Before skills training could take place, an appraisal scheme would therefore have to be designed.

- closed appraisal, especially at this particular time, would be viewed with great suspicion. It would be wiser to involve the managers and supervisors in the design of an appraisal scheme, opening up the entire design as well as the operational process from the start. Such an approach would also be consistent with the MD's other major need – to bind his managers and supervisors together into a close-knit managerial working team: the design task could start to build up that relationship.

- if the objectives of the appraisal scheme were simply to do with work review and planning and the diagnosis of training and development needs, then no rating or ranking system related to performance was needed. Furthermore, dispensing with it would further reduce fears of the managers and supervisors that there was some ulterior motive behind the exercise.

Profile of the learners

The third issue is the learners. What are their characteristics and situations in relation to the consultancy assignment? It is vital to get as much information about them at this early stage as possible.

Discussions on this issue confirmed that:

- the managers and supervisors were mainly in the 40–50 age range. Most had been with the store since their youth. In terms of learning styles and skills, they had no management training or education, although they had whatever technical and professional qualifications were needed. They would tend to be activists in the learning situation, distrustful of theories and simulated situations unless very clearly relevant to their work situation.

- over the last 10 years, with a rather old-fashioned, complacent and authoritarian leadership of the store, some managers had become disillusioned and pessimistic about their futures. Others felt that they had received little support from senior management in their attempts to perform well, and this had bred a lack of confidence as well as confusion and some stagnation. Although the MD had a high opinion of the managers' real levels of ability and potential, it was essential to restore their original enthusiasm. Also, one or two seemed to see no need to work harder or differently from the way in which they worked at present. What therefore would be the incentive for them to do any of the things desired by the MD?

- the MD believed that motivation would improve as they began to realise the possibilities that lay before them – a market that they could start to win back, and the opportunity to become a small, high-achieving professional team with rewards for those who proved their worth in meeting challenging standards. He was clearly determined to introduce appraisal and was fully committed to it. Also, his two directors would be positive in their support for the initiative. This should do much to convert any apathy, suspicion or apprehension into willingness to experiment. It would engender a commitment to make appraisal work, once there was a belief that this was not just one more 'flavour of the month' technique but a strategy offering real benefits.

- in terms of relevant skills and knowledge, few of the managers (including, said the MD, himself) knew anything much about appraisal.

Agreeing on a learning strategy

The final issue was to establish what the learning strategy should actually be and how it should be implemented. That is documented in the following section.

To conclude this part of the story, we can note that the agreement finally reached between myself as the consultant and the MD of the retail store was achieved first by my challenging the initial learning objectives that I was asked by the client to work to, and then by the two of us analysing the situation in depth until we were mutually satisfied that we had identified the real learning needs.

We were then able without difficulty to agree on:

- the purpose and objectives of learning

- the profile of the learning population

- a learning strategy to meet agreed needs.

Checkpoint

- Identify and explain the kind of information about the learners that you should seek to obtain beforehand in order to plan an effective learning event.

- A course tutor complains to you, as the programme manager, 'I can't do anything with these students – they just don't seem to *want* to learn!' Outline and justify your reply.

Stage 4: Establishing strategy, direction and management

The learning strategy

As we saw in Chapter 3, strategy is the route to be followed in order to realise vision and overall purpose. Learning strategy involves looking at alternative ways in which purpose and objectives for learning can best be achieved and then choosing the kind of events and delivery pattern which seem most likely to achieve the purpose.

A good fit must be achieved between learning strategy, the direction and management of a learning event, resources available to support it, and organisational context.

The direction and management of the learning event
Who is to lead the initiative, and who is to be responsible for its management? For simple events, those two roles can usually be combined. For more complex events (such as the programme described in the retail store case) they will have to be split. In that scenario there must be absolute clarity about lines of accountability and responsibility.

Resourcing the learning event
Who and how many will be needed to carry out the work involved in design, administration, delivery and evaluation? If the learning strategy to be pursued is one of training courses, then internal or external specialists will have to provide these, and will need careful selection, briefing and management (see Hackett, 1997). If the strategy includes an educational programme using day or block release, there will have to

be liaison with the educational institution concerned. Any requirement to assess workplace competencies and then use those for accreditation purposes will need extensive preparation, and may include training of workplace assessors. If there are to be elements of work-related learning, or a strategy of continuous development, relevant experiences and how best to organise them must be agreed with the managers concerned. Mentoring may have to be introduced. All options should be analysed in relation to their likely cost and outcomes.

The organisational context

It is important to reflect on organisational context (see Chapter 6) when planning a learning event, in order to determine which of a number of options for learning strategy is likely to be the most feasible. For example, if continuous development through the integration of learning and daily work is being considered, it will be vital to have a conducive workplace culture, as well as supportive human resource policies and practice. If another option is the delivery of learning through computer-based technology, then (as we saw in Chapter 11) there must be an effective infrastructure for that, and thought must be given to how best to prepare people – both learners and their managers – for this approach.

The climate in the workplace should also be one that will support learners who emerge from a planned learning event with new knowledge, skills and, probably, changed attitudes. Cultures are slow to change, and those who have 'been away' on a learning event may find invisible and possibly insurmountable barriers awaiting them on their return. New learning must be fertilised if it is to take root, but too often that process does not occur because no one in the organisation has seen the need to prepare the ground.

To demonstrate the importance of these issues, here is the conclusion of the story of the retail store project.

CASE STUDY: The appraisal project: conclusion

Once the overall purpose and learning objectives had been agreed in outline, the MD, the personnel officer (PO) and myself as the consultant spent considerable time together deciding how to carry out the project. The following points emerged:

Direction and management of the project

The management of the project was agreed without difficulty: the MD would approve the overall parameters of each stage of the project, leaving the detailed direction to me. The PO and I would manage the project together, working out the detail relating to staffing, materials and physical accommodation.

It was agreed that the project could encompass up to three stages, each involving the whole management and supervisory team and the MD: a workshop to design an appraisal scheme for the company (Stage 1), a workshop to develop appraisal skills (Stage 2), and – around six months later – a one-day event to review the outcomes of the two workshops (Stage 3). At the completion of each stage, a decision would be made on whether or not to progress to the next. It was also agreed that I would determine the behavioural objectives, both final and intermediate, of the workshops, and would be responsible for their design and delivery. If it was decided to run Stage 3, it could be run either by myself or by the PO. The PO would

CASE STUDY: continued

arrange pre-workshop and post-workshop briefing/debriefing sessions for all workshop members and their managers, with special reference to following up action agreed in the workshop. The PO would also organise longer-term evaluation a year after the entire project had ended.

Resourcing the project

Staffing posed problems. It needed more than one person to run a workshop – the first would require one more tutor, and the second would require four. It was decided that the PO would act as co-tutor on the first workshop, thus reducing costs and increasing internal training expertise. It was agreed to leave the matter of staffing of Stage 2 until a decision had been made about whether or not that stage would, in fact, go ahead.

Another resourcing problem was that, for the Stage 1 workshop (on the assumption that one would be needed), there would have to be *either*:

Option 1: one workshop for everyone, with consultant and PO there throughout the two or three days

or

Option 2: two workshops, with half the membership attending one, half attending the other, staffed by consultant and PO throughout on both occasions.

The direct cost of running the first option was less than the cost of running the second, because the first involved only one set of consultancy fees and only one sustained period of absence for the PO instead of two. However, difficulties of releasing all 15 store staff at the same time, together with obvious indirect costs incurred if these key people were all to be away from their departments for three days during a week, argued for the second option. On the other hand Option 2 would take longer to carry out than Option 1, and this again brought us up against the time factor. It would also split up the learning group, when keeping them together in order to build them up as a work team was an important objective.

In terms of physical resource, materials and equipment the workshops were relatively undemanding.

Accommodation proved more difficult. The store had conference accommodation, although of limited size, and at first the MD felt that, to reduce costs, all workshops should be held there. We then discussed the psychological advantages of taking the whole management and supervisory team of 15 away from the store to a local hotel for the duration of the workshops. This would quickly cement the relationship between consultant and programme members. It would give a powerful and sustained boost to the social, as well as task mastery, motivation of the programme members. It would also bring managers and supervisors together as a team for a sustained period, away from their usual work situation, and this would be a very positive way of starting to develop the managerial team identity that the MD saw as so crucial. It was therefore agreed to hold the workshops at a local hotel.

A flexible budget was drawn up for the entire three-stage project. It allowed for the possibility of some increase in initial costings over the period of the three stages.

Organisational context

After discussion, it was agreed that it would be sensible to proceed more slowly than originally hoped in order to give time for a positive climate about appraisal to be developed in the store. The MD also decided that the objective of building up a strong managerial team from the start was more important than his wish for the whole project to be concluded quickly. It was therefore decided that Option 1 would be followed, with the workshop held over a Bank Holiday weekend because the store would be closed then and all managers could attend. Such an arrangement was not unusual, being facilitated by flexible working procedures. The MD relaxed his initial time-scale so that Stages 1 and 2 could be spread over a five-month instead of a two-month period. This time-scale had the particular advantage of allowing time for a considered decision to be reached after the end of Stage 1 on whether to proceed to Stage 2.

Developing consultancy skills

In the task about the retail store's appraisal project that you had the opportunity to tackle earlier in the chapter, you were required to bring a holistic, integrative approach to bear on the subject matter of the case in order to reach a satisfactory conclusion. Here is another task to enhance the skills involved in that approach, while focusing on some operational tasks covered in this chapter.

Task 2

Produce a short brochure to market a training course that you have designed as part of a police force's overall strategy to reduce institutionalised racism in the force. The brochure should be aimed at the kind of learners whom you wish to attract onto the course, their managers/team leaders or equivalent, and anyone else you think should know about the course.

The brochure should pay particular attention to clarifying the overall purpose of the course, its learning objectives, those for whom it will be most relevant, its learning strategy, and the accountabilities it will involve.

CONCLUSION

Having read this chapter and completed its checkpoints and tasks, you should now:

- understand the importance of clear and appropriate purpose and objectives for a learning event

- know how to produce a profile of a learning population and relate this to a choice of learning strategies

- understand the practical issues affecting choice of learning strategies

- be able to draw up purpose, behavioural objectives and strategy for a learning event.

To test yourself against these objectives, what five-minute answers would you give to the questions on p300?

Review questions

As a consultant, outline and justify some of the *essential* questions (apart from those to do with financial resourcing and timescale for training) that you must ask your client in order to enable you to design a relevant and effective programme to develop a group of people to become a high-performing team in their organisation.

When a reputable consultancy firm delivers a short course that, as soon as it starts, produces complaints from participants that the consultants do not understand the organisation and are 'way out' in their approach, what should the organisation's training manager do, and why?

When drawing up the profile of a group of learners for whom you are designing a course, what are the main types of information you will need, and why?

Useful reference sources

Bass B. M. *and* Vaughan J. A. (1967) *Training in Industry: The management of learning.* London, Tavistock Publications.

Bee F. *and* Bee R. (1994) *Training Needs Analysis and Evaluation.* London, Institute of Personnel and Development.

Hardingham A. (1996a) *Designing Training.* London, Institute of Personnel and Development.

Robinson D. G. *and* Robinson J. C. (1989) *Training for Impact.* London, Jossey-Bass.

Facilitating Planned Learning Events: Stages 5 to 8

Introduction

This chapter concludes the analysis of the eight stages involved in facilitating planned learning events by looking at Stages 5 to 8 (see Figure 12 overleaf). These involve the selection of learners and the design, delivery and evaluation of learning events.

Stage 5: Selecting the learners

In an organisational context, the ideal is for the selection of learners for a particular learning event to be a decision that is shared between managers and those with formal responsibility for the design and delivery of that event.

Managers are directly responsible for the performance of those reporting to them, and for the effective and efficient deployment of all the resources for which they are accountable – people included. They must, therefore, play a key part in deciding who should participate in learning events. On the other hand, those with direct accountability for those events should share in the selection decision, since the involvement of inappropriate participants can reduce or destroy the possibility of a learning event's achieving its planned outcomes. Such failure will rebound adversely not only on the learning specialists but also on those who have authorised the investment of organisational assets (time, money and people) in the event – in other words, on management.

Real life differs, of course, from the ideal, and in many situations the choice of whom to take into a learning event is often out of the hands of

Figure 12 Eight-stage process to facilitate planned learning events – Stages 5 to 8

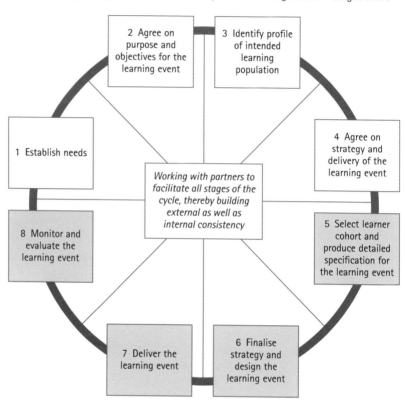

those planning and designing that event. However, if the criteria for selection are within their control, they should then identify the people for whom the overall purpose and intended outcomes of the learning event will clearly be relevant, and who have appropriate competencies and learner characteristics. Selection of learners will be greatly aided by availability of documentation detailing organisational, business unit and individual learning needs and plans, as outlined in Chapter 4.

Useful information about the extent to which potential learners are in fact 'trainable' for particular jobs can be obtained from procedures like trainability testing. Trainability tests were originally pioneered for manual workers by Sylvia Downs (1984) at the Industrial Training Research Unit at Cambridge. Such a test comprises the detailed instruction of a job applicant in a piece of work which is part of the job being applied for. The applicant then has to perform the task without further assistance, while under scrutiny from an assessor who observes how far the individual demonstrates that he or she has the potential needed to undertake training for the job. Similar procedures have been devised for supervisory and managerial positions, the most sophisticated form of which are assessment and development centres (see Chapter 17).

For all selection methods, two cost-benefit factors must be carefully assessed:

- *design and validation* – Tests and assessment centres have to be expertly designed and validated, so personnel involved in those processes have to be fully trained – a high-cost element.

- *operational cost* – A trainability test, for example, is a specialised instrument and so the expense can be high. Assessment centres too are very costly to operate, whether assessors are brought in from outside or are internal staff who have been trained for the work. Both procedures are time-consuming and require excellent administrative support systems – two more areas of cost. With trainability testing, a further cost relates to special insurance against accidents, which must be taken out for non-employees who take the tests.

There are frequent mistakes in selecting learners. The danger is probably greatest with externally provided courses, because when places are hard to fill, the temptation is strong for the provider to accept people whose needs or abilities may not adequately match the course profile. A menu-driven approach to the provision of learning events tends to lead to an insufficiently discriminating selection process. Organisations quickly become wary of internal as well as external providers who try to 'sell' off-the-shelf products rather than produce tailored initiatives.

Stage 6: Finalising strategy and designing the learning event

Finalising strategy

Once the participants in a learning event have been selected, it is essential to confirm or modify the learning strategy and design initially proposed. Although in most cases confirmation will be all that is called for, from time to time the more detailed information gained when examining the needs of the participants may indicate a requirement to change strategy or design, sometimes radically. Occasionally, the information may even indicate that the objectives or purpose set for the learning event are misconceived. Ignoring such indicators will put at risk the viability of the whole event.

Designing the learning event

It is important to adopt a systematic approach to the design of learning events. There must also be a process to achieve external consistency, as Table 9 (overleaf) indicates.

Table 9 Designing effective learning events

DESIGNING LEARNING EVENTS				
Achieving consistency		**Choosing content, media and methods**		**Applying principles of learning**
Internal consistency	*External consistency*	*Media*	*Examples of related methods*	
Systematic cycle of functional tasks	Effective partnerships	Oral (spoken word)	Talk, discussion, seminar	
		Printed (written word)	Handouts, books, flexible learning materials	1 Design structure and culture
				2 Stimulate the learners
		Electronically delivered; computer-based; radio, TV	Wide variety of methods	3 Help understanding
		On-the-job	Learning from supervisor or 'buddy'; trial and error learning; training manuals, etc; job rotation, secondments	4 Incorporate relevant experiences
				5 Build on learning
		Off-the-job	Mentoring; work shadowing	6 Guide learners
		Vestibule	Simulated work situation in training room or other premises adjacent to workplace	7 Aid retention of learning
				8 Ensure transfer of learning

In the following case, the need for external as well as internal consistency was clear from the outset, and increased as time went on. As we shall see from the concluding part of the case at the end of this chapter, there is little doubting the impact achieved by the programme. However, it was the process of involving the parties from the start, as much as the systematic approach to the tasks of programme design, that explains the unanimity with which the different parties judged it to have been successful. The importance of process in L&D work has been stressed throughout this book. Here again process emerges as crucial to the outcomes of that work.

The case concerns the planning and design of a lengthy learning event. It illustrates key points made in the previous chapters and in this one so far. Again, it was a project in which I was involved, this time as the programme director for the business school in question.

CASE STUDY: A management development programme for clinical directors: Part 1

Throughout the first eight months of 1991 staff at the then Northern Regional Health Authority (NRHA) and the University of Durham Business School (UDBS) worked together to plan, design and jointly manage a three-year management development programme for 24 clinical directors (CDs) in the region. The programme was funded by the National Health Service's Management Executive (ME), so decisions about overall purpose, ultimate objectives, learning strategy and the outline structure of the programme had to be made at the stage when funding was being sought – in the event, a year before the programme itself began.

Overall purpose

The purpose of the programme, which was evaluated by two external bodies as well as by the NRHA and UDBS, was to help senior clinicians in, or preparing to take on, a CD role to effectively fulfil the managerial demands of that role in order to ensure high standards of patient care. There were 24 participants, split into three cohorts of eight over the 1991–94 period to enable an individualised learning system to drive the cycle of three overlapping repeat programmes. Figure 13 shows the configuration of learning events characterising each programme and their timescale, using the first run of the programme as the reference-point.

Analysis of learning needs

Once funding had been obtained to run the programme (early in 1991), the NRHA and UDBS programme designers spent eight months expanding a base of initial information on learner- and job-related needs in order to produce a sound specification for the programme. The CD role was a new one within the radically changed NHS structure introduced in April 1991. It was sparsely documented at any level, and proved to be different in its interpretation and operation across virtually every organisation in which it existed. The initial eight participants too (selected in mid-1991 for entry that September to the first of the series of three programmes) were very heterogeneous in their professional, managerial and personal characteristics. NRHA and UDBS staff interviewed each of them and their managers at length during that summer, to identify needs and expectations of these key parties in relation to the programme. They repeated this exercise with each cohort, and made adjustments to their programmes accordingly.

The planning team used a problem-centred approach and role to identify and analyse learning needs. However, the needs proved so diverse that it was difficult to agree on how to interpret findings and to classify and prioritise the needs. There were three sets to reconcile:

Organisational needs derived from the overriding concern of the ME to improve the quality of patient care by ensuring effective management in the reorganised NHS. They also derived from needs expressed by the NRHA client and the participants' organisations – the NHS units who nominated them for the programme and gave them the time and other support to attend. These needs set the focus and direction of the programme, and helped to generate its overall purpose and objectives.

Group needs were derived from those areas of skill, knowledge and competency that all programme participants – and their organisations – saw as essential in a programme to enable them to learn quickly how to become not only managers but, in most cases, managers who had a significant strategic role at business-unit level in their local organisations.

Individual needs were identified both in the interviews and in the diagnostic workshop held as the first stage of the learning event (see below). They were expressed in personal development plans

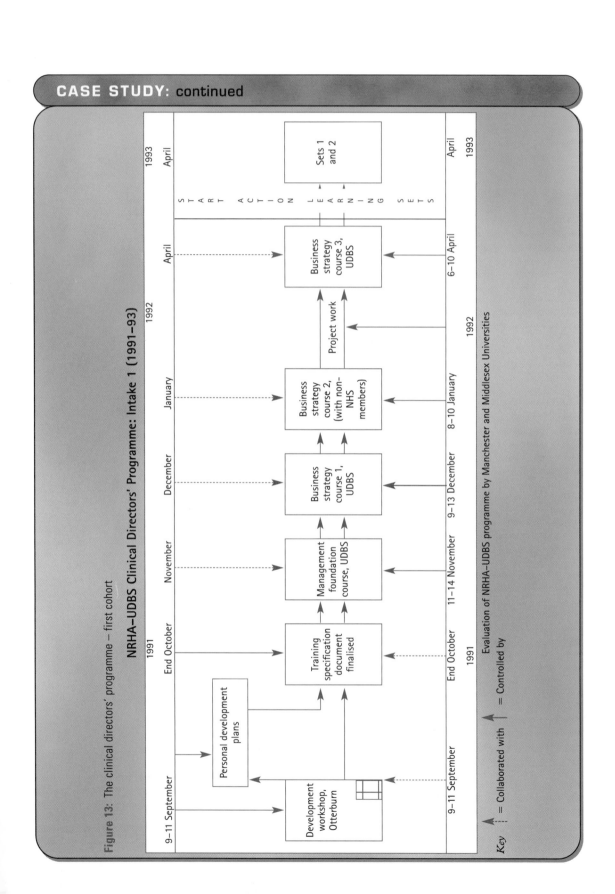

Figure 13: The clinical directors' programme – first cohort

NRHA–UDBS Clinical Directors' Programme: Intake 1 (1991–93)

Evaluation of NRHA–UDBS programme by Manchester and Middlesex Universities

Key ◄----- = Collaborated with | = Controlled by

CASE STUDY: continued

(PDPs) that were followed up by NRHA and NHS mentors throughout the programme. These helped to drive the programme and achieve objectives related to the provision of a tailor-made sequence of learning events that would help each individual to understand fully the new role and perform confidently and competently. They thus helped to ensure instrumental, dialogic and self-reflective learning (see Chapter 13).

The core NRHA/UDBS team that identified and analysed these needs was initially composed of four: two directors and two programme managers. This team was in close touch throughout with NHS senior management in the various locations where programme members worked. In mid-1991 the team expanded to include two external management consultants, recruited by UDBS for their particular NHS-related expertise, to help in the initial design process and to lead the delivery of the programme. During this period the School's programme staff had to guide both design work and a complex process of human interactions in order to ensure an effective two-way flow of information and ideas. Over the same time, NRHA and the UDBS personnel strove to make sense of a mass of often incomplete data and to develop shared perceptions and language about the programme.

There were many tensions. They related to matters of interpretation and focus and to the relative roles to be played by the NRHA and UDBS in the selection of learners, the organisation of the diagnostic workshop, and the monitoring and evaluation of the ongoing programme. It was often difficult for NRHA and UDBS personnel to make sense of a mass of often incomplete data and to develop shared perceptions and language about the programme. However, the agreement to take the overall purpose and objectives of the programme as the base reference-point in all discussions enabled differing views eventually to be reconciled and workable compromises to be reached. By August 1991 the core team had produced a draft job training specification, and an agreed plan for the first programme was almost ready for delivery in September.

Programme design and delivery

At this point flexibility was crucial, since a three-day personal development diagnostic workshop organised for the first cohort of CDs by the NRHA staff was to take place a few weeks before the formal programme started. It incorporated team-building through an outdoor development period; analysis of a previously completed computerised assessment questionnaire about the CDs' managerial competencies and needs as identified by themselves and a sample of their managers, subordinates and peers; and work on personal learning goals and plans. The insights obtained from this exercise had to be incorporated into the final programme plan.

Every programme component had its own stated purpose and three or four clearly defined final learning objectives. Within each formal module, interim objectives were established for each session. These interim and final objectives became the criteria against which the learners were asked by the programme planners to evaluate the modules. During each programme continuous fine-tuning took place in order to adapt the programme to emerging needs. The growing cohesiveness of the core team facilitated this process. Its members worked increasingly effectively together, and developed over the first year a shared language and philosophy about the programme that facilitated joint action on any problems in delivery.

At the conclusion of the formal components, each programme moved for a six- to eight-month period into action-learning sets (see Figure 13), each comprising four clinicians with an experienced set adviser. To design this component, the planning team had once more been expanded to incorporate two international action-learning experts contracted by UDBS. Again, the planning process was

CASE STUDY: continued

initially hampered by differences in views between the experts and both groups in the core team about how best to integrate the formal and action-learning components of the programme. Again, it was the overall purpose and ultimate objectives of the programme, together with the shared commitment of the parties to achieving them, that helped to resolve differences and drove that essential period forward.

Source: Harrison and Miller, 1993; Harrison, Miller and Gibson, 1993; Kessels and Harrison, 1998

Choosing content, media and methods

In designing any learning event, it is essential to choose media and methods that achieve best fit. We can distinguish between media and methods thus:

- Media of learning are the routes, or channels, through which learning is transmitted to the learner.

- Methods of learning are the ways in which that learning is transmitted.

'Learning technology' is a phrase commonly used to refer to the way in which learning media and methods are incorporated into the design and delivery of a learning event, and interact with those delivering that event. L&D professionals must be highly knowledgeable about the wide choice of media and methods, and should be creative as well as cost-conscious in selecting those most likely to add value.

Most learning events need a combination of different media and methods, and must be flexible enough to enable changes to be made if learning problems develop. Table 9 (p304) shows some major media together with examples of the kind of methods most frequently associated with them. It is important to be clear that there is no single best medium or method, whether in relation to a particular kind of learning objective, learner or learning event. Certain media and methods may enjoy current popularity, yet there is no evidence to support a generalised superiority of any one medium or method. Choice must be determined by the specifics of the situation.

In the latter connection, the budget that is available for the learning event will clearly be a major determinant, but so will organisational context. For example, some senior managers may not see the value of external courses as a way of developing their line managers, while others may see such courses as an essential part of the developmental process, and fully support them as a learning route for their staff. Information on past effectiveness of certain media and methods in organisational learning events should also be checked, as should best practice.

For a full discussion of media and methods there are regular articles in personnel and training journals. One of the clearest discussions remains that in Gagne's book (1977), which not only offers excellent practical advice about the design of learning events but illuminates it at the scholarly level, with his discussion of the psychology of learning.

Checkpoint

- You are designing a one-day workshop on time management for 20 participants. The intended outcome of the workshop is that its members should understand and be able to apply six methods of time management to their daily workload. Identify and justify the main considerations that will guide your choice of media and methods.

Applying principles of learning to the learning event

In Chapter 13 we examined learning theory, relating it there to the management and development of individual performance. Here, we need to look at learning theory from a different viewpoint in order to determine guiding principles for designing learning events. In providing a set of eight guidelines, this section draws significantly on Gagne's (1977) ideas.

1 Design an appropriate structure and culture
In this context, 'structure' means the framework of a learning event – the way it is shaped and the type of interactions planned to occur within it. 'Structure' also refers to how tightly or loosely controlled the event should be.

'Culture' refers to the learning environment established for the event – the style and pattern of relationships between the parties and the values they will be encouraged to share in the learning situation.

2 Stimulate the learners
This involves ensuring that the purpose and objectives of the event are perceived by the learners to relate directly to their needs. To guarantee continued stimulation throughout the learning event, choose media and methods that will actively involve them. Key points in learning must stand out and become memorable – in other words, they must achieve 'perceptual distinctiveness'. It is the beginning and end of a learning event that make most impact, so intended outcomes should be outlined at the start, and at the end learning should be summarised in a way that takes the learners back to those outcomes. This closes the learning loop.

3 Help understanding
Choose content that strikes a chord with the learners, and regularly check on their understanding of it as the event unfolds. Be ready to go

back to difficult points and to vary the learning pace and approach when learners need to gain a better grasp of the material and concepts.

4 Incorporate relevant learning activities

Activities in which the learners are involved during the event must involve situations or the use of skills and knowledge that are relevant to their real-life environment and roles, that carry the learning process forward, and that build expertise and confidence. Remember three aspects of motivation noted in Chapter 15: unpredictability, individual differences and dynamism. Be ready to adapt the learning situation to emergent learning needs.

5 Build on existing learning

Initially (until a strong positive relationship has been established between learners and those guiding the learning event), it is helpful not to fight against what learners think, feel or are sure they know. Instead, aim to make past learning and current mindsets an aid to the learning process. If brought to the surface in a non-judgemental way, they can be tested naturally by problems and activities built into the learning event. Unlearning and relearning are complex processes and can be painful, yet they are essential to the acquisition of much new learning. The skill lies in creating an atmosphere in which entrenched learning can become clear and can then be treated in such a way as, in time, to become integrated with new learning or – where irrelevant – gradually fall away. Sometimes the tensions between old and new learning are too great to resolve. Such a breakdown in the learning process indicates possible faults in the original diagnosis of needs, or in the purpose set for the event, or in the selection of learners.

6 Guide the learners

There must be regular feedback and guidance on learning progress. The instructor or facilitator will need technical competence to carry out instructional functions, and also interpersonal skills to ensure a supportive relationship with the learners as they struggle with areas of difficulty.

7 Ensure that learning is retained

There are two major issues to consider here – practice and rewards.

- *Practice* is clearly needed in order to reinforce learning until the point is reached when the behavioural patterns become habitual. But how much practice, and what distribution of it? Learning curves are important here. A learning curve means the average amount of time it takes to achieve mastery of what is to be learned. Curves vary greatly from task to task and person to person, being related to the difficulty of the task, the characteristics of the learners, and the duration and spacing of practice.

  We can rarely provide the ideal amount and spacing of practice that each learner requires. We should therefore select the most critical and/or the most difficult learning tasks and give those priority. Thus, for example, throughout this book I have built in various learning aids around issues that are critical to the mastery of L&D theory and practice, and also around those that commonly cause difficulty. The case studies, checkpoints and tasks have also been designed and spaced to stimulate and maintain interest in what would otherwise soon become a mass of indigestible material.

Designers of learning events should record typical learning curves for various roles, jobs and tasks. However, careful monitoring of the learning process will always remain necessary since learning curves can be at best only generalised predictors.

- *Rewards* help to reinforce effective behaviour in the learning situation, and often need be of only a quite simple kind in order to be motivating – a word of praise, prompt feedback confirming success in a task, rapid movement through to the next stage of learning, can all raise confidence and stimulate the learner.

'Punishment' of incorrect responses is less predictable in its consequences. A critical comment, a harsh word, a misplaced joke may frighten, anger or shame the learner into renewed effort, but equally may inhibit further learning. In an extreme case the learner may simply give up. There are many ways in which initial failures can be overcome, given skilful learning facilitators and the basic ability to learn. Where the ability or motivation to learn is and remains manifestly lacking, this may well indicate that there has been a selection error. In longer programmes, especially, there should always be provision for the counselling and guidance of learners in such situations. There should also be carefully planned exit-points from the learning event, to deal with the eventuality that some learners may not be able to complete the event.

8 Ensure transfer of learning

There are two points at which transfer of learning must be effective – transfer of learning into a learning event, and from it upon its completion. Past learning will transfer positively into the event if that learning can be used in the new situation. It will transfer negatively if it seems to the learner impossible to apply or if it contradicts what is being taught in the new situation.

The same principles hold true for the transfer of learning from the learning event into the workplace situation. Successful transfer at that point will depend on how far:

- the event has been appropriate to the learners' needs in their work situation

- its learning tasks have been within the capability of the learners and been mastered by them

- it has achieved stimulation and relevance of learning throughout its duration

- participants will be enabled and encouraged to use their new learning in the workplace.

The process of achieving external consistency is one that leads to the achievement of these aims. It does so by committing the external parties so powerfully to the learning event that their support for the transference of its outcomes is thereby ensured. (Illuminating case studies on transfer of learning are contained in Marchington and Wilkinson, 1996, Chapter 10.)

Task 1

You have been asked to speak for an hour and a half to a local meeting of your CIPD branch on 'How to decide on training methods'. Produce an outline of the talk, including its purpose and main objectives, and explaining how its design incorporates key principles of learning. (For further advice, see Fowler, 1995.)

Stage 7: Delivering the event

In delivering as well as in designing a learning event, the political, interactive and managerial processes involved are as critical as technical expertise. Delivery should pose few problems provided that:

- the event itself is agreed by the parties concerned to be an appropriate response to needs

- learning strategy, learners, and those delivering the learning event have been well chosen

- the event has been effectively designed

- the planning and managerial processes are collaborative and expertly handled.

Adaptability is essential. Going back to the case example, fine-tuning of focus and delivery had to continue throughout the clinical directors' programme. It was carefully negotiated in order to gain the agreement of the partners who were responsible for the joint running of the programme and to gain commitment from the learners.

Stage 8: Monitoring and evaluating the event

In contrast to the discussion of assessment of the L&D process and its outcomes in Chapters 4 and 5, the purpose here is to move to the micro level and discuss the evaluation of specific learning events. The section does not provide a literature review or cover techniques in any detail. For that kind of discussion the reader is referred to specialist texts. Kearns and Miller (1996) provide particular value because they also show the importance of assessing the future impact of investing in planned learning events, and explain how this can be done.

Five key questions about evaluation

Monitoring takes the temperature of a learning event from time to time, picking up any problems or emerging needs. Evaluation looks at the total value of a learning event (in contrast to validation, which simply examines the achievement of learning objectives). It thereby puts the event into its organisational context and aids future planning. Faced with an evaluation task, there are five crucial questions to answer:

- *Why* evaluate?
- *What* to evaluate?
- *Who* should evaluate?
- *When* to evaluate?
- *How* to evaluate?

1 Why evaluate?
There are many reasons evaluation might be required in a specific situation. Perhaps cost has to be justified, or effects on learners, or impact on job performance, or outcomes relevant to the profitability, performance, flexibility or survival of the organisation as a whole. Each kind of aim involves the evaluator in a different set of activities and can provide the frame of reference for the four remaining questions.

2 What to evaluate?
A fourfold 'CIRO' framework is helpful here, drawn from models provided by Warr, Bird and Rackham (1970) and Hamblin (1974). The dimensions to be evaluated are:

- *context* within which the learning event has taken place
- *inputs* to the learning event
- *reactions* to the learning event
- *outcomes* of the learning event.

The CIRO framework is expanded upon under question 5.

3 Who should evaluate?
Depending on the answers to the first two questions, there will be a range of possibilities here. Trainers, line managers, the personnel function, top management, external consultants, the learners and their sponsors – all these parties will have particular interests in the evaluation process. However, because each will bring his or her own viewpoint and aims to the task, none can be relied upon to be free of bias. It is here that it becomes so important to understand the evaluation task and its purpose – failure to ensure a good choice of evaluator can make

the organisation very vulnerable to manipulation. Evaluation is a sensitive and technically difficult matter of which the outcomes can be only as reliable and valid as the process that produces them.

4 When to evaluate?

There are several choices possible here.

- If the purpose of evaluation is to find out how valid the learning event was in helping the learners to reach identified standards by its end, then monitoring standards reached before and at the end of the learning event may be sufficient. However, it would be advisable to evaluate at least once again, at a later date, in order to assess how far learning has been retained and to gauge its ultimate impact.

- If the cost-efficiency of the inputs has to be determined, evaluation using reactions of the learners during and at the end of the event, and pre- and post-tests of the learning they have acquired in relation to the objectives of the learning event, may well prove sufficient.

- If the cost-effectiveness of a programme must be assessed in order to decide whether the organisation should invest again in such a programme, it may prove necessary to evaluate by reference to job performance in the short term, and by reference to the longer-term impact on both job performance and overall organisational trends in, perhaps, profitability, morale and flexibility.

Timing must be appropriate. To evaluate in depth using sophisticated methods at five different points in time, for example, would be very costly. It may not be possible or justifiable given the benefits likely to accrue from the exercise. A simple form of monitoring carried out at fairly regular intervals is cheap. Evaluation can then be carried out only at the most critical points.

5 How to evaluate?

This depends on what is being evaluated and when evaluation is needed. The CIRO approach already outlined in our second question above offers a basic framework for evaluation. We look at it in detail in the next section in order to ensure a clear understanding of the parameters that any evaluation framework should take into account.

Checkpoint

- You are required to evaluate a training course in order to determine its cost-efficiency. Explain when you would evaluate.

- Take any formal learning event in your own organisation. Outline and justify how it should be evaluated, and by whom.

The CIRO evaluation framework

Context of the learning event

This involves establishing how accurately needs were initially diagnosed, why this particular kind of learning event was decided on as a solution, whether the right kind of learning purpose and objectives were set, what was done to ensure external consistency of the event, and its appropriateness given the organisational context.

Inputs to the learning event

Here the concern is to discover how well the learning event was planned, managed, designed and delivered. It involves determining how cost-efficient, cost-effective and feasible and well-chosen its major inputs were.

It is necessary to identify and, within reasonable limits, cost the resources used to meet learning needs (time, money, staff and expertise, physical accommodation, materials, and the natural learning resources in the organisation); to assess the cost and appropriateness of the chosen learning system, media, methods and content; and to establish how far selection criteria for the event were appropriate.

Reactions to the learning event

This involves discovering the learners' perceptions of the event – their immediate reactions to it. Establishing what people feel, as distinct (often) from what outcomes have actually been achieved, is vital. Those views will influence others, including future potential participants, and may explain any motivational problems or successes during the event. It also involves discovering the reactions of other parties directly involved in or with the learning event, and comparing them with the reactions it was hoped the event would achieve.

It may be important to monitor reactions after every session of an event, or after every key element, or – in a modular programme – at the end of every module. Evaluation of reactions must suit the needs of the exercise. Hamblin (1974) recommended the use of 'session assessments' on training courses, where each session can be looked at in terms of any aspects in which the evaluator is interested: enjoyment, length of time given to discussion, level of presentation, informational content, relevance, length of the session; or to monitor the progress of a practical activity, often in order to establish typical learning curves.

Outcomes of the learning event

This involves assessing what actually happened as a result of a learning event. Outcomes should be measured at any or all of the following levels, depending again on the object of the evaluation exercise and resources available for the task:

- *the learner level* – This involves recalling not only the reactions of the learners to the learning event, since they themselves are a type of outcome (as described above), but also establishing changes in the learners' knowledge, skills and attitudes at the completion of the training that can be objectively ascertained (for example, by tests) and comparing them with levels of knowledge, skills and attitudes identified at the start of the programme (by techniques such as appraisal, tests, repertory grids, etc).

- *the workplace level* – This involves identifying changes that subsequently take place in the learner's job behaviour. These can be measured by appraisal, observation, discussion with the learners' managers/peers/customers/clients, and performance records, as well as by the reactions (see above) of the learners themselves, and how far these are in line with the views of others about that performance.

- *the team/department/unit level* – This involves identifying changes that take place in part or all of a team, department or unit as a result of a learning event.

- *the organisational level* – This involves identifying changes that take place in the organisation as a whole after the completion of the training programme and that appear strongly related to that programme.

These last two kinds of outcome are the most difficult to evaluate, yet – with careful thought – meaningful evaluation even here should be possible. Success will depend on the setting of clear objectives for the learning event and on prior agreement on how achievement of those objectives should be measured. *At departmental level,* changes that could be involved include alterations in departmental output, costs, scrap rates, absenteeism, staff turnover, or accident frequency; improvement in productivity rates, labour costs, absenteeism and staff turnover rates; or the effectiveness in some other way of the total organisation. *At organisational level,* there might be change in the culture of the organisation, more flexibility and reduced levels of conflict in relation to the introduction of change, and enhanced ability to attract and retain valued workers.

The evaluation process

It is important to distinguish between an evaluation framework (such as CIRO), with its associated techniques, and an evaluation process. The latter is crucial to the success of any learning event, because through it the commitment of key parties to that event can be obtained and sustained. In other words, it can build external consistency.

Six factors can help to ensure an effective evaluation process:

- *Plan the evaluation in advance* of the programme – As you plan it you are likely to realise that adjustments should be made to aspects of planning in order to ensure that effective evaluation can be carried out.

- *Involve the key parties* in the decision about what evaluation framework and methods to use, and in the operation of the evaluation process. Identify time-scale, resources and practical arrangements for managing that process.

- *Establish strategic milestones* for the event, working backwards from the timing of its completion (when its final objectives should have been achieved) to its inception. (If you need to check on the meaning of 'strategic milestones', see Chapter 5). Monitoring progress at each milestone will enable information to be shared with key parties. They can then become involved in decisions about any adjustments that may be needed to the programme or its organisational context in order that the next milestone can be met.

- *Identify performance standards* related to interim and final learning objectives in order to decide how the achievement of outcomes related to each milestone is to be measured. If they do not enable meaningful evaluation to be done, change them.

- *Monitor the learning process*, ideally from a point before the learning event begins to some point subsequent to completion. Job training analysis and personal development planning as carried out in our case study (Part 1) will supply useful reference-points, as, of course, will the specified learning objectives.

- *Ensure feedback of outcomes* to the key parties in order to influence the planning of future events. The results of an evaluation process can go far beyond validation of a particular programme. Bee and Farmer (1995) described how a study that started life as a simple training evaluation task became an exercise in helping the management of change at London Underground.

Task 2

You are a training manager planning a six-month management development programme involving a mix of off-the-job formal modules and work-related projects, visits to external organisations and other experiential learning approaches.

Produce a draft paper recommending:
- an evaluation process for the programme (including information about who should be involved in the process, and in what capacity)
- an evaluation framework and some evaluation methods for the programme
- strategic milestones for the programme.

Completing the eight-stage process

We have now completed our examination of an eight-stage process to facilitate planned learning events. Throughout, there has been emphasis on the importance of a systematic approach to functional tasks, and of a process that actively engages key partners – including, crucially, the learners – without whose support no planned learning event can succeed.

So now for the conclusion of the case of the clinical directors' programme. Although this part of the story focuses mainly on evaluation methods, issues of partnership run through the narrative. They illustrate how essential it was long after the programme itself had ended to maintain the active support of all the stakeholders in this strategic initiative.

CASE STUDY: The clinical directors' programme: Part 2

Because of its strategic importance in the region, the programme was evaluated by two universities outside the region on behalf of the Northern Regional Health Authority (NRHA) and the Management Executive (ME). It was also monitored continuously by the programme staff at the NRHA and at the University of Durham Business School (UDBS). The latter used daily reaction sheets for the critical first module – the Management Foundation Course – to test perceptions of and reactions to the achievement of module objectives, and to its delivery and content. Subsequently, they distributed questionnaires only at the end of each module, testing reactions to each main component. This elicited essential information while avoiding what otherwise could have been an excess of questioning in view of evaluation exercises also being conducted at regional and national level.

Finally, UDBS organised a detailed evaluation exercise near the end of the programme in September 1993 and a longer-term evaluation in February 1995, both linked to review seminars. On each of these occasions evaluative data were obtained not only in the form of opinions from the key parties but also in the form of specific examples provided by the clinical director participants (CDs) and their managers of changes in knowledge, attitudes, behaviour and performance.

The information obtained demonstrated that the stakeholders had a shared perception of the purpose and objectives set for the programme, and that for the overwhelming majority both purpose and objectives were valuable and had been satisfactorily achieved. Caution must, of course, be exercised at this point. Distortions can be caused by biases of evaluators, by timing, by the design of questionnaires, and by concerns over who would see the evaluations and to what use they would put the data. That said, evidence of the programme's perceived effectiveness was wide-ranging and came from multiple sources through time.

Of particular significance was the impact of the longer-term evaluation exercise in relation to assessing the value of the action-learning (AL) component. In longer-term evaluation questionnaires, four CDs cited AL as one of the most valuable elements of the programme. The strategic role of these clinicians had steadily expanded since the conclusion of the programme. For three of them it had been fully supported by their organisational context where they received encourage-

CASE STUDY: continued

ment, support and, often, further training and development to fully practise that role in line with their new learning. For the fourth, the organisational context had been less favourable but by February 1995 it was at last changing in a positive way.

Of the eight other CDs who by then were also in markedly more strategic roles, but who had made no comment on AL, four rated the programme's formal modules highly, although their learning had not subsequently been supported by their organisational contexts; and one saw the programme's unique value in its 'focused, small-group, safe environment to explore and experience issues away from work'. Three had been critical of AL in their earlier evaluations. Both of the clinicians who were not by then in more strategic roles

failed to mention AL in their long-term evaluations.

This information indicates the critical importance of a supportive and developmental organisational context in ensuring the long-term positive impact of an AL period. It demonstrates the unique value of obtaining evaluations at some stage after the completion of a learning event. Had the evaluation process stopped on completion of the CD programme, perceptions of the value and impact of the AL component would have been quite different, and the planners would have been reluctant to use AL again in a similar programme, given its high cost in relation to the benefits evident at that point.

Source: Harrison and Miller, 1999; Harrison, 1996(a)

CONCLUSION

Having read this chapter and completed its checkpoints and activities, you should now:

- understand the issues involved in selecting learners

- be able to apply principles of learning to the design and delivery of a learning event

- be able to advise on appropriate media and methods for a learning event

- be able to choose an evaluation process and evaluation framework for a learning event.

To test yourself against these objectives, what five-minute answers would you give to the questions on p320?

Review questions

You are an employee development manager, seeking a consultancy firm to help you and your team to design and deliver a senior management development programme, the success of which is vital for your organisation. Outline and justify *four* essential criteria *apart from financial cost* to guide your choice of firm.

What are the main topics that you would include, and why, in a three-day course on 'Managing a training and development department', to be run by a consultancy firm for up to 15 newly qualified human resource professionals from a wide range of organisations?

Suggest and justify a realistic evaluation process for a major modular project management training programme for all team leaders in your organisation.

Useful reference sources

Bee F. *and* Bee R. (1994) *Training Needs Analysis and Evaluation.* London, Institute of Personnel and Development.

Bramley P. (1996) *Evaluating Training.* London, Institute of Personnel and Development.

Phillips J. (2001) 'How to measure returns on HR investment'. *People Management,* Vol. 7, 23. pp48–9. (A useful introduction to Phillips's widely used model for evaluating the benefits of training programmes.)

Stewart J. (1999b) 'Evaluating employee development contributions'. In J. Stewart, *Employee Development Practice.* London, Financial Times and Pitman Publishing, pp178–197.

Tennant M. (1999) 'Is learning transferable?'. In D. Boud and J. Garrick (eds), *Understanding Learning at Work.* London, Routledge, pp165–179.

BUILDING FOR THE FUTURE

Developing Careers

Introduction

In Part 4 of this book the focus is on strategies and processes that help an organisation and its employees to build for the future. The career development and management development processes play a central part in the retention and development of the human capability needed to secure the organisation's future. These processes are examined in this chapter and the next. In Chapters 19 and 20 I explore ways in which L&D activity can stimulate and sustain organisational change, can expand the organisation's knowledge base, and can aid strategic progress.

Career development, the subject of this chapter, has been defined as 'an organised, planned effort comprised of structured activities or processes that result in a mutual career-plotting effort between employees and the organisation' (Gilley and Eggland, 1989: 48). It is central to the psychological contract that binds the individual to the organisation, and when it is managed effectively it offers a unique opportunity to achieve organisational as well as individual growth.

To explain briefly, the relationship that binds individual and organisation is twofold. There is a legal contract that specifies duties, terms and conditions, and material rewards. It clarifies the legal obligations of the parties. There is also a psychological contract consisting of felt and perceived expectations, wants and rights. It provides the framework for the continuing relationship between the parties. If the organisation wishes to change the legal contract of employment, it can do so only on the basis of renegotiation and a new agreement between the parties. In the same way, if the basis of the psychological contract changes during the individual's career with the organisation, then that too should be acknowledged as cause for the parties to jointly identify the key issues raised by the changed situation, what each party wants in that new situation, and a renegotiation of what each will offer to the other.

Traditionally, the concept of 'career' has been one of upward movement (Sparrow and Hiltrop, 1994: 427) involving:

- entry criteria linked to educational attainment or vocational training

- a planned structure of job experiences and promotional steps

- progressive status and/or salary

- membership of an external professional or occupational body with its own codes and culture.

Although this concept may not have changed as radically as is sometimes assumed, it is shifting. Organisations are now less able to guarantee lifetime job security and, in many waves of de-layering, have produced flatter structures. The concept of the 'portfolio career' is increasingly common, and in the knowledge economy (see Chapter 11) many organisations find it more difficult to attract and retain valued knowledge workers. The phrase 'the talent war' suggests the problems here. Such trends lead to a greater emphasis on 'career' in the sense of increased employability security for the employees as they move through their time with the organisation. This security is gained by acquiring experience and qualifications valued in the external labour market, and by continuously and successfully tackling expanding job challenges and role responsibilities.

Schein (1978) observed that career development marks the point at which the shifting needs of an organisation's people confront the shifting nature of its work. The challenge it embodies is one of matching the needs of the organisation with those of the people who work for it, and doing so from entry into the organisation, through each career transition-point thereafter in order to achieve a mutually beneficial relationship over time. The concept of mutuality of interest lies at the heart of Schein's observations.

This chapter looks first at some of the main triggers to a changed approach to career planning in an organisation. It then examines ways of building and sustaining an integrated career management system. The chapter concludes with an outline of issues and approaches related to self-assessment and self-development.

Triggers to career planning

Typical triggers

Many changes can trigger a need for a more planned approach to the management and development of careers in an organisation. The following are typical:

- *a policy of continuous internal promotion and growth* in order to attract and retain scarce skills and ensure continuity of supply. The rigours as well as the organisational benefits of the strategy of recruiting high-calibre employees and then investing heavily in their internal development and promotion have been well documented (see, for example, White and Trevor, 1983 and Wickens, 1987). However, where external supply is weak or unreliable, and the need to obtain and retain scarce skills is urgent, 'growing our own' may be the only feasible policy for the organisation. This requires a planned approach to career development.

- *affirmative action programmes*, such as the Civil Service's and the National Health Service's in relation to female employees. Their implications mean that long-term career progression patterns have to be identified and career paths clearly established in the organisation.

- *a radical change in the organisation's strategic path*, involving a change of culture that will be aided by investing in a durable career development programme. A typical example would be the need, following downsizing, to develop the remaining employees into a flexible workforce and therefore to negotiate a new psychological contract focused on the career development process.

The common factor linking such triggers is an imbalance – due to external or internal changes – that has developed in the psychological contract between the individual and the organisation, and a consequent need to review and renegotiate that relationship. The following study provides a case in point.

CASE STUDY: SCO's approach to career development

SCO, a computer software company founded in the USA, was typical in the late 1990s of many young, fast-growing firms whose rapid rise depended on a judicious mix of acquisition strategy and restructuring in order to develop new skills and products. Career development in such firms is inevitably an uncertain process. Yet the type of employees needed – with rare and high-level technical skills – have to be attracted and then motivated to stay long enough to make an impact on the firm's growth that repays the investment in recruiting them.

Macaulay and Harding's (1996) account identified the trigger to change in SCO's approach to career development as the recognition by the company of the need to change traditional employee expectations about career development to one more consistent with that which SCO could offer. Internal surveys and focus groups revealed widespread employee discontent with the gap between expectations and reality: 'loyalty no longer guaranteed security or promotion' (Macaulay and Harding, 1996). Employees were also critical of the HR department which, they felt, did not offer the expected level of support or expertise in relation to personal development.

A 'best practice' review of other world-class organisations showed the need for a career development system that was closely aligned with the company's vision and direction, that attracted, motivated and rewarded high-performing people, and that communicated well. This led to a plan of action focusing on four parameters:

- building a learning culture through emphasising self-development and career management driven by the individual

- improved feedback and communication

- a more effective performance management system (PMS)

- increasing the ability of individuals to bring about change.

The authors explained the kind of practical interventions involved in this plan:

- the production and distribution to all employees of a self-development guide containing a variety of inventories and activities, and stressing the joint nature of development in the company

- career management workshops

- project teams for specific business issues, incorporating technical problem-solving workshops

- lunchtime training sessions on key company issues

- a move towards Total Quality and continuous improvement

- workshops on managing transition

- a review of the PMS.

Their account made it clear that these interventions were not trouble-free, and that the company was only at the start of a complex process requiring management's sustained commitment to invest heavily in time and effort over the long term if the desired rewards were to be achieved. SCO saw no alternative, however, if it was to survive and grow in its tough market environment.

Source: Macaulay and Harding, 1996

Shifting career patterns

Schein (1978) differentiated between the concept of the 'internal career' – meaning the individual's pursuit of an occupational path during his or her lifetime – and that of the 'external career' – meaning the developmental path established by the organisation for employees during their time with that organisation. There is another kind of differentiation: between those types of career path that involve repeated movement for the individual between the external and the internal labour market, whether primary or secondary (see Chapter 21) and those that offer meaningful progression within a single organisation for most of an individual's employed life. In today's economy, the latter is becoming less common than the former.

A report of research by the Institute for Employment Studies in the mid-1990s (Hirsch, Jackson and Jackson, 1995) made it clear that people need help in managing their careers. It is not enough for companies to allocate major resources to self-development. There must be a strategy that tackles career management in an integrative way, and line managers must be committed to its implementation.

In those organisations that can no longer offer long-term job security, open recognition of mutuality of interest seems more likely to generate high performance and adaptability than appeals to loyalty and commitment. Mutuality-based strategies build up and retain valuable skills and experience while at the same time giving support to individuals at critical transition points in their working lives. Without such an approach to career development, 'employability security' could prove to be just one more fad.

Checkpoint

- Outline some of the trends that have led to an increased emphasis on achieving employability security through the career development process.

- Identify and explain some of the ways in which an organisation can align its career development process with its vision and direction, and ensure that the process is motivating for those it involves.

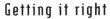

Getting it right

Ensuring mutuality

The 1995 IES research into career development just mentioned identified that organisations repeatedly fail to achieve:

- an appropriate and honest message

- workable career development processes

- a real intention to deliver.

Looking at these gaps and reflecting on the concept of mutuality, we can see the importance of four processes in any organisation's approach to career development (Herriot and Pemberton, 1995):

- informing
- negotiating
- monitoring
- renegotiating and/or exiting.

Informing

The provision of information should be a continuous process, starting at recruitment. The aim is to keep organisation and individual informed about what each expects of the other now and in the future. Vehicles for such information-sharing include the induction process, mentoring, appraisal discussions, employee satisfaction surveys and personal development plans.

Negotiating

This process should occur whenever employees' wants and needs significantly alter. Such a change may happen because of some altered personal circumstance on the individual's side, or on the organisation's side because of necessary changes in business goals and strategy, workplace environment or human resource (HR) policies.

Monitoring

There is a need for continuous checking to ensure that new skills and knowledge are being developed through a pattern of career paths that meet emergent organisational, team and individual needs.

Renegotiating and/or exiting

Disengagement or redeployment of individuals, whatever its cause, should be achieved with fairness, with mutual respect, and with supportive HR processes. I look at some ways in which this can be done in Chapter 19. There should be strategies to retain for as long as possible those whose skills, knowledge and disposition make them vital to the future of the organisation. This will also help to build a reputation in the labour market of being a fair employer with a genuine concern for employees' futures.

Critical success factors

It is commonly in the area of succession planning that organisations focus most of their career development effort. However, the organisation's career management process should be wider than that in its scope. Six factors are critical to its success:

- It must be a transparent process, to which line managers have real commitment.
- It must be a process that can evolve through time and is integrated with existing HR systems, ensuring fair operation of the internal labour market.

- It must be based on full information about people's career expectations and about business needs. This should ensure that the organisation has committed people in the right roles at the right time, with their capability for the future identified, developed and safeguarded.

- There must be measurement and monitoring of standards to show whether the system works.

- There must be clear communication to all employees about development processes and responsibilities and about career paths.

- There must be support for employees in planning their development.

Mayo (1994) observed that career management is made more difficult when an organisation has to operate in a rapidly changing and unpredictable world and in situations where there are structural trends such as flatter organisations, decentralised profit centres and elimination of central overheads. Nonetheless, as his many examples demonstrate, given strong direction from the top and effective integration of career development policy with business and human resource policy, much can be achieved.

Checkpoint

- How can some of the most common weaknesses in the management of the career development process be tackled?

- A senior colleague says to you, 'Look, I'm all for good career development in this organisation, but we've got to get it right. Tell me some of the critical success factors we should aim for.' Identify and justify *three* such factors.

Building integration

Strategic integration

For career management to be a coherent process rather than simply responding in *ad hoc* ways to each changing situation, it needs to be integrated at corporate, unit and operational levels of the organisation (Hall, 1984). Line managers as well as top management should appreciate that the career management process must be strategically driven if it is to bring real benefits to the organisation as well as to individuals.

- *At corporate level* it should be part of business strategy and planning, where it should be the direct responsibility of senior management. Only in this way can there be full commitment to developing objectives and a policy for career development throughout the organisation, and means to ensure that that policy is implemented. At this level the framework for career development is set by the decisions made about work to be done, the structure required for the organisation, the roles needed within the structure and the goals to be achieved across the organisation.

- *At business-unit level* it should be a formal part of the managerial role to carry responsibility for career development of employees. This responsibility should therefore be a key result area on which managers are appraised, and for which they are trained and recognised. The skills they need to acquire are those related to job design, career coaching and counselling, succession planning, the giving of feedback and the assessment of potential. Managers, working in partnership with the HR function (if there is one), can enhance career development by arranging job movements, including inter-unit co-operative arrangements such as transfers, secondments, special projects and other assignments.

- *At individual level* there should be a process of joint career planning that involves individual and manager (or some other person or body responsible for career development in the organisation) in exchanging information about wants and expectations, and in negotiating ways in which individuals' careers can be progressed to meet their and the organisation's needs.

Human resource policy integration
Schein (1978) showed how the HR system can act as the repository of those key processes by which the aims and interests of organisation and individual are matched. He suggested that a central integrative body (often a career or personnel development committee) should develop company-wide policy, systems and procedures for career development. Evaluation of career development activity can then reveal whether the system is achieving its success criteria, and whether chosen development programmes and other activities are providing the most mutually beneficial growth paths for individuals and for the organisation. This is particularly important when the organisation is undergoing fundamental restructuring leading to new pay systems and the identification of new competencies.

Operational integration
Some of the most intractable problems in developing career paths in an organisation are to do with trying to ensure consistency from one occupational or professional group to the next. In organisations like the NHS and the Civil Service the complexity of the occupational structure makes integration in this sense very difficult. Each group has its own historical patterns of recruitment, training, pay, and terms and conditions of service. Many have their own negotiating rights.

There are also taxing issues related to ensuring full access to career paths for minority groups in the organisation, whether in full-time or part-time positions; and about how to manage career breaks not only for women wishing to leave temporarily to have children (Hirsh, 1985) but – of increasing relevance given today's demographics – for those who have responsibility for the care of elderly family members. Few European companies have thought much about elder-care policies, comparing poorly in this respect with large US companies (Goodhart, 1994). However they tend to be more progressive in career-break policies that are sensitive to the stress factors involved in combining a full-time career with childbearing or elder-care, and to the adverse affects on productivity and performance that can result.

The integration of international career development planning into a company's career management process is a field of study in its own right. The literature is growing (see especially Sparrow and Hiltrop, 1994) as penetration of international markets increases. In leading European organisations career development has become the major challenge in human resource management (Evans, 1992), international careers becoming a common feature for so many senior, and even middle, managers. In this chapter there is no space to consider such issues in more detail. Readers are instead referred to specialist texts.

To summarise: without carefully planned integration at corporate level, all that will result from joint action planning at unit or operational levels of the organisation is a proliferation of initiatives without any overall coherency or purpose, bringing frustrated expectations as action fails to materialise. Schein (1978) quoted the example of a manager and employee agreeing that a functional move would be to the individual's benefit – but failing to set up any process or resource to evaluate the wider benefits such a move might bring, or to ensure that it could be implemented, monitored and evaluated. The HR or L&D function (or both) have key tasks to perform in carrying out those wider, integrating roles, as the next section illustrates.

The career planning system

Career transition points

From our examination thus far it can be seen that five different kinds of planning are needed to produce a planning system that enables the career management process to achieve its aims in an organisation. They are shown in Table 10 (overleaf).

Table 10 shows how the career development process can be built around key transition points in people's careers. At such points, it is important to develop a set of shared values and renegotiate, if necessary, the psychological contract between organisation and individual in order to promote mutual benefit. There should be strategies to blend on-the-job and other informal developmental processes with more formal development experiences at each career phase.

Table 10 makes it clear that the HR planners, L&D staff, management and the individual all have roles to play in ensuring that the needs and

Table 10 Integrating organisational and career development

HR planning	HR activity	Learning strategies	Career transition points
For staffing	Job analysis, job design. Audit of skills. Deploying personnel to build up a cohesive internal labour market.	Induction and basic skills training.	Entry to organisation.
For performance management and development	Establishing desired performance levels. Improving performance. Facilitating continuous development. Establishing reward systems. Assessment of potential. Planned approach to career development.	Coaching, mentoring and continuous feedback. Performance review and appraisal. Continuous learning and self-development. Promotions, job movement and access to continuing education and training opportunities.	Progress within particular areas of work. Mid-career with the organisation.
For change	New internal skills audit. Re-analysis of patterns of skill supply in external labour market. New balancing of skills and capabilities to adapt to changed internal and external situation. Achievement of consistency with wider HR policies and systems to facilitate and support change.	Retraining of individuals, teams, management sectors. Organisation development programmes to achieve cultural change and the development of new organisational and individual capabilities.	Changes in psychological contract with the organisation.
For levelling off and disengagement	Career counselling, joint planning, job redesign, disengagement counselling and planning.	Using experience and wisdom of those nearing final stages of their career with the organisation.	Later career with the organisation.
For replacement and restaffing	Policies to ensure retention of strategic capability of the organisation at corporate, unit and individual levels. Integrative approach to disengagement and new recruitment.	Supportive disengagement strategies and timely phasing in of new internal and external recruits.	End of career with the organisation. Retirement or return to the external labour market.

(Suggested by Schein, 1978: 201.)

aspirations of the individual are linked productively to those of the organisation in a continuous cycle of activity. For the career development process to be effective it must be simple, visible, fully accessible and well communicated.

In this cycle of activity, mid- and late-career stages can be particularly difficult to manage (Lewis and McLaverty, 1991). It is essential not only to facilitate the continued development of the high-fliers but also to help those unable to move up, on or out to see that they still have 'careers' in the sense of meaningful work, challenges and opportunities for achievement. The stimulation and growth of those who have reached their job ceiling can be enhanced by such developmental strategies as job rotation, cross-functional moves, job redesign, recognition and rewards for effective performance and for innovatory activity, and temporary assignments outside the company, including consultancy opportunities. More career-mobile employees should be kept informed about corporate career opportunities and high-level technical or professional positions available elsewhere in the company.

As some employees move towards the end of their careers with the organisation, it is important that the effects of low morale and stress caused by preoccupation with their forthcoming disengagement do not spread through the rest of the workforce. This is especially difficult in times of downsizing and redundancy, so it is essential in those scenarios to have positive career planning strategies in place (see Chapter 19).

The retirement challenge

It is estimated that by the year 2030 in the 18 Western European member-states of the Organisation for Economic Co-operation and Development (OECD), the size of the over-65 age-group will have risen to 70 million, compared with 50 million in 1990 (Willman, 1994). Over the same period the number of people of working age is likely to have fallen to fewer than three for every person aged 65, compared with five in 1994. These trends are similar across all leading world economies, but are much less marked in newly industrialised countries. The economic impact will be radical, but so complex as to be impossible to predict with any accuracy. The most likely outcome, however, will be a marked shift in competitive advantage from the old to the newly industrialised countries.

As Willman (1994) observed, once the flow of young people into organisations begins to diminish, so there will be a corresponding need to hold on to older workers and to attract back into employment those currently not in the labour market. Consumers too will be ageing, and so products and services will have to meet their distinctive needs. Retirement policies, once relatively simple and attracting little of management's attention (except in those organisations that advertised their status as benevolent employers) will have to carry a heavier burden of bottom-line responsibility. They will have the potential to make a direct negative or positive impact on a company's ability to remain competitive.

In the past in the UK, Inland Revenue rules have discouraged gradual retirement, even though such a strategy can mitigate most of the negative aspects of early retirement for the organisation and the individual. By the late 1990s, however, changes were opening up a range of possibilities for phased, partial or part-time retirement in the UK as in so many EU member countries. Imaginative planning can minimise organisational and personal disruption, help individuals to manage disengagement effectively, and ensure that those vital to the organisation's continued strategic capability are retained and remain committed to their work and roles (Reday-Mulvey and Taylor, 1996).

Task 1

Identify the career paths open to one or two occupational groups in your own organisation.

Analyse how far those paths are integrated into an overall planned career management system, and assess the extent to which that system meets the six critical success factors noted earlier in this chapter.

What are the main actions needed to improve the planning and/or operation of the system?

(*Before tackling this Task you may find it helpful to read Schein, 1978, Chapter 14.*)

Formal assessment processes

At the heart of any career management system there must be a process of assessment to establish the career needs and identify the potential of individuals.

Such assessment can be carried out in a variety of ways, through systems established by the organisation and/or processes initiated by the individual. In the former category, the appraisal process has an important role to play in identifying the career development objectives and proposed plans of an individual and in offering a vehicle for manager and individual to agree on appropriate action. (This was described in Chapter 13.) However, the formal appraisal discussion is not an adequate or appropriate occasion for comprehensive assessment of potential. Let us therefore now look at assessment and development centres.

Assessment and development centre methodologies

Stevens (1985) provided a definition of an assessment centre:

An assessment centre is a systematic approach to identifying precisely what is required for success in a particular job and then labelling these requirements in terms of a short-list of tightly defined criteria. Leadership, integrity, tenacity and team-building skill are typical criteria which might be included for a management position.

An assessment centre typically combines a series of exercises. As they tackle these, participants are observed by a trained team – usually, but not always, of company managers – whose members subsequently pool and discuss their information in order to reach as objective an assessment as possible of each individual. The aim is to ensure the identification of those who most closely fit the requirements of the job, and to build up a list of individuals' training and development needs.

Dulewicz (1991) noted many problems commonly associated with this methodology – poor design of exercises, inexpert assessors, lack of commitment of managers to ensuring transfer of learning to the workplace, and lack of long-term monitoring. He recommended the appointment of a mentor for each participant and concluded that the critical factor was the commitment of the individual, and how much the participant does to develop himself or herself.

Such accounts, while demonstrating some of the difficulties involved in the use of assessment centre technology, also provide evidence of their advantages, which typically include:

- *improved decision-making* – Decisions relating to the selection, transfer, promotion and training needs of staff are based on substantially more 'facts' than in the past.

- *improved feedback* – Assessment centre methodology offers an increased opportunity for meaningful feedback related to performance and potential, and this is especially valuable in relation to career and other counselling services.

You may have noticed that although the heading for this section includes reference to development centres, I have so far only discussed the use of assessment centres. What is the difference between the two? In both types of centre, groups of participants take part in a variety of job simulations, tests and exercises with observers who assess their performance against a number of predetermined job-related dimensions. If the collected data are used to diagnose individual training needs, facilitate self-development or provide part of an organisational development audit, then the most appropriate description would be *development centre* (Rodger and Mabey, 1987). If, however, the data are used primarily to feed into decisions about promotion or some other form of employee redeployment, the term *assessment centre* is more relevant.

It is essential that employees do not confuse the two. Bower (1991) told how Rover's assessment centres, used primarily for selection during the 1980s, brought only mixed success. Their decision to shift from assessment to development centres using competence-based criteria proved more successful because it gave 'greater visibility and credibility to the process, and ... spin-off benefits in performance appraisal, training objectives and for succession and development planning purposes'.

Career anchors

Development centres can offer a particularly valuable opportunity for the individual to clarify career anchors, notably by bringing personal values and motivation to the surface. Schein (1978) used the concept of career anchors to highlight the importance of the individual's self-perceived talents, motives and values in determining career-choice path. He identified five types of anchor:

- technical functional competence

- managerial competence

- security

CASE STUDY: Career planning at Allied Domecq Spirits and Wine

John Refausse, HR director (customer services and development) at Allied Domecq Spirits and Wine, described a career planning workshop, introduced in 1995 as part of a much wider programme of organisational change following some years of re-engineering and far-reaching strategic change in an international company formed by the acquisition of Allied Lyons – the mainly UK-based firm – and the Domecq group. Flatter management structures, significant job changes and movement into new markets all meant that there was a mismatch between organisational needs and expectations and those of individuals. In a climate of uncertainty for the business as well as for its workforce it was seen in the mid-1990s to be essential to help people adjust to the changes and become less focused on job security, more capable of planning their own future careers.

The workshop was piloted in 1995 for senior middle managers who confronted such uncertainties. Its aims were to help them 'take stock of their own achievements, identify the factors that had contributed to their past successes and understand how they matched up against the core competencies of the business' (Refausse, 1996).

Development centre methodology enabled participants to generate and handle a wealth of information that clarified their career anchors and helped them to assess these, and produce development plans and statements of their career aspirations. The workshop enabled individuals to gain insights into their fundamental motivation and talents, and into the past career choices they had made. This in turn 'helped them to look at their current roles and consider how these might be made to fit their aspirations and needs more closely' (*ibid.*).

Refausse described motivational outcomes for most of the eight participants. Two negotiated major career moves shortly afterwards: one, managing director of a wine subsidiary, achieved greater autonomy from her line manager; another applied successfully for promotion from a specialist to a general managerial post, having discovered during the workshop a 'creative professional' career anchor that he had never previously identified or considered.

Source: Refausse, 1996

- autonomy

- creativity.

Each anchor reflects a different type of underlying motive, need, values and perceived as well as discovered talents in the individual. Each is determined in part by experience and opportunity, and in part by latent talents and motives. A career anchor is thus significantly affected by those four processes to which attention has been drawn earlier in this chapter – informing, negotiating, monitoring and renegotiating. It may change or be reinforced at each of the main transition-points through which the individual's career in the organisation passes between entry and exit. The case study on p336 focuses on a 'career anchor' approach.

Ensuring value from development centres
Accounts of innovative and apparently successful development centres abound. To assess their true value, however, they ought to be followed up through time, and the views of participants as well as of observers and the organisation should be obtained. Iles and Mabey (1993), commenting on a range of empirical studies, found that some career development practices tended to be much better regarded by recipients than others, and that development centres, psychometric tests with feedback, and career review with superiors were particularly well viewed. The reasons were revealing:

- focus on the future as much as on the past and present

- promotion of reflection and insight as well as measurement of skills or competencies

- two-way, collaborative processes

- overt, with participants able to see clear evidence for assessments

- realistic, not only on account of the methodology used but also because managers were involved as assessors and because of the focus on the actual career criteria and activities used in the organisation.

Many of the 'third-generation' centres set up purely to develop people and therefore avoiding any focus on assessment for other purposes had run into difficulty by the late 1990s on grounds of affordability. As Woodruffe (1997) observed, there was a growing concern in some organisations to move away from that sole focus on development and to use the information generated by a centre also to 'influence their decisions about participants' careers and to decide on the further development that an individual will be offered'. This hybrid approach, which for participants may raise fears of assessment and selection for promotion and therefore of a divisive element, is the more likely in organisations whose approach to performance management tends towards the control rather than development end of the spectrum – as we saw in Chapter 13. Woodruffe's article provided helpful advice on how to mitigate the most demotivating effects of such hybrids when they are unavoidable (see also Woodruffe, 2000).

Six principles should guide the use of assessment and development centres.

- *Place the methodology in context* – The use of development centres must be placed in a firm context of major training and development programmes so that they are seen to be a positive aid, not a threat, to all who go through them.

- *Involve management* – Line management must be involved from the start in the development and operation of assessment/development centre methodology.

- *Ensure that there is expertise* – There must be a high level of skill in the design and operation of assessment and development centres and in the handling of feedback to participants. Dulewicz's article (1991) shows the damage that can be caused if this expertise is lacking.

- *Ensure openness, honesty and confidentiality* – Trust and commitment of the parties can be assured only if there is clarity and agreement about the true purpose – or purposes – of a centre, about who will have access to the information produced by the assessment processes, and about how that information will be used.

- *Achieve action* – The methodology must lead to action although, as Rodger and Mabey (1987) observed, 'for a whole host of reasons development activities may not happen immediately'.

- *Evaluate* – The results achieved by the use of such methodology must be evaluated, including analysis of the effects its introduction has had on personnel at various levels in the organisation.

Checkpoint

- Your senior management is interested in using assessment centre methodology in order to improve the career development process. What cautionary advice do you give, and why?

- A management colleague who is discussing concepts of career development with you says, 'You keep referring to "assessment centres" and "development centres". Are they two different things?' Outline a helpful reply.

Self-development

Self-development encourages active ownership of the career development process by the individual. However, taking responsibility for one's own development is not an easy matter. It requires an informed and objective assessment of the kind of skills and experience that will be relevant for the future, together with access to opportunities to develop those skills and acquire that experience. Where the future is impossible to predict, it will be difficult for the individual to find a focus for self-development in which he or she can feel confidence – yet it is precisely in that kind of scenario that taking responsibility for one's own learning becomes so important.

Self-assessment

The first step to take is to assess the individual's learning needs. This can be carried out by individuals on their own or with the help of others. Pedler, Burgoyne and Boydell (1978) recommended a four-stage process:

- *self-assessment* – This must be preceded by careful analysis on the part of individuals of their work and life situations. Self-assessment of learning needs then falls into an appropriate context.

- *diagnosis* – This is the stage of identifying the individuals' learning needs and putting them in an order of priority.

- *action planning* – This covers the identification of objectives, and of aids and hindrances to action, the determination of resources (including people) needed to carry out the action plan, and a timescale.

- *monitoring and review* – The individuals, either on their own or with the support of their managers or mentors, should determine how and at what points in time to monitor and review progress.

Self-assessment involves individuals in self-rating each area of skill in their job, and/or in each area of occupational competence. Questionnaires to facilitate the process can be completed by individuals working alone or with someone else. Tackling self-assessment with the help of another has the secondary advantage of developing diagnostic and counselling skills in that partner who, in the process of questioning, also has to practise and learn more about those skills of observation, listening, discussion and appraisal that are vital to the good coach. It is essential to identify barriers as well as aids to self-development, and to plan how best to tackle or use them.

Self-development

Companies like Company X (case study, Chapter 9) achieve a powerful organisational focus on self-development by making it core to their business and HR strategies that employees take responsibility for the process as part of their career development. As may be seen from re-reading that case study (p177), managers have clearly defined respon-sibilities to promote and facilitate that self-development process.

Many organisations now provide specific resources and facilities to aid self-development. These include:

- personal and career development workshops and seminars to encourage individuals to take responsibility for their careers

- resource centres giving access to a variety of facilities for self-directed and self-paced learning at the company's expense, although in the employee's time. Such centres can offer occu-pational guides, educational references, computerised self-assess-ment questionnaires and other diagnostic instruments to help people consider their career interests, values and competence, together with computerised educational and training programmes (see, for example, Dorrell, 1993).

- provision of access to career and counselling services of local col-leges and universities and to their vocational and non-vocational courses.

Development can take place not only at but away from work, and not only through formalised activities but in a wide range of informal ways. Belonging to activity and interest groups outside work can develop skills, knowledge and attitudes highly relevant to individuals' career aspira-tions and can expand their CVs.

Promoting self-development
It is easy to be complacent about one's own self-development. Unsurprising, then, that others often seem unconcerned about theirs. If HR professionals reflect on the dangers inherent in neglecting their own professional self-development (see Chapter 9), they should find it easier to gain the insights that will help them decide how to motivate and sup-port others in driving their own learning. The most important tasks for L&D practitioners here include:

- raising awareness of the centrality of self-development to the career development process – This is the vital link to make, and it has to be identified during the career development planning cycle. Self-development will then become from the start an integral part of the career development process.

- promoting awareness about the links between continuous improvement and the self-development process – This is another important link. L&D practitioners should use informal as well as formal situations in order to raise managers' awareness – for example, over coffee or lunch, or after meetings.

- using the personal development planning process – Many organisations now have a personal development planning process built into appraisal (see Chapter 13). When training appraisers and appraisees, the L&D practitioner has the opportunity to explain why self-directed learning matters and how it can be achieved. He or she can also produce guidelines on how to integrate self-development into personal development plans (see, for example, Forrest, 1993).

- introducing a focus on learning styles and skills – L&D practitioners should raise awareness across the organisation of the ways in which individual learning style and skills influence the effectiveness of the self-development process. Raising managers' awareness is particularly important, and one way in which this can be done is to draw attention to learning styles when discussing with them the learning needs of members of their units or teams (see Chapter 15). Another useful approach is to use Honey and Mumford's 'Learning Environment Questionnaire' (1996) to encourage managers to assess themselves in relation to four roles needed to build a workplace climate conducive to self-development and continuous learning – the role model, the provider, the system builder and the champion.

- resourcing the self-development process – L&D practitioners should advise their organisations on the affordability, feasibility and benefits of resources that can encourage and support employees' self-development – for example, a learning resource centre (Malone, 1997). People are resources too. Mentors, for instance, can do much to promote self-development in others, and managers can be encouraged to achieve NVQs at level 4 related to learning and development. This was done at Company X, as described in Chapter 9.

Task 2

Produce a discussion paper for your personnel director (or equivalent) outlining the ways in which a greater focus on the self-development process in your own organisation – or in a part of it with which you are familiar – could achieve benefits for the business as well as for individuals.

Identify in your paper processes and resources already available in the organisation that could help the self-development process. Conclude your paper with some short-term, feasible recommendations on how the process could be stimulated and supported, and outline who should have responsibility for the tasks this will involve.

Organisational change and the career development process

The following integrative case study demonstrates the challenges involved in an international company seeking to implement and sustain an effective career development process with mutuality at its heart. It shows, too, the importance of longitudinal research in order to establish 'what is really going on here' and the ultimate outcomes of various career development initiatives.

CASE STUDY: Career development at BP during the 1990s

When Robert Horton became chairman of BP in 1990 he published the following statement about BP's mission (Harrison, 1992).

BP vision, values and themes

BP is a family of businesses principally in oil and gas exploration and production, refining and marketing, chemicals and nutrition. In everything we do we are committed to creating wealth, always with integrity, to reward the stakeholders in BP – our shareholders, our employees, our customers and suppliers and the community.

We believe in continually developing a style and climate which liberates the talents, enthusiasm and commitment of all our people. We can then respond positively to the increasing pace of change in a rapid and flexible way to achieve real competitive advantage. With our bold, innovative strategic agenda, BP will be the world's most successful oil company in the 1990s and beyond.

As part of the process of developing a new culture and structure at BP, Horton promised vigorous promotion of career development and the recognition of both individual contribution and collective teamwork. Employees would be encouraged to strike a balance between their responsibilities to BP and to their home life. There was to be a particular focus on personal development, with the hope that every employee would agree a personal development plan with his or her manager.

The issuing of his statement coincided with the unveiling of Project 1990, announcing the radical restructuring of the group, with de-layering and decentralisation of authority. Job cutbacks were followed swiftly by programmes right across the group aimed directly at changing attitudes and behaviour (Butler, 1990).

In 1996 Hirsh and Jackson provided further information about career development at BP. They gave an illuminating insight into the problems that so often occur as companies attempt to implement and sustain career development strategies at times of complex business and organisational change.

Their article showed that the change process at BP did not go smoothly. There were tensions between the old corporately managed hierarchic career and the newer concepts of teamworking and empowerment, and fears for job security made it harder for those newer concepts to take root. By 1996 the focus in career development had moved from highlighting the need for self-management of careers to emphasising the need for partnership – a joint approach by individuals and the company to managing careers. Personal development planning remained a central concept, but initially it tended to founder for lack of sufficient assistance to individuals – sometimes because of failure in some parts of the devolved structure to put appropriate systems in place, sometimes

CASE STUDY: continued

because of a tendency to try *ad hoc* initiatives which were not sustained.

As is so often the case, the main focus of attention tended to be with the high-potential, fast-track managers, linking in to corporate succession planning. The needs and expectations of others in the workforce were felt by some employees to have been relatively neglected in that process.

Despite these setbacks, the authors saw positive signs for the future lying in three factors: the 'clear and honest communication about what has been happening to the business' that had 'helped staff to adjust their ideas about careers' (Hirsh and Jackson, 1996); the realisation by the company that career management is a long-term process and must be tackled as such; and the company's determination to ensure that changes were handled at local more than at corporate level, and that business-unit managers understood, accepted and carried out the responsibilities they held for the career development of all their staff.

Sources: Butler, 1990; Harrison, 1992; Hirsh and Jackson, 1996

CONCLUSION

Having read this chapter and completed its checkpoints and tasks, you should now:

- understand the importance of a strategic approach to career development in the organisation and the typical triggers for such an approach

- be able to advise on a career development process based on mutuality and the psychological contract between employer and employee

- be able to identify and explain major methods of assessing potential to aid career development

- be able to advise others on continuous self-development, and raise awareness of its centrality to the career development process.

To test yourself against these objectives, what five-minute answers would you give to the questions on p344?

Review questions

Briefly define what is meant by 'career development' and identify *three* typical triggers in organisations to a more systematic approach to the planned management and development of careers.

Identify *three* ways in which self-development could be – or is – promoted in your own organisation, and provide a rationale for such promotion.

What are some of the problematic issues involved in achieving 'intergration' of the career development process?

Useful reference sources

HERRIOT P. (1992) *The Career Management Challenge: Balancing individual and organizational needs.* London, Sage.

INDUSTRIAL SOCIETY (1997) 'Self-managed learning'. *Managing Best Practice.* No. 40. October. (Published monthly by the Industrial Society and available from the Communications Department, 020–7479 2127.)

JACKSON T. (2000) *Career Development.* London, Chartered Institute of Personnel and Development.

MEGGINSON D. *and* WHITAKER V. (1996) *Cultivating Self-Development.* London, Institute of Personnel and Development.

• Developing Managers

CHAPTER OBJECTIVES

After reading this chapter you will:

- understand what the management development process involves and the need to link management development to organisational goals and strategy

- be able to explain the characteristics of an effective management development process, and how to manage it

- be able to advise on the generalised design of a management development programme

- understand how to integrate succession planning within the management development process.

Introduction

One of the responsibilities of L&D practitioners is to aid the organisation to build for the future through the management development process (MDP). Managers are major decision-makers in any organisation. For that reason alone, an effective MDP is crucial to organisational success. Its generalised purpose can be described as one of increasing the organisation's present and future capability in attaining its goals (French, 1987).

For all organisations, the MDP is a potentially powerful 'strategic tool' (Osbaldeston and Barham, 1992). The development of managers takes on an additional dimension in those organisations – of whatever size, type or sector – that have to operate in an increasingly globalised and technology-driven environment. Such organisations must be able to rapidly set and achieve new productivity, quality and effectiveness standards, develop and implement new strategies, and change and sustain new corporate cultures.

The meaning and parameters of 'management' are expanding and changing. Using the International Labour Office's classification, Brewster and Tyson (1991: 218) defined managerial and professional staff as those who:

- are salaried members of an organisation

- have achieved a higher level of education and training or recognised experience in a scientific, technical or administrative field

- perform functions of a primarily intellectual character involving a high degree of judgement and initiative

- may hold delegated authority to plan, manage, control and co-ordinate the work of other organisational members

- do not occupy positions as first-line supervisors, foremen or top-level executives.

In many organisations today, however, this classification system is losing validity. Brewster and Tyson pointed to the blurring effects of technology on the lines of distinction between managerial tasks and the work of other occupations. De-layering and decentralisation involve devolution of problem-solving and decision-making. Decentralisation often results in 'supervisors' having to take on team management roles, while an increasing number of those occupying traditional middle management positions may find themselves in charge of semi-autonomous business units, and therefore involved in the strategy process. Professionals frequently have to assume more managerial responsibilities, some of a strategic nature (as in the case of the clinical directors described in Chapter 16).

Of fundamental importance in explaining these 'blurring effects' is 'the relentless drive to add value ... [that] is having a radical impact on the nature of everyone's work, from front-line staff to top management' (Guile and Fonda, 1998: *xi*). Companies and public services are seen less and less as hierarchies of 'command and control', more and more as chains and networks of processes that must be managed to this end.

With this new emphasis on partnership rather than control, and on processes that add value, there is a related focus on management behaviours. The 1998 Institute of Personnel and Development report on 'Performance Management through Capability', for example, highlighted 20 behaviours perceived to be essential to develop in future-oriented managers (Guile and Fonda, 1998). Managers still have to manage, but in today's increasingly unpredictable environment anyone planning their development has to answer searching questions concerning how they should manage, with whom they should collaborate as they manage, and how they should behave in order to achieve the desired outcomes.

The blurring in the meaning of 'management' in many of today's organisations has another implication for some, who argue that it means that the scope of the MDP should extend to all employees and should incorporate the total process of learning, continuous improvement and change in the organisation (Wille, 1990). The aim is to ensure a continuous supply of leaders and managers who best 'fit' the organisation through time. The point deserves reflection. It will not be pursued here, but will receive attention in the next two chapters.

This chapter looks first at a range of differing agenda and tasks for management development, and at critical success factors for the process. It then explores issues related to the design of the MDP and of programmes within it, looking in particular detail at competency-based MDP frameworks. The fourth part of the chapter explores issues of management succession, and the chapter ends by focusing on ways of improving the capability of strategic managers.

Checkpoint

- In what ways is the traditional management classification system becoming irrelevant?

- To what extent (if any) do you share the view that management development should incorporate all employees?

Tasks for the management development process

Tasks involved in the management development process (MDP)

Essentially, the MDP involves three tasks:

- the analysis of present and future management needs

- an assessment of the existing and potential capability of managers against those needs

- producing and implementing policy, strategy and plans to meet those needs.

These tasks involve decisions about individuals' career routes, about management succession, and about organisational performance. The decisions can be complex, depending on how far the focus of the MDP is only on the micro or is also on the macro level.

- If it is mainly on the micro level, it is perhaps more accurate to refer to it as *manager development*. The aim here is to improve the performance and develop the potential of individual managers (singly or in groups) in order to remedy specific performance gaps, and to ensure that they are competent in their jobs and are well prepared for future responsibilities.

- If it also operates at a macro level, then it is essentially to do with making decisions about how to develop management as a whole, across the organisation. It is indeed about *management development*. The aim here is one of building a shared culture across the whole management sector and enhancing management capability throughout the organisation.

Agenda for the MDP

Tasks for the MDP are complicated by the fact that the MDP's agenda can vary considerably from one organisation to the next, every agenda having its own characteristics, assumptions and typical outcomes. The different focuses of three types of development programme can be particularly problematic (Mabey and Salaman, 1995):

- *functional performance*, typified by the Lead Body Standards framework for management competencies, and centred on improvement in the performance of managers' functional tasks. A rational, systematic, task-oriented approach typifies programmes in this kind of MDP. As is evident later in the chapter, this agenda may not produce effective managers but simply managers who can perform their functional tasks competently.

- *political reinforcement*, where those in charge of the MDP are mainly concerned that however it is designed and whoever it involves, the process should sustain the current political order in the organisation. In such a scenario, management development methods are selected accordingly. They are unlikely to include any that will lead to challenges to the status quo, and consequently to radically new managerial thinking and action.

- *compensation*, where management development is offered as a reward to secure 'loyalty' and commitment to the organisation rather than as a process to improve effectiveness and develop future-oriented skills and values.

Critical success factors for the MDP

Despite these variations in MDP agenda, Sadler and Barham (1988) argue that six features always produce an effective process. Osbaldeston and Barham (1992) expanded on them:

- a clear MDP mission, linked to the organisation's business strategy

- specific programme objectives that relate to the external challenges that the organisation is facing

- a focus also on major internal organisational issues

- programmes tailored to organisational and individual needs

- the systematic assessment of management development needs, aims and outputs

- a professional, business-led approach to the MDP.

Looking at the final point, in order to ensure effective management of the MDP, it is essential that:

- management development is owned by managers and achieves strong external consistency. Managers, any human resource (HR) practitioners and other key stakeholders should work as business partners in this and be clear as to their respective roles and responsibilities.

- the MDP has a vision and strategy that are understood and supported by the managers involved in its operation. The process must be driven by business needs as well as being responsive to individual needs. It must enable the continuous identification, assessment and development of potential and be grounded in an agreement between managers and HR specialists as to its purpose and management.

- managers are trained in the processes involved in training and developing others and must have a shared commitment to implementing the MDP across the organisation. HR specialists need a thorough knowledge of the business, its goals and strategy in order to advise on the design, delivery and evaluation of management development strategy and programmes.

- the MDP is integrated with wider employee resourcing policy and practice in order to achieve consistency across the processes of planning, recruitment, selection, appraisal, rewards and development. This is an argument for the human resource function to have a central involvement in planning and managing the MDP. However, such specialists must not dominate the MDP, or it will not achieve management ownership.

- when the organisation is decentralised, the units as well as the centre are actively involved in planning, operating and evaluating the MDP. While management development must be 'owned' by units, it must also be well integrated across the whole of the organisation. The danger of loosening central control is that divisions/units will take too much power into their own hands and end by doing things their own way according to their own cultures. The danger of putting central control into the hands of a personnel function is that its specialists may hold insufficient power and be seen as 'outside' the real management system of the organisation.

Task 1

Collect information about the MDP in your organisation. Then draft a paper for discussion with your L&D/personnel manager giving your analysis of the following, and concluding with appropriate recommendations:
- the formal purpose of your organisation's management development activity, and the agenda that activity seems to serve
- how far the MDP focuses on 'manager development' and how far on 'management development'
- how well or badly managed the MDP appears to be.

Management development design

For those whose responsibility it is to advise on, or implement, management development design in an organisation, there are some testing issues to resolve. Some of the most common are described below.

Achieving realism

Management development design is often dominated by a highly systematic approach, leading to blocks of training and development aiming to 'teach' managers (and potential managers) their roles and tasks in an orderly, sequential fashion and to help them acquire sets of functional skills. However, organisational life is not entirely rational, ordered or predictable. Simply learning how to perform specific functional tasks is not enough to be effective in management roles. Managers have to operate at the heart of complex webs of social and political interaction. They have to continuously adapt to changing internal and external pressures and opportunities. They have to think and operate across many internal boundaries, and often across external boundaries too.

The MDP should therefore be designed to stimulate a holistic and integrative approach to management tasks. It should ensure that managers have the adaptability and flexibility of skills and disposition to move through often rapidly changing managerial roles and organisational circumstances. It must raise awareness about the bounded rationality of decision-making and action, help to develop the skills to deal with this, and promote effective approaches to the management of conflict (see Chapter 6).

Dealing with values

Lippitt (1983: 38) declared that:

> *The most meaningful aspect of personal change resulting from a management development process is the examination and alteration of attitudes within the organisation. Reinforcement will need to be related to meaningful renewal systems.*

Dogmatic attitudes among managers mean that they are unlikely to be able to function effectively in a changing world because they cannot accept that they themselves need to change. Management development that does not focus on attitudes can, unwittingly, simply ensure the perpetuation of old mindsets to the detriment of new learning.

When designing management development programmes it is essential to consider the kind of workplace that will be conducive to the acquisition, retention and full utilisation over the longer term of learning, knowledge and values that participants acquire. How many graduate trainees, for example, quickly leave the organisation they have joined because, despite promises of fast-track advancement and the stimulus of an inno-vative MDP, the reality of life in that organisation increasingly contra-dicts the expectations that the MDP has encouraged them to hold? How many managers, eager to put into practice new ideas and new ways of managing and behaving, are unable to do so because there is no sup-port for such changes among their colleagues and superiors?

There must be a real willingness in the organisation to accept the changed managerial values and attitudes, as well as the new competen-cies, that can result from a powerful management development pro-gramme, if that investment is to realise its value. If the 'renewal' it offers is resisted by those who hold the most powerful positions in the organ-isation, it can only indicate that the true agenda for the MDP is a politi-cal one: the process is not intended to produce fundamental changes in the status quo.

The points raised above introduce other issues in their turn. For example: in order to ensure that the organisation has an adequate supply of managers whose attitudes and values are future-oriented, who are adaptive to change, and who are receptive to new ideas, what bal-ance should there be between investing in internal management devel-opment and buying in from outside? And at what point and organisational level should any buying in start?

Task 2

Your training manager has asked you to produce an outline design for a management development course that will begin to change deep-rooted managerial attitudes held by its 20 or so long-serving middle management participants.

Produce the design, showing the structure, generalised content, methods and evaluation process for the course. It can be of any length you wish and can be organised in whatever way you think best, but you must provide a convincing rationale for the design, relating it back to the purpose set by your training manager.

Using experiential learning

Mabey and Salaman (1995: 140) distinguished between *training* and *learning*. Most of the reports on management development focus on the former, yet it is the process and outcomes of work-based experiential learning that make the most fundamental impact on managerial capa-bility. As we saw in Chapter 12, even though in many smaller organis-ations there may be few signs of a systematic, formalised approach to training, a good deal of productive learning goes on. Mumford, Robinson and Stradling's 1987 report on the development of directors concluded that the possession of a management qualification is of little relevance – what promotes the most effective learning is day-to-day, work-based experience and role models. Most of the directors studied did not attribute their success to any formal development processes. This explained the emphasis of the report on the value of self-development in a greatly diversified range of roles over a variety of organisational settings.

Such a view of the need to put experiential learning at the heart of any management development process is widely held. Work-based learning can be stimulated in many ways. Currently the most popular methods and processes include development through project work, self-development, action learning, coaching and mentoring. A balanced mix of these in the MDP can prove effective, relatively cheap and beneficial to the organisation as well as to participants in the MDP. Such methods can also provide a powerful bridge between externally based programmes and work-based learning (see the clinical directors' development programme, in Chapter 16), ensuring effective two-way transfer of learning and experience between work role and job and programme.

No single approach to development can guarantee an effective management development process. It is important to consider what kind of work-based experiential learning will achieve improved performance and strengthen the ties between managers and the organisation. But it is equally important to consider the benefits that are offered by in-house or external training and educational programmes. These formalised methods may not be located in the workplace, but they can incorporate a variety of work-based scenarios in their design. Their advantages are that, precisely because they take current and potential managers out of their daily work environment, they can broaden their vision, challenge their customary ways of thinking and behaving in the organisation, and expand their intellectual capacity. They have a vital educational role in the widest sense of that word.

Incorporating educational programmes

No MDP should rely exclusively on educational programmes, but they do offer particular value for four types of individual or group:

- young potential managers who have yet to decide what they want to specialise in and what kind of managerial role will best suit their disposition as well as their abilities

- managers involved in structural and role change in their organisation – they need help in developing new abilities, understanding and social skills to perform effectively in that new situation

- managers who are set in their ways – they are so focused on their customary ways of thinking, behaving and performing that they are blocking the development both of themselves and of their teams. Such managers need the challenges that powerful educational programmes can provide if the barriers they are unwittingly creating are to be demolished.

- managers who are being prepared for more strategic roles in

their organisations and need an interplay of on-the-job development and demanding intellectual activity in order to help them in
that transition (as in the clinical directors' programme, Chapter
16).

It is important to gain a balanced perspective on accredited educational
programmes. The real question to ask is not 'Why don't we have enough
qualified managers?' It is 'Will qualifications make our managers more
effective?' (Chambers, 1990). The Japanese and the Germans virtually
ignore the Master of Business Administration (MBA) route to management development, yet as a sector their managers are highly regarded.
In both Japan and Germany recruits have a high standard of educational
attainment by the time they enter employment – the same tends not to
be true of the average new recruit to employment in the UK. The case
for the educated employee is therefore clear; the case for the manage-
ment-educated manager rather less so. Let us look at this issue in a
little more detail.

Country comparisons
Low standards of education in managers can lead to low levels of ability
to cope with new technologies, to manage and develop people, and to
think and act strategically. Most well-educated Germans do not join a
large company until around 27 years of age, because they tend to have
followed an apprenticeship after school and then pursued a degree and
often a higher degree in subjects such as engineering, law or economics. In Japan and in Britain, the average age for joining such a
company is 22, but in Japan, the potential manager studies law or engineering at a top university, and, after entry to a large firm, goes through
a 'rigorous process of job rotation, private study and classroom learning which can last for up to 15 years' before being promoted to the first
level of management (Handy, 1987).

In France, the route to management in a larger organisation is either
through business or engineering at one of the Grandes Ecoles, or
through some other educational pathway leading to the same kind of
functional qualifications as in Japan and Germany. In France, too, the law
requires all firms to spend 1.1 per cent of the wage bill on continuing
education and training, and corporations with more than about 2,000
employees spend three times that amount, about one-third going on
management training. Such investment is common across most of
mainland Europe and the USA, but not in the UK.

In the UK during the 1970s and 1980s the low participation rate in
management education came under critical fire, with the publication of
a stream of reports pointing to the urgent need for improvement if our
economy was to become more competitive. One message emerging
from these reports was that those who are uneducated, untrained and
undeveloped themselves are unlikely to be committed to the education,
training and development of others – so in every organisation, a low
level of management education threatened the future supply of

educated managers also. During the 1990s that situation changed. Managers became steadily better qualified, and the MBA award achieved rapid growth that has been sustained. Business studies is now one of the most popular undergraduate programmes. However, the UK still lags considerably behind France, Germany, Japan and the USA in terms of basic educational attainment, while emerging industrial countries invest heavily in their education systems in order to produce capable leaders and workforces for the future.

Checkpoint

- Your personnel manager asks your view on the value that educational programmes can have within a long-term management development strategy. Outline a convincing but brief reply.

- A manager who has been converted by the works of Alan Mumford says to you forcefully, 'Management development? No two ways about it – learning on the job, in the workplace is the only real way. Give them a good job pathway and plenty of role models and mentoring – and you'll find their development takes care of itself.' Outline your reply.

Competency frameworks for management development

The subject of competency frameworks was introduced in the context of National and Professional Standards in Chapter 8. We returned to it briefly in Chapter 13 and in more depth in Chapter 14 when we examined competency-based analysis. Now we should look at it specifically in relation to the MDP.

Management competencies are the set of character features, knowledge and skills, attitudes, motives and traits that comprise the profile of a manager and enable him or her to perform effectively in the managerial role. A competency framework provides a template against which teams as well as individuals can be developed, since no individual will have more than a few of the competencies needed for superior organisational performance. It provides a clear set of performance criteria both at organisational and at individual levels and identifies the expected outcomes of achieving those criteria. Competency frameworks are widely used but are also expensive to design, install and monitor. If they are not well conceived or adequately evaluated through time, they can prove an expensive mistake for the organisation. The main types of competency framework are outlined and discussed below.

Functionally based frameworks

These have been popularised in the UK through the work of the Management Charter Initiative (MCI). The MCI was established in the late 1980s to improve the performance of UK organisations by increasing the standard and accessibility of management education and development. It led to the establishment of national professional management qualifications at three levels, with existing qualification courses such as the Diploma of Management Studies and MBA being integrated into a national, hierarchical structure. The national standards relating to this functionally-derived MCI framework are expressed as a ladder of qualifications to complement the continuous development of managers in the workplace. Many organisations value them as aids to staff recruitment, appraisal, training and development. They also enable first-level management trainees to get a national certificate qualification.

The aim of the MCI framework is to improve the capability of managers by applying standardised criteria to the description of their roles and tasks and by appraising their performance against clearly defined, measurable behavioural and task targets. This approach is most relevant for those working in relatively stable, hierarchical structures with specified managerial career pathways. Despite this, some organisations have applied the framework to contexts such as newly decentralised units where middle managers face radically changed roles and tasks. The rationale for the use of the MCI framework in these scenarios is less convincing, although a future-oriented thrust is often attempted by including a development centre component from which every participant leaves with a development programme specifying 'present competency levels, appropriate developmental priorities, learning targets, and a timetable of training and development methods' (Colloff and Goodge, 1990: 52)

In 2001 the MCI's existence was terminated without explanation by the government. In 2002 a new 'Council for Excellence in Management and Leadership' published a rival management competency framework in a report to government on improving management skills in the UK (Perron and Burgoyne, 2002). Whereas the MCI's framework identifies three discrete sets of competencies – technical, personal and those to do with knowledge and understanding needed to perform the management role – the CEML offers a single framework incorporating 83 separate competencies, grouped under eight major categories that (however) roughly correspond to the MCI's three types. Rankin (2002: 44) finds the CEML framework has the virtue of addressing the latest facets of the work of a manager or leader, and has a clear structure, but is 'short on detail and explanation'. He concludes that neither framework in its present form is likely to meet most employers' requirements for a full matrix of managerial skills, fit for purpose, but that the two together do offer 'a rich resource of ideas and inspiration for those developing their own competencies for managers' (ibid: 46).

The Chartered Institute of Personnel and Development's 'Core Management' standards are aligned and broadly consistent with the national

MCI management standards finalised in 1997. They take more account of the need for managers to have higher-level holistic, integrative and political skills as well as functional competence. They do not represent so much 'competency-based frameworks' as a set of generalised performance indicators for those entering or preparing to enter first-level management positions.

Generic frameworks

Generic frameworks derive mainly from work carried out by the American Management Association in the 1970s (Cave and McKeown, 1993: 123). Boyatzis (1991) distinguished between threshold and superior management competencies, and between surface and core elements of competency in the individual. Core motives and traits that influence competency are seen as the least amenable to development, being embedded in personality. Surface, or explicit, skills and knowledge are seen as the most amenable as a basis for developmental activity.

Checkpoint

- What are the main differences between functional and generic competency frameworks?

- For what kind of situation would you advise the use of a functional framework, and why?

Concerns about competency frameworks

The competency-based approach to management development, whether based on generic or functional frameworks, has many supporters – see, for example, the case study in Chapter 13. It also has many critics. Critics' concerns are that it is an insufficiently discriminating approach to analysing and meeting managerial needs, except in that minority of cases where the managerial role can be adequately described by reference to a number of discrete components that remain relatively constant and standardised through time. Mintzberg (1973) found managerial roles to be highly variable, involving the often simultaneous pursuit of a variety of objectives in changing ways according to the judgement of the individual manager in the particular situation. They required managers to have quite wide discretion to determine how best to operate, what tasks to tackle and how, at any one point in time.

Some of the concerns are examined in more detail below.

The manager's world
Partridge (1989: 205) stated that:

Managerial work across all levels ... is characterized by pace, brevity, variety and fragmentation ... It is hectic and fragmented, requiring the ability to shift continuously from relationship to relationship, from topic to topic, from problem to problem.

Even first-level and middle managers use a range of skills that cannot easily be categorised. Many of those skills are, and must be, integrated in their practice, and this may lead to a synergetic effect – that is to say, one in which the outcome of management action is greater than the sum of its parts. Such skills have been styled as 'overarching competences' (Burgoyne, 1989) and are to do with achieving synthesis, balance and perspective.

The development of managers and of the management sector in an organisation must be related closely to the organisational context in which they work. This is the main reason why many argue for the MDP to be based on the ongoing management process in the organisation rather than on educational and training programmes, however they are designed. That context is pressured and can be highly politicised. Research shows that management is not an objective and consistently rational activity. It involves constantly trying to find 'a way through contradictory demands in a world of uncertainty' (Edwards, 1990). Political skills and creative ability, as well as purely functional skills, are crucial in enabling managers to cut through these complexities in order to produce the results for which they are responsible.

The changeability of managers' roles and jobs
Sir Geoffrey Holland, in the Foreword to Guile and Fonda (1998), observed that:

Competition between companies and countries is no longer dominated by access to capital, equipment, systems or location. It is the capability of people to generate, share and deploy knowledge for value-added purposes which makes the difference.

This IPD report in 1998 amplified on those fundamental changes to show that 'the new corporate capabilities of organisations and the individual capabilities of people will need to be managed as a single process'. As noted earlier in the chapter, the authors identified 20 capabilities that managers now need to operate in roles and jobs that, for many, continue to change dramatically. Can functionally based competency frameworks adequately cope with such a rapid pace of change? And what is the cost, in time, money and expertise, in regularly updating them in order that they can attempt to do so?

Strategically focused competency frameworks
Organisational competencies are those unique and core capabilities

that enable an organisation to innovate and gain competitive advantage. A distinguishing feature in many competency frameworks is the attempt to formalise and link both individual and organisational competencies to strategic priorities and to human resource systems (Alvarez, 1996).

One example of a strategically focused competency framework was that of British Petroleum (BP) in the 1990s, described by Sparrow and Hiltrop (1994). It embodied 67 essential behaviours related to four organisational culture dimensions, and involved a lengthy and apparently successful process of cross-national, cross-cultural implementation. It was part of a strategy to radically change the structure, culture and strategic performance of the organisation worldwide – as has already been described in Chapter 17 – and was supported by extensive changes to BP's HR policies and systems.

A fundamental concern here is whether a competency framework might simply reinforce any given strategy, regardless of its quality. Alvarez (1996) expressed the fear that such frameworks could dangerously narrow managerial perspectives, inhibiting the intellectual independence needed to question given strategy in the light of an ever-changing environment. Certainly, a competency framework is likely to develop from, and become part of, the dominant logic of an organisation, defined as 'the way in which managers conceptualise the business and make critical allocation decisions' (Prahalad and Bettis, 1986 – for those interested, their concept is examined further in Chapter 22).

Looking at the managers themselves, those operating at strategic levels or with strategic tasks to perform as part of their managerial roles do need to develop some functional competencies related to their strategic tasks. For example, for many managers at unit level, formal planning and the specific techniques and skills it requires are still central to their work. However, there is continuing debate about how far higher-level capacities – especially needed by strategic managers – to do with judgement, intuition, mental elasticity, abstract thinking and tolerance of risk and ambiguity can be viewed in the same light as more measurable 'competencies' (Mintzberg, 1994 and 1994a). There is a clear danger that reliance on functional frameworks when planning the development of strategic managers will mean that 'the integrated work of managing still gets lost in the process of describing it' (Mintzberg, 1994a: 11).

Balancing the arguments

What conclusions can be drawn about competency-based MDPs? I suggest the following:

- In the short term, and in the more stable organisations, a competency-based approach to management development can produce excellent results, enabling the linking of performance criteria, development activity and performance outcomes at individual and organisational levels.

- There is evidence to show that a competency-based approach can also be of value when the business is moving into changed conditions, provided that there is a high degree of certainty and agreement on the kind of future-oriented qualities and skills needed by those who will have to cope with those conditions.

- However, competencies should always be analysed in the context of the particular organisation and be agreed as meaningful and relevant by the key parties involved in and affected by the MDP.

- Where it is clear that tomorrow's environment will be radically different from today's, with complex, unfamiliar problems and no certainty as to the exact nature and interrelationship of the competencies needed to deal with it – in other words, when that environment is turbulent – then an alternative framework for the MDP should be considered.

Checkpoint

- Your L&D manager is sceptical of competency-based management development processes. Produce some arguments to convince her that they have a value.

- A student on a CIPD course says that competency frameworks for management development purposes are 'useless in rapidly changing business environments'. How will you reply?

Succession planning and the management development process

As we saw earlier, planning for the future is one of the three main tasks of any MDP. Gratton and Syrett (1990) emphasised that systems for management succession planning should be tailored to the needs of business strategy in the organisation and should take account of any changes in organisational structure. They also noted that, despite the importance of building the needs of the individual into succession programmes if key personnel are to be retained and committed, many companies still focus succession planning on career structures that have been imposed on participants instead of being planned with them. The concept of mutuality, discussed in Chapter 17, therefore goes to the heart of succession planning for managers.

The traditional model

Conventionally, succession planning has been based on a model of identifying needs related to the business plan, identifying high-fliers at an early stage and grooming them over an extended time-scale for positions at the top of the organisation. Development has usually been a matter of initial formal training followed by specialisation until a late stage, when those still left in the race have been rotated through various functions in order to become 'generalists'. Assessments, often using incomplete, unreliable and subjective information, result in a diminishing number of the original cohort continuing to climb steadily up the ladder, others falling from it at various points into permanent positions in the structure. Wastage, in this model, can come arbitrarily. It can mean that some of the most valued people leave the organisation unpredictably, with consequent gaps at various stages that may prove difficult or impossible to fill.

This traditional model assumes that there is a long-term business plan, that it is accessible to those responsible for management development planning, that it is sufficiently detailed to enable succession planning needs to be identified from it, that the longer-term future of the organisation can be forecast, and that it is unlikely to be radically different from the past. The model also presupposes a stable, hierarchical structure of positions through which people are developed and progress along specified career pathways that remain in place through time. Finally, it assumes the exercise of centralised rather than localised control over the whole process, with ownership of career development by the centre and/or by HR specialists rather than by individuals and their managers.

Succession planning in turbulent environments

The traditional model is not relevant to an organisation that operates in a turbulent environment in which threats and opportunities are likely to be complex, unfamiliar and unpredictable. Moreover, in organisations that have decentralised, the kind of managers and competencies needed will have changed. Managing strategic business units requires a profound knowledge and understanding of the business and its environment, as well as entrepreneurial skills that can come only from multi-functional experience and adaptability to rapidly changing situations. In such an organisation, succession planning and management development policy based on competencies defined by reference to the current roles and tasks of those in senior positions cannot be a valid approach to succession planning. An attempt to identify and put in place a specific successor to every key position will also be unrealistic and unjustifiably costly.

The following task is intended to help the reader review all the material in this chapter so far, and then to reflect on it in the context of a real-life situation. That situation can be drawn from experience, from reading, or from some other source. Reflection on failure can be a great aid to learning – hence the nature of this task!

Task 3

Do some research to discover information about a real-life *ineffective* management development strategy or programme. Then produce a brief paper (perhaps in the form of a report to management, or of an article for a professional journal) in which you:

- explain what the purpose of the strategy/programme was
- outline its key features and its organisational context
- identify and analyse what you see to have been the reasons for its failure.

Improving strategic management capability

A well-designed MDP can make a powerful contribution to improving the quality of strategic management in an organisation. To do that, it has to make a direct link between management development and competitive advantage. It should ensure that managers are developed in ways that improve their abilities to generate strategic options, choose strategies that fit the company's situation, and make high-quality strategic decisions that are effectively implemented across the company. It must also help managers to acquire ways of thinking and behaving, and the dispositions, that are required in order to be effective in strategic roles. Where obstacles emerge, the company's top management must look again at their strategic management selection process.

To conclude this chapter, a case study presents an example of the way in which a particular programme within an MDP can help to build strategic management capability in an international organisation. It also illustrates many of the points made thus far about principles of good planning and process design.

CASE STUDY: Hewlett Packard's management development programme

In the 1980s a programme was designed to develop Hewlett Packard's European managers. It centred on groups of managers carrying out project work related to the 10 most important strategic issues facing Hewlett Packard Europe. Top management took a leading role in identifying and explaining the issues, agreeing the projects, evaluating them, and being committed to their implementation. Relationships with the Business Schools involved in the programme proved very effective because of the many ways in which they responded positively to the perspectives and needs of the managers.

The company had always been characterised by high innovation and quality, but moving into the 1980s it faced globalised competition and a fast-changing business environment. With key markets on the decline, new technology needing heavy investment, major competition from small, fast-growth companies and low-cost foreign companies, and costs rising rapidly within the

CASE STUDY: continued

company, these managers now had to become much more entrepreneurial.

This produced an urgent need at Hewlett Packard to change the attitudes and improve the current effectiveness of their European managers. The managers came mainly from a technical background, and fewer than 40 per cent had any formal business education. Most had worked for years in the company, and because of the company's long-standing success and high profit ratios, few had needed to pay much attention to costs. Managers were also used to the autonomy and local cultures of the company's functional matrix management system. Many tended to pay more attention to local needs of their units than to the wider business scenario.

The management development programme

Working with a number of leading business schools, personnel and training specialists at Hewlett Packard, staff designed a management development programme to develop the company's European managers. The programme was designed to make the vital link between management development and strategic advantage (interested readers can learn more about this link in Chapter 22). It was part of a management development process of which the underlying purpose was to build up a management sector that would make the organisation more effective now and for the longer term.

Key criteria for the programme were that it must:

- be business-focused, cost-efficient, have the involvement of senior company executives, and reflect corporate issues

- have an international, not a local, focus

- be capable of being delivered by each of the company's regional training teams, and within their resources

- emphasise managers' responsibility for self-development and stimulate them to an active commitment in this respect

- have teamwork as a key feature, so that participants would learn from and support each other in the learning processes and develop project management and team skills

- focus on making the target population more effective in their current roles as well as focus on developing future-oriented skills and values.

With these criteria in mind, the designers produced a programme with these key features:

- a focus on the real strategic business issues that the company faced – One measure of the success of the programme was the extent to which it enhanced managers' ability to understand and deal effectively with those issues.

- methods that involved learning from and through experience, in order to increase competence and test it on real issues – Methods used on the programme included live project work, practical assignments, the use of benchmarking and best practice to suggest improvements to business strategy at corporate and unit levels, and tools and processes to improve strategic planning and decision-making.

- the knowledge and techniques needed to tackle strategic issues provided in part by theoretical inputs, in part by help in various forms (not only talks, but also mentoring, coaching, secondments, and so on) from skilled senior executives in the company, and in part by external educationalists – Teamwork was developed through group-based projects supported by informal networking systems extending beyond the programme back into the various workplaces of the participants. (Action learning is often used in management development programmes to achieve this.)

CASE STUDY: continued

active involvement of the company's training staff during the programme – This was achieved through a rotation of regional training staff in the delivery of the programme, as well as through their involvement in programme design.

the working of the training staff with their external business school partners to design and deliver the programme – The schools were chosen because of their excellent reputation, and because of their ability to work collaboratively, making no attempt to impose ivory-tower attitudes or content on the programme. Business school staff formed part of the core planning team. They were in that way able to partner managers on the programme and respond to participants' need for 'a blend of internal knowledge and external wisdom which participants can exploit, particularly in developing their projects' (Carter and Lumsdon, 1988).

The programme produced major results for Hewlett Packard whilst also gaining the commitment of top management and the European managers who were programme members. It focused on both manager and management development, and it took account of attitudinal factors and organisational values (Lippitt, 1983). Through the learning strategies it involved, it broadened participants' knowledge and began to change the culture of the whole management sector.

Source: Carter and Lumsdon, 1988

CONCLUSION

Having read this chapter and completed its checkpoints and tasks, you should now:

- **understand what the management development process involves and the need to link management development to organisational goals and strategy**

- **be able to explain the characteristics of an effective management development process, and how to manage it**

- **be able to advise on the generalised design of a management development programme**

- **understand how to integrate succession planning within the management development process.**

To test yourself against these objectives, what five-minute answers would you give to the questions on p364?

Review questions

- The six members of the top management group in an organisation do not work well together as a corporate team, and strategic direction is suffering in consequence. Identify *three* possible causes of this failure, and against each suggest a training or other developmental approach to tackle the problem.

- You have been told that management development in your organisation is poorly managed. What criteria would you use to decide if this is really the case – and why?

- What are *three* of the most critical factors for the success of a management development process, and why would you describe them as 'critical'?

Useful reference sources

GUILE D. *and* FONDA N. (1998) *Performance Management through Capability*. London, Institute of Personnel and Development.

MILLER L., RANKIN N. *and* NEATHEY F. (2001) *Competency Frameworks in UK Organisations: Research Report*. London, Chartered Institute of Personnel and Development.

MUMFORD A. (1997) *Management Development: Strategies for action*. 3rd edn. London, Institute of Personnel and Development.

PERREN L. *and* BURGOYNE J. (2002) *Management and Leadership Abilities: an analysis of texts, testimony and practice*. Council for Excellence in Management and Leadership, www.managementandleadershipcouncil.org.

RANKIN, N. (2002) 'The rivals: two national frameworks of management competencies'. *Competency & Emotional Intelligence Quarterly*. Vol. 10 1. pp40–46.

• Aiding and Sustaining Change

CHAPTER OBJECTIVES

After reading this chapter you will:

● understand what is involved in the L&D professional's role as change agent

● be able to advise on how to provide L&D initiatives to facilitate and embed organisational change

● be able to advise on process and strategies for culture change.

Introduction

We saw at the start of Chapter 8 that Pettigrew and his colleagues (1982) identified the 'change agent' as a key training role. One of the most important tasks of L&D practitioners is to help to introduce and embed organisational change. To do this, they must develop in themselves and promote in others the skills and attitudes needed to work effectively in changed or changing organisational roles, structures and working environments. They must also advise on, and work with others to introduce, L&D strategies and initiatives that can support organisational culture change.

Change can take many forms, but by definition it always involves a need to learn and to adapt. It is common, for example, for L&D staff to organise initiatives responding to a new drive for customer care or total quality, a forthcoming downsizing programme, the introduction of new tasks, patterns of work organisation or new technology, or new legislation that has direct implications for organisational members. Change in all such cases is driven by a need for the organisation to find new ways of improving its performance in the pursuit of current goals, or to generate and develop the capability to achieve new goals essential to its progress.

Whereas major advances in achieving competitive advantage come from a combination of new patterns of social organisation and from new technology, it is new patterns of social organisation that are the crucial factor (Storey, 1994a). These patterns need to be planned first, not emerge accidentally after new technological strategies have been introduced. L&D initiatives are sometimes used as a token gesture prior to the implementation of change, but this can be a costly error. The social reorganisation of the workplace cannot be achieved by a quick fix. It calls for (Starkey and McKinlay, 1993: 2):

> *deep analysis rather than superficial prescription, concentrated reflection upon the way we act and often painful learning to undo existing patterns of thought and behaviour.*

This chapter is not about specific change management techniques. It is about the crucial issues upon which L&D practitioners should reflect when preparing to carry out their 'change agent' role. In the first part of the chapter I identify some criteria to guide the planning of L&D change initiatives. The second section examines how L&D initiatives can tackle internal barriers to change. The third section explores the territory of culture change, and the fourth comprises an integrative case study.

Checkpoint

- If major change had to be introduced in your organisation, or one with which you are familiar, what do you think would be *three* of the main barriers that would stand in its way, and how might these be tackled?

- What is meant by describing the L&D professional as a 'change agent', and what do you see to be the core skills that such a role involves?

Contributing to organisational change

It is essential to the success of any major organisational change that:

- the organisation's purpose and driving goals are understood and communicated to everyone, and are embedded in the L&D process so that they inform all L&D activity

- there are the skills to design and use management systems and business processes that will enable decision-making to be pushed down to the levels where quick responses can be made to competitive forces – and management is aware that this is a crucial task

- there is effective team leadership, teamwork and project management

- those who take on cross-functional roles, in which influence and persuasion are more relevant than the exercise of direct control and authority, have the skills to operate in those roles

- managers and team leaders accept the importance of building a

Figure 14 Eight-stage process to facilitate planned learning

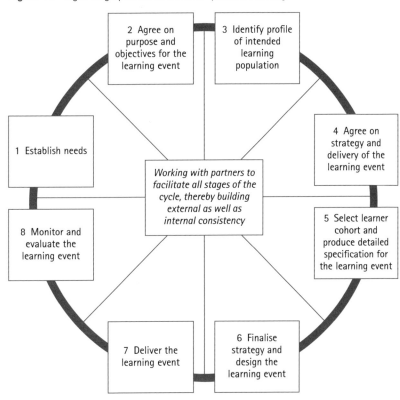

workplace environment that facilitates learning and change, and have the skills and support to do this.

There are clear implications here for those with L&D responsibilities. To ensure the effectiveness of the initiatives that they advise or produce, they should use the same process that relates to the facilitation of all planned L&D activity. It formed the framework for our discussions in Chapters 14 to 16, and is shown (again) in Figure 14.

The most important questions that need to be answered in organising L&D change initiatives relate to the eight stages of the facilitative process:

1 Have we carried out adequate needs analysis?

Where major organisational change is involved, auditing through the use of a diagnostic process (as outlined in Chapter 5) is often the most relevant approach. It will enable force-field analysis, identifying those forces likely to cause resistance to change, and those likely to support it.

What must be avoided is any unnecessarily time-consuming or mechanical approach. For example, comprehensive training needs analysis (see

CASE STUDY: Training for change at Pindar Set

1 Pindar Set was a small, family-owned Yorkshire business that until May 1995 was a one-customer, one-site, highly profitable company with a 10-year contract to design and set advertisements for *Yellow Pages'* customers (Crabb and Johnson, 2000). At that point, however, *Yellow Pages* decided that it wanted to move to a shorter, more demanding type of contract. It offered Pindar Set three design studios to incorporate into its business.

2 The company therefore had to rapidly expand to occupy four sites, three of them new, increasing its workforce virtually overnight from 80 to almost double that number. By 2000 the workforce size was 235, turnover had increased by a third, and production costs had dropped substantially.

3 In 1995 the strategy to turn the business round, achieve a more flexible relationship with its customer, and improve its innovative capability put people management at its heart. After a fundamental rethink of its vision, strategy and organisational structure, management at Pindar Set worked with the HR director to introduce a programme of new HR policies and practices focused on multi-skilling, teamworking, the introduction of new team leader roles and of training for those roles, twilight shifts, flexible working, and a new financial reward scheme.

4 The modular training programme covered personal as well as technical, financial, personnel management and change management skills. These had been identified as the core skills needed by team leaders, who had to take on direct responsibility for financial, operations and people management, running their sites as semi-autonomous businesses with their own profit and loss accounts.

5 The team leader training was crucial to the programme. It was devised in the form of an 18-month process involving 30 days' training for each team leader at a cost of £3,000 per person. The process incorporated modular skills-based training, personal development plans to facilitate putting learning into practice, and supervisors' handing responsibilities over gradually to the future team leaders acting as their deputies while being trained. A pool of new team leaders as well as 21 current team leaders was established, giving eight current and five newly appointed personnel their training in the first 18 months.

6 An integrative but pragmatic approach to the introduction and embedding of change was crucial to the success of the reorganisation at Pindar Set. One problem that arose was that in one of the studios taken over by the company, there was a 'traditional printing industry culture with a strong union presence' (Crabb and Johnson, 2000). Staff at that studio opposed the introduction of overtime working and the idea of individuals' volunteering to join the scheme in favour of a collective approach to negotiating terms and conditions of service. Anxious to avoid an industrial relations problem, the company conceded and omitted the studio's existing employees from the scheme. The success of this approach became clear when the studio's staff participated fully in all other aspects of the change programme, and when, through time, four new teams joined at that site, all working flexibly.

Source: Crabb and Johnson, 2000

Appendix 3) is irrelevant to a situation in which the main requirement from the L&D function is to help all employees, no matter what their existing knowledge and skills, to quickly acquire quite new competencies and a commitment to a different organisational culture.

Consider the analytical approach that evidently underpinned the change process in the study on p368. The paragraphs are numbered in order to provide reference-points for further examination following the case.

The analytical thrust in this situation was to develop a vision, corporate strategy and set of organisational values that would achieve commitment across the organisation and shape future organisational context. It was also to determine what core skills were needed in order for company personnel (especially the new team leaders) to operate effectively in their new roles.

2 What is our purpose for the learning process, and what specific outcomes do we want it to achieve?

Once the implications of organisational vision, goals and design have been identified, it becomes easier to agree where help is needed most from the L&D process. It is at this stage that the overall purpose of L&D change initiatives has to be clearly established, and ultimate objectives set for them to achieve – as exemplified in points 3 and 4 of the Pindar Set case.

3 Who will the learners be?

For the major organisational change that was introduced at Pindar Set, key learners were the new team leaders and team members right across the organisation. In all such change processes it is essential to integrate L&D initiatives with human resource policies and work practices. At Pindar Set, the effective merging of planned learning with the work system indicated in point 5 and the pragmatic approach to potential industrial relations problems outlined in point 6 both demonstrate the commitment to such integration.

4 Who is going to be responsible for planning, leading and managing the L&D initiatives, and what resources and expertise will they need?

Responsibilities must be clearly allocated, a time-scale determined and a provisional budget agreed. There must be clarity about who is to be ultimately accountable for the outcome of the initiatives. Organisational change requires effective business partnerships if it is to succeed and become embedded. HR practitioners on their own can never sustain the complex outcomes that such change requires, as is demonstrated in point 3 of the Pindar Set case.

5 to 7 What kind of L&D initiatives will we produce, and how will they be delivered?

Options need to be generated and evaluated, using 'pay forward' when deciding on which are likely to provide most added value (see Chapter 4). The interests of key stakeholders must be fully taken into account here, with particular attention paid to the likely reactions and levels of motivation of the intended learners and their managers/team leaders.

Many organisations prefer initiatives that they can link to National Vocational Qualifications (NVQs) or other qualifications, provided this can be done without compromising the overall purpose of the initiatives (see, for example, the Egg plc case study in Chapter 6). Such a link enables individual competence to be recognised and accredited to National Standards, thereby helping to build an organisation-wide competency framework and also adding value for employees by enhancing their employability security.

It is essential to identify any special issues relating to the learners who will be involved in the initiatives. Examples would include health, safety and equal opportunities legislation applying to various cohorts of learners, professional or occupational codes and standards of practice that govern their training, and so on. Again, there must be clarity about implications the new initiatives have for wider HR policy and practice in the organisation, since any inconsistencies here will put the whole change process under threat.

Internal staff may have the necessary expertise to deliver the learning initiative/s. Alternatively, it may be more cost-beneficial to outsource some or all elements of design and delivery. For major organisational change initiatives, a common pattern is for internal staff to work with a number of external partners through time, as was the case with the clinical directors' programme in Chapter 16. All lines of responsibility and accountability related to design and delivery tasks must be confirmed at this stage, and there must be agreement on how to co-ordinate and monitor the L&D initiatives as they progress.

8 How will the initiatives be evaluated?

Decisions about the evaluation process to be used must be made well in advance of the launch of the initiatives so that everyone is clear about what is to be measured, how, by whom, when, and in what ways (see Chapter 16).

> **Task 1**
>
> Take a particular L&D change initiative that has been introduced into your own organisation or an organisation with which you are familiar. Collect information to enable you to understand why and how the initiative was organised, its essential features, its cost and time-scale, and the extent to which its intended outcomes were achieved.
>
> Then write a brief case study on the initiative or programme to convey key facts and learning points about the initiative.

Developing adaptability

We noted in Chapter 4 that when a company is de-layering and down-sizing and needs to build an adaptable workforce, it will require L&D strategies related to team-building and multiskilling. It should also produce positive HR strategies related to any redeployment or disengagement of employees.

Reducing cross-functional learning and performance barriers

There are many initiatives to reduce cross-functional barriers to learning new skills and approaches, and to performing in new ways. Examples include:

- cross-functional business improvement groups to tackle fundamental business problems

- virtual learning centres: an Internet-based learning resource allowing employees to access data on business initiatives and engage in discussions with other staff members on them

- cross-functional mentoring, shadowing and job rotation

- regular cross-functional team reviews of teamwork and team processes

- newsletters and other initiatives to publicise and encourage cross-functional learning achievements and inform staff of forthcoming learning events

- training events (including outdoor development programmes) to promote cross-functional learning and working.

Such initiatives should always be integrated with wider HR policy and workplace practices, in order to ensure their support in the workplace.

Teambuilding and team leadership

Changes in teamworking place some of the most taxing demands on the L&D process. One of the three components of L&D strategy at

CASE STUDY: Developing teamworking at Yardley Cosmetics

By the late 1990s, Yardley's manufacturing site in Basildon employed around 650 people, mainly women. Yardley had been taken over by the US group Wasserstein Perella in 1990, and a radical programme of strategic change and organisational restructuring then commenced. The need was to improve customer service in a company that had been a traditional functional hierarchy, with poor communication across the business and little control over sourcing and supply of materials for its large range of products.

Steve Reddington, the new business director, came from Unilever to Yardley in 1990 with experience in co-ordinating a Total Quality programme. Initial changes were to do with breaking down functional barriers by setting up cross-functional management teams. The concept of internal customers and suppliers was developed, and clear and interrelated targets were set for all managers in the supply chain. Triggered by the need to focus on customer service and quality in order to improve competitive edge, it was decided to invest in employee development, particularly via a new training centre with a training co-ordinator.

A 'common-sense' approach to teamworking was a natural consequence of the new order, but some formalisation rapidly became necessary. As production controllers were replaced by production managers, so supervisors were replaced by team leaders 'whose role was to help people achieve their goals and work as members of their own team' (Arkin, 1995a).

Team development had received little attention in the years before the take-over. Now, with three production units – cosmetics, fragrances and body-care – it was clear that there must be a carefully integrated plan to select, train and develop teams and their leaders. The plan involved a number of stages:

- A project team was set up to identify the skills and attributes needed by team leaders and members in their new work environment.

- Training consultants then designed a programme to improve team communication and problem-solving skills while also focusing on understanding the teamworking concept so that people would be thinking, as well as working, together.

- As the first stage of the programme, current supervisors and other employees went through an assessment centre in order to identify those to be given team leader positions. Not all supervisors made the transition, while some employees who had previously held only operator positions were found to have the necessary potential.

- Presentations were held on-site to explain the team training programme, and then four half-day modules were organised first for workers in the cosmetics production unit. They were also attended by the training co-ordinator and a training adviser who would later deliver the same programme to those working in the two other production units.

- In parallel, modules were delivered that focused on 'helping team leaders think of themselves as coaches rather than supervisors' (Arkin, 1995a).

Meanwhile the company was moving into another key stage of restructuring – the creation of integrated business units. Purchasing and planning departments were disbanded and those working in them were brought into the manufacturing units which, in turn, took responsibility for all aspects of production. Each unit was given clear goals and had to operate as a competitive unit benchmarked against other companies. At this point it became clear that team leaders would need further training, especially in running team briefings, in order to give the teamworking initiative sustained impetus within the new business-unit context. This was duly arranged.

Source: Arkin, 1995a

Cummins Engine (case study, Chapter 4) related to developing effective teams. This proved to be a particularly challenging task, the key issue being how to develop supervisors into new-style team leaders.

Team leaders carry the responsibility for organising and managing people, ensuring the quality and profitability of products or services, improving safety, and controlling costs. Their tasks require them to possess a considerable knowledge of the commercial, economic and customer-care aspects of a business. They also need mastery of many interpersonal skills and processes. The competencies and disposition needed to perform well in team leader roles are specific to the particular organisational context (Warr and Bird, 1968), so training must be fit for the purpose. Many team training programmes ignore the needs of those who come to team leader roles with experience of supervising sections or individuals but without an understanding of the processes involved in managing flexible and autonomous teams, and without an awareness of how different the roles of team leader and of a traditional hierarchical supervisor are. In the case of Pindar Set, there was a clear recognition of the kind of training and development needed to produce new-style team leaders.

An example of an integrative approach to breaking down cross-functional barriers, and to analysing and responding to the learning and training needs involved in new forms of teamworking, is presented in the case study opposite.

The Yardley case offers many lessons in how to produce L&D initiatives to facilitate organisational change:

- *It demonstrates the ways in which external factors can trigger a need for internal changes in strategy and structure that have consequences for the L&D function.* In this case, the initial triggers were to do with a more competitive environment. Investment in L&D, especially the setting up of a training centre, was an acknowledgement of training's crucial role in ensuring achievement of the new business goals.

- *It demonstrates the importance of aligning new L&D initiatives with business strategy.* Changes in Yardley's business strategy led to organisational restructuring as well as to new goals for customer service and quality. Customised training gave employees the skills to achieve those goals and to operate effectively in the new structure.

- *It demonstrates the value of business partnerships.* The speed with which the first stage of training was organised at Yardley in response to those triggers owed much to the effective partnership that was forged between external and internal training consultants. External consultants can bring benefit to the organisation in many ways, especially when changes in mindsets as well as in skills are needed, and when internal L&D staff must themselves quickly acquire new skills and learn how to become expert in change management.

- *It demonstrates the expertise needed in planning, designing and evaluating new learning initiatives.* It is easy to see how the eight stages involved in planning, designing and delivering a learning event were followed in this case study. What should also be noted is the way in which the company ensured that as business and organisational changes continued, training was adapted to respond to them.

- *It demonstrates the importance of accurate analysis of learning needs.* In this case, the identification and analysis of learning needs in the roles and jobs concerned (by the project team) was paralleled by the assessment of those selected to occupy those roles and carry out those jobs (through the medium of the assessment centre).

- *It demonstrates the need to focus on leaders as well as members in team training initiatives.* The power of a team lies in the way in which its leader and members interact. In this case there was a focus both on developing team skills within a team and on helping team leaders to function effectively in their new roles.

L&D strategies for downsizing and redeployment

One of the unwelcome outcomes of organisational restructuring is the human wastage that it often involves. Take acquisitions. Crozier estimated in 1998 that since the mid-1980s in the UK fewer than 25 per cent of deals had generated economic value for the buyer. He attributed much of the failure here to the ineffective human resource planning and activity that so often accompanied or followed in the wake of acquisitions. Management turnover, for example, was typically between 39 per cent and 54 per cent. Too often, as also in redundancy situations, the competent people on whom much of the firm's future depends leave, and those who stay fall prey to loss of focus, reduced commitment and ultimately loss of performance with its consequent adverse impact on productivity. As Crozier observed, when a company's intellectual capital and competitive knowledge base departs with the executives who possess it, the cost is incalculable.

When downsizing and redeployment of employees is being planned, HR professionals – including those with L&D responsibilities – must work with management to promote positive strategies that can help the business and individuals. Random initiatives are of no value. What is needed is a comprehensive strategy that embraces those who are leaving, those who are staying on (usually in changed roles and with new tasks to perform) and those who have to manage the change process.

Any strategy should be phased, and L&D initiatives should also be planned in the context of wider HR policies in order to ensure horizontal integration. The kind of L&D activity that is helpful is exemplified here:

L&D activity before the changes take place

- training for those who will have to communicate the changes to the workforce

- training for managers in how to handle the departure of some of their staff, and the redeployment of others (for example, training in coaching, counselling and mentoring skills).

L&D support and opportunities for those leaving the organisation

- financial support, perhaps in the form of a training grant for all leavers, matched by one from a local Learning and Skills Council, in order to aid the acquisition of new skills

- internal courses or the use of an outplacement consultancy to aid job search

- outplacement activities to help people prepare for redundancy or retirement

- special training aid for those who cannot find work by the end of the redundancy period (the older, the disabled, those from ethnic minorities and those with few skills-based or educational qualifications tend to find it the most difficult to gain new employment)

- pre-retirement programmes for those who choose the retirement option.

L&D initiatives to equip those staying in the organisation to handle new roles and tasks

- a training grant or other facility to aid redeployment on an individual basis and to re-energise people in a climate of low morale and uncertainty

- team-building and teamwork training for those who are going to work in or manage new teams.

Checkpoint

- Identify and justify ways in which to break down cross-functional barriers to change in an organisation.

- Your organisation is about to go through major restructuring that will involve staff redeployment and redundancies. What kind of L&D strategy will you propose to management in order to ensure as positive an approach as possible to the situation?

Changing culture

When any significant change has to be introduced in an organisation, it invariably calls also for culture change. In Chapter 6, culture was defined as an expression of the identity of people and of the organisation that, collectively, they produce and perpetuate through their actions. Culture affects behaviour by providing people with a 'toolkit' of material such as symbols, stories, procedures, habits and skills that influence their actions and perceptions (Dougherty, 1999: 182) and is reinforced or weakened by structure – the network of roles and relationships by which responsibilities and activities are allocated across the organisation.

There is a distinction between primary and secondary cultures in the workplace. Primary culture relates to the fundamental values, norms and behaviour that typify the organisation at large. Secondary cultures are to do with the myriad attitudes and interpersonal relationships that characterise particular parts of the organisation.

As we also saw in Chapter 6, although culture and structure form the immediate context within which employees learn and work from day to day, they are powerfully shaped by the interplay of three forces: top management's vision, management's style and actions at different organisational levels, and the employment system of the organisation. It is therefore essential to target those forces when it is necessary to build a new organisational context in which employees should operate in the future.

Because of culture's deep roots in the history and identity of the organisation, such change cannot be rushed. Culture takes years to develop, and so can take years to alter. Many so-called L&D culture-change initiatives prove in retrospect to have had only a passing impact. Reasons for this fall basically into three categories:

- a failure of those who have responsibility for the initiatives to secure stakeholders' commitment to them. Culture change initiatives must be owned by all because they affect all.

- a failure of expertise in facilitating and sustaining the L&D initiatives. Goodman and Dean (1982) reported that over time the majority of organisational change programmes that they examined had become 'deinstitutionalised' because of a failure to develop the structures and management environment needed to carry their outcomes forward. This takes us back to the point already made about the importance of targeting the primary forces that shape organisational context.

- a failure to recognise the need for a paradigm shift when radical organisational change has to be achieved – and a failure to achieve that shift.

Let us look further at that last point. What does it mean, and what does it involve? Below is a brief case study that illustrates an issue of 'paradigm shift' – to which we shall return in Chapter 20.

In Chapter 6 and again in Chapter 13 we noted the concepts of single- and double-loop learning. They were originally developed by Chris Argyris (1996), who argued that what he called single-loop learning cannot produce radical change, only continuous improvement. This is because it focuses on responding to the symptoms of problems rather than on the kind of questioning that uncovers the causes of those problems.

Argyris explained the limitations of single-loop learning by reference to the 'skilled incompetency' that it can produce. Skilful actions of individuals and groups, acquired through training in specific competences and reinforced by repetition, can eventually lead to defensive routines that, spreading across the organisation, produce a culture that avoids confrontation. In such a culture it is not possible to test or challenge the basic assumptions that people hold about the organisation. Vital issues become undiscussable until 'something occurs that blows things open' (Argyris, 1996). That 'something' is usually trauma in the form of a threat to the organisation's survival, and/or the bringing in of new blood at the top. Argyris used the example of the 1986 Space Shuttle disaster to make his point here: only when that tragedy happened 'were the mixed messages and defensive routines used during the decision to launch exposed. The disaster made it legitimate for outsiders to require insiders to discuss the undiscussable' (Argyris, 1996: 87).

CASE STUDY: Change at Ford, Europe, in the 1980s

Starkey and McKinlay (1993) carried out detailed research on how change was managed in the Ford Motor Company in Europe when, during the 1980s, in response to intense Japanese competition, it had to find a new way forward. To make this possible, Ford's leadership had to transform its HR function from one focused on administration to one acting as an internal consultancy, identifying where HR initiatives and processes could best support business strategy.

Ford's leaders and managers had to radically change an organisational context that severely limited its competitive capability. That context was characterised by bureaucracy, management-worker divisions, alienation of workers, demarcation barriers, and separation of thinking from doing. Radical change of this kind requires a paradigm shift – put simply, a complete and permanent change in the established pattern of thinking by organisational members about the work organisation. At Ford, the dominating paradigm had always been that of the mass-production system, served by human beings performing set tasks in fixed routines. However, the strategic challenges faced by the company in the 1980s made that paradigm inappropriate. They highlighted instead the importance of quality and service, and of differentiation allied to cost. This required a new paradigm: one of the work organisation as a social system that depended on trust, collaboration, and creativity to achieve a new technology of production based on teamwork, on flexibility of skill, on good communication, and on surfacing and using workers' tacit knowledge.

Source: Starkey and McKinlay, 1993

Even trauma is not enough to change organisational culture if its consequences are not acted on and then sustained through time. Hendry (1995) identified two typical approaches to changing culture: programmatic, and critical path. The programmatic approach assumes that behaviour can be altered by a planned experience or set of experiences, and that spreading such experience/s across the organisation will be sufficient to change its primary culture. Critical path adopts a more incremental, long-term approach that recognises the often insuperable problems involved in culture change, the tendency of culture to continually regress – especially at times of crisis – and therefore the need for a sustained change process. Quinn's paper offers the classic rationale for this approach (Quinn, 1993).

A programmatic approach, while not enough in itself to produce and sustain major culture change, can have a powerful thrust within a critical path framework. The approaches to change adopted at Pindar Set and Yardley were of this combined type. Change processes such as that advocated by Burack (1991: 94–5) use a combination of programmatic and critical path approaches to move the organisation through three well-known change stages: unfreezing, reframing, and refreezing:

- *unfreezing* – the planning of new directions, when old features of the organisation's culture have to be 'unlocked' and 'internal behavioural benchmarks' begin to emerge

- *reframing* – the consolidation of new directions, when communications help to indicate the growing successes in shifting culture, values and behaviours, and when new forms of communication and behaviour become established

- *refreezing* – reinforcement, when key values become 'internalised' and the culture is reinforced by 'a growing nucleus of organisational processes, relationships, leadership styles, analysis approaches and rituals'.

Chapter 20 gives expanded detail on L&D practitioners' role in promoting learning that can aid unfreezing and reframing.

Task 2

You have been asked by your HR director to produce a discussion paper giving your advice on the contribution that the L&D process can make to producing culture change in the organisation (which can be any type you wish to use for this task).

Draft this paper, which must include a clear identification of the need for change and of forces that you believe will act as barriers and of support to the change process. Do not be concerned in your paper to provide any detail on L&D initiatives – just focus on the general ways in which you think L&D activity can support the kind of change process that you advocate.

Responding to the challenges of change

If those with L&D responsibilities are to respond effectively to the challenges of change, they need to take a holistic view, putting new demands and opportunities in the context of where the organisation stands at present, and what outcomes have to be achieved if it is to move forward. To end this discussion, a case study draws together the material covered in this chapter and demonstrates what is meant by taking 'a holistic view'. Morgans is a fictional company, but First Quench, mentioned at the end of the study, is a real organisation.

CASE STUDY: Morgans, the hotel chain

Morgans is a company that owns sixteen four- and five-star 'country house' hotels across the country. The 'Learning and Development Group' (LDG) plans and organises the company's training and development activity. Most of this activity is carried out by in-house trainers, who in turn train the hotel staff, sometimes centrally in the LDG's Training School, sometimes on site.

Until recently the company was a leader in its market, but over the past two years it has been losing its way. Profits and customer share have been declining under pressure of competition from consortia of privately owned hotels and from some large hotel chains that are now focusing part of their business on the 'country house' sector. Morgans's hotels are usually rated highly on their food, accommodation and facilities. However, there are persistent complaints about the service provided by customer-contact staff — receptionists, portering, housekeeping, bar and dining room staff.

In the past year, many changes have taken place in the company's management. There is a new chief executive and a new chairman of the board, both committed to investing in L&D activity and human resource policy changes that will achieve improved human capability and commitment across the company. Middle management has been slimmed down. The company's strategy, structure and processes have been overhauled and re-focused. A new company vision has been produced: 'Our customers lead the way.'

The company has always prided itself on its long-serving hotel staff. However, those staff do not seem to feel particularly committed to the company. The main reason they stay appears simply to be that they enjoy pay, conditions and a work environment that most of them could not get elsewhere. Most of them show no awareness of a need to change. Staff generally show little interest in self-development, and few customer-contact staff have occupational qualifications.

The LDG manager joined the company recently from a bigger hotel chain. She is a well-qualified professional who welcomes the recent changes. She is particularly pleased that she and the director of personnel have just been asked by top management to come up quickly with a plan to show what contribution the two departments can make to helping the hotel group regain its competitive edge. The previous bureaucratic organisation structure made it impossible for them to work closely together. Now, she and the director of personnel are looking forward to the chance to create a progressive personnel and development service for the company.

The LDG manager has identified immediate priorities for the LDG:

- producing a set of L&D goals and a strategy that will convince Morgans' new leadership that the L&D process can make a value-adding contribution to business recovery. From now on, all L&D activity must be

CASE STUDY: continued

focused on the company's new customer-driven vision and must fit well with the new, flattened structure of the company.

- ensuring that the LDG forms effective business partnerships at Morgans in order to successfully implement L&D strategy across the organisation

- aiding major culture change by integrating L&D activity with the company's performance management process (which is currently being overhauled by the director of personnel in collaboration with top management). This means producing initiatives to improve induction, basic skills training, appraisal and continuous development, and career planning. The results will help staff at the 16 hotels to understand and become committed to the new company vision, will equip them with the skills and targets to transform their approach to customer service, and will ensure that they become adaptive in the face of new demands and opportunities.

- aiding culture change also by focusing powerfully on management training and development. Without changes in management style and actions, any improvements that training produces in customer contact staff will not take root.

- equipping LDG staff with any new skills that they need in the changed company situation.

The LDG manager decides to propose to the director of personnel a short-term strategy similar to that used at First Quench in the late 1990s. In September 1998 the newly merged retail company, formed from two rival high-street chains —

Thresher and Victoria Wine — needed 'little short of a miracle to get everyone on board and maintain profitability' (Tyler, 2000). Yet it achieved that miracle in an 18-month period, during which HR staff, directors and management worked together to implement and support a programme that they called 'Alchemy' — a reference to the quest to 'turn base metals into gold' by getting the new organisation quickly on track and maintaining profits.

Once the board had been helped by an external consultant to produce new organisational vision, mission and values, the following programme was put in place:

- an in-house two-day culture-change programme, designed and delivered by in-company staff and piloted on 60 head office staff, in order to train the company's key communicators first

- the cascading by 21 of those staff, who were given special training as coaches, of a 'team kit' of the programme throughout mixed-level groups that encompassed 600 people

- a subsequent rapid roll-out of the programme until it had covered all 15,000 of the workforce, again through mixed-level groups.

The Alchemy programme was set in a context of many changes to HR policies and practices. These were put in place for the long term, since the company recognised that 'effective change is not a one-off event' and that the changes achieved in the first 18 months would need to be built on carefully thereafter if their outcomes were to achieve a lasting transformation in company culture and performance (Tyler, 2000).

CONCLUSION

Having read this chapter and completed its checkpoints and tasks, you should now:

- understand what is involved in the L&D professional's role as change agent
- be able to advise on how to provide L&D initiatives to facilitate and embed organisational change
- be able to advise on process and strategies for culture change.

To test yourself against these objectives, what five-minute answers would you give to the following questions?

Review questions

What might be the reasons for failure to achieve hoped-for levels of teamwork in an organisation despite a good deal of teamwork training and a de-layered organisation structure?

You have to design a programme to train managers in the management of culture change. What core skills would you aim to develop in them, and why?

You are introducing a number of L&D initiatives in order to facilitate major change in your organisation. What principles guide you in planning and providing these initiatives?

Useful reference sources

ANTHONY P. (1994) *Managing Culture*. Buckingham, The Open University Press.

MABEY C. *and* MAYON-WHITE B. (1993) *Managing Change*. 2nd edn. London, The Open University and Paul Chapman.

• Generating and Managing Knowledge

CHAPTER OBJECTIVES

After reading this chapter you will:

- understand some major notions of knowledge and their implications for L&D practice in the organisation

- be able to contribute to the development of effective work-based learning

- understand how organisations can become 'knowledge-productive'

- be able to advise on L&D roles and tasks related to the 'management of knowledge'.

Introduction

Following on from our discussion in the previous chapter on L&D professionals' role as change agents, it is natural now to discuss their responsibility for promoting learning that will produce organisationally valuable knowledge and stimulate strategic thinking and action. The UK body, the University Forum for HRD, has provided the following rationale for this role (University Forum for HRD, 1998):

> *As the strategic significance of organisational learning as a source of competitive advantage gains recognition, a strategic need arises for appropriately positioned 'learning architects' with the distinctive competencies to orchestrate learning initiatives on behalf of organisations.*

In the CIPD's professional L&D Standard (CIPD, 2001), the role involves:

- developing learning initiatives and processes to promote strategic awareness and the identification of strategic issues at all organisational levels

- using L&D processes to aid unlearning and relearning, and to stimulate challenges to established routines and prescriptions in ways that will help the organisation

- identifying and helping to tackle barriers to understanding the knowledge process, and to generating, sharing and disseminating knowledge

- promoting internal and external learning partnerships that can produce or expand knowledge valuable to the business

- understanding and performing effectively roles and tasks related to 'knowledge management'.

As organisations internationalise and increasingly globalise their operations, a failure to generate new knowledge can lead to the repetition of old and increasingly irrelevant strategic recipes, and prevent responsiveness to new strategic issues that are emerging 'out there'. Changing patterns of competition, of employment, of work and of organisation all focus attention on the need for the adaptability and foresight that comes from continuous learning and the ability to generate new knowledge. Such knowledge can lead to two valuable outcomes:

- the production of new strategic assets

- an enhanced quality of strategic thinking and decision-making.

However, behind these apparently straightforward statements there is uncertainty. What exactly is knowledge? How does it relate to learning, and how do those two processes operate? What is an organisation's 'knowledge-base' and how can it be 'developed and regenerated'? In this chapter I explore different notions of 'knowledge' and discuss issues related to the 'learning organisation' and to changing organisational context. I then look at the role of work-based learning in developing new knowledge, and conclude by identifying some of the challenges facing those with a responsibility for 'knowledge management'.

Checkpoint

- Outline and justify some of the key tasks involved in L&D practitioners' acting as 'learning architects'.

- Why do you think that the CIPD's 2001 Standard for L&D identifies the development of knowledge as a key area of responsibility for L&D professionals?

Notions of knowledge

Knowledge development is a confused field. There is as yet no common language with which to unite disciplines or practitioners. To start at the beginning: what do we mean by 'knowledge'? Consider the following definitions:

> ***Knowledge***: representations of facts (including generalisations) and concepts organised for future use, including problem-solving.
>
> (Gregory, 1998)

> **Knowledge**: tacit and explicit mental models, beliefs and perspectives that influence perceptions and behaviour.
>
> (after Nonaka, 1991)

These different interpretations of knowledge underline the fact that every definition is problematic. Notions are widely debated, and emerge from a bewildering variety of theories. Classification systems, models and concepts overlap, while also being applied in differing ways by different theorists. There are no clear-cut boundaries between the various schools of thought, nor is it invariably the case that the most meaningful theories are those produced most recently. We may have more information about 'knowledge' now, but that does not necessarily mean that we understand the field any better than we did decades ago.

In this section I have chosen to examine two notions of knowledge. Each has its flaws, but each yields important insights. The notions are linked yet are discrete:

- knowledge as a commodity (Gregory's interpretation)

- knowledge as a relational process (Nonaka's interpretation).

Knowledge as commodity

Let us go back briefly to Chapter 1, to the discussion of scientific management and of systems theory. To engineers like Taylor, the organisation was a machine, and knowledge was central to its control. In this view, accurate knowledge enables the orderly and efficient organisation of people and operations in order to achieve a shared purpose. It provides the means by which to substitute a scientifically based uniformity of treatment for ineffective, arbitrary and often inequitable decision-making and management.

To systems theorists like Trist and Bamforth knowledge, acquired by accurate information-processing, makes possible the intelligent decision-making that is thought necessary to keep the organisation in equilibrium with its environment. Open systems theorists do, however, admit that information-processing systems do not function perfectly, and that decision-making processes are not fully rational. They attribute weaknesses partly to the complexity of much of the information 'out there' and its frequent lack of 'accuracy' or 'truthfulness', partly to lack of proficiency in processing and communicating information, and very much to the 'bounded rationality' of human beings that we noted in Chapter 3.

In both these views, knowledge is a type of commodity – something 'out there' that can be tracked down and acquired, assessed, codified and distributed across the organisation. It is an intangible asset that can have unique competitive value. This notion is lodged in a view of the world as an objective external entity, and of knowledge as a body of 'facts', truths, that explains the world.

Knowledge as relational process

A very different notion of knowledge stems from a view of the world not as a given external reality, as conceived in open systems theory, but as a socially constructed state. 'There is no objective reality. Reality is socially created' (von Krogh, Roos and Kleine 1998: 43). In this perspective, knowledge is both object *and* subject. It is an outcome of the learning process, but it is also a process, powerfully shaped by human relationships.

The notion of knowledge as a process emerging from within ourselves but intimately shaped by our relations with others, changing as our understanding and interpretation of the world around us changes, draws attention to the workplace where so many of our social interactions take place. The learning that is situated in those 'communities of practice' (Spender, 1994) can produce vital insights, as it did in the case of the photocopier repair technicians (case study, Chapter 1).

Much of the methodology underpinning research in the knowledge field has been criticised for its lack of rigour (see especially Hodgkinson's critique, 1996). Nonetheless, the relational view provides us with illuminating insights. What emerges in study after study, regardless of methodology, is that:

- 'knowing' is about relational and emotional as well as rational processes, social as well as psychological factors

- in organisations, cognition does occur in a social context or through a social process (Daft and Weick, 1984)

- both practical and social competencies are crucial in helping to explain the extent to which people behave intelligently in the context in which they find themselves (Ginsberg, 1994, p.155).

Once we view learning and knowledge in organisations as interactive processes that are situated primarily (although not exclusively) in the workplace, then we begin to appreciate that the workplace is a potential source of profound change. This helps to explain the major emphasis now being placed on workplace learning in national policy (Chapter 2).

However, we must be cautious. If an organisation's base of knowledge is regarded as essentially generated 'in here', this can create a problematic scenario for management. Knowledge that is embedded in social relationships is not a commodity. It cannot be owned by the company, as tangible assets can. Because it resides in people it cannot easily be transferred. Sometimes, although it can be observed in action (as in the case of the photocopier repair technicians), it cannot be fully articulated by those who possess it.

At this point I need to be more precise. I have already noted that the relational view of knowledge sees knowledge in two ways: as the outcome of learning, and as a process in itself. Nonaka (1991) explained knowledge outcomes, or types of knowledge, in the following way:

- *Tacit knowledge* is the knowledge that is embedded deep in the individual or collective subconscious, expressing itself in habitual or intuitive ways of doing things that are exercised without conscious thought or effort.

- *Explicit knowledge* is the knowledge that, once articulated, is written down, codified in protocols, guidelines, checklists, reports, memoranda, files, training courses or other tangible forms. At that point, it does indeed become a type of commodity, to be protected in patents and other legal formulae.

It is not clear how tacit knowledge is formed or how it changes through time, so such knowledge is difficult, if not impossible, to copy or to poach. It is for this reason often regarded as the source of the organisation's most distinctive competencies. However, by definition (as already indicated), this kind of knowledge cannot be wrested from people. They must agree to put it at the service of the collective whole. But what if they do not? What if 'knowledge' becomes a bargaining counter? Or what if actions that may be genuinely intended by management to foster the development and management of knowledge to the benefit of all are perceived by 'the managed' to be exploitative, and are therefore resisted?

It is here that the concept of the 'learning organisation' may seem to come to the rescue.

Checkpoint

- What is the difference between *explicit* and *tacit* knowledge?

- To what extent do you agree that there is more competitive value in tacit than in explicit knowledge?

The 'learning organisation'

Issues of collective learning

One of the most widely quoted definitions of the learning organisation is that of Pedler, Burgoyne and Boydell (1991): 'an organisation which facilitates the learning of all its members and continuously transforms itself'.

Such a statement suggests that organisations have a life of their own, and are themselves capable of learning (Matthews and Candy, 1999). This is unrealistic, and such claims do not lend themselves to practical implementation or measurement (Coopey, 1995). They appear to assume that the 'the learning organisation' and 'organisational learning' are synonymous processes, yet they are not. There are many research studies to show that organisational learning is not the aggregate of the learning of individuals and groups across the organisation. Collective learning is an area of considerable uncertainty in the literature, but we do know that to spread the learning of individuals or groups across the organisation needs carefully planned processes and systems. The following study is a case in point.

CASE STUDY: Learning at Toyota and Volvo

Adler and Cole (1993) compared data on two car manufacturing plants: the Toyota–GM NUMMI plant in California, representing the 'lean production' model favoured in recent years, and Volvo's Uddevalla plant in Sweden, set up to demonstrate and reap the benefit of 'human-centred' ways of organising the labour-intensive production of standardised products typified in the research of earlier US organisational psychologists like Hertzberg.

The researchers concluded (Adler and Cole, 1993: 86)

> although elements of the Uddevalla approach do indeed promise a higher potential for individual learning, NUMMI is the more effective model for encouraging organizational learning.

They found that NUMMI had created both world-class performance and a highly motivating work environment even though its work organisation followed the 'democratic Taylorism' model. At Uddevalla, management had provided a wide range of personal learning opportunities for its employees, focusing especially on team autonomy and decision decentralisation, in the belief that an increase in individual learning would automatically lead to an increase in collective organisational learning. In fact, 'this emphasis on individual learning had no counterpart in organizational learning' (Adler and Cole, 1993: 92).

Source: Adler and Cole, 1993.

Issues of power and politics

The notion of the 'learning organisation' is persuasive because of its human attractiveness and its claimed potential to aid organisational effectiveness and advancement (see, for example, Senge, 1990; Mills and Friesen, 1992). The emphasis is on openness, support, a climate of trust and challenge, learning from reflection and experience, and a focus on a commitment to the learning that can resolve hitherto intractable organisational problems. Yet this emphasis stems from a unitary view of the organisation, and can ignore issues of who controls that organisation and the uses to which new learning will be put. (We examined the difference between unitary and pluralist views of organisations in Chapter 6.)

Because what scholarly commentators refer to as the 'practice-oriented, prescriptive literature' of the 'learning organization' (Argyris and Schon, 1996: 180) rarely pays enough attention to issues of power, conflict and control, the extent to which the 'learning organisation' offers a genuinely new approach to management and workplace learning is questionable. It provides, after all, no convincing response to our concerns at the conclusion of the previous section, exemplified by such questions as:

- 'Who decides that this will become a learning organisation?'

- 'Why?'

- 'Who then is most likely to control and gain increased power from the new learning that such an organisation will presumably achieve?' (Coopey, 1995).

Too often, the answers are likely to be 'management' rather than 'all the members of the organisation'.

Other practical issues

There are other practical difficulties associated with the 'learning organisation' concept. If it is to become a reality, it requires the implementation of integrated business processes and developmental approaches that will encourage a search for organisationally valuable knowledge. One commentator has observed that this requires creating a 'rich landscape' of learning and development possibilities (Kessels, 1996). Such a landscape requires a skilful balance between formal systems and informal features that in practice is extremely hard to achieve. It presupposes a sophisticated approach to the knowledge process in organisations that (as we shall shortly see) does not fit easily with the lack of expertise and awareness that research indicates actually prevails in the field.

There is a contradiction, too, between the prescriptive framework of guidelines, questionnaire surveys and self-checks that typify the literature of the 'learning organisation' and the uncertainties that surround the knowledge and strategy processes. For example, we saw in Chapter 3 that the strategy process is not entirely rationally based. Yet UK exponents of the learning organisation such as Morris (1991) and Pedler and Boutall (1992) do appear to regard strategic change as essentially to do with rational activity, with the finding of better ways of tackling existing problems and of reorganising work. That kind of approach encourages single-loop learning. It is questionable, however, whether it can ever generate the double-loop learning that, by seeking out the root causes of those problems, can open the door to radical change.

Recently, there has been a reformulation of the learning organisation model, accompanied by a robust rebuttal of the claim that the concept or the practice is in decline (Burgoyne, 1999, 1999a). Unipart University has been used as a model of this new approach to the 'learning organisation' defined (Miller and Stewart, 1999: 43) as one in which:

- learning and business strategy are closely linked

- the organisation consciously learns from business opportunities and threats

- individuals, groups and the whole organisation are not only learning but continually learning how to learn

- information systems and technology serve to support learning rather than to control it

- there are well-developed processes for defining, creating, capturing, sharing and acting on knowledge

- these various systems and dimensions are balanced and managed as a whole.

This renewed attempt to apply generalised prescriptions to complex theoretical territory where there is still no consensus on basic concepts and issues does not convince everyone. For those like Critten (1999), Burgoyne's proposal that the learning organisation formula needs to follow a similar trajectory to Total Quality Management 'puts it right back into another box'; it is now time (he says) to let the whole concept go. This, however, is to disregard the very real interest in 'learning organisations' that is still evident in many organisations today. The following task recognises that interest and requires the reader to put it into a practical context.

Task 1

Do some research to find out how the 'learning organisation' model is intended by its advocates to be put into practice. Then draft a paper, either for your management or for your HR colleagues, in which you:
- produce and justify criteria to determine how far (if at all) it would be appropriate to transform your organisation into a 'learning organisation'
- assess what actions would be needed to achieve that transformation
- identify and explain the barriers and aids that you would expect to encounter in any attempt to implement those actions.

Changing the organisational context

Leadership's role

There are, then, no easy answers to our questions about how to ensure that people seek and share potentially valuable knowledge across an organisation. What does seem clear is that the emphasis should not be on management systems to 'control' learning or to 'manage' knowledge. Rather, attempts should be made to find 'new ways to encourage people to think creatively and feed their thoughts back into the organisation' (Russell and Parsons, 1996) and to provide the skills and support systems needed to manage the projects that arise from that creativity.

The main onus here lies with organisational leaders. If they create the right kind of vision and sense of purpose, then it is likely that people will increasingly seek and use new knowledge in order to drive the business forward. To do this, leaders need to understand the importance of signposting, facilitating and rewarding the development and sharing of knowledge as essential organisational tasks. If they take the initiative and ensure that managers support it in the workplace, the result can be new ways of understanding business issues, new ideas and new solutions that will enable the organisation and its people to make significant progress.

What we are confronting here is the need for leaders to create a new organisational context (Chapter 6) by providing new vision and values, and then by reshaping management style and actions and building a new kind of employment system.

Management actions and human resource strategies

Management structure and actions, HR strategies and the employment system of an organisation will significantly determine the extent to which knowledge is mobilised or constrained in the organisation.

Organisations are complex social institutions. Within them, formal and informal networks facilitate or impede the generation and transfer of knowledge. In particular, professional and occupational networks influence the development and application of knowledge both within and between organisations. For example, a highly segmented labour force operating in a hierarchical structure within which there are differentiated human resource systems relating to recruitment, rewards, career development and disengagement, will produce highly differentiated work communities. Those communities will be disposed to hoard rather than share knowledge, and will be in many cases unaware of, or uninterested in, any wider quest for knowledge than that likely to improve earnings or job-retention prospects at the individual level, or bargaining strengths at the institutional level. In such a system there is little hope of encouraging knowledge creation by 'tapping the tacit ... insights, intuitions and hunches of individual employees and making those insights available for testing and use by the company as a whole' (Nonaka, 1991).

Tasks for HR practitioners

What can those HR practitioners with L&D responsibilities contribute in order to help build an organisational context that is conducive to the development and sharing of strategically valuable knowledge?

They can use their expertise and business partnerships to:

- raise management's awareness, through training initiatives and through formal and informal learning processes, of the need to promote the development and spreading of new knowledge across the workforce and to ensure its effective application and its retention

- work with organisational leaders, local managers and team leaders to develop a culture in which workplace learning is understood as essential to the organisation's strategic progress, and help them to acquire the skills that they need to stimulate and support work-based learning

- raise awareness of the need for a performance management process that will encourage and reward knowledge-productive learning and contribute ideas on how that could be achieved

- introduce or propose initiatives and processes that enable an inclusive approach to learning, in order to access and share knowledge embedded in the grass-roots of the organisational community.

Beaumont and Hunter (2001) have explored the role of HR professionals in the knowledge process. Their findings highlight the need for culture change and for building internal competencies if knowledge is to be developed, transferred and retained across the organisation. They confirm the importance of establishing communities of practice that are shaped by the common interests of participants rather than by organisational structure. Their real-life case studies demonstrate the many ways in which this can be done.

What emerges clearly from such studies is that L&D practitioners should be pragmatic in carrying out such tasks, particularly because of the problematic issues that they can involve. For example:

- One of the barriers to achieving real inclusiveness in a community context is a domination of the learning environment by the customary players. The danger is that when new ideas do emerge from the grass-roots, they will be perceived as a threat to those players. It is here that the activities of local champions, who should have a direct involvement with learning initiatives from the start, are likely to be crucial to their success.

- Another barrier can be reluctance or apathy, from whatever cause, of certain individuals and groups in the workplace. Again, local champions are important here, as are ways of recognising and rewarding everyone's contributions to the development and dissemination of knowledge.

- There should be sufficient oversight and direction of workplace learning to ensure that valuable knowledge is identified and utilised, without thereby erecting a formal superstructure that becomes rigid, top-heavy and bureaucratised.

- Although a shared sense of purpose is important in stimulating the knowledge process, it should not be of a kind that stifles individual and group initiative. Challenges to fixed ways of thinking and behaving can act as spurs to creativity and produce innovation that benefits the organisation.

[The author's acknowledgements for these suggestions are due to Richard Bromiley, doctoral research student in the Department of Geography, University of Durham, who in 1999 carried out initial field-work for her and for the Northeast Regional Development Agency – ONE NorthEast – to test this template in a context of community learning and regeneration.]

Task 2

Taking the points noted in this section, draft a discussion paper for your management that makes practical suggestions for L&D practitioners to facilitate the development and sharing of knowledge in the organisation. Pay particular attention to the skills and support that those practitioners will need in performing the tasks you propose.

Building learning partnerships

We have been looking at learning partnerships. Increasingly, as organisations enter and compete in global markets there must be intra-organisational as well as internal learning alliances. Such networks are vital to the process of questioning and challenge that is 'especially essential during times of crisis or breakdown when a company's traditional categories of knowledge no longer work' (Nonaka, 1991: 103). The more people within an organisation, and organisations themselves, interact positively with one another, the stronger the tendency to adopt shared belief systems and common frames of reference and to develop a common language to fuel discourse.

A learning partnership that operates as a long-term strategic alliance can generate knowledge and creativity that produce increasing value through time. It does this through commitment to the idea that 'learning is about increasing your capacity to create that which you previously couldn't create' (Senge, 1990). Such a partnership requires a shared commitment to a long-haul approach, with the partners often closely co-operating on a number of interlinked projects over time, all under the umbrella of a clear long-term purpose. Stakeholders who invest in the partnership must be prepared to sacrifice immediate profitability for longer-term strategic success. The partners must be committed to working together at close quarters, and must have the skill to drive their partnership forward through an effective strategic management process. To do this, they must forge a shared work ethos that values and promotes trust, mutual support and continuous learning.

One example of a such an alliance is General Electric's Crotonville Centre, where in the later years of the twentieth century seconded university staff worked in close partnership with GE leaders, HR professionals and successive cohorts of GE executives to leverage major strategic change.

CASE STUDY: Crotonville: 'staging ground for corporate revolution'

The launch and development of Crotonville

Crotonville, General Electric's Management Development Institute, was launched in 1956 by chief executive officer Ralph Cordiner, with a 13-week advanced management programme as a direct lever for change, enabling multi-functional general managers to run a decentralised company. It was built in a campus-like setting in Ossining, New York, and its curriculum design drew on the expertise of academics across the USA. From the start, it was to be the breeding-ground for a new type of leader in a company that had to find a way of quickly developing the talent to enable it to capitalise fully on the post-World-War-II market opportunities.

Under the next CEO, Borch, it was used to introduce strategic planning to GE. During the 1980s and 1990s it was used by Jack Welsh, the famed CEO (who retired only in 2000 aged over 80 after an outstandingly successful and innovative 19-year régime), as a key lever in the radical transformation of the company's culture and to facilitate de-layering, downsizing and change. He wanted 'a revolution to start at Crotonville. I want it to be part of the glue that holds GE together' (Tichy, 1996: 244–5).

Noel Tichy managed the Institute from 1985 to 1987 when he was on two-year sabbatical leave from the University of Michigan.

Mission and strategy for Crotonville

When Tichy arrived at Crotonville in 1985, it had a new mission:

> To leverage GE's global competitiveness, as an instrument of cultural change, by improving business acumen, leadership abilities and organisational effectiveness of General Electric professionals.

Taking in about 8,000 learners a year, Crotonville now had to fuel the company's transformation. This meant the need for a 'shift in the Crotonville mindset from a training to a workshop mentality', and this led to radical changes in programme design. In 1987, following Tichy's departure, Crotonville's portfolio expanded further, with all technical education at GE brought under one manager's direction, along with recruitment and initial training for new college hires. In this way, Crotonville became CE's 'integrating device' for co-ordinating developmental activity from new entry to leadership levels.

The transformational thrust

In 1989, the Centre was used by CEO Jack Welsh to move the bureaucracy of the company from its 'old way' to a 'new way', led by its middle management. The new way was to be non-hierarchical, fast-paced and flexible (Tichy, 1996). To do this, officer workshops under the title of 'Workout' were designed to mobilise 30,000–40,000 middle managers, working in every GE business. The workshops brought together business heads and all their middle-level managers to work on unresolved company-wide issues, with Welsh's active participation also.

A career model of leadership development was used to identify key transition points in people's careers – 'moments of opportunity' – and to provide L&D initiatives at those points to produce shared values and leadership characteristics. There were therefore tailored programmes for:

- entry-level graduates
- functional contributors
- new managers
- experienced managers
- functional leaders
- business leaders.

There was also a portfolio of 'elective programmes', changing through time to meet changing company needs.

Crotonville achieved lasting success, due in large measure to the personal involvement of the CEO, Jack Welsh, who used development 'as a lever for change and as a creator of the new shared values in leadership'.

Source: Tichy, 1996

Reflecting on the Crotonville case, certain principles emerge related to building and maintaining successful strategic learning partnerships. These include the need for:

- a powerful and challenging vision that will provide a cohesive purpose for the partnership through time

- mutuality of interest and of goals, and a common language

- a shared commitment to openness, trust, collaboration, productive conflict and knowledge-sharing

- a formal infrastructure to support the partnership through time, and an agreed process for managing the partnership

- partners with the necessary capability, commitment and resources to fuel and sustain the relationship.

Task 3

Produce a discussion paper for your HR director/ or equivalent, setting out your ideas for an innovative learning partnership that will produce fresh thinking, new skills and changed relationships in the organisation, and will add value for the business and for individuals.

Enhancing learning in the workplace

Government help to improve work-based learning

So far, the emphasis has been on the importance of the learning that occurs naturally within communities of practice situated in the workplace. However, not all workplace learning occurs as part of a natural relational process. A great deal is formally planned. In 2000 the practitioner community in England engaged in funded training numbered between 95,000 and 110,000. That did not include subcontracted activities where providers outsourced some tasks. Work-based assessment and internal verification are among the most commonly outsourced activities. (The following comments are based on a consultation document distributed by the Department for Education and Employment in 2000.)

Work-based learning practitioners include:

- managers, resource and programme co-ordinators

- tutors/occupational trainers and assessors

- supervisors

- administrators

- other support staff.

Improving the competence of such practitioners is now an official priority. Reports from Training Standards Inspectors and other official bodies have expressed much concern about the quality of planning, delivery and support of work-based learning, identifying a serious lack of skill and knowledge in those carrying out work-based learning roles. There are also many concerns about quality assurance processes. One problem is the wide range and varying levels of qualification held by work-based learning practitioners. Providers question the utility of some of these qualifications. The greatest take-up is of qualifications centred on work-based assessment and verification. Generic qualifications for vocational trainers and tutors are significantly less widespread. Other qualifications – in particular those focused on the management of training and quality and related planning activities – are much less widely supported.

This uneven pattern of take-up is also of concern. In December 2001 the Chancellor announced in a pre-budget report that the government would be investing £40 million in a pilot initiative to boost workforce training, due to begin in September 2002 (Roberts, 2001). Ultimately some £7 billion per year will be delivered into workplace training and education, and 'the government is anxious that the delivery of this investment is by competent people in the training area' (Employment National Training Organisation, 2001). Organisations will have to demonstrate that they meet the qualifications and competency requirements that are a condition of funding.

The Employment National Training Organisation (EmpNTO), the body responsible for setting standards for work-based learning in the UK, has been working with the Department for Education and Skills (DfES) to produce new standards and related qualifications for those who plan, deliver and assess such learning. So far three qualifications have been approved by the English and Scottish qualifications and curriculum authorities (see Chapter 8). The activities covered by these qualifications relate to:

- managing the training and delivery process
- planning and developing integrated programmes of work-based training
- identifying trainees' abilities and needs in relation to programmes of work-based training
- providing appropriate work-based training opportunities
- supporting trainees and monitoring progress against an agreed training plan (for example, through mentoring)
- assessing trainees' achievements on work-based programmes
- monitoring and evaluating effectiveness of work-based programmes

● developing and monitoring professional competence.

The Chartered Institute of Personnel and Development also has grave concerns about work-based learning provision, as noted in Chapter 2 (p33). In its 2001 Professional Standards it produced a revised Certificate of Training Practice and a new suite of L&D Standards at professional qualifying level to guide the performance and improve the competence of all those with L&D responsibilities. The L&D Standards cover (CIPD, 2001):

● learning and development

● managing organisational learning and knowledge

● managing the training and development function

● training design and delivery

● management development.

Checkpoint

● Explain why work-based learning is a cause of current concern at national level.

● Identify and discuss ways in which national and professional bodies are giving help to work-based learning practitioners.

Building a knowledge-productive organisation

In all the discussion so far, what have really been explored are qualities, processes and activities that can build a 'knowledge-productive' organisation. What does that mean? Simply, it is an organisation where there is an approach to the processes of work and learning that leads to the expansion of existing knowledge and the generation of new knowledge for the organisation (Kessels, 1996).

To be knowledge-productive, learning is not enough. There must also be unlearning and relearning. 'Relearning' refers to the need to transfer old learning to new contexts, and to make the necessary adjustments that this process involves. Its significance in relation to all types of change situation is clear and in consequence it receives much attention in major organisational change programmes. Yet in the achievement of such change 'unlearning' is arguably of even greater importance. The process involves the removal of any barriers to relearning and to new learning that are presented by previously acquired knowledge, skills, attitudes and cognitions. One of the paradoxes of becoming a 'successful' organisation is that the longer success is sustained, the less likely it is that organisational leaders will be able to achieve the unlearning needed to produce radically different strategies when external challenges require them.

An example of an organisation in which leaders recognised and acted on the need for such unlearning is given below. It continues the story of Ford begun in Chapter 19.

CASE STUDY: How Ford Europe gained competitive edge in the 1980s

We have already seen in Chapter 19 how it came to be recognised by Ford's leaders in the 1980s that the old 'economies of scale' paradigm had become increasingly inappropriate. A new paradigm was needed, focused on the importance of quality and service, of differentiation allied to cost.

Learning how to think about a different pattern of links between the nature of the market and of organisation and job design was impeded by the fact that no one in the company had any concept of an alternative pattern. The regular importation of new information, and the continuous stimulation of reflection, debate and experimentation across all sectors of the organisation through a variety of changed business and decision-making processes and workplace practice had to take place over a long period of time before unlearning finally occurred and a new paradigm emerged. Slowly, as people were brought together in new ways in the workplace, and through the creation of new routines, new business processes, new ways of decision-making, a new comprehension of the organisation became established – one of Ford as a social entity, with a social organisation of production based on teamwork, skill flexibility, and communication processes that tapped into workers' tacit knowledge.

In the view of the researchers, transformation at Ford Europe was only gained by the sustained vision and purpose of corporate leaders in ensuring the pursuit across Ford of 'often painful learning to undo existing patterns of thought and behaviour' (Starkey and McKinlay, 1993: 2). Those leaders did not impose change. They facilitated it. They worked with other employees to develop new self-descriptions for the organisation, effective languaging and knowledge connectivity. They provided a generalised steering process, as everyone at Ford went through often painful unlearning and relearning processes before achieving new learning and knowledge.

Source: Starkey and McKinlay, 1993

This example supports comments made earlier about the need for organisational leaders to produce vision and values that encourage new learning, and to build an organisational context where that learning can take root.

Issues of 'knowledge management'

How should an organisation 'manage' its knowledge-base? It seems logical to argue that the way in which knowledge is managed in an organisation should largely be determined by its type and uniqueness (Hall, 1996). Some codified, explicit knowledge is of such value to the organisation that it has to be managed as a legal entity, often with property rights (for example, patents, copyright and licences). Some may be so sensitive that access to it has to be restricted. Other information may be related to particular jobs, positions, tasks or functions and so may need to be recorded in training manuals.

Tacit knowledge, on the other hand, cannot be 'managed', as we have seen earlier in the chapter – but it can be enhanced by socialisation

(Hall, 1996) and by a workplace climate that encourages and facilitates teamwork, informal meetings and discussions, exchanges of views and observations of internal 'best practice'. Such methods are likely to lead to tacit knowledge being shared widely among organisational members without that knowledge having to be made explicit (Nonaka, 1991). When uniquely valuable tacit knowledge is embedded in a number of people rather than a few, it is less likely to become explicit and thereby vulnerable to copying or poaching. The issues involved in its transfer are therefore very different from those involved in transferring explicit knowledge (see also Dixon, 2000).

Current problems in knowledge management

Research carried out for the CIPD (Scarbrough, Swan and Preston, 1999) showed that different organisations have different perspectives on what is loosely called 'knowledge management' (KM). In some, especially financial institutions, knowledge is valued as intellectual capital. In some, knowledge is exploited as intellectual property, and is viewed as a commodity that is essential to competitive strategy (eg pharmaceutical organisations). In some, what is important is to capture the knowledge gained from learning that has taken place in individual projects, disseminating it across the organisation to promote creativity and innovation (eg consultancies and professional service organisations).

When discussing knowledge 'management' it is common to stress the value of electronic information-processing. Yet we must be cautious here. Information is not knowledge. It is simply one stage in the process of developing knowledge. Information has to be put in order and interpreted by people before 'knowledge' emerges from it (Von Krogh, Roos and Slocum, 1994). Furthermore, a preoccupation with the notion of knowledge as commodity indicates a Tayloristic approach that fails to take sufficiently into account the human element, infinite in its perversity and variability. It is essential to get the right balance between encouraging the generation of knowledge (through focusing on the people issues involved) and facilitating its dissemination and codification (where new technology can offer important ways forward). Managers, HR practitioners and IT specialists should be aware that (Nahapiet and Ghoshal, 1998):

> the availability of electronic knowledge exchange does not automatically induce a willingness to share information and build new intellectual capital.

This warning seems to have had little effect (Scarbrough *et al*, 1999). There still appears to be a preoccupation with systems to process and spread information. Continued dominance of this narrowly conceived approach may well lead to an 'obsession with tools and techniques' that ignores or minimises the centrality of people throughout the knowledge process (*ibid.*).

Table 1 Building learning and development into the business

Strategic level	L&D's strategic focus is on:	L&D must:	Crucial processes for: L&D	L&D specialist/manager needs to:
1 Corporate	• formulating L&D mission, goals and strategy to achieve corporate goals • influencing and developing strategic thinking and planning	• 'fit' with wider HR strategy • be aligned with corporate strategy • help to secure appropriate balance between corporate goals for survival and for advancement • produce L&D strategy that is capable of implementation at Level 2	• collaboratively developing mission and goals for L&D • strategic planning and thinking • influencing key stakeholders • adding value through L&D activity	• have board-level position/access and skills • be pro-active as well as reactive • have deep knowledge of competitive environment • fully understand the value chain and strategic assets of the business • speak the language and logic of the business • work in business partnerships
2 Business unit/managerial	• developing L&D policies and systems in line with strategic needs of the business unit • ensuring achievement of business targets • influencing and developing strategic thinking, organisational capacity and human capability	• 'fit' with wider HR policies and systems • be aligned with business unit policy • have a clear plan within the overall business plan, with agreed evaluation measures • ensure feedback on policies to Level 1	• working with HR and business unit managers to produce policies and plans for acquisition, retention, growth/redeployment of workforce • developing key performance indicators • strategic thinking and business planning • adding value through L&D activity	• work in business partnership with managers and others • have collaborative relationships with other HR specialists • have deep knowledge of competitive environment of company and of business units • fully understand how strategic assets can be developed • speak the language and logic of the business units
3 Operational	• ensuring individual and team performance targets are met • improving acquisition, quality and motivation of people for the business.	• adapt to needs of the business and needs and aspirations of people • ensure L&D activity is expertly carried out and appropriately evaluated • ensure feedback of outcomes to Level 2.	• working with teams and individuals to implement business plans for L&D • appraisal, personal development planning to achieve targets and improve core competencies and capabilities.	• working in partnership with internal and external stakeholders • have effective and efficient systems and procedures • have deep knowledge of culture of the workforce • be expert and continuously self-developing.

To prevent this from happening, HR professionals – including those with L&D responsibilities –should be working in partnership with management, project leaders and external partners to discover ways of effectively developing, disseminating and using knowledge. As yet, they seem to be rarely doing so. More worryingly, they are often unaware of the need to do so. Many, perhaps most, seem unfamiliar with the KM field and have no shared language amongst themselves or with management for entering it. General management is often hampered by a similar lack of understanding. In such a situation, it is unsurprising that IT 'experts', who appear to 'speak the language' and to offer an impressive array of 'solutions', lead the action.

It is these concerns that explain why the CIPD's 2001 L&D Standard emphasises the tasks for L&D professionals outlined at the start of this chapter. Once again, we can look (on p399) at the table used in Chapter 1 – this time to appreciate how to build such tasks into the business.

Task 4

Read back through this chapter. Then consider your own organisation, or one with which you are familiar. Identify some ways in which you see knowledge being developed, shared, and put to valuable use in the organisation. Analyse how this is being done, and relate your analysis back to the theory you have been studying thus far.

The 'thinking organisation'

We have mentioned at intervals throughout this book the importance of HR practitioners' being 'thinking performers'. This chapter points to the need for 'thinking organisations' also. Below is a case study which demonstrates the meaning of that phrase and pulls together much of the material in this chapter. It offers three particularly important lessons:

- It shows how to achieve flexibility and innovation through a strong base of education and training, appropriate HR policies, and effective selection, deployment, conditions and rewards, flexibility and disengagement.

- It shows how unlearning and relearning can be promoted. Relying on natural learning processes in the organisation is not enough here, because those processes can be blinkered, concentrating too much on existing strategic goals and on tasks in hand. At Hydro Polymers in 1982, it needed new ownership to produce a change in strategic direction. That new leadership, together with the crisis faced by the company, enabled the old culture and mindsets to be overturned. The subsequent threefold thrust of education and training, flexibility and technological innovation ensured the durability of that change. Further 'traumatic events' around 1990 in the external environment led to a dramatic acceleration in learning, capability and performance of the company.

- It shows the valuable role that effective, expert training can play in improving not only competence and performance, but also learning skills and the generation and sharing of knowledge in the workplace.

CASE STUDY: Hydro Polymers, Aycliffe, Co. Durham 1982–97

History and context

Between 1946 and 1963 Bakelite Ltd, a US company well established in the UK, carried out chemical processing at a site in Newton Aycliffe, Co. Durham. After various changes in corporate structure, Norsk Hydro, Norway's largest industrial company, purchased the PVC Resin and Compound Facility at Aycliffe in 1982, merging vinyl production with their existing loss-making Vinatex plants at three other sites in the UK to form Norsk Hydro Polymers Ltd (NHPL).

In 1982 the Aycliffe plant was characterised by traditional restrictive working practices and attitudes, and a low-morale workforce. It compared badly in terms of both productivity and product quality with competitors, many of whom were already using sophisticated microprocessor production control techniques. In 1983 new strategic aims were announced for NHPL in order to enable it to improve its position in an increasingly competitive market. Flexible working practices and a larger investment programme were seen as essential to prevent further decline in performance.

In 1984 the company, at that time 90 per cent unionised, was restructured following a negotiated agreement on radical changes in working practices and payment systems. A Statement of Intent was issued, with goals of harmonisation of terms and conditions (including sick pay), improved flexibility in the workforce, a regular weekly wage for all and the removal of bonus schemes. Job losses were unavoidable but most

were achieved by natural wastage and voluntary redundancy.

1985–97: the 'thinking organisation'

In 1985 a drive started to improve the educational and competency base of the company in order to enhance its performance and its adaptability. A £6 million investment programme enabled its employees to commence training courses to broaden their skills and raise their level of educational attainment. The aim was training to standards and for competence.

Thereafter, the aim consistently remained to educate, not just train, the workforce in order to create a 'thinking' culture – explained by senior company personnel as an organisation in which everyone thinks strategically, looking out into the environment for new challenges and ideas, and thinking for the future as well as for immediate improvements. People at Hydro Polymers are not paid to learn – there are no bonuses or special payments for attaining qualifications – but they are encouraged to do so both in the nature of the work that they do and in the opportunities offered for self-learning. Open learning is a major part of the culture, and there is access to the Open College, Open University (OU) and MBA courses (there are on-site tutorials for OU students). The mentoring process is an important one. Everyone has a self-development plan. The level of vocational qualification attainment is high.

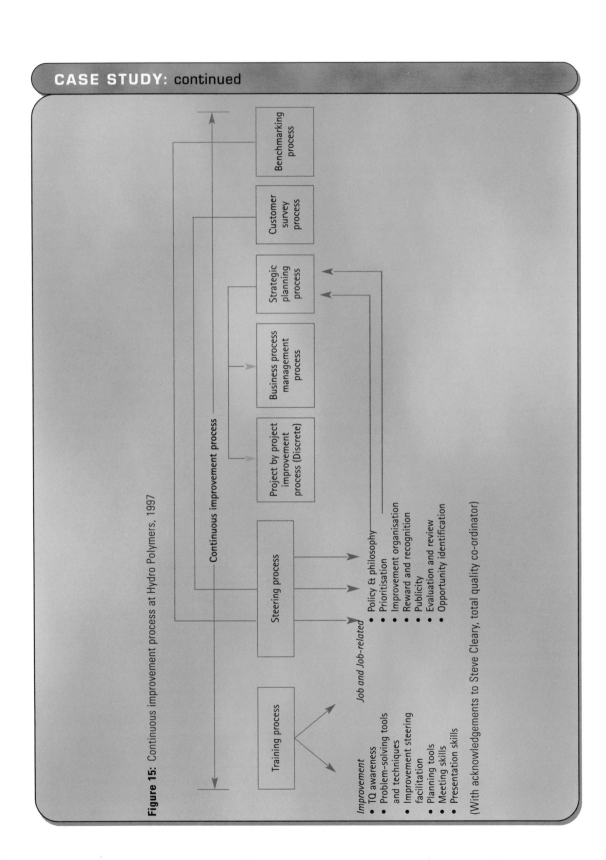

Figure 15: Continuous improvement process at Hydro Polymers, 1997

(With acknowledgements to Steve Cleary, total quality co-ordinator)

CASE STUDY: continued

Organisational change

By 1997, the style of relationships in the workplace at Hydro Polymers had fundamentally changed. It had become one of participative dialogue, not of the confrontational behaviour that in the early 1980s so divided management from the rest of the workforce. Close relationships were built too with suppliers and local firms, involving them in various training and team events. A project-based organisation structure reinforced this style. Figure 15 (opposite) shows the structure of the continuous improvement process at Hydro Polymers, designed to achieve integration between training, steering of projects, project management, strategic planning, benchmarking and customer-surveying.

Collective learning

The company relied on continuous improvement, accelerated learning and innovation to build a secure future for the business and its people. There was no suggestion scheme because it was thought to be divisive in a situation where the aim was to achieve teamwork, collective learning and shared commitment to new ideas. Financial rewards for new ideas were tried out for teams, but made far less impact than other forms of recognition now given regularly to successful projects. These included features in the company newsletter, presentation of projects to top management by those responsible for running them, Christmas hampers and gifts from Norway (more valued than the former annual bonus even though the cost was much less), and celebratory events in which the local community was involved.

The strategic role of middle management and supervisors

Once the company's structure had been flattened, there could not be any 'ladder of success' (a term used by a senior executive), so there had to be other motivators. Money was not used for this purpose: basic pay was good, and attracted a high calibre of recruit to work for the company. The motivation was intended to be provided by the workplace environment. It was one in which people felt that they were fulfilling a valued role and that they were a crucial part of the company's outstanding success.

The supervisors had a key role. They drove the quality programme and they were the team leaders. Competent people at any level had the opportunity to take on new roles, and as a result of this many managers were now more involved in strategic planning, a process that at Hydro Polymers had a specific meaning. It referred to obtaining information from a wide variety of sources and generating a wide range of options, systematically analysing them, and doing all this with a longer- rather than shorter-term perspective.

1997: Outcomes

By 1997 a culture of training, learning and involvement was well embedded at Hydro Polymers. It had become accepted that the person doing the job was the one with most knowledge about it; all employees had a say in what happened in their plant, the processes and the business; they all held responsibility for change and were trained to be aware of the need for quality throughout all their work.

By many quantifiable measures, striking improvements had gone on being made through the projects introduced across the business, saving more than £5 million in five years, helping the company to remain profitable and building security for employees. In 1995–96 alone, 57 new projects were introduced and 55 completed, with savings of £712,407 achieved. Business processes were understood and were being steadily improved on by the workforce. Hydro Polymers, like Cummins Engine Co. at Darlington, was a company that was 'in it for the long haul'.

It may be argued that project management of the kind that helped to lead this advance is likely to produce only continuous improvement, not the real

CASE STUDY: continued

innovation that generates discontinuous change — that is to say, change of a quite different kind from any experienced in the past (Chesbrough and Teece, 1996). On the other hand, there is considerable evidence to indicate that the sustained and wide-ranging changes that took place at Hydro Polymers for over 13 years were of the fundamental kind most likely to develop capacity for radical innovation. The landscape of corporate learning in a company like this has become so rich and its internal competencies so well developed that the company's capacity to advance seems unarguable.

(With acknowledgements to the company and to Ennew and Ford, 1990.)

CONCLUSION

Having read this chapter and completed its checkpoints and tasks, you should now:

- understand some major notions of knowledge, and their implications for L&D practice in the organisation
- be able to contribute to the development of effective work-based learning
- understand how organisations can become 'knowledge-productive'
- be able to advise on L&D roles and tasks related to the 'management of knowledge'.

To test yourself against these objectives, what five-minute answers would you give to the following questions?

Review questions

Describe *three* ways in which an emphasis on creative methods of workplace learning, rather than on external training and educational courses, can benefit an organisation.

One of the managers in your organisation asks you what you mean by a 'learning alliance' with external partners, and what value such a partnership might bring for the organisation. Outline a convincing reply.

An organisation's employees do not show enough awareness of the organisation's long-term goals and of changing trends and threats in its environment. Suggest *three* L&D initiatives to improve strategic awareness across the organisation.

Useful reference sources

BEAUMONT P. *and* HUNTER L. (2002) *Managing Knowledge Workers*. London, Chartered Institute of Personnel and Development. (Incorporates 15 case studies from the private and public sectors.)

BOUD D. *and* GARRICK J. (EDS) (1999) *Understanding Learning at Work*. London, Routledge.

EVANS K., HODKINSON P., KEEP E., MAGUIRE M., RAFFE D., RAINBIRD H., SENKER P. *and* UNWIN L. (1997) *Working To Learn – A work-based route to learning for young people*. London, Institute of Personnel and Development.

SCARBROUGH H. *and* SWAN J. (EDS) (1999) *Case Studies in Knowledge Management*. London, Institute of Personnel and Development.

STERN E. *and* SOMMERLAD E. (1999) *Workplace Learning, Culture and Performance*. London, Institute of Personnel and Development.

PART 5

ENHANCING STRATEGIC PROGRESS

• International Policy Frameworks

CHAPTER OBJECTIVES

After reading this chapter you will:

- have a context for understanding the international – and especially the European – scenario relating to vocational education and training

- understand the key differences between national vocational education and training systems in major competitor countries and the UK

- be able to identify lessons that such comparisons offer both for UK government policy on vocational education and training and for L&D policy in organisations.

Introduction

In this final part of the book we come full circle. We return in this chapter to the external policy context of L&D activity covered in Chapter 2 and broaden it to incorporate international comparisons. In Chapter 22 we discover the finishing point of that journey through L&D territory that we began in Chapter 1. There are no concluding review questions in these chapters, because at this advanced level the issues are not amenable to any brief analysis or prescriptions. Some checkpoints and tasks are included, however, in order to stimulate learning and reflection.

The aim in this chapter is to place the L&D process in the context of vocational education and training (VET) policies followed in some key competitor countries. It is not in the scope of the chapter, or indeed of this book, to look more widely at L&D issues related to internationalised businesses and to globalisation. Those are complex matters that require specialist treatment (although as an introduction interested readers are referred to Brewster, Harris and Sparrow, 2001). Here, we first outline and explore the European VET framework, then make some cross-country VET comparisons. We conclude with some lessons for the UK that emerge from those comparisons.

Vocational education and training policy in Europe

This section provides a basic conceptual framework for European VET policy. It involves three interacting parameters: the socio-economic, the labour market and the educational.

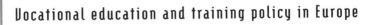

1 The socio-economic parameter

The Single European Market (SEM) has two aims (Hendry, 1994: 93):

- the removal of all artificial barriers to the stimulation of trade within the European Community (EC)

- the improvement, by means of their restructuring and internationalisation resulting from that stimulation, of European firms' competitive capability in the global market.

These two aims produce tensions between economic and social interests. The European Commission's vision of VET is one of many powerful contributors to the development of the EC, meeting a range of social and economic public policy objectives (Commission of the EC, 1989). This vision may seem essentially the same as the vision for VET policy in the UK, but the way in which policy is formulated and implemented across most of the EU is very different from the UK's non-regulatory approach.

At Community level, the Directorate General for employment, industrial relations and social affairs holds responsibility within the Commission for training. Policy is executed by a Task Force on Human Resources, Education, Training and Youth. An advisory committee for vocational training and an education committee meet regularly with union and employer bodies to discuss training as part of the 'social dialogue'. 'Social dialogue' is a key term. It refers to a process involving the social partners in training policy in order to encourage employers to contribute to long-term profitability and economic performance rather than training only for immediate needs. This dialogue enables stakeholder interests, in the shape of organisations representing employers and unions, to agree on policy that is informed by practical knowledge and expertise, and increases the likelihood of successful implementation.

Together, the Community's social partners have produced a series of joint Opinions endorsing the importance of education and training within the SEM (Rainbird, 1993). Most member states (apart from the UK) mirror this Community-level approach by having some form of regulation of the VET system, and by incorporating employer and trade union interests into the policy-making process.

2 The labour market parameter

A country's labour market, like an organisation's, can be divided broadly into two segments (van der Klink and Mulder, 1995):

- *primary* – Entry to this segment requires professional qualifications and sometimes specific vocational training. Those in the primary segment of the labour market usually enjoy favourable terms of employment and working conditions, relatively high job security and good promotion prospects.

- *secondary* – In this segment most jobs involve manual/semi-skilled work. What training there is tends to be focused on improving productivity on the job, not on opening up career paths for individuals. There are few of the advantages enjoyed in the primary segment, since there are minimum training requirements, poor terms of employment and little job security.

The labour market itself has two sectors:

- *external* – people waiting for employment, including relatively large numbers of school-leavers, the unemployed and women returners

- *internal* – comprising the human resource base of the organisation, where employee resourcing policy can produce an integrated flow of people into, through and out of the organisation, with a particular focus on performance management, personnel development, career paths and an interlinking L&D policy.

Use of this fourfold matrix can show the extent to which a country's labour market links its educational system to its business needs. The matrix can be applied to an organisation's internal labour market and educational system in the same way.

Task 1

Use the fourfold matrix just described to examine your own organisation and to identify people resourcing and development policies.

Record on the matrix approximately what proportion of your organisation's employees is in the primary sector (highly qualified/professional/highly trained and skilled employees) and what proportion is in the secondary sector (semi-skilled and unskilled).

Then, looking at these two sectors, record the kind and proportion of employees in each to be customarily recruited from the external labour market, and to be customarily recruited from internal sources.

What does your completed matrix suggest to you about the operation of your organisation's internal labour market, and about its recruitment, development and retention policies?

There are many factors affecting the way in which, in Europe, the interaction between educational system and labour market operates. Below, we look at four of the most powerful – routes that are used to achieve competitive advantage, barriers to flexibility of labour, the plight of the unskilled underclass, and the labour market that operates within organisations.

Europe's routes to competitive advantage
Although competing on efficiency and low costs are two possible routes

to competitive advantage, their benefits can cancel each other out in net terms. It is the quality route, focusing on high added value, that promises to minimise the immediate costs of the SEM and to maximise its longer-term benefits. That route involves 'capital investment in new production techniques and products, an expanding knowledge-base, and a more highly skilled workforce' (Hendry, 1994: 98). A high-skill strategy requires a strong and successful VET drive. Without this, a large proportion of the labour force will remain trapped in the secondary segment of the labour market and it will not be possible to sustain a drive for quality and innovation.

The UK, like Spain and Greece, is disadvantaged in a drive for long-term quality, being competitively strong only in some (perhaps one-third) of its industrial sectors. Germany, on the other hand, possesses competitive strength in most of its sectors, with 73 per cent of its employment in the primary segment of the labour market. Another source of disadvantage for the UK is that its large firms distribute significantly more of their profits to investors and significantly less to employees than do such firms elsewhere in Europe. This means that employees have less sense of ownership, and also that there is a lower level of investment in those areas that fuel innovation and growth – research and development and L&D – than is the case generally across the rest of Europe. Typical consequences of this culture of short-termism and of shareholder domination in the UK include a low level of average wage and of productivity, reflecting and reinforcing lack of adequate investment in education and training for skills and in employee rewards.

Hendry (1994) pointed out that in the UK's low-wage economy, which is also more internationalised than any other economy in the EC, workers are particularly vulnerable. Internationalised companies require strong social controls in order to avoid exploiting low-wage economies, but the UK has consistently resisted the Social Chapter's attempts to provide such controls.

It would be easy to conclude from the above comments that in a European Community where the quality route is the one being chosen by the majority of countries, the few that, like the UK, are low-wage economies with relatively unregulated labour markets are likely to lose out. However, there is another viewpoint that puts the UK's labour and VET policies in a rather different perspective.

Barriers to a flexible labour market
It was always predicted that there would be job losses on a major scale in the first few years of the SEM's existence as administrative barriers came down, but the position was expected to correct itself after about six years. In reality, unemployment rates across most of the European Union (EU) are still high – averaging over 8 per cent in early 1997 – and job creation has been low. However, economies like those of the USA and the UK which have deregulated labour markets and more labour flexibility have generated more service-sector jobs than has continental

Europe. Many of these jobs have been part-time, and many taken by women (Wolf, 1994). These countries have also achieved lower youth and female unemployment rates. The USA has had the additional advantages of a mobile population and (until very recently) a thriving domestic economy. Traditionally it has therefore avoided the persistent divide between high and low unemployment regions that characterises Europe and the UK.

The EU also suffers from poor export performance and slow growth of output. An important factor here is its heavy labour costs, to which three major contributors are protective labour legislation, relatively high taxation, and a flabby and highly bureaucratised public sector. The steady appreciation of European currencies against the US dollar has added to the EU's competitive disadvantage.

These failures to achieve the expected benefits of the SEM are putting increasing pressure on a hitherto highly differentiated labour market across Europe. Signs of convergence are becoming evident. Country differences rarely explain comparative competitive advantage, since weaknesses in one area of practice tend to cancel out gains in another, leaving the total package of labour costs, flexibility and skill levels similar across Europe (Goodhart, 1994a). Now, as Balls and Goodhart identified (1994), wage restraint is becoming a trend across Europe. There have been, however, few signs of significant social dumping – a process that involves such measures as lowering wage costs, cutting social benefits, increasing hours of work and reducing restraints on employers. Reductions in direct wages and job cuts have occurred, but by the end of the twentieth century they were proving to be the consequence less of a deliberate dumping policy or of the feared cheap labour/low-cost competition from Far East countries, more of technical and organisational change.

Flexibility is the issue here. Rising real wages and failures in training and education systems are leaving European countries ill-equipped to match competitors in future high-tech products, in the same way as cheap imports from low-wage developing countries are undercutting the expensive products of European manufacturers of medium- and low-tech goods (Balls and Goodhart, 1994). As the shift towards more sophisticated technology grows in advanced economies and as fewer, better-educated workers are employed in manufacturing, wage and labour flexibility become vital for Europe. Failure to adjust is in time bound to lead to high and persistent unemployment.

This suggests a need for more labour market deregulation in the EU. It must be sufficient to give the necessary wage and labour flexibility but not enough to threaten the level of job security needed to maintain workers' commitment. Many commentators feel that the labour market models of the UK and the USA are proving more relevant for the future than the tightly regulated Germanic model spreading across the Netherlands, Belgium and France (Ashton, Sung, Raddon and Powell, 2001).

However, there is a downside here. In an article summarising research undertaken by academics at Sheffield Hallam University, Paterson (2000) noted that although official UK figures showed record numbers of people in work (a trend that has subsequently continued), joblessness was at a 20-year high. Despite an expansion in vacancies, the number of economically inactive men (those neither in work nor registered as unemployed) now appeared to exceed by two to one the number regis-tered as unemployed. Female participation in employment, on the other hand, was rising steadily. Whatever the reasons for this kind of situ-ation, it carries worrying implications, not least because a substantial proportion of the long-term male sick are highly skilled manual workers. Also, because of its poor training record the UK lacks the large pool of skilled workers essential to competitiveness and has much more ground to make up in that direction than most of its competitors.

The plight of the unskilled underclass
In Chapter 2 we saw the plight of the educational underclass, and noted its potential implications for the economy. For those emerging from that underclass into semi-skilled or manual jobs at best, unemployment at worst, the future is bleak. To be unskilled in today's global market place is to belong to the most vulnerable of groups in the labour market. Employment creation inevitably favours the more highly-skilled workers, and in 20 countries across Europe there is strong evidence to indicate that the labour market has an overall bias against less skilled or lower-paid workers (Wood, 1994). The underclass consistently forms between 10 per cent and 20 per cent of all earners, and its plight is growing, par-ticularly with the influx of the cheap unskilled labour that gives Third World countries their competitive edge. In any country, the size of the underclass will not decrease unless basic educational standards improve – the cause of the concern of educationalists and the govern-ment in the UK.

In the UK and the USA the effects have been worse in this respect than elsewhere, even though in terms of per capita earnings unskilled workers have done better in recent years than in mainland Europe (Marris, 1995). Whether, as in the UK, the unskilled tend to form the bulk of the unemployed, or whether, as in the USA, they tend to form the bulk of the very poorly-paid, they consistently fare worst in the competi-tion for jobs and wages. Their lack of a good basic education compounds their vulnerable position.

There has to be an investment in training that will give core workers sound basic education and the opportunity to invest and reinvest in workplace skills. Although in terms of good basic education Europe over-all compares favourably with the USA, it compares unfavourably with Pacific Rim countries. At higher educational level it also compares unfavourably with the USA, only 30 per cent of young Europeans moving into tertiary education, as opposed to nearly 70 per cent of young Americans. In Chapter 2 we reviewed the ways in which in this country the government is in the process of radically overhauling the education system in order to remedy skills shortages and improve the UK's competitive capability. An important aim here is to reduce and ultimately remove occupational barriers in a hitherto rigidly divided labour market through a national system of vocational qualifications and closer partnership with unions and employers.

Task 2

Consider the following arguments that underpin the belief that 'training as social engineering won't work', and then provide an opposite viewpoint.

'Profit comes first, then training,' said a *Daily Telegraph* editorial in 1996, continuing with the argument that in a period of steady growth and low inflation, such as was then being enjoyed, the provision of training by employers rises naturally without the need for government intervention, because successful companies spend money on training when they can afford it. Naturally they are wise to reduce investment in hard times, because training adds to costs, and in hard times rising costs are not affordable, leading usually to higher unemployment. Therefore the government should focus its investment not on improving national vocational training schemes – which in any case have high drop-out rates and are ill-equipped to meet the real needs of industry – but on improving the basic education system (as in Japan and the USA) so that young people have the necessary standards of literacy and numeracy for skills development in-company when they enter the labour market.

Smith (1996) also believed that training as social engineering will not work: the role of training is to improve the labour market position of those who receive it, not to change the unemployment figures. He observed that Sweden spends four times as much on training as a share of national income than Britain, but it has a higher unemployment rate, which extensive national training programmes, especially for young people, have not dented. On the other hand Britain has grown faster than Europe in recent years despite a poor VET record. He concluded that investment in training can make a real difference to emerging economies, lifting them to a position where they can compete internationally, but that thereafter it has little impact on competitive capability.

Sources: Smith, 1996; *Daily Telegraph*, 1996

The operation of internal labour markets
L&D policies in organisations can do much to improve the pool of skilled labour locally and nationally. However, if – as is so often the case – there is a rigid division of labour within an organisation, it then becomes very

difficult for manual workers to acquire the professional competencies that could gain them entrance to the primary sector of the labour market (van der Klink and Mulder, 1995). New technologies, and especially the Internet, are increasingly providing the impetus to integrate hitherto rigidly separated categories of work, but for that to happen, employees must be able to acquire the necessary competencies. If their educational background is weak and their grasp of practical skills poor, retraining may be impossible. When that happens a company will be forced to maintain its division of labour, buying in the requisite skills but not resolving the fundamental weakness of a workforce that cannot respond rapidly and creatively to market changes because it is so segmented and inflexible.

Inescapably, therefore, the lack of an adequate VET system will lead to a labour market geared mainly to the manufacture of comparatively cheap mass products, because that is what it has the competencies to produce. In such an economy there will be a declining demand for skilled employees. This, in turn, reinforces lack of investment within organisations in the vocational education and training that could produce more people capable of entering the primary rather than the secondary labour market segment. Caught in such a vicious cycle it is not surprising that British companies have not been keen to invest in L&D, and that the internal labour market is not generating sufficient skills needed by the economy.

Checkpoint

● Outline some key problems and advantages that the UK has, related to achieving flexibility of labour.

● What kind of impact does the choice of competing either on efficiency or on low costs tend to have on a country's labour force?

On p417 is a case study about a company, Sentex, that has chosen a high-quality route to competitive advantage and is operating in an increasingly competitive international market. The company's name has been changed to preserve its anonymity.

There are a number of issues at Sentex that have a wider resonance. One is that because of the high-quality route it has chosen to competitive advantage, it must have a flexible, highly adaptable workforce without rigid divisions of labour. This competitive strategy has obvious implications for recruitment, selection, pay, training and continuous and career development systems.

Another issue typifying practice in many such companies relates to some of the trends in HRM at Sentex. It is clear that there are tensions between the need for cost-efficiency and high immediate productivity,

CASE STUDY: Sentex Engineering Company Ltd

Context

Sentex Engineering Company Ltd, formed in 1950, manufactures small, high-quality electronic machines for use in a specialised field. Six years ago the business was operating in a narrow and declining market in which its product was a high-quality mechanical specialist machine. However, after a management buy-out and the development and piloting of a prototype electronic machine, a more multifaceted machine was produced. This rapidly captured the British market and moved successfully into the wider European market. Now, the firm has secured about 40 per cent of the world market within its specialised sector but faces increasing competition as it seeks to expand its European market base. With the world population for the specialist product rising, the aim for Sentex is growth by acquisition and diversification.

Corporate strategy

The firm has a strong vision of trail-blazing, excellence and world-class products. The MD's style is open and communicative, but he believes that participation in strategy is best restricted to those at the top unless there is genuine difficulty or failure to agree. He has set one long-term corporate goal, which relates to the need for continuing growth. Within that goal the directors annually draw up shorter-term objectives for their own functional areas and agree with their staff on how these can be achieved. Particular issues such as product reliability, quality and standards are targeted over an agreed time-scale.

Strategic strengths and weaknesses

The major strengths of the firm are its 300 employees, especially the management team and certain key individuals; excellent basic products; good tools and machines; strong capability in research and development (R&D) and engineering; a first-class network of licensees; and a secure financial base.

Main weaknesses arise from the fact that the firm has been very slow to make the transition from mechanical to sophisticated electronic manufacturing and is still trying to master the complexities of operating in an international market.

Human resource management issues

The MD has not until now felt the need for an explicit HR strategy. Now, however, human resources are becoming a priority issue because the firm must have more flexibility of skills. Currently, the main skills shortages are in R&D, where there is also very high staff turnover. There are also regular shortages in production and services. In the component assembly area such problems are tackled by buying in. The assembly operation is amateurish, and there is no mechanism for ideas for improvements coming from the shop floor. The new manager there takes the view that anyone who performs inadequately after basic training must leave, and that any but job-related training is an unaffordable cost to the business. Service staff are particularly difficult to obtain. They also take years to train in the variety of skills they need and have to be away from home for up to nine months of the year, making training difficult. Training has been limited to only a few of this staff's skill areas; for the rest, they have to pick things up as they go along.

The MD sees a bigger and more strategic investment in training as an urgent priority. However, with the company developing so fast, it is difficult to foresee exactly what training will be needed. Staff are continually firefighting, and usually they are so busy that time off for training cannot be found.

and the need to develop skills and competencies for the future. Since that future is unpredictable, investing in an integrated well-educated workforce is essential, with strategic thinking and creativity encouraged in every employee.

Finally, there are positive signs at Sentex of a growing alignment of the L&D process both with HR strategy and with corporate goals. Its MD is committed to a more strategic investment in training and development, a vision focusing on world-class excellence and long-term growth, and high-calibre employees. In such a situation an expert HR manager can make a strong case for a better balance of the short and the longer term in L&D strategy, and especially for interventions to improve the vocational attainments and competencies of the workforce. There must also be a drive for management development to ensure managerial style and skills better suited to achieving the high-quality world-class goals essential to the success of the business over time.

3 The educational parameter

A country's educational system determines its levels of basic education and also the potential to acquire work-based competencies. That system can be either full-time or dual (van der Klink and Mulder, 1995: 159).

- In the full-time system students do most of their training at a state (or independent) institution of study – a school, college or university – and least in-company. In such a system the main emphasis is on obtaining theoretical qualifications. Funding is likely to be split, the state helping to resource external provision and the employer carrying the main responsibility for funding training in employment. The UK system is of this kind.

- The dual system is a partnership in which vocational training is largely provided on the job with less, but complementary, provision in institutions of study away from the company. In such a system there is bound to be a dominating emphasis on students obtaining the practical competencies they need to practise their profession. Theoretical qualifications are focused on acquiring knowledge that underpins such competencies. Funding is likely to be shared between state and employers. The German system is of this kind.

The socio-economic and labour market contexts described earlier in the chapter explain why the European Commission in its educational policy must do two crucial things:

- improve the level of basic education in certain states

- spread scarce skills more efficiently across the Community and increase the stock of those skills. Greater mobility will make the labour market more efficient, and so the Commission is working for common vocational standards, transferability of qualifications and student exchanges.

International comparisons in vocational education and training

Within as well as across countries, VET systems are influenced not only by socio-economic, labour-market and educational differences but also by differences to do with legal systems, history and tradition, and work-related values and other cultural dimensions. Meaningful comparative data are difficult to obtain. That said, there are still insights to be achieved by some generalised comparisons. These must be regularly updated, using the kind of information sources noted at the end of the chapter.

Vocational education and training

Although the school-leaving age across Europe varies from 14 to 16, there is already a major emphasis on extending full-time education and training to the age of 18 in Sweden, Belgium, Luxembourg, Greece and the Republic of Ireland. There is a similar emphasis in France, but there both full-time vocational and apprenticeship training are important for the age-group. In Germany and the Netherlands, part-time attendance at a school or college is compulsory up to age 18. In Denmark the emphasis is on young school-leavers moving into the apprenticeship system, as it is in Germany where, however, the term covers most jobs that 16-year-olds can be employed to do. In the UK in 1990 only 53 per cent of children were staying on in school or college, but by 1994 the figure had reached nearly 73 per cent and it has continued to rise subsequently. However, in 1995 it was estimated that only 50 per cent of such UK students could be considered to be in vocational training, compared with 80 per cent in Germany (Smith, 1995). As was noted in Chapter 2, the present government is trying to boost this percentage significantly with its new NVET policy, but it will be some time yet before the practical effects begin to make themselves felt across the economy.

In Greece, vocational education can start at 15. In France, technical subjects can start at 13 or 14, as they can in Belgium, Luxembourg, the Republic of Ireland and the Netherlands. By 1986 only 15 per cent of young French people left full-time education without completing a vocational course, and more than 70 per cent of 16- to 18-year-olds were staying on in full-time education, compared with just over 30 per cent in Britain (Steedman, 1990).

Across most of Europe there is a major emphasis on competency-based occupational training tied to the attainment of national standards, and on control of examinations by independent institutions or by partnerships of employers, unions and educationalists. Except in the UK, youth wages are low until a significant level of vocational qualification has been achieved, and it is widely assumed that young people will either have a degree or vocational qualification. In Germany, where the aim is that no-one without a satisfactorily completed apprenticeship should enter the labour market, it is illegal – as it is not in the UK – to stop youth training before it has gone full term, or to stop the off-the-job element during the training period.

Vocational qualification rates

In Germany, 75 per cent of the population is skilled to craft level, whereas in Britain the comparable figure is only 30 per cent. In Britain too, 20 per cent of adults are 'without qualification, literacy or numeracy' (Gracie, 1999, in conversation with the head of the National Skills Task Force). Reports from the independent National Institute for Economic and Social Research continue to show that the UK still lags significantly behind many competitor countries in terms of its basic education and training. This means that once young people enter the labour market, they are likely to have access only to the secondary segment and to remain trapped there. The need for dramatic improvement is the greater because of changes in jobs that will take place over the next 20 years or so. Higher-level professional, scientific, technical, managerial and administrative jobs will continue to grow fast, and the proportion of knowledge workers continue to increase, against a backdrop of an ageing workforce into which there will not be large inflows of new young workers because of a demographic downturn likely to continue for at least two more decades.

At this point, comparison with the situation of France in the 1960s is instructive. France then had more acute problems of skills shortages and educational levels than the UK faced at the end of the 1980s. There was also, as in the UK, a widespread reluctance of employers to take a lead in the vocational training of young people. In the 1970s and 1980s the pace of technological and skills change in the French economy was great, yet France managed to equip her workforce to cope effectively with all the demands that faced it. The key to success was the use of government-set targets of vocational attainment using full-time education to provide courses leading to the combined craft and general education CAP certificates. 'A coherent range of qualifications means that practically the whole ability range can gain nationally-recognized qualifications which are frequently rewarded by higher pay' (Steedman, 1990). A set of vocational A-levels was added in the late 1980s, based on the craft-level CAP (equivalent to City and Guilds craft certificate and several GCSE passes) but still able to lead to higher education. Subsequently, there were concerns about CAP, and new legislation in the early 1990s aimed to improve the quality and flexibility of apprenticeship in France. The similarities with current curriculum and other VET reforms in the UK are obvious.

Occupational standards

In most EU countries (except the UK) youth wages are low until a significant level of vocational qualification has been achieved. In most competitor countries, too, occupational training is tied to the attainment of national standards, and it is widely assumed that young people without a degree will be vocationally qualified. In Germany the aim (achieved in 1984 by over 90 per cent of its young people) is that none without a satisfactorily completed apprenticeship should enter the labour market. It is also illegal in Germany, as it is not in the UK, to stop youth training before it has gone full-term, or to stop the off-the-job element during the training period.

There has been growing concern since the late 1980s in a number of European countries (for example, Greece, France, the Irish Republic and Portugal) to improve the legal framework governing apprenticeship. Some have introduced more flexibility at local level to vary course length and content to suit local needs (for example, the Netherlands and France). Even in Germany, the dual system that remains a model for the rest of Europe has attracted criticism relating to inflexibility, length, its over-theoretical nature and the lack of co-ordination between examining bodies, leading to inconsistent standards (Incomes Data Services, 1993).

The UK, then, is not alone in its struggle to improve occupational standards and we have seen in Chapters 2 and 8 the ways in which it has recently revised those standards and is linking them to a national qualifications structure. That structure will ultimately link to a European-wide structure that was agreed on 19 June 1999 in a joint Declaration of European Ministers of Education at Bologna, to which 29 countries were signatories.

Task 3

In this book it has not been possible to include any detail on apprenticeship. However, in any attempt to improve a country's skills base apprenticeship training has a vital role to play. Consult some of the reference sources at the end of this chapter to identify:
- current concerns about the work-based learning of young people in the UK
- national policy changes to improve apprenticeship training in the UK
- critical comparisons between apprenticeship policy in the UK and in other European countries.

Continuous learning and development

In our major competitor countries there is a wide acceptance of the need for continuing education and training in order to ensure advancement and adaptation. In Germany and France, local chambers of commerce make available training for employed workers, and in most countries there are now arrangements to train the unemployed – often, too, to help those likely to become unemployed. In the UK under the Labour government, lifelong learning is central to national VET policy and is being supported by funded initiatives in the workplace (see Chapters 2 and 20). However, as we saw in Chapter 2, there are many practical barriers to the realisation of the lifelong learning vision. It also remains the case that the distinction between education and training, like the distinction between vocational and non-vocational education and training, is more marked here than in most of our competitor countries. Areas in which the UK emerges worst from cross-national comparisons (Stern and Sommerlad, 1999: 79) are to do with:

- the readiness or preparedness of workers for continuous training and learning in the workplace

- the organisation and management of training in the workplace including employers' attitudes

- regulatory polices and frameworks, including incentives for training.

Coverage of industrial training

Westwood (2001) stated that:

 There is a very simple training divide in the UK between those who can access it and those who cannot.

Per head of the workforce Germany was by the mid-1980s training each year twice as many mechanics, electricians and construction workers, and even more office and distributive trade workers, as the UK (Prais and Wagner, 1981; Prais, 1985). In the UK, managerial and supervisory training tends to receive the highest level of investment, followed by technical and professional training, and then by blue-collar worker training. Our clerical training has traditionally been poor in both quantity and quality compared with France and Germany. This uneven coverage of the training investment in the UK raises the likelihood of a serious shortage of skills in the middle and lower ranks of workforces, which in turn will impede the implementation of technological change and more flexible work patterns.

Training for manual workers in the UK has been almost entirely in the form of apprenticeships, with the cost carried by employers. Since the introduction of the Modern Apprenticeship scheme in 1993, UK governments have made significant attempts to reverse the disastrous decline that occurred in manufacturing (as in other) apprenticeships between 1964 and 1986. Apprenticeship has been given a further boost by measures put in place in 2001 (see Chapter 2), but grave causes for concern remain (Evans, Hodkinson, Keep, Maguire, Raffe, Rainbird, Senker and Unwin, 1997).

Investment in vocational education and training

Inter-country comparisons of levels of investment in VET are particularly fallible because of the differences in the way data are collected and analysed, and because relatively little is known about in-company investment and its outcomes. Evaluation of the effectiveness of training, for example, is weak in most European countries (although, interestingly, stronger in the UK). It is therefore impossible to know much about the true value added by investment in training in those countries. In this section, only the most obvious differences between key countries are outlined.

Most of our competitor countries invest substantially in education and training, sharing the cost between the main stakeholders. German employers voluntarily bear the burden of most of the cost and effort involved, working closely with unions and the authorities to provide a high-quality and rigorously administered and controlled NVET system. In Japan the costs are shared by the education system and the employer, with only limited state-sponsored public-sector provision. In France collective agreements usually link pay to vocational and technical qualifications, and small means-tested allowances are available to pupils in secondary and tertiary education.

In the UK the cost of industrial training is carried mainly by employers, but there is a state-funded primary and secondary education system. The government now exercises significant control over the funding of schools as it attempts to develop an education system offering more integrated and comprehensive academic and vocational pathways and more sensitivity to market needs. Recent funding changes in the further- and higher-education sectors mean that students are bearing a heavy cost in fees and maintenance.

In Sweden the state pays for the integrated upper secondary school; in Italy, France, Belgium, Luxembourg and the Netherlands the state pays for full-time training. In both France and Germany apprentices receive only a modest income, whereas in the UK starting wages at 16 years old can be high, and until recently (with the Modern Apprenticeship scheme) they have not been tied to vocational qualifications. The French have a training tax, set at a minimum level of expenditure (1.1 per cent of total payroll) to be invested in training by qualified trainers. As was the case with the now defunct British levy-grant system, it has been widely felt to lead to irrelevant training that has not played any central part in the successful building up of a skilled, highly qualified workforce.

In the USA, as in the UK, the NVET system has traditionally been market-driven. However, as Ashton et al. (2001: 48) explain, two factors are now changing levels of, and approaches to, training and development in many organisations. The introduction of high-performance practices such as self-managed teams and quality circles in most larger companies is leading to higher training levels: and the 1998 Workforce Investment Act has centralised many activities hitherto performed by various agencies, with the aim of encouraging states to work in partnership with local governments to achieve 'more streamlined universal workforce development systems' (ibid). The 'One Stop Centres' in the USA offer integrated services similar to those provided by the UK's Business Links.

After World War II Japan, Germany and the Netherlands rebuilt their education systems, and students today in their schools lead the world in advanced maths, science and other technical subjects. In Japan and Germany teaching is a highly paid and prestigious profession. In Germany teacher-training is rigorous and operates at a high academic standard, every type of school requiring its own kind of training course. In the UK, by contrast, teaching has until recently been a relatively poorly-paid and low-status profession, with questionable standards of teacher-training. Our secondary education system has not focused adequately on science and technology pathways, and this has led to a critical undersupply of teachers in those subject areas and to poor teaching standards. A good deal is now being done to tackle these problems in the UK but, as we saw in Chapter 2, there are still grave problems within the teaching profession.

The USA tends to invest more money on buildings and administration, with proportionately less going on teacher salaries. There has been considerable concern at poor standards of teaching and attainment, especially in relation to maths and science instruction, but the participation of young people in the American university system is very much higher (at around 70 per cent) than in European countries overall.

Checkpoint

- Looking at key differences between NVET in the UK and in leading competitor countries, identify and explain *three* of the main weaknesses in the UK system.

- What are the main differences in involvement of employers in VET in the UK and in leading competitor countries?

Lessons for the UK

As we saw in Chapter 2, the UK faces many challenges in its attempts to invest in learning and development that will achieve both social and economic aims of its NVET policy. Pulling together the material covered there and in this chapter, we can conclude by identifying the main needs as the following:

Improved basic educational standards
OECD statistics in 2000 showed that the proportion of those aged 16 to 19 who were not attending school and were not employed was 19.4 per cent in the UK. That was higher than in 13 other member countries, over three times the rate in France and four times the rate in Germany (Clare, 2000b).

An effective, competence-based qualification system
The government seeks to establish three routes into the world of work: a work-based route through NVQs, the General National Vocational Qualification (GNVQ), GCSE and A-level route, and the 'academic' route. Success is proving difficult, and there is a need to learn from practice across most other European countries. Both a practical and a theoretical grasp of tasks must be developed and tested – preferably by external examiners in order to ensure uniformity and consistency of skill standards – before a qualification is awarded.

Testing needs to be more rigorously linked to the needs and characteristics of the workplace. This should be not only in terms of standards reached but also in terms of reliability, punctuality and quality. Poor assessment methods applied to work-based learning are a major cause of official concern (DfEE, 2000).

A reduction in the training divide
A formula has still to be found to ensure adequate investment across different sectors of training, particularly in the field of craft and technician training. As noted, there is a deep divide in training across the UK, caused by unequal access and provision. Such a divide perpetuates the plight of the educational and labour market underclass, and militates against the closing of major skills gaps in the UK economy.

Improved education and training for flexibility
When future patterns of demand for skills are so unpredictable, flexibility of skills at an early age is vital. This can be achieved only by a good basic education, together with well-integrated academic and vocational pathways. This also gives young people a wider career choice. Modern apprenticeships and current developments in the NVQ field may right the balance in the UK in due course, but as explained in this chapter and in Chapter 2, there is considerable progress still to be made.

Improved work-based learning processes and standards
On the Continent, adult education and training are taken seriously by individuals, employers, trade unions and governments alike. In the UK, it remains to be seen whether the present government's undoubted commitment to lifelong learning and continuous development both in and out of work can win the support needed by employers in order to bring about real change in the workplace. The quality and provision of

work-based learning is a key issue here, and, as we saw in Chapter 20, there are currently serious criticisms about both.

Stronger stakeholder involvement

In Chapter 2 we examined the new VET implementation framework that has been in place since April 2001. Concerns were summarised about the new system, particularly those relating to the need for adequate resourcing and for active involvement of key stakeholders in the framework's operation. Without that involvement, the new system will be no more effective than the old in achieving a strong commitment from all parties – especially employers – to NVET policy.

There are serious doubts about the ability of the present market-driven system to achieve that commitment. In the UK employers are expected to carry a heavy burden of responsibility for training. It seems clear that if this continues, short-termism will increasingly dominate (Keep, 2001). If that happens, the country's available workforce will not be adequately prepared for the future, and the current geographical and socio-economic disparities in the availability of, and access to, training will continue. At organisational level it is essential to provide employers with incentives to reduce rigid divisions in the internal labour market and enhance basic education and occupational standards. There is also a need for improved management styles and competencies, especially in those operating at international level (Whitfield, 1995).

Unless such needs are met, organisations – and therefore ultimately the economy – will lack the improved capacity that is needed to secure competitive advantage and the innovation essential to growth. It will also prove dauntingly difficult for those in lower-level jobs to improve their skills and so to be able to compete on more equal terms for entry to the primary segment of the internal as well as external labour market.

CONCLUSION

Having read this chapter and completed its checkpoints and tasks, you should now:

- have a context for understanding the international – and especially the European – scenario relating to vocational education and training

- understand the key differences between national vocational education and training systems in major competitor countries and the UK

- be able to identify lessons that such comparisons offer both for UK government policy on vocational education and training and for L&D policy in organisations.

Useful reference sources

CHARTERED INSTITUTE OF PERSONNEL AND DEVELOPMENT (2001) *Workplace Learning in Europe* [summary of the European Workplace Learning Seminar, London, 2 April]. London, CIPD, available to download from: www.cipd.co.uk

EVANS K., HODKINSON P., KEEP E., MAGUIRE M., RAFFE D., RAINBIRD H., SENKER P. *and* UNWIN L. (1997) *Working To Learn – A work-based route to learning for young people.* London, Institute of Personnel and Development.

STERN E. *and* SOMMERLAD E. (1999) *Workplace Learning, Culture and Performance.* London, Institute of Personnel and Development.

WILSON D., LANK E., WESTWOOD A., KEEP E., LEADBEATER C. *and* SLOMAN M. (2001) *The Future of Learning for Work.* London, Chartered Institute of Personnel and Development.

The information in Chapter 4 will require to be regularly updated, especially by reference to:

- the *International Journal of Training and Development*, Oxford, Blackwell, *Human Resource Development International*, London, Routledge, and similar journals with an international focus on VET policy and practice.

- the quality press – and especially the Sunday 'heavies' and the *Financial Times* – for their regular articles and editorials on matters relating to VET in Britain and competitor countries, and to patterns of employment and movements in the economies of those countries.

- (for students) your university or college library, whose staff will advise you on relevant publications and websites. One of the most relevant websites is www.dfes.gov.uk, which gives comprehensive information about progress with NVET policy in the UK and has European links.

- the website for overview of European Community educational policy: http://europa.eu.int/pol/educ/index_en.htm

- the CIPD's website, from which students and members can download fact-sheets and policy documents on matters related to many of the issues in this chapter: www.cipd.co.uk

- the business section of your local public library, whose information officer will be able to direct you to up-to-date sources of information (especially on the Internet) on L&D in competitor countries.

• Building Strategic Capability

Introduction

In this final chapter we move away from learning and development activity in its international setting to return to the main focus of this book: learning and development as an organisational process. The book began with a journey through gateways of the L&D territory. It ends with an exploration of the holistic contribution that the L&D process can make to organisations that are pursuing their strategic route in increasingly turbulent environments.

For this purpose, a conceptual framework is used that is related to an organisation's key capabilities, laying stress on 'strategic capability' and the learning and knowledge underpinning it. The aim in this chapter is to generate ideas, to reflect and to discuss, not to prescribe. There are few checkpoints or tasks, and no final review questions. The complexity of the issues, and their unresolved state in theory and in practice, argue against any quick responses to the puzzles that they generate.

Understanding strategic progress

The case of BTR, presented even in outline form overleaf, illustrates the rapidity with which the strategic direction of an organisation can founder. Such stories raise questions about how that risk can be reduced, when turbulence – in the sense of profound commotion, disturbance – in the business environment is increasing. Prahalad and

CASE STUDY: BTR

BTR's extraordinary downfall is a story of how a winning strategy in the fragmented markets and corporate inefficiency of the 1970s and 1980s produced an unmanageable empire up against increasingly strong competitors in the 1990s. It is also the story of how management failed to adapt as engineering and manufacturing turned upside around the world (Potter, 1998).

BTR, built on the base of the tiny Birmingham Tyre and Rubber Company in 1963, reached its peak as an industrial conglomerate in the 1980s, being one of the 10 largest corporations in Britain and retaining a premium rating from the stock market. By the 1990s its strategic direction was beginning to drift. It was announced in November 1998 that it was to merge with Siebe, another UK manufacturing giant. In reality, the merger was widely viewed as a takeover by Siebe. How could such a reversal have occurred?

In 1993 BTR's founding father, Sir Owen Green, had retired, to be succeeded by Norman Ireland, former finance director. It was a curious and unsuccessful appointment. The world was changing rapidly. Advances in information technology and crumbling capital barriers allowed manufacturing to go global (Potter, 1998) and by 1994 BTR's margins were beginning to slide. The real problem, however, was at the top, where Ireland and Alan Jackson, who had been appointed chief executive in 1991, continued to be dominated by the old BTR mindset – cyclical acquisitions, cost-cutting, adding value at the margins, and then seeking bids to move through the cycle once again. By the early 1990s that prescription was fast becoming inappropriate. The fashion was for focus and specialisation, for re-engineering. Also, in the low-growth environment of the time the risks involved in con-

tested takeovers did not seem to make sense – yet still Jackson concentrated on sticking to that old BTR knitting.

Lorenz (1995) observed BTR's new vulnerability to the turbulent climate, doubly worrying as its top men retired and its traditional stock of home-grown replacements ran out. For three decades BTR had nurtured its own top management and resisted even the appointment of external non-executive directors. After September 1994, however, its performance had slowed down and become erratic, for two reasons: 'It is facing a seismic shift in its business environment; and the people who must lead BTR's response to this fundamental change will be men with no previous connection with the company.' But by the time Ian Strachan took over as CE at the end of 1995, it was really too late.

By 1998, Siebe – the UK's most highly rated engineering stock – sought out BTR because of its process controls and power-drives businesses. These would enable Siebe to sell more systems rather than get stuck in the increasingly unproductive components-manufacturing end of the business. Commentators feared that it might have taken on too much. BTR was the bigger enterprise of the two, and it might be too complex for its partner to understand and to manage. There might not be the organisational capacity or the effectiveness of strategic direction to make the new conglomerate work. It might then founder (Potter, 1998). In the event, BTR ultimately became Invensys, and although in the early 2000s it was having difficulties, at the time of writing its profits and share price were enjoying a rally.

Sources: Potter, 1998; Lorenz, 1995

Hamel (1994) have identified many ways in which organisations' competitive space is changing. Causes include deregulation, structural changes brought about by technology and customer expectations, excess capacity inviting radical restructuring, and mergers, acquisitions and alliances. They also include the impact of environmental concerns, reduction in protectionism leading to exposure of inefficiencies, techno-logical discontinuities spawning new industries, the emergence of trading blocks that are changing the basis and patterns of trade, and global competition that affects even the most localised of businesses.

The rapidity and complexity of all these changes call into question the strategic approaches and tools of the past. There can be no reliance on traditional prescriptions or on detailed long-term planning in a world of such unpredictability. Workforces must be increasingly fast-reactive to change. They must have flexible skills and mindsets. They must be strongly committed to aiding the realisation of the organisation's vision, no matter what changes in direction and fortunes that may involve.

Survival and advance

Many companies do not survive for long, and some may not wish to do so. A third of the Fortune 500 industrials listed in 1970 had vanished by 1983. On the other hand, a small group had lasted for more than 70 years, some 'sticking to their knitting' but doing it increasingly well, others from time to time completely changing direction in order to remain profitable. The latter type manage to innovate radically at key stages in their existence in order to leapfrog over their rivals and secure durable advantage. They survive, but they also advance (a dis-tinction explained clearly in von Krogh, Roos and Slocum, 1994: 64).

It is relevant at this point to consider the issue of 'turbulence'. For Ansoff and Sullivan (1993) it can be analysed by reference to four vari-ables:

- complexity of events in the environment (the extent to which those events are difficult to interpret)

- familiarity of the successive events (the extent to which those within the organisation recognise the type of event from past experience)

- rapidity with which the events evolve after they are first perceived

- visibility of the consequence of these events (the extent to which those consequences quickly become clear).

The greater the levels of turbulence, the more profound the implications for the direction of the organisation and the greater the difficulty in deciding how to move forward. At the stable end of the environmental spectrum, the past can act as a good guide for the present, and stra-tegic decision-makers will need formal strategic planning skills together with competence in financial and human resource management and a focus on continuous improvement. At the unstable end, however, there must be increasing reliance on entrepreneurial skills, on collective learn-ing and on adaptability. Change is likely to be discontinuous, so the past will no longer be an adequate guide to the future. In fact, it may act as a distorter, and there will be an ever greater danger of the organisation's becoming trapped in its customary ways of thinking and doing. Sticking to the knitting will then no longer be a recipe for survival but a swift route to corporate failure.

What is needed if an organisation is to be able not just to survive but, when necessary, to transform itself?

Capacity for change

There must be enough stability in the organisation to ensure that current operations can be performed consistently and well. There must be structure, systems and processes to ensure that it can alter its portfolio of products or services and its operational effectiveness in line with a need for improved achievement of its strategic goals.

However, there must also be the capacity to experiment, learn and innovate, so as to make possible change of a kind that completely 'reinvents' corporate character and to ensure the generation of a quite different type of strategic asset (Lorenz, 1992). At this point I should define what is meant by 'strategic assets'. They are 'those unique, hard-to-copy, durable products, services or processes that are valued in the external market and so become the firm's source of competitive advantage' (Amit and Schoemaker, 1993).

'Transformational' change (to use a term that tends to be applied indiscriminately to a good deal of change that is in reality nothing of the kind) enables the organisation to advance in its environment rather than simply survive from day to day. The capability to advance needs key decision-makers in the organisation who can think in lateral ways about the company, what it should be doing and where it should be going. Capacity to advance depends on organisational structure and systems, on material and financial resources, and on the adaptability of the workforce. Only by having both capability and capacity can an organisation conceive and implement plans for new patterns of provision of services for a quite different type of product (as when Marks & Spencer and Virgin entered the personal pension field), or for a radically new process.

Adaptive and generative learning

If what an organisation needs in order to make progress towards its strategic goals is, essentially, continuous improvement, then this will put a premium on the learning that produces adaptive knowledge (Senge, 1990). This is the kind of knowledge that by producing understanding of the gaps with competitors that relate to productivity, quality or operational flexibility and cost, enables the steady closing of those gaps. When, on the other hand, new classes of assets and strategies are needed, and corporate character may require to be reinvented. This calls for learning that will produce, and sustain, discontinuous change.

Senge has described this as 'generative learning', a concept very similar to that of double-loop learning, by which the very goals, norms and assumptions of the organisation itself have to be questioned.

As we saw in Chapter 19, transformation in a company may be stimulated by a sudden, one-off and usually traumatic event, but much more than that is needed to sustain it. That requires a series of systemic changes that achieve a 'mesh of the formal and the flexible' (Lorenz, 1992) by tackling formal and informal aspects of the organisation in an integrated and consistent way through time. This involves creating new structures, processes and behaviours across the organisation that are so profound and wide-ranging in their nature and effects that they can be loosely termed 'genetic' – a way of distinguishing them from the programmed changes that are more narrowly focused and more short-lived.

In the following section, I propose a conceptual framework – a construct – that focuses on capacity and capability, making links between an organisation's key capabilities, its learning and knowledge processes, and its strategic progress.

Checkpoint

● In the case of BTR, what seems to you to be the most likely explanation for the failure in the company's strategic progress?

● What kind of learning can help an organisation to continuously improve, and what kind do you think is needed to enable it to advance?

The strategic capability framework

Capabilities and the organisation

Capabilities refer to 'the capacity for a team of resources to perform some task or activity' (Grant, 1991). In the literature of business strategy and competitive performance, the so-called 'resource-based view of the firm' highlights organisational resources and capabilities as critical in explaining variations in the ability to become and remain profitable (Penrose, 1959; Wernerfelt, 1984; Barney, 1991; Rumelt, 1991; Peteraf, 1993; Schendel, 1994).

A capability must be 'valuable' if it is to be a differentiator of firm performance in the competitive environment. It must enable the firm to exploit opportunities and reduce threats, and so must have a number of characteristics:

● It must meet or create a market need.

● It must have uniqueness (scarcity value).

- It must – therefore – be hard to copy (so it must be difficult to understand in terms of its basic components and how they interact).

- It must be so deeply embedded in the organisation, and in such complex ways, that there is little possibility it can be transferred to any other organisation (therefore making it easy for competitors to poach).

In the literature, the term 'strategic capability' is used frequently yet ambiguously. Johnson and Scholes, for example, used it in a generalised sense to indicate the 'organisation's ability to pursue strategies which it is capable of sustaining', and described it as being 'best understood in relation to other [competitive] organisations. It is the distinctive competence of the organisation vis-à-vis competitors or other providers ...' (Johnson and Scholes, 1993: 83). Grant (1991: 109) used the plural noun to indicate the 'distinctive competencies ... activities that the firm can perform better than competitors'. Kay (1993) related the term to the ability to identify and utilise the distinctive capabilities of the firm that are to do with innovation, reputation, strategic assets and architecture. Floyd and Wooldridge (1994: 48) used it in relation to the strategic roles that middle managers can play in 'sustaining an adaptive balance between industry forces and organisational resources'. They distinguished the latter from 'strategic resources' of knowledge and skills of members and other strategic assets. Such examples tend either to be operationally unclear or to concentrate on specific outcomes to be achieved by strategic managers through the quality of their strategic planning process.

Another problem is the tendency in the resource-based literature for the terms 'organisational capability' and 'strategic capability' to be used as synonyms, to do with those processes and systems by which unique synergies are created that help the organisation to respond effectively to environmental turbulence (see, for example, Stalk, Evans and Schulman, 1992: 62).

Despite these problems of classification (convincingly identified by Collis, 1994), the literature indicates three internal types of capability to be interactively linked to the firm's competitive performance. They are described here under the headings *resource-based, organisational,* and *strategic* (see Figure 16 overleaf).

Figure 16 indicates that the impact the three capabilities actually achieve will be mediated by the outcomes of policy decisions in the business and by the firm's strategic position at any given time – its 'positional capability' that, arising from the interaction of a range of external factors that produce a munificent or hostile environment for the organisation, broadly decides its potential for growth and profitability (Porter, 1980, 1985; Coyne, 1986; Hamel and Prahalad, 1993).

Figure 16 The key capabilities of an organisation and its strategic progress

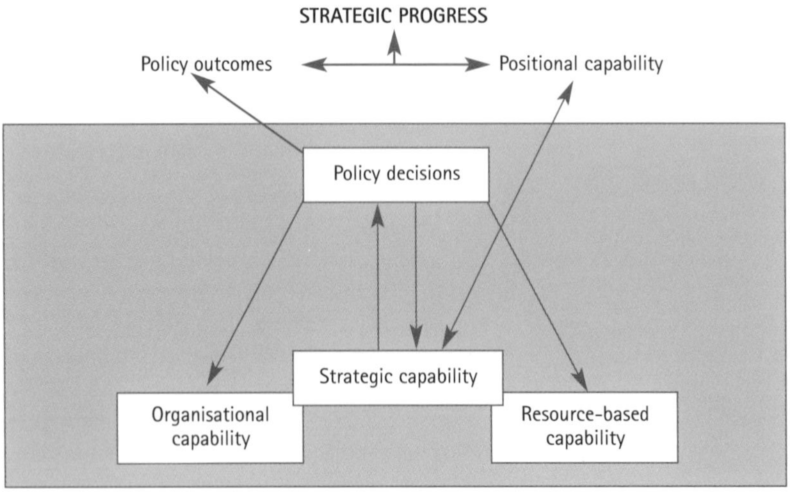

STRATEGIC PROGRESS

Policy outcomes ⟵⟶ Positional capability

Policy decisions

Strategic capability

Organisational capability

Resource-based capability

In this chapter the focus is not on the outcomes of policy decisions or on how the enterprise should deal with external factors in order to improve its competitive position. It is on how to integrate and direct those internal capabilities that are the source of the organisation's present and future strategic assets.

Resource-based capability

This capability represents the potential offered by the firm's bank of resources for the development of strategic assets to underpin a firm's competitive position in a particular market (Markides and Williamson, 1994: 150). Resource-based capability can be described loosely as what the firm 'knows and can do', vested primarily in the legacy of knowledge, strategic assets, networks and reputation conferred by its past human resources, and the knowledge and skills of its current workforce (Badarraco, 1991; Hall, 1993).

The task for the L&D process in relation to resource-based capability is one with which few managers or HR practitioners are not familiar. It is to help to build up the levels and kinds of educational and knowledge-base, and the human competence, motivation and commitment that the business needs to achieve its goals. This is part of L&D's value-adding function and we have spent a good deal of time exploring it in Parts 2 and 3 of this book. To give just three examples here, those with L&D responsibilities can:

- raise awareness in the organisation of the ways in which the development of people can add value for the business and for individuals, and thereby achieve commitment to the L&D process

- aid the recruitment, selection and performance management processes by organising induction, training and development that will motivate learners, achieve competent performance and build commitment to organisational goals and values

- advise on and contribute to processes to stimulate continuous improvement and personal development.

Organisational capability

Resources cannot be deployed and utilised to their maximum potential unless they are supported by an appropriate organisational system (Nelson and Winter, 1982; Wheelwright and Clark, 1992; Miles and Snow, 1995). 'Organisational capability' involves building and adapting to changing needs the structure, the business processes, and the routines and procedures that enable resources (including people) to be deployed, combined and recombined through time in strategically productive ways. It is about having networks of stable contacts between internal and external parties that form the firm's 'strategic architecture' (Baud and Scanlan, 1995: 112–13). It also involves developing an organisational culture that can be a unique source of competitive advantage when it enables rapid learning, unlearning and relearning throughout the organisation. If resource-based capability is about 'can do', organisational capability is about enabling the resource-base to realise its fullest potential.

Part 4 of this book has focused on ways in which the L&D process can help to expand organisational capability through:

- well-chosen competency-based frameworks, and strategically focused processes and systems for career planning and management development

- processes to aid change of organisational culture and structure, including strategic learning alliances

- processes and culture to build knowledge productivity.

Strategic capability

I have formulated a concept of 'strategic capability' to express a number of features that, from reading and research, appear to be central to an organisation's ability to achieve and sustain effective strategic direction:

Strategic capability provides the vision, the rich and sustained learning and knowledge development, the integrity of purpose and the continuous direction and scope to the activities of the firm that are needed to secure long-term survival. It is based on a profound understanding of the competitive environment, of the resource-base, capacity and potential of the organisation, of the strategy process, and of the values that engender commitment from stakeholders to corporate goals.

In this view, strategic capability significantly determines the extent to which the organisation achieves the best fit between its unique assets and the position it occupies in its environment. It is to do with:

- choosing and communicating the most appropriate vision, long-term goals and objectives for an enterprise

- achieving a quality of life in the organisation that generates the sustained commitment of internal and external stakeholders to the organisation's corporate goals (Harrison and Smith, 2001)

- managing the development of strategically valuable knowledge

- determining and managing the courses of action and the allocation of resources necessary for achieving strategic goals (Chandler, 1962; Grant, 1991; Barney, 1991).

- selecting and ensuring the development of unique strategic assets.

It is my view that the effective interaction of resource-based, organisational and strategic capabilities explains much of an organisation's ability not only to survive but also when necessary to advance in its environment; and that it is primarily upon the quality of its strategic capability that the effectiveness of that interaction depends. An organisation's resource-base may be well-developed, and its people may be high-performing, adaptive and creative. Its organisational capability may be strong. However, it is hard to envisage how those advantages can work to their fullest potential unless there are a clear focus for activity, decisions about an appropriate route to follow, goals to act as stimuli and to give purpose, and the flexibility of systems as well as people to change direction as need be in turbulent conditions.

To summarise: I see strategic capability to be in part about directing, developing and interacting positively with organisational capability. I see it to be in part about directing, developing and interacting positively with the organisation's resource-base, particularly its people.

To enhance the quality of strategic capability in its interactions with resource-based and organisational capabilities, those with L&D responsibilities can help with:

- initiatives to raise awareness of the variety of strategy process modes that can be used to ensure that there is broad-based knowledge and experience informing the strategy process, and that set ways of thinking and of decision-making are challenged (Hart and Banbury, 1994; Ginsberg, 1994)

- processes and initiatives to develop 'thinking performers' at all levels and to ensure skilled use of the organisation's strategic processes and routines (for example, through informational processes to do with environmental scanning, scenario-building, the identification of strategic issues, and the generation of wide-ranging strategic options)

- processes and initiatives to continuously improve the cognitive abilities of strategic managers and teams – especially at middle management level, where strategic orientation may be critical for organisational performance yet where many feel ill-equipped to deal with their newly acquired strategic roles (Floyd and Wooldridge, 1994)

- processes and initiatives to improve skills related to the implementation of strategy – for example, skills in setting and monitoring plans and targets, and in evaluating their impact in the workplace

- the stimulation of the search for strategically valuable knowledge

Figure 17 Understanding organisational learning and knowledge development

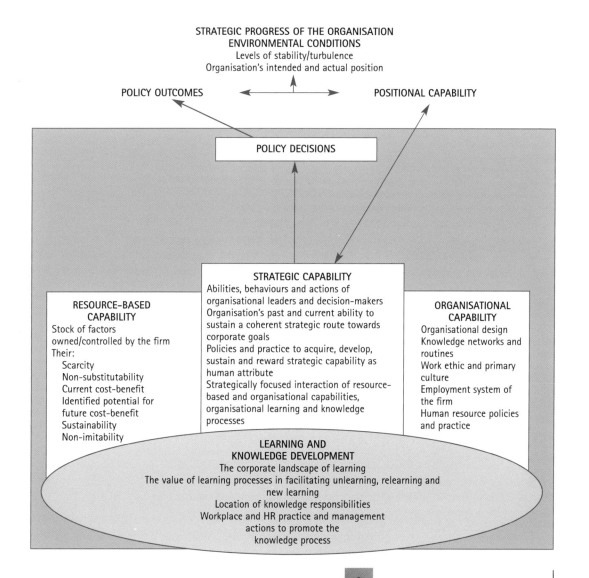

throughout the organisation through work-based learning processes.

What emerges strongly from these practical suggestions is, as we saw in Chapter 20, the vital role of individual and collective learning. In Figure 17 (p437) I have tried to capture the flavour of the relationship between learning, development and the key capabilities of the organisation.

The conceptual framework suggested in this section rests on the assumption that the quality of interaction between an organisation's three key capabilities can help to explain and influence strategic progress through time, and that L&D processes and activity can add to the value of those capabilities. For those who carry responsibility for L&D in their organisation, the strategic capability framework suggests two things, to both of which other HR writers and researchers have repeatedly drawn attention – notably Ulrich (1987), Hendry (1995) and Huselid (1995), all of whose views we noted in Chapter 3:

- the need for a profound understanding of the organisation in which they operate, its strategy process, and its business environment

- the need for a clear grasp of where to focus effort and investment in L&D – and what kind of efforts those should be – in order to ensure that well-integrated L&D and other HR practices enhance the organisation's key capabilities.

Task 1

Choose an organisation with which you are familiar, and where you will be given good access – it may be your own, but need not be. Your task is to assess what would be the most useful and feasible ways in which L&D could begin to enhance some aspect of strategic capability in that organisation, or in a major division, unit or section of it (choose whatever context in this respect is most feasible for you).

The assignment should be tackled in five steps:
- preliminary reading
- decisions on methodology
- gathering data
- an analysis of findings and a diagnosis of issues
- conclusions and recommendations.

Linking management development and strategic capability

Tasks for the management development process (MDP)

Stalk, Evans and Schulman (1992) attributed the US retail firm Wal-Mart's extraordinary success in the 1980s to a strategic vision, a set of business decisions and a competitive capability that in a short space of time took the company from nowhere to a dominating position not only in the USA but throughout the world. They concluded that the strategic choices that managers make increasingly determine organisations' fates. This signals the importance of the MDP. In Chapter 19, the Crotonville case was a striking example of the kind of contribution that the MDP can make to the strategic capability of an organisation.

An important task for the MDP is to produce skills required by managers working in highly innovative organisations – those with a need to regularly generate quite new strategic assets. There are tensions here. Such organisations operate in a pressured world. They are more complex and demanding, more uncertain in their work patterns and routines than the traditional type of organisation. As more people learn how to initiate ideas, activities and projects that create work for still others, and are encouraged by the organisation to do so, there is a danger of losing the balance between operational and creative activity to the point that neither is satisfactorily being achieved. 'Empowered' employees working in organisations with a high degree of innovatory activity are not easily managed. Too often they become disillusioned and cynical as fear of losing authority and control causes management to retrench, as once-effective teams become split by rivalries, and as strategic cohesion breaks down. There is also reduced employment security in such organisations, and increased stress levels when not all can pursue the ideas and assignments that bring the most attractive rewards.

Through the MDP, managers working in such organisations can become equipped with the knowledge and skills to achieve a balance in their teams between routine and innovatory activity, and learn how to foster creativity without endangering the performance of operational tasks.

To make any impact on strategic capability, the MDP must encompass a critical mass. Who should be developed in order to provide this? A growing body of research suggests that across most of today's more decentralised organisations it is the management team, broadly defined, rather than the chief executive, that most affects the quality and outcomes of strategy-making (Ghoshal and Bartlett, 1994; Hedlund, 1994). The MDP in such organisations must therefore focus on the development of middle as well as senior managers. Their strategic role can have a direct impact on the performance of the organisation, especially in those de-layered structures where innovation and market-sensitivity are essential to innovation and the advancement of the business in its competitive environment (Floyd and Wooldridge, 1994). Many would go further, as we saw in Chapter 18, in the belief that the scope of management development should take in every employee and focus on the total process of learning, continuous improvement and change in the organisation.

Managerial learning and the knowledge process

In Chapter 20 the notion of knowledge as a process was emphasised. Imagine now that the organisation is a continuous 'stream of knowledge' (von Krogh, Roos and Slocum, 1994: 54). Imagine the ways in which different approaches to the development of managers in the organisation can affect that stream of knowledge. They can change its shape and course, give it new outlets, or increase its force so that it can refresh and revitalise the sometimes barren territory of strategic decision-making. Finally, imagine knowledge as the firm's powerhouse, within which are stored the mental maps, the values and ideas, the customary ways of thinking, that can generate in organisational members a shared way of looking at and making sense of their organisational worlds and the environment around it.

By using our imagination in these ways we can begin to grasp the planned connections that can be made between the MDP, the knowledge-base of the organisation and strategic process. If the MDP is to enhance strategic capability, it must use approaches that result in the development of knowledge that can then be shared and utilised in ways beneficial to the business. It should help managers to unlearn ways of thinking and acting that are no longer appropriate given the organisation's changing environment. It should help them to reorganise and apply in different ways – relearn – much of the learning they already possess.

This kind of MDP contribution was illustrated in the clinical directors' programme in Chapter 16. There, new information had to be absorbed; old ways of thinking and behaving that were inconsistent with becoming a strategic manager had to be challenged so that they could be unlearned; yet at the same time, in order to be able to occupy both the professional role they still held and the new managerial role they now occupied, the clinical directors had to reorganise old knowledge, skills and values so that they could cope adequately with the demands of both roles – relearning as well as learning had to be achieved (Harrison and Miller, 1999).

We saw in Chapter 18 that arguably the most effective form of development for strategic managers is organisation-based and grounded in their ongoing tasks. New approaches can be reinforced, and sometimes activated, by changes in business processes. Unlearning and relearning can take root when supported by organisational systems. The concept of the dominant logic has a particular significance here. It has been explained (Prahalad and Bettis, 1986: 491) as:

> *a mindset or a world view or conceptualisation of the business and the administrative tools to accomplish goals and make decisions in that business and stored as a shared cognitive map among the dominant managerial coalition in the organisation, expressed as a learned, problem-solving behaviour.*

The dominant logic is not a well-grounded concept, in the sense of one that is supported by convincing research evidence. However, it does produce a memorable image of the danger of ways of thinking and behaving so deeply embedded in mindsets that they can prevent even the awareness that change is needed, let alone the willingness to achieve that change.

One of the paradoxes raised by the dominant logic is that the more successful a business becomes, the less likely is it that it will be able to achieve the unlearning needed to produce a different logic when internal or external changes may require it. We look at an example of this in the closing case study (p442).

Checkpoint

- What do you see to be the 'dominant logic' that prevails in your own organisation – or a division or unit of it with which you are fully familiar?

- Assess the extent to which that logic seems to inhibit or facilitate innovation and adaptability to change in the management sector.

- In the organisation's management development strategy, is there or should there be a focus on changing managerial cognitions and dominant logic?

Interpreting strategic progress

Levy (1994: 170, 172) stated that:

> *Capabilities acquired during previous competitive episodes shape the context for future competitive battles. Moreover, the accumulation of competitive advantage can be self-reinforcing. ... One can only learn strategies [for successful play] after experiencing the complexities of interactions on the chessboard. Indeed, because of the complexity of strategic interactions, one does not always know why a particular strategy is successful.*

I now want to return to an issue raised at the start of this book: one that is critical in any discussion of 'strategic progress'. The question, in Chapter 1, was 'What is really going on here?'

That, of course, is the question that all researchers must ask. It is easy to be wise after the event – for example, about the causes for BTR's decline. Given any theory, it is not too difficult to give it weight by being selective about the data one uses to illustrate it. In reality, however, the picture can be far less clear. To repeat John Storey's warning (1992: 17), what you meet on the ground can turn out to be very different from accounts received at second hand.

It is my belief that the 'strategic capability' construct is helpful in promoting a holistic approach to the L&D process, suggesting ways in which L&D practitioners can produce integrative strategies to help the organisation move forward even in turbulent conditions. I believe, too, that it has a particular value if used as a type of lens with which to scan data about an organisation's history, helping to identify patterns of behaviour that explain 'why we are where we are now'. In highly turbulent conditions history is unlikely to repeat itself. Little can therefore be extrapolated from old strategic recipes that will aid the formulation of new ones. Yet in such a scenario historical enquiry still has a value. Lessons can be learned from the past. They are lessons about the extent to which an organisation has demonstrated through time an ability to adapt quickly and effectively to changing conditions. They are lessons about processes and generalised strategies that aided or hindered adaptability.

In the following case study there are insufficient data to be sure about the causes of past events. However, there is clear evidence of an inability to break with past logics and to recognise and deal effectively with major new strategic issues. Scanning the case through the lens of strategic capability suggests some insights that would repay fuller investigation.

CASE STUDY: Marks & Spencer

Until December 1998 M&S was a bellwether of the British economy, and arguably the biggest retailer in Europe. A home-grown retail store, it is based on what was until recently a steady industry – food and clothing. As the end of the 1990s approached, the business remained in the hands of the Marks, Sieff and Sacher families who, in the 1920s, set it up as a penny-market. Its reputation for quality and value was for most of its history second to none.

M&S invests heavily in its resource-based capability. Its business-focused L&D strategy is implemented largely through expert line-managed in-store learning and development. Its organisational capability, too, is impressive. There are famously close links with suppliers, and stores are strategically located across the UK. There is a network of business routines, systems and processes to achieve the effective and efficient transformation of inputs into high-value-adding outputs.

The group's corporate culture, however, was described as an impregnable fortress buttressed by consistently rising profits – 'those who question the Company Way tend not to stay' (Weaver, 1988). Under Lord Rayner in the 1980s, an evangelistic glow acted 'like a nuclear furnace in firing the engines of expansion' but by 1998 increasing concerns were being expressed by business commentators about the extent to which corporate decision-makers were shielded from external criticism. M&S's stranglehold on clothing was by then being broken by changing high-street design trends and shifts in customer purchase patterns. At the same time there were aspirations to be a multinational mega-group that spanned countries and market sectors but uncertainty as to how exactly to handle that change of strategic direction. The investment needed ate into the group's profit-base.

Between 1996 and 1998 there was increasing

CASE STUDY: continued

boardroom unease about M&S's strategic direction, and a perception that the posts of CEO and chair of the company must be separated. Although conceding that point, Sir Richard Greenbury (62 years old) fiercely resisted making any announcement about succession. A company man, he had taken on the combined post from Lord Rayner in 1991 and was the first chief executive from outside the founding families. A feared autocrat, he dominated M&S. But in 1998 six months of sustained conflict broke out between him and his deputy chair, Keith Oates, not regarded as a real insider and not Greenbury's choice for successor.

Matters came to a head on 2 November 1998. Greenbury, about to board a plane for India for meetings with suppliers there, announced a 23 per cent fall in half-year profits due to recent poor trading. He confessed that this had come as an 'awful shock' to him and the rest of the board. No sooner had his plane taken off than Oates contacted the non-executive directors, expressing his wish to become chief executive. A bitter fight erupted, and M&S's largest investors complained directly to the company's divided board and to its stockbroker, Cazenove. On 9 November an enraged Greenbury cut short his India trip and returned, determined that Peter Salsbury, a seasoned company man and his personal choice, would be appointed CEO. By the end of November Greenbury had won, at some cost. Salsbury was appointed by unanimous vote and Oates left — but Greenbury had to agree to retire in July 2000 instead of on his 65th birthday in July 2001, a date previously announced by the board.

For Greenbury, it was a public climb-down of previously unthinkable proportions, and the adverse publicity for the company arising from the protracted boardroom indecision had damaging effects on shareholder confidence. When it was announced in January 1999 that the previous year's profit level would be halved, M&S shares plunged. With M&S, of course, all things are relative. Its profits were still high, and the decline was attributed internally to excessive winter overstocking. Organisational capability was tackled by establishing three new business units and a new post of marketing director. However, the board remained unwieldy, key faces were too familiar, and there was no liberation of young talent. The search for a new chairman appeared for some time to be deadlocked and the appointment of Woolworth's marketing director 'failed to impress the market' (Rush, 1999).

Of course no company can remain excellent indefinitely. As Professor Peter Doyle at Warwick University observed in the *Guardian*, 30 January 1999, yesterday's strategic assets become today's liabilities, and the average life of a public company in Britain and the USA is less than 20 years. On that basis, M&D had long been due for decline. But in this case, there was more to it than that. Problems at board level continued. Salsbury, 49, was little known in the City and was very much in the company image, with the same grooming as Greenbury and a record of deferring to him. Whether he could break the mindset represented by Greenbury, and whether he could handle the new turbulence facing M&S became increasingly uncertain.

By December 1999 shares were at their lowest level since August 1992, and morale at the company's head office was 'terrible', many believing that it had been a mistake for the non-executive directors to allow Greenbury to stay on (Rankine, 1999). Rumours of mergers and takeovers subsequently spread, and many senior company personnel departed or were moved on or out (including Salsbury). It was 2001 before signs of a halt in the decline of the company began to appear. How, initially, was it possible for such major strategic miscalculations to be made? Why did the decline persist for so long? And will the apparent reversal be sustained (Crabb, 2001)?

Sources: Rankine (1999), Rush (1999), Weaver (1988)

One reading of the situation is that despite its superior resource-based and organisational capability, lack of strategic capability in latter years was a direct contributor to the undermining of M&S's market position. Over a considerable period of time there was a steady deterioration in the quality of the organisation's strategic direction, perceived and tackled too late. The case suggests that problems were encountered when new learning was needed because the learning process was consistently blocked by failure to shed entrenched values and ways of thinking. For too long, it appears, a dominant logic continued to hold sway at M&S that prevented the unlearning and relearning that are essential in order to produce radical strategic change.

What has come under particular criticism at M&S is the failure to listen until too late in the day to those lower down the hierarchy (for one of the problems here was indeed a rigid, hierarchical structure) who had important information, suggestions and views to offer that had a bearing on strategic issues facing the firm. In organisations operating in conditions of increasing turbulence, it is no longer possible for the chief executive to 'learn for the organisation'. There must be an integration of strategic thinking at all levels for this kind of company to make continued progress (for an expansion on this, see Harrison 2000).

Of course what we are also seeing here is the bounded rationality of the strategy process first examined in Chapter 3. All that is proposed in this chapter is subject to the proviso – the very significant proviso – that rationality is a concept that can only go so far in explaining the twists and turns of organisational life. One of the salient features of the Marks & Spencer case was the power battle that was fought in and outside the boardroom between the key players. Much of what followed was fall-out from that battle.

Task 2

The case of Marks & Spencer continues. Gather as much information as you can about the company's progress subsequent to the above account, and also try to obtain more data about the period covered by the account. Then analyse your expanded narrative through the lens of the strategic capability framework. What conclusions does that analysis suggest? And to what extent were the tentative conclusions formed at the end of the account in this section borne out by later events?

CONCLUSION

Throughout this book themes of challenge, business partnership, strategic alignment, professionalism, and the contribution that the L&D process can make to improving human performance and aiding strategic progress have all been pursued. Theories, frameworks and prescriptions have jostled for place in an attempt to express both the intellectual rigour involved in the study of L&D and the need for it to achieve outcomes that will substantiate its claim as a value-adding process.

There are, however, two words that have appeared little if at all in the book so far, yet they go to the heart of its matter. The words are *wisdom* and *humility* – the wisdom to search for the fundamental questions to ask, and the humility to realise that some may never be possible to answer. In a book where themes of turbulence, of uncertainty, of irrelevant logics and of human fallibility have figured large, it is appropriate at this last point to recall the difference between learning and knowledge. The book began with a quotation from Dickens. Now, a writer (Janette Turner Hospital, 2001) from quite a different century and country (Australia) offers a crucial insight at its close:

> When we learn that we are too ignorant to formulate intelligible questions, we learn a great deal. We begin to cross the divide, to think with 'forked brain', to become a different self, one which is no longer at ease in the old dispensation. From that moment, we understand how very strange our own unexamined assumptions are and, like T. S. Eliot's Magi, we begin to feel foreign in our own country.

Wisdom and humility are the trademarks of the true professional. The acknowledgement of the need to 'think with forked brain', the realisation of how little we know, how much more we need to discover, and the determination to constantly unlearn in order to learn – these are the human qualities that offer to the profession its best hope of moving forward with its partners both in and beyond the organisation.

This book has involved a long journey across the corporate landscape of learning and knowledge. Sometimes that landscape has seemed barren, sometimes rich, and always the way ahead has seemed uncertain. This, however, is no new experience in the long history of learning and development. At the end of World War I a distinguished educationalist (Bobbitt, 1918) made an observation that we could as well make today:

> The controlling purposes of education have not been sufficiently particularized. We have aimed at a vague culture, an ill-defined discipline, a nebulous harmonious development of the individual, an indefinite moral character-building, an unparticularized social efficiency, or, often enough, nothing more than escape from a life of work.

But this is more than a commentary on dilemmas that still face our educational system. For those in the field of learning and development there is particular resonance in the phrases 'nebulous harmonious development' and 'escape from a life of work'. The seventeenth-century mystic Henry Vaughan* wrote of how 'the liberated soul ascends, looking at the sunset towards the west wind, and hearing secret harmonies'. But Bobbitt spoke of 'nebulous' harmonies, and that is the most telling observation. In learning and development it is indeed a constant struggle to reconcile the business imperative with the noble aspiration to transform individuals through the realisation of their human potential.

Since harmony is the product of the resolution of tensions, it should not surprise us that the history of learning and development is one of a continuing search for a satisfactory balance between responding to the needs of the economy, of the organisation, and of the individual. It is a search that should be viewed as a challenge, not as a fruitless endeavour. Bobbitt's commentary must not become an epitaph for human resource professionals. The last message should rather be one of hope, like Vaughan* the mystic who journeyed on 'looking towards the west wind, and hearing secret harmonies' . . .

Useful reference sources

GUILE D. *and* FONDA N. (1998) *Performance Management through Capability*. London, Institute of Personnel and Development.

STALK G., EVANS P. *and* SHULMAN L. E. (1992) 'Competing on capabilities: the new rules of corporate strategy'. *Harvard Business Review*. March–April. pp57–69.

STARKEY K. (ED.) (1996) *How Organizations Learn*. London, Thomson International Business Press.

* In previous editions I confused Henry Vaughan, religious poet and mystic, with his brother Thomas, the noted alchemist and magician. In view of the dazzling sleights of hand that are to be observed in some L&D practice and theory, perhaps this was a Freudian slip!

• The Chartered Institute of Personnel and Development's Learning and Development Standard (CIPD, 2001) (Extract)

Purpose

The organisational process of developing people involves the integration of learning and development (L&D) processes, operations and relationships. Its most powerful outcomes for the business are to do with enhanced organisational effectiveness and sustainability. For the individual they are to do with enhanced personal competence, adaptability and employability. It is therefore a critical business process, whether in for-profit or not-for-profit organisations.

Anyone working in the L&D field has interrelated responsibilities to:

- the organisation(s) they work for
- the people they are helping to develop
- the human resource (HR) community to which they belong.

To make the essential professional-level contribution to organisational as well as to individual performance and progress, the L&D practitioner must be concerned with integrative activity and future planning, as well as with developmental operations here and now.

This standard:

- requires the mastering of a body of operational expertise in L&D practice at the level of a generalist practitioner, and calls for a broad-based understanding of the contribution that people development can make to the performance and progress of the organisation and the individual

- requires those with L&D responsibilities to consistently demonstrate in their values, behaviour and practice that they are both business partners and ethical practitioners

- provides the integrating performance framework to shape the activity of anyone in an L&D role.

No personnel or development activity exists in a vacuum. So it is inevitable that this standard reinforces some of the core operational and knowledge indicators that appear in the People Management and Development standard, and in the specialist standards related to learning and development.

It is relevant for:

- any personnel/HR practitioner at a relatively early stage in their career, responsible for a range of basic personnel operations and wanting to develop deeper and broader knowledge and skills to enable them to make a professional contribution to the L&D process. Such a practitioner is likely to aspire to a senior HR or L&D position ultimately.

- line managers who need to build broad-based L&D skills and knowledge because they hold L&D responsibilities

- externally based consultants, such as training providers, and those working in training and L&D agencies – providing advice and services in many organisational types, sectors and settings.

To be effective in their performance, L&D generalists must be holistic in their approach and integrative in their operations. They must continuously relate their operations and advice to wider HR and business policy and practice in their organisations. They must also act as business partners, creating and maintaining collaborative and business-focused working relationships with those most involved in, and affected by, planned L&D processes.

In addition to the knowledge that underpins their operational expertise, L&D generalists must have a broad-based understanding of the L&D field. In order to have credibility they must be informed about, and be able to explain, the L&D implications of a wide range of issues.

Performance indicators

Operational indicators

Practitioners must be able to:

1. co-operate with L&D stakeholders in L&D policy, strategy and plans, in order to integrate L&D activity with wider personnel and business policy

2. advise on how to achieve a well-managed, appropriately staffed and value-adding L&D function

3. contribute to L&D that will aid the processes of recruitment and performance management

4. contribute to L&D that will help the organisation retain the people it needs for the future

5. contribute to L&D that will expand the organisation's overall capacity and competence, and will help to introduce and embed organisational change

6. promote learning that will stimulate strategic awareness, and will

develop and help to disseminate organisationally valuable knowledge

7 contribute to the design and provision of effective learning processes and activity, using new technology as appropriate

8 evaluate learning outcomes, and help to assess the returns on the organisation's past and planned investment in L&D

9 identify and promote L&D processes and practices that meet or exceed legal, mandatory and ethical requirements

10 continuously develop their own expertise, professionalism and credibility in the L&D field.

Knowledge indicators

Practitioners must understand and be able to explain:

1 the integration of L&D activity and organisational needs, with special reference to:
   1 the organisation's business environment and internal context
   2 the goals of the stakeholders in L&D, and the building and sustaining of partnerships that will produce and communicate effective L&D processes and initiatives
   3 the formulation of the organisation's L&D goals and strategy, and their implementation at different organisational levels.

2 the provision of a value-adding L&D function:
   1 how the L&D process adds value for the organisation and the individual
   2 the organisation, management and evaluation of the L&D function and roles
   3 the delivery of organisationally focused projects to time, cost and quality
   4 aids and barriers to effective performance as an L&D consultant.

3 L&D's contribution to the recruitment and performance management processes:
   1 induction, basic skills training and continuous improvement that will motivate learners, achieve competent performance, and build commitment to organisational goals and values.

4 L&D's contribution to employee retention:
   1 career and management development processes that help identify, develop and use people's potential and adaptability and aid their continued employability.

5 L&D's contribution to building organisational capacity and facilitating change:
   1 the skills and attitudes needed to work effectively in

changed/changing organisational roles, structures and working environments, and how they can be developed

2   L&D strategies for organisational culture change.

6 the stimulation of strategic awareness and the development of knowledge

1   L&D initiatives and processes to stimulate strategic awareness, creativity and innovation

2   learning strategies and processes to develop, share and disseminate knowledge that is valuable to the organisation.

7 the design and delivery of L&D processes and activity:

1   the planning, design and delivery of learning processes and activity that will add value for the organisation and for individuals

2   the appropriate application of new technology to training and learning.

8 the evaluation and assessment of L&D outcomes and investment:

1   methods and models for:

- evaluating the outcomes of L&D processes and activity
- evaluating the organisation's past L&D investment

2   the identification and assessment of L&D processes and activity that will benefit the organisation in the short- and longer-term future.

9 the role and tasks of the ethical practitioner:

1   the impact on, and implications of, diversity of people, style, and employment contracts for L&D policies and practice and organisational learning strategies

2   the information and actions needed to identify and achieve legally compliant and ethical L&D practices and processes.

10 the importance of continuing professional self-development:

1   methods and processes of continuing personal and professional development, including coaching, counselling and mentoring

2   databases and information sources that provide up-to-date information about current and emergent theory, practice and issues in the field.

• The Framework for National Vocational Standards and Qualifications

Note: The phrase 'NVQs' is used throughout as a shorthand to cover both English and Scottish qualifications.

Vocational qualifications are those that relate directly to a person's competence in employment. By 1986 less than one-third of the UK labour force held vocational qualifications, compared to two-thirds in Germany and significantly less than in other competitor countries.

The National Council for Vocational Qualifications (NCVQ) was set up in 1986 by the government following the White Paper *Working Together – Education and Training.* That White Paper endorsed the recommendations of the *Review of Vocational Qualifications in England and Wales* produced by the CBI and TUC in the same year. The Council was an independent body, sponsored jointly by the Secretaries of State for Employment, and for Education and Science, for Northern Ireland and for Wales. Its main role was to produce a national framework incorporating vocational qualifications that meet national standards of occupational competence within a simple structure of 5 levels. Links have been established with all the awarding bodies in the UK (currently around 250 examining bodies and 150 industrial training bodies) and with the European Commission. The longer-term aim is to have a harmonised European system of vocational qualifications, with consistency of standards across Europe in all occupations and professions.

In 1997 the NCVQ and the Schools Curriculum and Assessment Authority were merged to form the Qualifications and Curriculum Authority (QCA). This, with the equivalent Scottish and Welsh bodies, now oversees the UK qualification system.

National Vocational Qualifications

A NVQ represents a statement of competence confirming that the individual can perform to a specified standard in a range of work-related activities, and also possesses the skills, knowledge and understanding which makes possible such performance in the workplace.

NVQs are not awarded by a qualification authority but by various examining bodies such as BTEC and the City and Guilds, RSA and Pitmans, whose courses incorporate standards, on a scale from 1 to 5, laid down by the various industry lead bodies. The courses have been QCA-accredited, and certificates carry both the NVQ stamp and that of the examining bodies.

Support for NVQs from the various industries and professions stems from the fact that their representatives formed the membership of the

150 Lead Bodies that produced 'Lead Body Standards' in 1996 for different occupations and professions (see below). Given that the NCVQ's membership was also employer-dominated, it could fairly be claimed that it was employers and the professions, not some central government body insensitive to employers' needs, who 'drove' the NVQ movement and who give its products their seal of approval.

Lead Body Standards were developed by a lengthy analytical and consultative process, involving the breaking down of a job first into general areas of competence, each comprising abilities and skills, and then more detailed elements of competence. Each approved qualification is currently assigned to one of five levels within the NVQ framework (a new qualification structure is to be introduced in 2002). The levels indicate the level of competence achieved. Levels 1 and 2 ('basic' and 'standard' levels) typify the kind of competence needed in many routine jobs and occupations of a predictable character. They are below the level of any occupational standards operating in France or Germany, but the argument is that attaining level 1 will encourage movement onto level 2, and that level 2 will offer a foundation for further training. Levels 3 and 4 range through existing craft, technician and lower-level professional areas of skill, while level 5 is intended to equate in most cases with the higher-level professional qualifications – although there is considerable debate about this among the professions. Some qualifications are easier to integrate into the NVQ system than others, because many professions have a highly structured system for gaining qualifications, some of which include competencies whereas others are more educationally based.

Assessment of prior learning

Since performance in the workplace, or activities which realistically simulate it, is part of NVQs, assessment of workplace competence has to be widely used, in ways and by assessors agreed between colleges, training organisations and/or employers. This has clear implications for appraisal schemes and also for the identification of training needs and the design of training courses in order to ensure that they both meet job-related needs and can achieve NVQ accreditation.

Credit accumulation and transfer

This is a comprehensive and flexible system that enables people to achieve a level of competence through various methods of training and work experience, at various centres and over varying periods of time and thereby also to acquire vocational qualifications. It is intended to design all qualifications in such a way that they can be offered on a modular basis and tested by judging someone's competence in the job. This is similar to the highly successful French vocational training and education schemes.

A 'unit' is a measure of an outcome of learning, and each NVQ is made up of a number of units of competence. Credits are given for the acquisition of 'units of competence'. Through the credit accumulation and transfer system a workplace supervisor with training responsibilities might be able to gain one or two units of a 'Training profession' NVQ mainly through having his or her workplace performance assessed as meeting the standards laid down in those units, without immediately having to complete an entire course of study. He or she would then be seen as competent in those specific areas of activity, and could add to them or not as he or she chose.

Each unit builds up the credit balance of an individual's 'competence account'. The aim is to express all existing qualifications in terms of units; units certificated by different awarding bodies can then be accumulated within the common system, and units common to two or more qualifications can be transferred in order to avoid repetition in training and assessment. CIPD Professional Qualifications introduced in 1996 are, for example, cross-mapped with National Vocational Qualifications, and were introduced in the same year. Following the revision of the CIPD's Professional Standards and of the National Vocational Qualification structure in 2002 (see Chapter 8), new cross-mapping will be announced during 2002.

Individuals can continually register their achievement in an NVQ Record of Competence that is opened when an individual embarks on a programme or seeks certification for the first time. This record moves with the individual, providing a recognised record of competence throughout the individual's life.

All National Occupational Standards were revised following extensive country-wide consultation between 1999 and 2001. They were produced in their new version by the end of 2001, with a new National Vocational Qualification structure to follow during 2002 (for updating information, see www.empnto.co.uk and www.qca.org.uk).

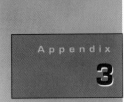
The Comprehensive and the Problem-centred Approaches to Identifying and Analysing Organisational L&D Needs

These two approaches are based on the same general principles, but in their detailed operation they cater for different kinds of situation.

The *total, or comprehensive, approach* involves a systematic, full-scale analysis of all the organisation's learning and development needs, identified by discussions with managers (and unions as relevant), by analysis of the corporate business plan, and by examination of any other sources of likely change affecting people in the organisation. Its product is an organisation-wide L&D plan containing unit and individual plans for the forthcoming year (a year is usually the planning period for this kind of approach). It can be relevant for organisations where the environment is relatively stable, and where longer-term training plans can feasibly be produced and pursued, although it is unlikely to be used unless there is a specialist personnel/training function. If you are following this approach you must ensure that you have the necessary time and other resources, and that it will justify such expenditure.

For organisations operating in an unpredictable environment, facing severe pressures, and/or (like many small to medium-sized firms) lacking the resources or expertise for the 'total' strategy, something more selective and immediate in its payback is needed. For them, the 'problem-centred' analytical approach may be the most appropriate.

The *'problem-centred' approach* focuses on urgent problems facing the organisation and requiring a training/development response. It places minimum reliance on paperwork. The assumption here is that the planning of L&D must be ongoing and focused on immediate needs, with long-term strategy at a minimum. There may be no formalised L&D plan other than papers that from time to time have to be drawn up for budgetary or external purposes. L&D must respond quickly to any urgent needs, and so flexibility in the function and its operations is essential.

Both approaches are systematic; it is the timescale and scope of assessment and planning that are the major differentiating factors. Here is a step-by-step guide to their implementation.

The total, or comprehensive, approach

Step 1: Identify major needs

The first step is to study the organisation's business strategy and plan. L&D/personnel staff should then discuss with every manager the learning and development needs for their units. At this stage, they need to bring into the discussions implications of any impending organisational changes, new technology initiatives, new plant and machinery and new staff coming into the organisation. In establishing L&D needs they should be influenced by managers' interpretation of events as well as by areas of need identified in corporate strategy.

Step 2: Agree possible solutions

During this phase of the discussion, the degree to which L&D can contribute to meeting departmental needs must be assessed. Performance targets and outputs of the department must be examined, together with any other data that will give substance and objectivity to the discussions. Information about many L&D needs may come from the results of appraisal interviews. Where an appraisal system is not yet operative, information will come from such sources as managers' views and the views of any other key parties, performance records, career plans and potential reviews.

Problems perceived initially by managers to have an L&D solution may on analysis prove to be problems needing some other solution, and vice versa. It is therefore essential to be clear as to the real nature of a problem. If performance is poor, for example, it may be because of inadequate or non-existent training, but it could as easily be because of poor motivation, ineffective management or faulty equipment.

Thus in this second step the L&D manager (with help as needed) has detailed talks with line management to ensure that the departmental and individual needs they raise will be best and most cost-effectively tackled by some form of training or development. They will also need to jointly define and agree those needs and apply a prioritisation system that reflects overall objectives established in the organisation's corporate L&D policy.

Step 3: Select L&D options

At this point it is important to discuss options for L&D, with a view to the process being as cost-efficient as possible. Initially the possibility of on-the-job events to achieve the required learning should be discussed rather than looking at external courses of action as a priority. Such discussion can lead to a significant shift from a reliance on external courses to an emphasis on in-house training, much of it delivered by consultants. It can also lead to line managers, supervisors and other non-specialist L&D personnel in the organisation taking significant responsibility for design and delivery of L&D activity once they have acquired the necessary level of competence. Such a shift must obviously be accompanied by appropriate training and development of such external and internal personnel and by careful monitoring of processes and outcomes.

Step 4: Create learning and development plan

Next, the L&D manager constructs the first draft of the annual L&D plan, which identifies each department's and each individual's learning needs and the relevant courses of action agreed with the managers of those departments and individuals.

Step 5: Prioritise learning events

The budgeting process conducted by the L&D manager starts at this point, when, within the L&D plan, he or she classifies L&D needs and events on a scale (which could simply be an 'A' to 'E' rating system, A being 'essential training/development', E being 'desirable but not necessarily this year') according to priorities established in corporate L&D policy. This means that each learning event is prioritised in accordance with corporate business needs, so that when finalised the L&D plan is geared to make an optimum contribution to the achievement of business objectives as well as to individual needs.

Step 6: Apply budgetary constraints

After L&D activity has been categorised, the L&D manager should then estimate the costs involved in the initial draft of the L&D plan, including the options that were discussed with managers. Costing should be done using current costs (an inflationary factor can be added later), examining both direct and indirect costs.

In an organisation where managers are required to submit departmental budgets for the coming financial year in, say, late January, total budget figures need to be allocated before the beginning of the financial year. This will enable managers to allocate resources appropriately according to their budget allocation, based on their January submissions. Once the L&D manager receives his or her budget allocation, adjustments to the plan are quite straightforward if it has been built up on a prioritised pyramid of costs, descending from 'essential' to 'can be deferred if necessary'. Reappraisal of the options available may result, for example, in the use of more internal training, or in dropping some training in the category that lists training agreed to carry lowest priority. In the latter event, subsequent reassessment of the original need should be carried out, to see whether or not training is still appropriate and needs to be done in the next budget year.

Step 7: Communicate results

Once the L&D plan has been fully costed and agreed by the board, a copy of the relevant sections should be given to each manager as an *aide-mémoire* and plan for each department. This then becomes an essential tool of reference for the review meetings the L&D manager holds with managers throughout the forthcoming year.

Step 8: Monitor and evaluate implementation

A continuous appraisal of progress and budgetary control should be maintained by the L&D department, using information supplied by management and those who go on L&D programmes. The task is not a difficult one when the L&D plan has been costed in relation to specific learning events and departments, with clear categories covering course fees, travel and related expenses, and fees paid to external consultants and trainers. Monitoring is vital for two reasons:

- It enables a tight control to be exercised over ongoing L&D activity, so that if at any point in time costs are exceeded, appropriate action can be taken. If, on the other hand, it should happen that costs fall below estimate, then there is flexibility to either include any hitherto-deferred activity or to organise L&D activity to meet some unexpected contingency.

- It enables the L&D manager to build up a 'value for money' statement that can be included in the annual report on the L&D plan. This can include statements related to key parameters like:

  - outcomes of L&D activity, in relation to key needs it was intended to serve (using quantifiable and qualitative measures)

  - expenditure overall on L&D activity, compared with last year

  - number and cost of person days of L&D activity, compared with last year

  - number and cost of person days of L&D activity carried out externally and in-house, compared with last year.

The problem-centred approach

Here is how the eight steps can be applied using the problem-centred approach. (Throughout, reference is made to 'the training manager' but this should be taken to mean anyone who carries the responsibility for formulating L&D policy and an L&D plan for the organisation.)

Step 1: Identify major needs

The training manager should identify with managers on a continuing basis the most urgent problems or challenges they face, for which it is felt that some form of training or development would be the best solution. Analysis itself is carried out in a similar way to that outlined in the comprehensive approach. At regular intervals (determined by the length of the business planning cycle) the training manager must check on any information available about business plans and likely future changes, to see if training is needed to feed into those.

Step 2: Agree possible solutions

Here, as with the 'total' approach, the training manager must analyse whether particular problems are not only relevant for L&D activity to tackle, but are problems to which such activity would be the most cost-effective and cost-efficient response. In making a decision consideration must be given, within the constraints of corporate policy and employee resource systems, to alternative options such as changing equipment, jobs, people or organisation structure.

With the problem-centred approach priorities are determined by the extent to which one problem, if resolved, would make a greater impact on immediate business performance than another. Areas of weakness that are currently impeding achievement of results crucial to the company's survival must therefore be tackled first. Longer-term issues such as succession planning needs must also be tackled on an ongoing basis in the light of their importance to ensuring continuity and calibre of uniquely valuable personnel.

Step 3: Select L&D options

Here, agreement must be reached on who is to be trained or developed, how many, and when, where and how L&D will be organised. L&D activity can be done in any cost-effective, feasible and agreed way, but must take place in or near the work environment wherever possible, both to reduce costs and to ensure immediate relevance and transferability of learning. Events selected under the problem-centred approach must be mainly concerned to achieve results in the shortest possible time, and in the most efficient manner.

Step 4: Create L&D plan

Training to meet certain major needs will usually be planned and agreed some time in advance (for example, health and safety training, retraining to cope with redundancies or redeployment of workers, or training to enable key workers to operate new technology). That apart, the L&D plan will be informal rather than heavily documented. A record should, however, be kept of the number and names of the learners, of L&D objectives, of the type, location and timing of the learning event, and of its timing, cost and outcomes related to objectives.

Step 5: Prioritise learning events

Although L&D activity, with the problem-centred approach, is organised on a rolling basis rather than on the basis of an annual plan, attention must still be paid to prioritising events. Planning no more, probably, than a few weeks or months ahead, the training manager must still ensure that effort is put into those problem areas across the company where there will be the most significant return in terms of impact on the business. So, as with the prioritisation of departmental or divisional L&D

needs, attention must be given first to those areas having a critical impact on the firm's survival, and crucial to its future stability and growth.

Step 6: Apply budgetary constraints

The training manager may not have a budget (or may only hold a small central budget for core training and development needs), but be paid from the budgets held by line managers. It is therefore particularly important that he or she has a clear idea of what the business overall, and particular departments within it, can afford for the L&D they are requesting. All L&D activity must be carefully costed. When line managers hold budgetary control, particularly close attention needs to be given to 'hidden' costs like lost opportunity and lost production, replacement or other costs involved in covering for people away from their jobs for a period of time. The training manager must be able to convince that L&D activity can offer the value needed to offset costs.

Step 7: Communicate results

With the problem-centred approach, initial requests for L&D must be acted upon quickly, and information about L&D activity that will be going ahead must be communicated to the managers concerned as soon as possible.

In situations where the problem-centred approach is used, certainty can rarely be built into any stage of the cycle. Even at the last minute action plans may have to be cancelled or postponed because of some contingency. Communications at that point must work particularly well in order to ensure that everyone is informed about the reasons for the changes, and that wherever possible alternative ways of responding to the initial request (assuming it is still valid) can be agreed.

Step 8: Monitor and evaluate implementation

Evaluation is essential in order to ensure that scarce resources (including time) are being used effectively. The initial clear specification of the nature of the problem and the exact outcomes that L&D activity is intended to produce, together with agreement between training manager and line managers about how those outcomes will be measured, should ease the task of evaluation. Identifiable improvements in competencies, and measurable impact on the indicators chosen beforehand – for example, material wastage rates, levels of employee absenteeism, turnover, learning times, indices of customer satisfaction, speed and quality of service provided – should all be used in order to assess the extent to which L&D activity has had an impact on the problems it was intended to resolve or reduce.

Appendix

4

• Extract from the CIPD's Code of Professional Conduct and Disciplinary Procedures

Copyright CIPD, 2000

4 Standards of professional conduct

CIPD members are expected to exercise relevant competence in accordance with the Institute's professional standards and qualifications.

4.1 CIPD members provide specialist professional knowledge, advice, support and management competence in the management and development of people. In all circumstances they:

4.1.1 must endeavour to enhance the standing and good name of the profession; adherence to this code of professional conduct is an essential aspect of this

4.1.2 must seek continually to improve their performance and update and refresh their skills and knowledge

4.1.3 must, within their own or any client organisation and in whatever capacity they are working, seek to achieve the fullest possible development of people for present and future organisational needs and encourage self-development by individuals

4.1.4 must, within their own or any client organisation and in whatever capacity they are working, seek to adopt in the most appropriate way the most appropriate people management processes and structures to enable the organisation to best achieve its present and future objectives

4.1.5 must promote and themselves maintain fair and reasonable standards in the treatment of people who are operating within the scope of their influence

4.1.6 must promote and themselves seek to exercise employment practices that remove unfair discrimination including but not limited to gender, age, race, religion, disability and background

4.1.7 must respect legitimate needs and requirements for confidentiality

4.1.8 must use due diligence and exercise high standards of timeliness, appropriateness and accuracy in the information and advice they provide to employers and employees

4.1.9 must seek to recognise the limitations of their own knowledge and ability and must not undertake activity for which they are not yet appropriately prepared or, where applicable, qualified.

4.2 In the public interest and in the pursuit of its objectives, the Chartered Institute of Personnel and Development is committed to the highest possible standards of professional conduct and competency.

To this end members:

4.2.1 are required to exercise integrity, honesty, diligence and appropriate behaviour in all their business, professional and related personal activities

4.2.2 must act within the law and must not encourage, assist or act in collusion with employers, employees or others who may be engaged in unlawful conduct.

• References

ABBOTT B. (1994) 'Training strategies in small service sector firms: employer and employee perspectives'. *Human Resource Management Journal*. Vol. 4, 2. pp70–87.

ADLER P. S. *and* COLE R. E. (1993) 'Designed for learning: a tale of two auto plants'. *Sloan Management Review*. Vol. 34, 3. pp85–94.

AIKIN O. (1999) 'The right to learn'. *People Management*. Vol. 5, 13. p23.

AIKIN O. (2001) 'Select advice for employers'. *People Management*. Vol. 7, 17. p20.

AIKIN O. (2001a) 'No more secrets'. *People Management*. Vol. 7, 21. p23.

ALLEN R. E. (1990) *The Concise Oxford Dictionary of Current English*. 8th edn. Oxford, Clarendon Press.

ALLISON G. J. (1971) *Essence of Decision: Explaining the Cuban missile crisis*. Boston, MA, Little, Brown.

ALRED G., GARVEY B. *and* SMITH R. (1998) *The Mentoring Pocket Book*. Alresford, UK, Management Pocket Books Series.

ALVAREZ J. L. (1996) 'Are we asking too much of managers?' *Financial Times*. 12 July. p13.

AMIT R. *and* SCHOEMAKER J. H. (1993) 'Strategic assets and organizational rent'. *Strategic Management Journal*. Vol. 14, 1. pp33–46.

ANDREWS K. R. (1965) *The Concept of Corporate Strategy*. Homewood, IL, Dow Jones-Irwin.

ANNETT J., DUNCAN K. D., STAMMERS R. B. *and* GRAY M. J. (1979) *Task Analysis: Department of Employment and Productivity Training Information Paper, No. 6*. London, HMSO; reprinted Sheffield, Department of Employment.

ANSOFF H. I. (1965) *Corporate Strategy*. New York, McGraw-Hill.

ANSOFF H. I. *and* SULLIVAN P. A. (1993) 'Optimizing profitability in turbulent environments: a formula for strategic success'. *Long-Range Planning*. Vol. 26, 5. pp11–23.

ANTHONY P. (1994) *Managing Culture*. Buckingham, The Open University Press.

ARAGON S. R., HATCHER T. *and* SWANSON R. A. (eds) (2001) 'Ethics and integrity in HRD: Case studies in research and practice'. *Advances in Developing Human Resources*. Vol. 3, 1. February. (Quarterly journal of the Academy of Human Resource Development, USA.)

ARGYRIS C. (1957) *Personality and Organization*. New York, Harper & Row.

ARGYRIS C. (1977) 'Double-loop learning in organizations'. *Harvard Business Review*. September–October. pp115–24.

ARGYRIS C. (1982) *Reasoning, Learning and Action*. San Francisco, CA, Jossey-Bass.

ARGYRIS C. (1996) 'Skilled incompetence', in K. Starkey (ed), *How*

Organizations Learn. London, International Thomson Business Press, pp82-91.

ARGYRIS C. *and* SCHON D. A. (1978) *Organizational Learning: A theory of action Perspective.* Reading, MA, Addison Wesley.

ARGYRIS C. *and* SCHON D. A. (1996) *Organizational Learning II: Theory, method and practice.* New York, Addison Wesley.

ARKIN A. (1991) 'A springboard to equal opportunities'. *Personnel Management.* Vol. 23, 2. pp57-8.

ARKIN A. (1995) 'Breaking down skills barriers'. *People Management.* Vol. 1, 3. pp34-5.

ARKIN A. (1995a) 'More than just a cosmetic change'. *People Management.* Vol. 1, 8. pp30-31.

ARKSEY H. (2001) 'How to support staff who are carers'. *People Management.* Vol. 7, 17. pp44-5.

ARMSTRONG M. *and* BARON A. (1998) *Performance Management: The new realities.* London: Institute of Personnel and Development.

ASHTON D., SUNG J., RADDON A. *and* POWELL M. (2001) 'National frameworks for workplace learning'. In Chartered Institute of Personnel and Development *Workplace Learning in Europe* [summary of the European Workplace Learning Seminar, London, 2 April]. London, CIPD, pp35-60. Available to download from: www.cipd.co.uk

BADARACCO J. L. (1991) *Knowledge Link: How firms compete through strategic alliances.* Boston, MA, Harvard Business School Press.

BALLS E. *and* GOODHART D. (1994) 'Can Europe compete? The high price of social cohesion'. *Financial Times.* 28 February. p11.

BARNEY J. (1991) 'Firm resources and sustained competitive advantage'. *Journal of Management.* Vol. 17. pp99-120.

BARON A. (2000) 'Advance beyond intuition'. *People Management,* Vol. 6, 15. pp30-31.

BASS B. M. *and* VAUGHAN J. A. (1967) *Training in Industry: The management of learning.* London, Tavistock Publications.

BATCHELOR J., DONNELLY R. and MORRIS D. (1995) 'Learning networks within supply chains'. *Working paper, Coventry Business School.* Coventry, Coventry University, Priory Street, Coventry, CV1 5FB.

BAUD D. C. *and* SCANLAN G. (1995) 'Strategic control through core competencies'. *Long-Range Planning.* Vol. 28, 2. pp102-14.

BEAUMONT G. (1996) 'Review of 100 NVQs and SVQs'. *A Report submitted to the Department for Education and Employment.* 25, Albion Road, Chesterfield, S40 IBR (Freepost SF10305), Beaumont.

BEAUMONT P. *and* HUNTER L. (2002) *Managing Knowledge Workers: The HRM dimension.* London, Chartered Institute of Personnel and Development.

BECKER G. (1975) *Human Capital: A theoretical and empirical analysis with special reference to education.* 2nd edn. New York, Columbia University Press.

BECKET M. (1996) 'Small business packs statistical punch'. *Daily Telegraph Business Monitor* section. 12 August. p27.

BEE F. and BEE R. (1994) *Training Needs Analysis and Evaluation*. London, Institute of Personnel and Development.

BEE F. and FARMER P. (1995) 'HR projects on the right track'. *People Management*. Vol. 1, 16. pp28–30.

BENTLEY T. (1990) *The Business of Training: Achieving success in changing world markets*. Maidenhead, McGraw-Hill.

BLUNKETT D. (2000) 'How partnerships can aid failing schools'. *Daily Telegraph*. 15 March. p22.

BLUNKETT D. (2000a) 'Digital dimensions'. *Guardian Higher Education Supplement*. 15 February. p1h.

BOUD D. and GARRICK J. (EDS) (1999) *Understanding Learning at Work*. London, Routledge.

BOWER D. (1991) 'Case study: Rover', in V. Dulewicz, 'Improving assessment centres', *Personnel Management*, Vol. 23, 6, pp52–3.

BOYATZIS R. E. (1991) 'Building on competence: the effective use of managerial talent', in G. Salaman (ed.), *Human Resource Strategies*. London, Sage.

BOYDELL T. and LEARY M. (1996) *Identifying Training Needs*. London, Institute of Personnel and Development.

BRAMLEY P. (1996) *Evaluating Training*. London, Institute of Personnel and Development.

BRATTON J. and GOLD J. (1994) *Human Resource Management: Theory and practice*. London, Macmillan.

BREWSTER C. and TYSON S. (EDS) (1991) *International Comparisons in Human Resource Management*. London, Pitman.

BREWSTER C., HARRIS H. and SPARROW P. (2001) 'On top of the world'. *People Management*. Vol. 7, 21. pp37–42.

BROWN J. S. and DUGUID P. (1991) 'Organisational learning and communities-of-practice: towards a unified view of working, learning and innovation'. *Organization Science*. Vol. 2, 1. pp40–57.

BROWN P. (2000) 'Trained to cope with anything'. *Times*. 22 February. p45.

BUCKINGHAM M. (2001) 'What a waste'. *People Management*. Vol. 7, 20. pp36–40.

BURACK E. H. (1991) 'Changing the company culture – the role of human resource development'. *Long-Range Planning*. Vol. 24, 1. pp88–95.

BURGOYNE J. (1989) *Management Development: Context and strategies*. Aldershot, Gower.

BURGOYNE J. (1999) 'Design of the times'. *People Management*. Vol. 5, 11. pp39–44.

BURGOYNE J. (1999a) *Develop Yourself, Your Career and Your Organisation*. London, Lemos & Crane.

BUTLER E. (1999) 'Technologising equity: the politics and practices of work-related learning', in D. Boud and J. Garrick (eds), *Understanding Learning at Work*. London, Routledge, pp132–150.

BUTLER G. V. (1986) *Organization and Management: Theory and practice*. London, Prentice-Hall International, in association with the Institute of Personnel Management.

BUTLER S. (1990) 'Cutting down and reshaping the core'. *Financial Times*. 20 March.

CAMBRIDGE UNIVERSITY SMALL BUSINESS RESEARCH CENTRE (1992) *The State of British Enterprise: Growth, innovation and competitive advantage in small and medium-sized firms*. Cambridge, Small Business Research Centre.

CANNELL M. (1997) 'Practice makes perfect'. *People Management*. Vol. 3, 5. pp26–33.

CANNELL M. (1998) *The IPD Guide on Training Technology*. London, Institute of Personnel and Development.

CANNELL M. (1999) 'Tradition before technology'. *People Management*. Vol. 5, 7. p35.

CARNALL C. (1999) 'Positive e-valuation'. *People Management*. Vol. 5, 17. pp54–7.

CARTER P. *and* LUMSDON C. (1988) 'How management development can improve business performance'. *Personnel Management*. Vol. 20, 10. pp49–52.

CAULKIN S. (2001) *Raising UK Productivity: Why people management matters*. London, CIPD.

CAVE E. *and* MCKEOWN P. (1993) 'Managerial effectiveness: the identification of need'. *Management Education and Development*. Vol. 24, 2. pp122–37.

CHAMBERS C. (1990) 'Self reliant'. *Times Higher Education Supplement*. 6 April. p26.

CHANDLER A. (1962) *Strategy and Structure*. Cambridge, MA, MIT Press.

CHARTERED INSTITUTE OF PERSONNEL AND DEVELOPMENT (2000) *CIPD Code of Professional Conduct and Disciplinary Procedures*. London, CIPD.

CHARTERED INSTITUTE OF PERSONNEL AND DEVELOPMENT (2001) *CIPD Professional Standards*. London, CIPD.

CHARTERED INSTITUTE OF PERSONNEL AND DEVELOPMENT (2001) *Workplace Learning in Europe* [summary of the European Workplace Learning Seminar, London, 2 April]. London, CIPD. Available to download from: www.cipd.co.uk

CHARTERED INSTITUTE OF PERSONNEL AND DEVELOPMENT (2001a) *Training and Development 2001 Survey Report*. London, CIPD.

CHESBROUGH H. W. *and* TEECE D. J. (1996) 'When is virtual virtuous? Organizing for innovation'. *Harvard Business Review*. January–February. pp65–73.

CHRISTIAN-CARTER J. (2001) *Mastering Instructional Design in Technology-based Training*. London, Chartered Institute of Personnel and Development.

CIPD *see* Chartered Institute of Personnel and Development.

CLARE J. (1996). 'Dearing seeks to cut examination gap between schools and work'. *Daily Telegraph*. 28 March. p4.

CLARE J. (2000) 'Sponsors to take over bad schools'. *Daily Telegraph*. 15 March. p1.

CLARE J. (2000b) 'Any questions?'. *Daily Telegraph Education Section.* 9 February. p20.

CLARE J. (2001) 'Teaching profession "cannot be sustained"'. *Daily Telegraph.* 31 August. p2.

CLEGG S. R., HARDY C. *and* NORD, W. R. (1999) *Managing Organizations: Current issues.* London, Sage.

COLLIS D. (1994) 'Research note: How valuable are organizational capabilities?' *Strategic Management Journal, Winter Special Issue.* Vol.15. pp143–152.

COLLOFF S. *and* GOODGE P. (1990) 'The open track to elite status'. *Personnel Management.* Vol. 22, 11. pp50–53.

COMMISSION OF THE EC (1989) *Education, Training, Youth.* Brussels, Task Force for Human Resources, Education, Training and Youth.

COOPER C. (2000) 'Southall rail crash report orders review of training'. *People Management.* Vol. 6, 5. p17.

COOPER C. (2000a) 'The Met fails inspection on race and recruitment'. *People Management.* Vol. 6, 2. p11.

COOPERS AND LYBRAND ASSOCIATES (1985) 'A challenge to complacency: changing attitudes to training'. *A Report to the Manpower Services Commission and the National Economic Development Office.* Sheffield, MSC.

COOPEY J. (1995) 'The learning organization, power, politics and ideology'. *Management Learning.* Vol. 26, 2. pp193–213.

COULSON-THOMAS C. (2001) 'Fashion victim'. *People Management.* Vol. 7, 17. p51.

COURT S. (1998) 'Lessons for life'. *Association of University Teachers' Bulletin.* April. pp6–7.

COYNE K. P. (1986) 'Sustainable competitive advantage – what it is and what it isn't'. *Business Horizons.* January–February. pp54–61.

CRABB S. (2001) 'The thrill of the purchase'. *People Management.* Vol. 8, 1. pp26–31.

CRABB S. *and* JOHNSON R. (2000) 'Press for success'. *People Management.* Vol. 6, 22. pp28–36.

CRITTEN P. (1999) 'To embrace the new, release the old'. *People Management.* Vol. 5, 12. p29 (letters page).

CROZIER A. (1998) 'Follow these rules – or takeovers could be bad for your wealth'. *Sunday Times Business Section.* 29 November. pp3–4.

CROZIER M. (1964) *The Bureaucratic Phenomenon.* London, Tavistock.

CULLY M. (1998) 'The state we're in'. *People Management.* Vol. 4, 2. pp69–72.

CYERT R. M. and MARCH J. G. (1963) *A Behavioural Theory of the Firm.* Englewood Cliffs, NJ, Prentice-Hall Inc.

DAFT R. L. *and* WEICK K. E. (1984) 'Toward a model of organizations as interpretation systems'. *Academy of Management Review.* Vol. 9, 2. pp284–295.

DAILY TELEGRAPH (1996) 'Training can cost jobs'. 21 September. p19.

DAILY TELEGRAPH (2000) 'Blunkett's schooling'. *Daily Telegraph* editorial. 15 March. p29.

DARLING J., DARLING P. *and* ELLIOTT J. (1999) *The Changing Role of the Trainer*. London, Institute of Personnel and Development.

DEARING R. (1996) *Review of Qualifications for 16–19-Year-Olds*. London, SCAA.

DEARING R. (1997) 'Higher education in the learning society'. *Report of the National Committee of Inquiry into Higher Education*.

DEPARTMENT FOR EDUCATION AND EMPLOYMENT (1996) 'Learning to Compete'. *White Paper*. London, HMSO.

DEPARTMENT FOR EDUCATION AND EMPLOYMENT (1998) 'The Learning Age'. *Green Paper*. London, HMSO.

DEPARTMENT FOR EDUCATION AND EMPLOYMENT (1998a) 'Lifelong Learning'. *Green Paper*. London, HMSO.

DEPARTMENT FOR EDUCATION AND EMPLOYMENT (1999) 'Learning to Succeed'. *White Paper*. London, HMSO.

DEPARTMENT FOR EDUCATION AND EMPLOYMENT (2000) *Raising Standards in Post-16 Learning: Building practitioner skills and qualifications in work-based learning funded by the Learning and Skills Council and Employment Service: Technical Consultation Document*. Cheshire: DfEE Consultation Unit, August.

DEPARTMENT FOR EDUCATION AND EMPLOYMENT. (2001) 'Schools, Building on Success'. *Education Green Paper*. London, HMSO.

DfEE *see* Depatment for Education and Employment

DIXON N. (2000) *Common Knowledge: How companies thrive by sharing what they know*. Boston, MA, Harvard Business School Press.

DOLAN S. (1995) 'A different use of natural resources'. *People Management*. Vol.1, 20. pp36–40.

DORRELL J. (1993) *Resource-Based Learning, Using Open and Flexible Learning Resources for Continuous Development*. Maidenhead, McGraw-Hill Training Series.

DOUGHERTY D. (1999) 'Organizing for innovation', in S. R. Clegg, C. Hardy and W. R. Nord (eds), *Managing Organizations: Current issues*. London, Sage, pp174–189.

DOWNS S. (1984) 'Trainability testing'. *Personnel Management*. Vol. 26, 10. p79.

DRUCKER P. (1993) *Post-Capitalist Society*. Oxford, Butterworth-Heinemann.

DULEWICZ V. (1991) 'Improving assessment centres'. *Personnel Management*. Vol. 23, 6. pp50–55.

EDWARDS P. (1990) 'Uncertain worlds'. *Times Higher Education Supplement*. 6 April.

ELFRING T. *and* VOLBERDA H. W. (2001) 'Schools of thought in strategic management: fragmentation, integration or synthesis', in H. W. Volberda and T. Elfring (eds), *Rethinking Strategy*. London, Sage, pp1–25.

EMPLOYMENT NATIONAL TRAINING ORGANISATION (2001) Employment Newsletter NTO. Leicester, EmpNTO, Spring.

ENNEW E. *and* FORD C. (1990) *The Management of Change: Reflections of change at Norsk Hydro Polymers Ltd, Newton Aycliffe, County*

Durham, 1984–1990. London, Advisory Conciliation and Arbitration Service Work Research Unit.

EVANS K., HODKINSON P., KEEP E., MAGUIRE M., RAFFE D., RAINBIRD H., SENKER P. *and* UNWIN L. (1997) *Issues in People Management No. 18: Working To Learn – A work-based route to learning for young people.* London, Institute of Personnel and Development.

EVANS P. (1992) 'Developing leaders and management development'. *European Management Journal.* Vol. 10, 1. pp1–9.

EWINGTON T. (2000) 'Teach yourself the lot'. *Sunday Times*, Section 9: Culture ('Doors'). 26 March. pp55–7.

FAIRBAIRN J. (1991) 'Plugging the gap in training needs analysis'. *Personnel Management.* Vol. 23, 2. pp43–5.

FIELD A. (2001) 'How to work with the new ISO 9001'. *People Management.* Vol. 7, 24. pp48–9.

FLOYD S. W. *and* WOOLDRIDGE B. (1994) 'Dinosaurs or dynamos? Recognizing middle management's strategic role'. *Academy of Management Executive.* Vol. 8, 4. pp47–57.

FOMBRUN C., TICHY N. M. *and* DEVANNA M. A. (EDS) (1984) *Strategic Human Resource Management.* New York, Wiley.

FONDA N. *and* BUCKTON K. (1995) *Reviewing the Personnel Function: A toolkit for development.* London, Institute of Personnel and Development.

FONDA N. *and* ROWLAND H. (1995) 'Take me to your (personnel) leader'. *People Management.* Vol. 1, 25. pp18–23.

FORREST A. (1993) *Fifty Ways to Personal Development.* London, Industrial Society. November.

FOWLER A. (1992) 'How to: structure a personnel department'. *Personnel Management Plus.* January. pp22–3.

FOWLER A. (1995) 'How to: decide on training methods'. *People Management.* Vol. 1, 25. pp36–7.

FOWLER A. (1999) *Induction* London, Institute of Personnel and Development.

FRENCH W. L. (1987) *The Personnel Management Process: Human resources administration and development.* 6th edn. Boston, MA, Houghton Mifflin.

GAGNE R. M. (1977) *The Conditions of Learning.* New York, Holt Saunders.

GALBRAITH J. R. *and* NATHANSON D. (1978) *Strategy Implementation.* St Paul, MN, West Publishing.

GARNER R. (2001) 'Four years on'. *Independent 'Education' section*, 3 May. p2.

GARNETT J. (1992) 'My biggest mistake'. *Independent on Sunday.* 8 March.

GHOSHAL S. *and* BARTLETT C. A. (1994) 'Linking organizational context and managerial action: the dimension of quality of management'. *Strategic Management Journal, Special Summer Issue.* Vol. 15. pp91–112.

GILLEY J. W. *and* EGGLAND S. A. (1989) *Principles of Human Resource*

Development. Wokingham, Addison Wesley and University Associates Inc.

GINSBERG A. (1994) 'Minding the competition: from mapping to mastery'. *Strategic Management Journal, Winter Special Issue.* Vol. 15. pp153–174.

GOODHART D. (1994) 'Fresh thinking needed on old labour problem'. *Financial Times.* 8 March. p14.

GOODHART D. (1994a) 'Can Europe compete? Convergence in the work-force'. *Financial Times.* 28 February. p11.

GOODMAN P. S. *and* DEAN J. W. (1982) 'Creating Long-Term Organization Change', in Goodman, P. S. (ed.), *Change in Organizations.* San Francisco, Jossey-Bass.

GORMAN T. (2000) 'C's the opportunity'. *People Management.* Vol. 6, 7. p57.

GRACIE S. (1999) 'Despairing firms do their own training'. *Sunday Times Business Section.* 3.9. December. p10.

GRAHAM G. (1994) 'Lack of training shuts out poor'. *Financial Times.* 14 March. p4.

GRANT R. M. (1991) *Contemporary Strategy Analysis: Concepts, techniques, applications.* Oxford, Blackwell.

GRATTON L. *and* SYRETT M. (1990) 'Heirs apparent: succession strategies for the future'. *Personnel Management.* Vol. 22, 1. pp34–8.

GREEN K. (1999) 'Offensive thinking'. *People Management.* Vol. 5, 8. p27.

GREGORY R. L. (ED.) (1998) *The Oxford Companion to the Mind.* Oxford, 1998.

GUARDIAN (2001) 'Labour fails the 11-plus: Two tiers will create more inequity'. *Guardian* editorial leader. 13 February. p21.

GUEST D. E. (1990) 'Human resource management and the American dream'. *Journal of Management Studies.* Vol. 27, 4. pp377–97.

GUEST D. *and* BARON A. (2000) 'Piece by piece'. *People Management,* Vol.6, 15. pp26–30.

GUEST D. *and* KING Z. (2001) 'Personnel's paradox'. *People Management.* Vol.7, 19. pp24–9.

GUILE D. *and* FONDA N. (1998) *Performance Management through Capability.* London, Institute of Personnel and Development.

HACKETT G. (2001) 'Architect of AS-level doubts own exam'. *Sunday Times* 'News' section, 10 June. p1.5.

HACKETT P. (1997) *An Introduction to Training.* London, Institute of Personnel and Development.

HALL D. T. (1984) 'Human resource development and organisational effectiveness', in D. Fombrun, N. M. Tichy and M. A. Devanna (eds), *Strategic Human Resource Management.* New York, Wiley, pp159–181.

HALL R. (1993) 'A framework linking intangible resources and capabilities to sustainable competitive advantage'. *Strategic Management Journal.* Vol. 14. pp607–618.

HALL R. (1996) 'Supply chain management – the challenges for the 21st century'. *Paper presented to the CIPS Conference at Durham*

University Business School, 9 May. Durham University Business School, Mill Hill Lane, Durham City, DH1 3LB.

HAMBLIN A. C. (1974) *Evaluation and Control of Training.* Maidenhead, McGraw-Hill.

HAMEL G. *and* PRAHALAD C. K. (1993) 'Strategy as stretch and leverage'. *Harvard Business Review.* Vol. 71, 2. pp75–84.

HAMLIN B. (1999) 'The national context', in J. Stewart, *Employee Development Practice.* London, Financial Times and Pitman Publishing, pp22–36.

HAMLIN B. *and* DAVIES G. (1996) 'The trainer as change agent: issues for practice', in J. Stewart and J. McGoldrick (eds), *Human Resource Development: Perspectives, strategies and practice.* London, Pitman, pp199–219.

HANDY C. B. (1985) *Understanding Organizations.* 3rd edn. Harmondsworth, Penguin.

HANDY C. B. (1987) 'The making of managers'. *A Report for the National Economic Development Council, the Manpower Services Commission, and the British Institute of Management on Management Education, Training and Development in the USA, West Germany, France, Japan and the UK.* London, National Economic Development Office.

HANDY C. B. (1989) *The Age of Unreason.* London, Business Books.

HARDINGHAM A. (1996) 'Improve an inside job with an outside edge'. *People Management.* Vol. 2, 12. pp45–6.

HARDINGHAM A. (1996a) *Designing Training.* London, Institute of Personnel and Development.

HARRIS V. (1995) 'Moving ahead on cultural change'. *People Management.* Vol. 1, 6. pp30–33.

HARRISON J. *and* LORD P. (1992) 'Investors in People and the accreditation of training in SMEs', in *Proceedings of the 15th National Small Firms Policy and Research Conference, Southampton.* November. Northern Ireland Small Business Institute, United Kingdom Enterprise Management Research Association.

HARRISON ROGER (1972) 'How to describe your organization'. *Harvard Business Review.* September–October.

HARRISON R. (1988) *Training and Development.* London, Institute of Personnel Management.

HARRISON R. (1992) *Employee Development.* London, Institute of Personnel and Development.

HARRISON R. (ed.) (1993) *Human Resource Management: Issues and strategies.* Wokingham, Addison Wesley.

HARRISON R. (1993a) 'Thorn Lighting Ltd., UK – a learning organization', in R. Harrison (ed.), *Human Resource Management: Issues and strategies.* Wokingham, Addison Wesley, pp375–380 (feedback notes in Instructor's Manual).

HARRISON R. (1993b) 'Strategic human resource management at HMH Sheetmetal Fabrications Ltd, 1993', in R. Harrison (ed.), *Human*

Resource Management: Issues and strategies. Wokingham, Addison Wesley, pp335–9.

HARRISON R. (1996) 'Developing human resources for productivity'. Module 13 in J. Prokopenko and K. North (eds), *Productivity and Quality Management: A modular programme: part II.* Geneva, International Labour Office and Tokyo, Asian Productivity Association, pp1–53.

HARRISON R. (1996a) 'Action learning: route or barrier to the learning organization?' *Employee Counselling Today, The Journal of Workplace Learning.* Vol. 8, 6. pp27–38.

HARRISON R. (1999) *The Training and Development Audit: An eight-step audit to measure, assess and enhance the performance of your organisation's training and development.* Cambridge, Cambridge Strategy Publications.

HARRISON R. (2000) 'Learning, knowledge productivity and strategic progress'. *International Journal of Training and Development.* Vol. 4 (4). pp244–258.

HARRISON R. *and* MILLER S. (1993) 'Doctors in management: two into one won't go – or will it?' *Journal of Executive Development.* Vol. 6, 2. pp9–13.

HARRISON R. *and* MILLER S. (1999) 'The contribution of clinical directors to the strategic capability of the organisation'. *British Journal of Management.* Vol. 10, 1. pp23–39.

HARRISON R. *and* SMITH R. (2001) 'Practical judgement: its implications for knowledge development and strategic capability', in B. Hellgren and J. Lowstedt (eds), *Management in the Thought-Full Enterprise: European Ideas on Organizing.* Bergen, Fagbokforlaget Vigmostad and Bjorke AS, pp195–213.

HARRISON R., MILLER S. *and* GIBSON A. (1993) 'Doctors in management, part II: getting into action'. *Journal of Executive Development.* Vol. 6, 4. pp3–7.

HARRISON ROY. (1999) 'Faster-track learning'. *People Management.* Vol. 5, 18. p69.

HART S. *and* BANBURY C. (1994) 'How strategy-making processes can make a difference'. *Strategic Management Journal.* Vol. 15. pp251–69.

HEALY M. (1995) 'Innovators beware!' *People Management.* Vol. 1, 6. pp24–5.

HEDLUND G. (1994) 'A model of knowledge management and the N-Form corporation'. *Strategic Management Journal, Special Summer Issue.* Vol. 15. pp73–90.

HENDRY C. (1994) 'The Single European Market and the HRM response', in P. A. Kirkbride (ed.), *Human Resource Management in Europe: Perspectives for the 1990s.* London, Routledge, pp93–113.

HENDRY C. (1995) *Human Resource Management: A strategic approach to employment.* London, Butterworth-Heinemann.

HENDRY C., JONES A., ARTHUR M. B. *and* PETTIGREW A. M. (1991) 'Human resource development in small to medium-sized enterprises'. *Research Paper No. 88.* Sheffield, Employment Department.

HENDRY C., PETTIGREW A. M. *and* SPARROW P. (1988). 'Changing patterns of human resource management'. *Personnel Management.* Vol. 20, 11. pp37–41.

HERRIOT P. (1992) *The Career Management Challenge: Balancing individual and organizational needs.* London, Sage.

HERRIOT P. *and* PEMBERTON C. (1995) 'A new deal for middle managers'. *People Management.* Vol. 1, 12. pp32–4.

HERTZBERG F. (1966) *Work and the Nature of Man.* London, Staples Press.

HILL R. *and* STEWART J. (1999) 'Human resource development in small organizations'. *Human Resource Development International.* Vol. 2, 2. pp103–123.

HILLS H. (2000) 'Not in the net yet'. *People Management.* Vol. 6, 5. p33.

HILLS H. *and* FRANCIS P. (1999) 'Interaction learning'. *People Management.* Vol. 5, 14. pp48–9.

HIRSH W. (1985) *Women, Career Breaks and Re-Entry.* London, Institute of Manpower Studies.

HIRSH W. *and* JACKSON C. (1996) 'Ticket to ride or no place to go?' *People Management.* Vol. 2, 13. pp20–25.

HIRSH W., JACKSON C. *and* JACKSON C. (1995) 'Careers in Organisations – Issues for the future'. *Institute for Employment Studies Report.* London, IES.

HODGKINSON G. P. (1996) *The Cognitive Analysis of Competitive Structures: A review and critique. Working Paper.* Leeds, School of Business and Economic Studies, University of Leeds, June.

HODGKINSON G. P. *and* JOHNSON G. (1994) 'Exploring the mental models of competitive strategists: the case for a processual approach'. *Journal of Management Studies.* Vol. 3. pp525–551.

HOMAN G. *and* SHAW S. (2000) 'Reframing the role of higher education in the process of lifelong learning – a UK perspective'. *Paper presented at the Conference on Convergence and Divergence in the European HRD Agenda: Comparing and Contrasting Research and Practice.* Kingston, Kingston University. 15 January.

HONEY P. *and* MUMFORD A. (1992) *A Manual of Learning Styles.* 3rd edn. Maidenhead, Honey.

HONEY P. *and* MUMFORD A. (1996) *Managing Your Learning Environment.* Maidenhead, Honey.

HOSPITAL J. T. (2001) 'Strangers in a strange land'. Talk on Radio 4. 7.45–8.00 pm, 18 August.

HUSELID M. A. (1995) 'The impact of human resource management: an agenda for the 1990s'. *International Journal of Human Resource Management.* Vol. 1, 1. pp17–43.

ILES P. and MABEY C. (1993) 'Managerial career development programmes: effectiveness, availability and acceptability'. *British Journal of Management.* Vol. 4, 3. pp103–11.

INCOMES DATA SERVICES (1993) *European Management Guides: Training and development.* London, Institute of Personnel Management.

INDUSTRIAL SOCIETY *Managing Best Practice.* (Monthly reports on achieving excellence in the key areas of managing people.) Available by sub-scription or as single copies: 0121 410 3040.

INDUSTRIAL SOCIETY (1997) 'Self-managed learning'. *Managing Best Practice. No. 40.* October. (Available from the Communications Department, 020 7479 2127.)

INKPEN A. *and* CHOUDHURY, N. (1995) 'The seeing of strategy where it is not: towards a theory of strategy absence'. *Strategic Management Journal,* Vol. 16. pp313–323.

INSTITUTE OF PERSONNEL AND DEVELOPMENT (1999) *Managing Diverstiy: Evidence from case studies.* London, IPD.

JACKSON L. (1989) 'Transforming managerial performance – a com-petency approach', in *Proceedings of Institute of Personnel Management National Conference, Harrogate,* October. London, IPM.

JACKSON T. (2000) *Career Development.* London, Chartered Institute of Personnel and Development.

JENKINS S. (1999) 'Whitehall farce'. *Times.* 17 December. p24.

JENNINGS P. L., RICHARDSON B. *and* BEAVER G. (1992) 'Improving the role of accreditation in the training and development of small business owner/managers', in *Proceedings of 15th National Small Firms' Policy and Research Conference, Southampton.* November. Northern Ireland Small Business Institute, United Kingdom Enterprise Management Research Association.

JOHNSON G. *and* SCHOLES K. (1993) *Exploring Corporate Strategy: Texts and cases.* Hemel Hempstead, Prentice-Hall

JOHNSTON R. (1996) 'Power and influence and the HRD function', in J. Stewart and J. McGoldrick (eds), *Human Resource Development: Perspectives, strategies and practice.* London, Pitman, pp180–95.

JONES R. A. *and* GOSS D. M. (1991) 'The role of training strategy in reduc-ing skills shortages: some evidence from a survey of small firms'. *Personnel Review.* Vol. 20, 2. pp24–30.

KAPLAN R. *and* NORTON D. (2001) 'Marked impact'. *People Management.* Vol. 7, 21. pp52–57.

KAPLAN R. *and* NORTON D. (2001a) *The Strategy-focused Organization.* Boston, MA, Harvard Business School Press.

KAY J. (1993) *Foundations of Corporate Success: How business strat-egies add value.* Oxford, Oxford University Press.

KEARNS P. *and* MILLER T. (1996) *Measuring the Impact of Training and Development on the Bottom Line.* Technical Communications.

KEASEY K. *and* WATSON R. (1993) *Small Firm Management: Ownership, finance and performance.* Oxford, Blackwell.

KEEP E. (2001) 'The skills system in 2015', in D. Wilson, E. Lank, A. Westwood, E. Keep, C. Leadbeater and M. Sloman, *The Future of Learning for Work: Executive briefing.* London, Chartered Institute of Personnel and Development, pp24–31.

KEEP E. *and* MAYHEW K. (1994) *Scoping Paper for the 'What Makes Training Pay' Project.* London, Institute of Personnel and Development.

KELMAR J. (1990) 'Measurement of success and failure in small business – a dichotomous anachronism', in *Proceedings of the 13th National Small Firms' Policy and Research Conference, Harrogate.* November. Northern Ireland Small Business Institute, United Kingdom Enterprise Management Research Association.

KEMENY L. (2001). '£6bn boost to job skills'. *Sunday Times* 'Business' section. 25 March. p3.3.

KESSELS J. W. M. (1996) 'Knowledge productivity and the corporate curriculum', in J. F. Schreinemakers (ed.), *Knowledge Management: Organisation, competence and methodology: proceedings of the Fourth International ISMICK Symposium,* 21–22 October, Rotterdam, the Netherlands, Würzburg, Ergon-Verlag, pp168–74.

KESSELS J. W. M. *and* HARRISON R. (1998) 'External consistency: the key to management development?' *Management Learning.* Vol. 29, 1. pp37–68.

KINGSTON P. (1999) 'Reaching the learners others cannot reach'. *Guardian Further Education.* 16 November. pp1f and 4f.

KIRBY D. A. (1990) 'Management education and small business development: an explanatory study of small firms'. *UK Journal of Small Business Management.* Vol. 28, 4. pp78–87.

KOLB D. A., RUBIN I. M. *and* McINTYRE J. M. (1974) *Organizational Psychology: An experiential approach.* Englewood Cliffs, NJ, Prentice-Hall.

LATCHFORD P. (1999) 'Past imperfect, future tense'. *People Management.* Vol. 5, 16. p31.

LAVE J. *and* WENGER E. (1991) *Situated Learning – Legitimate Peripheral Participation.* Cambridge, Cambridge University Press.

LE CARRÉ J. (2001) *The Constant Gardener.* London, Hodder & Stoughton.

LEE R. (1996) 'The "pay-forward" view of training'. *People Management.* Vol. 2, 3. pp30–32.

LEES S. (1992) 'Ten faces of management development'. *Management Education and Development.* Vol. 23, 2. pp89–105.

LEGGE K. (1998) 'The morality of HRM', in C. Mabey, G. Salaman and J. Storey (eds), *Strategic Human Resource Management: A reader.* London, The Open University and Sage, pp18–29.

LEVY D. (1994) 'Chaos theory and strategy: theory, application, and managerial implications'. *Strategic Management Journal, Special Summer Issue,* Vol.15. pp167–178.

LEWIS J. *and* McLAVERTY C. (1991) 'Facing up to the needs of the older manager'. *Personnel Management.* Vol. 23, 1. pp 32–5.

LIKERT R. (1961) *New Patterns of Management.* New York, McGraw-Hill.

LINDBLOM C. E. (1959) 'The science of muddling through'. *Public Administration Review.* Vol.19, 2. pp79–88.

LIPPITT G. (1983) 'Management development as the key to organisational renewal'. *Journal of Management Development.* Vol. 1, 2. pp36–9.

LOCKETT J. (1992) *Effective Performance Management: A strategic guide to getting the best from people*. London, Kogan Page.

LORENZ A. (1995) 'BTR breaks the mould'. *Management Today*. May. pp44-8.

LORENZ C. (1992) 'Different routes through the minefield of change'. *Financial Times*. 20 November. p14.

LORENZ C. (1994) 'Dissent in the measurement ranks'. *Financial Times*. 25 March. p16.

LYLES M. (1990) 'A research agenda for strategic management in the 1990s'. *Journal of Management Studies*, Vol. 27, 4. pp363-75.

LYMER A. (1996) 'Educational impacts of the World-Wide Web'. *Account*. Vol. 8, 1. pp9-10.

MABEY C. and MAYON-WHITE B. (eds) (1993) *Managing Change*. 2nd edn. London, The Open University and Paul Chapman.

MABEY C. and SALAMAN G. (1995) *Strategic Human Resource Management*. Oxford, Blackwell.

MACAULAY S. and HARDING N. (1996) 'Drawing up a new careers contract'. *People Management*. Vol. 2, 7. pp34-5.

McGOLDRICK A. (ED.) (1996) *Cases in Human Resource Management*. London, Pitman.

McGREGOR D. (1960) *The Human Side of Enterprise*. Maidenhead, McGraw-Hill.

McILROY A. J. (2001) 'No charges over Paddington rail crash'. *Daily Telegraph*. 25 October. p11.

MAGER R. F. (1984) *Preparing Instructional Objectives* Fearon, CA, CEP Press.

MALING G., WRIGHT J. and HESSEY P. (2000) 'Three-point turn'. *People Management*, Vol. 6, 15. pp32-5.

MALONE S. A. (1997) *How to Set up and Manage a Corporate Learning Centre*. Aldershot, Gower.

MANWARING T. and WOOD S. (1985) 'The ghost in the labour process: job redesign', in D. Knight (ed.), *Critical Perspectives on the Labour Process*. Aldershot, Gower.

MARCH J. G. and SIMON H. A. (1958) *Organizations*. New York, John Wiley and Sons.

MARCHINGTON M. and WILKINSON A. (1996) *Core Personnel and Development*. London, Institute of Personnel and Development.

MARCHINGTON M. and WILKINSON A. (2002) *People Management and Development*. London, Chartered Institute of Personnel and Development.

MARKIDES C. C. and WILLIAMSON J. P. (1994) 'Related diversification, core competences and corporate performance'. *Strategic Management Journal, Summer Special Issue*. Vol. 15. pp149-65.

MARLOW S. and PATTON D. (1992) 'Employment relations, human resource management strategies and the smaller firm', in *Proceedings of the 15th National Small Firms' Policy and Research Conference, Southampton*. November, Northern Ireland Small

Business Institute, United Kingdom Enterprise Management Research Association.

MARRIS R. (1995) 'Worrying fortunes of the Anglo-Saxon underclass'. *Times*. 28 September. p29.

MARSTON P. (2001) 'Railway "was riddled with complacency"'. *Daily Telegraph*. 20 June. p4.

MARTON F. *and* RAMSDEN P. (1988) 'What does it take to improve learning?', in P. Ramsden (ed), *Improving Learning: New perspectives*. London, Kogan Page.

MASIE E. (1999) 'Joined-up thinking'. *People Management*. Vol. 5, 23. pp32–6.

MATTHEWS J. H. *and* CANDY P. C. (1999) 'New dimensions in the dynamics of learning and knowledge', in D. Boud and J. Garrick (eds), *Understanding Learning at Work*. London, Routledge, pp47–64.

MAYO A. (1994) *Managing Careers*. London, Institute of Personnel and Development.

MAYO A. (1998) *Creating a Training and Development Strategy*. London, Institute of Personnel and Development.

MEGGINSON D. *and* WHITAKER V. (1996) *Cultivating Self-Development*. London, Institute of Personnel and Development.

MEZIROW J. A. (1985) 'A critical theory of self-directed learning', in S. Brookfield (ed.), *Self-Directed Learning: From theory to practice*. San Francisco, CA, Jossey-Bass.

MIDGLEY S. (2001). Comments on the reorganisation of the DfEE into the new Department for Education and Skills, *Guardian* website, 19 June.

MILES R. *and* SNOW C. (1995) 'The new network firm: a spherical structure built on a human investment philosophy'. *Organizational Dynamics*. Vol. 23, 4. pp5–18.

MILLER L., RANKIN N. *and* NEATHEY F. (2001) *Competency Frameworks in UK Organisations: Research Report*. London, Chartered Institute of Personnel and Development.

MILLER R. *and* STEWART J. (1999) 'Opened university'. *People Management*. Vol. 5, 12. pp42–6.

MILLER S., HICKSON D. J. *and* WILSON D. C. (1999) 'Decision-making in organizations', in S. R. Clegg, C. Hardy and W. R. Nord (eds), *Managing Organizations: Current issues*. London, Sage, pp43–62.

MILLS D. Q. *and* FRIESEN B. (1992) 'The learning organisation'. *European Management Journal*. Vol. 10, 2. pp146–56.

MILLS G. E., WAYNE PACE R. *and* PETERSON B. D. (1988) *Analysis in Human Resource Training and Organization Development*. Wokingham, Addison Wesley.

MINTZBERG H. (1973) *The Nature of Managerial Work*. New York, Harper & Row.

MINTZBERG H. (1994) *The Rise and Fall of Strategic Planning*. Hemel Hempstead, Prentice-Hall.

MINTZBERG H. (1994a) 'Rounding out the manager's job'. *Sloan Management Review*. Vol. 36, 1. pp11–26.

MINTZBERG H. and WATERS J. (1985) 'Of strategies, deliberate and emergent'. *Strategic Management Journal*. Vol. 6. pp257–272.

MOORBY E. (1991) *How to Succeed in Employee Development: Moving from vision to results*. Maidenhead, McGraw-Hill.

MORGAN G. (1997) *Images of Organization*. 2nd edn. London, Sage.

MORRIS J. (1991) 'Action learning: the long haul', in J. Prior (ed.), *Handbook of Training and Development*. Aldershot, Gower, pp611–628.

MOXON G. R. (1943) *The Functions of a Personnel Department*. London, Institute of Personnel Management.

MOYNAGH M. and WORSLEY R. (2001) 'Prophet sharing'. *People Management*. Vol. 7, 25. pp24–6, 28–9.

MOYNAGH M and WORSLEY R. (2001a) *Tomorrow's Workplace: Fulfilment or stress?* The Tomorrow Project, tel. 0115 925 1114.

MUMFORD A. (1997) *Management Development: Strategies for action*. 3rd edn. London, Institute of Personnel and Development.

MUMFORD A., ROBINSON G. and STRADLING D. (1987) *Developing Directors: The learning processes*. Sheffield, Manpower Services Commission.

NADLER L. (1970) *Developing Human Resources*. Houston, Tex., Gulf.

NADLER L. (1992) 'HRD – where has it been, where is it going?' *Studies in Continuing Education*. Vol. 14, 2. pp104–14.

NAHAPIET J. and GHOSHAL S. (1998) 'Social capital, intellectual capital and the organizational advantage'. *Academy of Management Review*, Vol. 23, 2. pp242–266.

NATIONAL COMMISSION ON EDUCATION (1993) *Learning to Succeed – A radical look at education today and a strategy for the future*. London, Heinemann.

NCE *see* National Commission on Education.

NELSON R. R. and WINTER S. G. (1982) *An Evolutionary Theory of Economic Change*. Cambridge, MA, Harvard University Press.

NEWTON T. and FINDLAY P. (1998) 'Playing God? The performance of appraisal', in C. Mabey, G. Salaman and J. Storey (eds), *Strategic Human Resource Management: A reader*. London, The Open University Business School and Sage, pp128–143.

NICHOLLS A. (1997) 'Thames Valley: a new line on learning'. *Guardian Higher*. 21 January. piii.

NICHOLLS A. (1997a) 'Towards new horizons'. *Guardian Higher*. 21 January. pii.

NOEL L., JAMES N. L. and DENNEHY R. F. (1991) 'Making HRD a force in strategic organisational change'. *Industrial and Commercial Training*. Vol. 23, 2. pp17–19.

NONAKA I. (1991) 'The knowledge-creating company'. *Harvard Business Review*. November–December. pp96–104.

NONAKA I. (1996) 'The knowledge-creating company', in K. Starkey (ed.), *How Organizations Learn*. London, International Thomson Business Press, pp18–31.

NORDHAUG O. *and* GRØNHAUG K. (1994) 'Competences as resources in firms'. *International Journal of Human Resource Management.* Vol. 5, 1. pp89–106.

OLDFIELD C. (1996) 'Quarter of small firms say they want to sell up'. *Sunday Times Business Section.* 15 December. p2.

O'LEARY J. (2001) 'Flagship academy's sponsor lacks cash'. *Times.* 22 January. p2.

O'LEARY J. (2001a) 'Bad omens for Mr Blunkett'. *Times.* 1 February. p2.

ONIONS C. T. (ED.) (1973) *The Shorter Oxford English Dictionary.* 3rd edn. Oxford, Oxford University Press.

ORR J. E. (1990) 'Sharing knowledge, celebrating identity: community memory in a service culture', in D.S. Middleton and D. Edwards (eds), *Collective Remembering.* Newbury Park, SA, Sage, pp169–198.

OSBALDESTON M. *and* BARHAM K. (1992) 'Using management development for competitive advantage'. *Long-Range Planning.* Vol. 25, 6. pp18–24.

OTTO C. P. *and* GLASER R. O. (1972) *The Management of Training.* London, Addison Wesley.

PARTRIDGE B. (1989) 'The problem of supervision', in K. Sisson (ed.), *Personnel Management in Britain.* Oxford, Blackwell. pp203–21.

PATERSON L. (2000) 'Hidden jobless must not be ignored'. *Times.* 16 February. p31.

PATTERSON M. G., WEST M. A., LAWTHOM R. *and* NICKELL S. (1997) *Impact of People Management Practices on Business Performance.* London, Institute of Personnel and Development.

PAWSEY V. (2000) 'Police pooling evidence to bolster training standards'. *People Management.* Vol. 6, 1. p12.

PEARSALL J. *and* TRUMBLE B. (EDS) (1996) *The Oxford English Reference Dictionary.* 2nd edn. Oxford, Oxford University Press.

PEDLER M. *and* BOUTALL J. (1992) *Action Learning for Change: A resource book for managers and other professionals.* Eastwood Park, Avon, NHS Training Directorate.

PEDLER M., BURGOYNE J. *and* BOYDELL T. (1978) *A Manager's Guide to Self-Development.* Maidenhead, McGraw-Hill.

PEDLER M., BURGOYNE J. *and* BOYDELL T. (1991) *The Learning Company: A strategy for sustainable development.* Maidenhead, McGraw-Hill.

PENROSE E. T. (1959) *The Theory of the Growth of the Firm.* Oxford, Blackwell.

PERREN L. *and* BURGOYNE J. (2002) *Management and Leadership Abilities: an analysis of texts, testimony and practice.* Council for Excellence in Management and Leadership, www.managementandleadershipcouncil.org.

PERROW C. (1970) *Organizational Analysis.* London, Tavistock.

PETERAF M. A. (1993) 'The cornerstones of competitive advantage: a resource-based view'. *Strategic Management Journal.* Vol. 14. pp179–91.

PETTIGREW A. (1973) *The Politics of Organizational Decision-making.* London, Tavistock.

PETTIGREW A. M., ARTHUR M. B. *and* HENDRY C. (1990) 'Training and human resource management in small to medium-sized enterprises: a critical review of the literature and a model for future research'. *Research Paper No. 56.* Sheffield, Employment Department.

PETTIGREW A. M., JONES G. R. *and* REASON P. W. (1982) *Training and Development Roles in Their Organisational Setting.* Sheffield, Manpower Services Commission.

PHILLIPS J. (2001) 'How to measure returns on HR investment'. *People Management*, Vol. 7, 23. pp48–50.

PICKARD J. (1995) 'Food for thought'. *People Management.* Vol. 1, 20. pp30–31.

PICKARD J. (1997) 'A yearning for learning'. *People Management.* Vol. 3, 5. pp34–5.

PICKARD J. (2001) 'How Abbey are they?'. *People Management.* Vol. 7, 25. p27.

POLICY STUDIES INSTITUTE (1993) *Employment in Britain Survey.* London, PSI Publishing.

PORTER M. E. (1980) *Competitive Strategy.* New York, Free Press.

PORTER M. E. (1985) *Competitive Advantage.* New York, Free Press.

POTTER B. (1998) 'The rise and fall of a corporate Goliath'. *Daily Telegraph Business News.* 28 November. p33.

POTTINGER J. (1989) 'Engineering change through pay'. *Personnel Management.* Vol. 21, 10. pp73–4.

PRAHALAD C. K. *and* BETTIS R. A. (1986) 'The dominant logic: a new linkage between diversity and performance'. *Strategic Management Journal.* Vol. 7. pp485–501.

PRAHALAD C. K. *and* HAMEL G. (1994) 'Strategy as a field of study: why search for a new paradigm?' *Strategic Management Journal.* Vol. 15. pp5–16.

PRAIS S. J. (1985) 'What can we learn from the German system of education and vocational training?', in G. D. N. Worswick (ed.), *Education and Economic Performance.* London, Gower, pp40–51.

PRAIS S. J. *and* NATIONAL INSTITUTE of ECONOMIC and SOCIAL RESEARCH TEAM (1990) 'Productivity, education and training: Britain and other countries compared'. *National Institute Economic Review.* London, NIESR.

PRAIS S. J *and* WAGNER K. (1981) 'Some practical aspects of human capital investment: training standards in five occupations in Britain and Germany'. *International Institute of Economic and Social Research Review.* November. pp46–65.

PURCELL J., KINNIE N., HUTCHINSON S. *and* RAYTON B. (2000) 'Inside the box'. *People Management.* Vol.6, 21. pp30–38.

QUINN J. B. (1980) *Strategies for Change – Logical incrementalism.* Homewood, IL, Irwin.

QUINN J. B. (1993) 'Managing strategic change', in C. Mabey and B. Mayon-White (eds), *Managing Change.* 2nd edn. London, The Open University, pp65–84.

RAINBIRD H. (1993) 'Vocational education and training', in M. Gold (ed.),

The Social Dimension: Employment policy in the European Community. London, Macmillan, pp184–202.

RANA E. (1999) 'NTOs debate radical plans for voluntary investment'. *People Management.* Vol. 5, 18. p17.

RANA E. (1999a) 'Recipe for succession'. *People Management.* Vol. 5, 16. pp32–7.

RANA E. (1999b) 'Firms fear being sidelined in skills council overhaul'. *People Management.* Vol. 5, 21. p12.

RANA E. (1999c) 'E-learning "will fail" unless it is focused on the users'. *People Management.* Vol. 5, 24. p11.

RANA E. (1999d) 'Failure to embrace online learning will hit firms hard'. *People Management.* Vol. 5, 16. p19.

RANA E. (2000) 'IIP revamp aims to cut back on bureaucracy'. *People Management.* Vol. 6, 8. p14.

RANA E. (2001) 'Low skills, low interest'. *People Management.* Vol. 7, 18. pp24–30.

RANKIN N. (2002) 'The rivals: two national frameworks of management competencies'. *Competency & Emotional Intelligence Quarterly.* Vol. 10, 1. pp40–46.

RANKINE K. (1999) 'M&S nervous as shares fall again'. *Daily Telegraph.* 25 September. p27.

REDAY-MULVEY G. *and* TAYLOR P. (1996) 'Why working lives must be extended'. *People Management.* Vol. 2, 10. pp24–9.

REFAUSSE J. (1996) 'Self-knowledge to lift career spirits'. *People Management.* Vol. 2, 10. pp34–5.

REID M. A. *and* BARRINGTON H. (1997) *Training Interventions: Managing employee development.* 5th edn. London, Institute of Personnel and Development.

REYNOLDS J., CALEY L. *and* MASON R. (2002) *How do People Learn? Research Report.* London, Chartered Institute of Personnel and Development.

RILEY K. *and* SLOMAN M. (1991) 'Milestones for the personnel department'. *Personnel Management.* Vol. 23, 8. pp34–7.

RITCHIE J. (1993) 'Strategies for human resource management: challenges in smaller and entrepreneurial organisations', in R. Harrison (ed.), *Human Resource Management: Issues and strategies.* Wokingham, Addison Wesley, pp111–135.

ROBERTS A. (2001) 'Brown boosts training'. *People Management.* Vol. 7, 24. p8.

ROBERTS K. H *and* GRABOWSKI M. (1999) 'Organizations, technology and structuring', in S. R. Clegg, C. Hardy and W. R. Nord (eds), *Managing Organizations: Current issues.* London, Sage, pp157–173.

ROBINSON D. G. *and* ROBINSON J. C. (1989) *Training for Impact.* London, Jossey-Bass.

RODGER D. *and* MABEY C. (1987) 'BT's leap forward from assessment centres'. *Personnel Management.* Vol. 19, 7. pp32–5.

RUMELT R. P. (1991) 'How much does industry matter?' *Strategic Management Journal*. Vol. 12, 3. pp167–85.

RUSH D. (1999) 'Baldock stays on in M&D chair'. *Sunday Times Business Section*. 26 September. p3.

RUSSELL C. *and* PARSONS E. (1996) 'Putting theory to the test at the OU'. *People Management*. Vol. 2, 1. pp30–32.

RYAN C. (2001) 'The biggest test for raising standards'. *Sunday Times 'Education' section*, 5 August. p6.13.

SADLER P. *and* BARHAM K. (1988) 'From Franks to the future: 25 years of management training prescriptions'. *Personnel Management*. Vol. 20. pp48–51.

SAINT AUGUSTINE. *Confessions*. Tr. R. S. Pine-Coffin (1964). London, Penguin Classics.

SALMON G. (2001) 'Far from remote'. *People Management*. Vol. 7, 19. pp34–36.

SCARBROUGH H. *and* SWAN J. (EDS) (1999) *Case Studies in Knowledge Management*. London, Institute of Personnel and Development.

SCARBROUGH H., SWAN J. *and* PRESTON J. (1999) *Knowledge Management: A literature review*. London, Institute of Personnel and Development.

SCHANK R. (1999) 'Courses of action'. *People Management*. Vol. 5, 20. pp54–7.

SCHEIN E. H. (1978) *Career Dynamics: Matching individual and organizational needs*. Reading, MA, Addison Wesley.

SCHENDEL D. (1994) 'Introduction to "Competitive organizational behaviour: toward an organizationally-based theory of competitive advantage"'. *Strategic Management Journal, Winter Special Issue*. Vol. 15. pp1–4.

SCHUCK G. (1996) 'Intelligent technology, intelligent workers: a new pedagogy for the high-tech workplace', in K. Starkey (ed.), *How Organizations Learn*. London, International Thomson Business Press, pp199–213.

SCHUMPETER J. A. (1934) *The Theory of Economic Development*. Boston, MA, Harvard Business School Press.

SENGE P. M. (1990) *The Fifth Discipline: The art and practice of the learning organization*. New York, Doubleday.

SILVERMAN D. (1970) *The Theory of Organizations*. London, Heinemann Educational Books.

SIMON H. A. (1945) *Administrative Behaviour*. 2nd edn. New York, Free Press.

SIMON H. A. (1955) 'A behavioural model of rational choice'. *Quarterly Journal of Economics*. Vol. 69. p99–118.

SKINNER D. *and* MABEY C. (1995) 'How do organisations conceive, design and implement human resource strategies?' *Working Paper*. Open University Business School, Centre for Human Resource and Change Management.

SLOMAN M. (1994) 'Coming in from the cold: a new role for trainers'. *Personnel Management*. Vol. 26, 1. pp24–7.

SLOMAN M. (2001) *The E-Learning Revolution*. London, Chartered Institute of Personnel and Development.

SMITH A. (1999) 'Get with the programme'. *People Management*. Vol. 5, 11. p33.

SMITH A. D. (1995) 'Europe has a multitude of systems and certificates'. *Guardian*. 30 May.

SMITH D. (1996) 'The training that just isn't working'. *Sunday Times*, 28 April. p8.

SMITH D. (2000) 'Why the New Deal isn't working'. *Sunday Times News Review*. 16 April. p6.

SOLOMON N. (1999) 'Culture and difference in workplace learning', in D. Boud and J. Garrick (eds), *Understanding Learning at Work*. London, Routledge, pp119-131.

SPARROW P. (1996) 'Too good to be true'. *People Management*. Vol. 2, 24. pp22-7.

SPARROW P. and HILTROP J-M. (1994) *European Human Resource Management in Transition*. London, Prentice-Hall.

SPENDER J-C. (1994) 'Knowing, managing, learning: a dynamic managerial epistemology'. *Management Learning*. Vol. 25, 3. pp387-412.

SPURLING M. and TROLLEY E. (2000) 'How to make training strategic'. *People Management*. Vol. 6, 8. pp46-8.

STALK G., EVANS P. and SHULMAN L. E. (1992) 'Competing on capabilities: the new rules of corporate strategy'. *Harvard Business Review*. March-April. pp57-69.

STAMMERS R. and PATRICK J. (1977) *The Psychology of Training*. London, Methuen.

STARKEY K. (ED.) (1996) *How Organizations Learn*. London, International Thomson Business Press.

STARKEY K. and McKINLAY A. (1993) *Strategy and the Human Resource: Ford and the search for competitive advantage*. Oxford, Blackwell.

STEEDMAN H. (1990) 'Speaking practically, the French have it'. *Independent*. 5 September.

STERN E. and SOMMERLAD E. (1999) *Workplace Learning, Culture and Performance*. London, Institute of Personnel and Development.

STERNBERG R. J. (1994) 'PRSVL: an integrative framework for understanding mind in context,' in R. J. Sternberg and R. K. Wagner (eds), *Mind in Context: Interactionist perspectives on human intelligence*. Cambridge, Cambridge University Press, pp218-232.

STEVENS C. (1985) 'Assessment centres: the British experience'. *Personnel Management*. Vol. 17, 7. pp28-31.

STEVENS J. and ASHTON D. (1999) 'Underperformance appraisal'. *People Management*. Vol. 5, 14. pp31-2.

STEWART B. (1996) 'Firms do better when EVA keeps the score'. *Sunday Times Business Focus*. 8 December. p2.5.

STEWART J. (1999) 'Policy and ethics in employee development', in J. Stewart, *Employee Development Practice*. London, Financial Times and Pitman, pp240-260.

STEWART J. (1999a) 'Resourcing the ED function', in J. Stewart, *Employee Development Practice*. London, Financial Times and Pitman, pp261-279.

STEWART J. (1999b) 'Evaluating employee development contributions' in J. Stewart, *Employee Development Practice*. London, Financial Times and Pitman Publishing, pp178–197.

STOREY J. (1992) *Developments in the Management of Human Resources*. Oxford, Blackwell.

STOREY J. (1994) 'How new-style management is taking hold'. *Personnel Management*. Vol. 26, 1. pp32–5.

STOREY J. (1994a) *New Wave Manufacturing Strategies: Organizational and human resource management dimensions*. London, Chapman.

SWIDLER A. (1986) 'Culture in action: symbols and strategies'. *American Sociological Review*. Vol 5. pp273–286.

TAYLOR C. (2001) 'ILAs' day of reckoning'. *People Management*. Vol. 7, 25. p8.

TENNANT M. (1999) 'Is learning transferable?', in D. Boud and J. Garrick (EDS), *Understanding Learning at Work*. London, Routledge pp165–179.

TERRY M. *and* PURCELL J. (1997) 'Return to slender'. *People Management*. Vol. 3, 21. pp46, 47.

THOMAS K. W. (1976) 'Conflict and Conflict Management' in M. D. Dunnette (ed.), *Handbook of Industrial and Organizational Psychology*. Chicago, Rand McNally, pp889–935.

THOMAS K. *and* MELLON T. (1995) *Planning for Training and Development: A guide to analysing needs*. London, Save the Children.

THOMAS M. *and* ELBEIK S. (1996) *Supercharge Your Management Role*. London, Butterworth-Heinemann.

TICHY N. M. (1996) 'GE's Crotonville: a staging ground for corporate revolution', in K. Starkey (ed.), *How Organizations Learn*. London, International Thomson Business Press, pp 243–257.

TIMES (2001) 'Church and school: a commitment to moral values in education is rewarded'. *Times* editorial leader. 12 February. p17.

TORRINGTON D. *and* HALL L. (1995) *Personnel Management: Human resource management in action*. London, Prentice-Hall.

TORRINGTON D. *and* WEIGHTMAN J. (1985) *The Business of Management*. London, Prentice-Hall.

TRADES UNION CONGRESS (1999) *Britain's Skills Gap*. Available from the TUC, tel. 020 7636 4030.

TRIST E. *and* BAMFORTH K. (1951) 'Some social and psychological consequences of the longwall method of coal-getting'. *Human Relations*. Vol. 4. pp3–38.

TUCKER B. (ED.) (1997) *Handbook of Technology-Based Training*. Aldershot, Gower.

TYLER E. (2000) 'Golden hello'. *People Management*. Vol. 6, 22. pp54–56.

ULRICH D. (1987) 'Organizational capability as a competitive advantage: human resource professionals as strategic partners'. *Human Resource Planning*. Part 4. pp169–184.

UNIVERSITY FORUM FOR HRD (1998) *Unpublished Report from the Standing Committee for Professionally-focused University Postgraduate*

Programmes in HRD to AGM. 1 May. Available from The Executive Secretary, UFHRD, 58, Picklers Hilll, Abingdon, OX14 2BB.

Van Adelsberg D. *and* Trolley E. (1999) *Running Training Like a Business – Delivering unmistakable value.* San Francisco, CA, Berrett-Koehler. Distributed in the UK by McGraw-Hill.

Van der Klink M. *and* Mulder M. (1995) 'Human resource development and staff flow policy in Europe', in A-W. Harzing and J. van Ruysseveldt (eds), *International Human Resource Management.* London, Sage, pp157–78.

Von Krogh G., Roos J. *and* Kleine D. (eds) (1998) *Knowing in Firms: Understanding, Managing and Measuring Knowledge.* London, Sage.

Von Krogh G., Roos J. *and* Slocum K. (1994) 'An essay on corporate epistemology'. *Strategic Management Journal, Summer Special Issue.* Vol. 15. pp53–71.

Vroom V. H. *and* Deci E. L. (eds) (1970) *Management and Motivation: Selected readings.* Harmondsworth, Penguin.

Vygotsky Lev S. (1978) *Mind in Society: The development of higher psychological processes.* Cambridge, MA, Harvard University Press.

Walker B. A. (1994) 'Valuing differences: the concept and a model', in C. Mabey and P. Iles (eds), *Managing Learning.* London, The Open University and Routledge, pp211–223.

Walsh J. (1999) 'HR "slow to gain input at board level"'. *People Management.* Vol. 5, 15. p15.

Walton J. (1999) 'Outsourcing: what stays in and what goes out', in J. Walton, *Strategic Human Resource Development.* Harlow, Financial Times and Prentice-Hall, pp279–99.

Walton J. (1999a) 'The emerging role of managers and staff in strategic human resource development', in J. Walton, *Strategic Human Resource Development.* Harlow, Financial Times and Prentice-Hall, pp181–209.

Walton J. (1999b) 'Human resource development and the corporate university', in J. Walton, *Strategic Human Resource Development.* Harlow, Financial Times and Prentice-Hall, pp412–437.

Walton J. (1999c) 'Working in the virtual organisation', in J. Walton, *Strategic Human Resource Development.* Harlow, Financial Times and Prentice Hall. pp.536–57.

Walton J. (1999d) 'Small and medium-sized enterprises and human resource development', in J. Walton, *Strategic Human Resource Development.* Harlow, Financial Times and Prentice-Hall. pp324–51.

Warman C. (2000) 'Face-to-face help'. *Times.* 22 February. p45.

Warr P. B. *and* Bird M. W. (1968) 'Identifying supervisory training needs'. *Training Information Paper No. 2.* London, HMSO.

Warr P., Bird M. W. *and* Rackham N. (1970) *Evaluation of Management Training.* Aldershot, Gower.

Watson R. *and* O'Leary J. (2001) 'New church schools to boost standards'. *Times.* 12 February. p1.

WEAVER M. (1988) 'Inside the spending factory'. *Daily Telegraph*. 1 September.

WELCH J. (1997) 'Charities face battle to recruit volunteers'. *People Management*. Vol. 3, 5. p12.

WERNERFELT B. (1984) 'A resource-based view of the firm'. *Strategic Management Journal*. Vol. 10. pp17–32.

WESTWOOD A. (2001) 'Drawing a line – who is going to train our workforce?', in D. Wilson, E. Lank, A. Westwood, E. Keep, C. Leadbeater and M. Sloman, *The Future of Learning for Work: Executive briefing*. London, Chartered Institute of Personnel and Development, pp17–22.

WHEELWRIGHT S. C. and CLARK K. B. (1992) *Revolutionizing Product Development*. New York, Free Press.

WHIDDETT S. and HOLLYFORDE S. (1999) *The Competencies Handbook*. London, Institute of Personnel and Development.

WHIPP R. (1999) 'Creative deconstruction: strategy and organizations', in S. R. Clegg, C. Hardy and W. R. Nord (eds), *Managing Organizations: Current issues*. London, Sage, pp11–25.

WHITE M. (1996) 'Flexible response'. *People Management*. Vol. 2, 6. p33.

WHITE M. and TREVOR M. (1983) *Under Japanese Management*. London, Heinemann.

WHITEHEAD M. (1999) 'Firms ignore staff needs in key areas of the economy'. *People Management*. Vol. 5, 3. p16.

WHITFIELD M. (1995) 'High-flyer hazards'. *People Management*. Vol. 1, 24. p9.

WICKENS P. (1987) *The Road to Nissan*. London, Macmillan.

WILLE E. (1990) 'Should management development be just for managers?' *Personnel Management*. Vol. 22, 8. pp34–7.

WILLMAN J. (1994) 'With a greyer picture of the future in mind'. *Financial Times*. 8 March. p14.

WILLS M. (2000) 'The new keys to learning'. *Daily Telegraph*. 16 March. p9.

WOLF M. (1994) 'Can Europe compete? A relapse into Euroscelerosis'. *Financial Times*. 24 February. p21.

WOOD A. (1994) *North-South Trade and Income Inequality*. Brighton, Institute for Development Studies.

WOODRUFFE C. (1991) 'Competent by any other name'. *Personnel Management*. Vol. 23, 9. pp30–33.

WOODRUFFE C. (1997) 'Going back a generation'. *People Management*. Vol. 3, 4. pp32–4.

WOODRUFFE C. (2000) *Development and Assessment Centres: Identifying and assessing competence*. 3rd edn. London, Chartered Institute of Personnel and Development.

WOODWARD W. (2001) 'Pupils to be steered into vocational path at 14'. *Guardian*. 24 January. pp1–2.

ZUBOFF S. (1988) *In the Age of the Smart Machine*. New York, Basic Books.

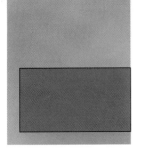

• Index